CAPTAIN GRONOW

*His Reminiscences of Regency and
Victorian Life 1810–60*

CAPTAIN GRONOW

*His Reminiscences of Regency and
Victorian Life 1810–60*

Edited and with Notes by

Christopher
Hibbert

This Selection of *The Reminiscences of Captain Gronow*
first published 1991 by
Kyle Cathie Limited
3 Vincent Square London SW1P 2LX

ISBN 1 85626 013 5

Introduction and notes copyright © Christopher Hibbert 1991

Based on the original four volumes by Gronow
published 1862, 1863, 1865 and 1866.

A Cataloguing in Publication record for this title
is available from the British Library.

Typeset by DP Photosetting, Aylesbury, Bucks
Printed by Richard Clay Ltd, Bungay

Contents

Introduction

WHEN INTRODUCING THESE reminiscences to a grateful public in 1862, their sprightly author claimed that it had been his lot to have lived through the greater part of one of the most eventful centuries of England's history and to have known most of the remarkable men of his day. He had been endowed, he continued immodestly, with a strong memory so that he could recall, 'with all their original vividness, scenes that took place thirty years ago, and distinctly recollect the face, walk and voice, as well as the dress and general manner' of everyone whom he had met.

These were not idle boasts. It has to be conceded that Captain Rees Howell Gronow was not a profound thinker, that he was not deeply interested in the political or social questions of his day, that he was not even much concerned with the hidden springs of human behaviour, and that he was not always to be relied upon when writing of people he did not know. But as an observer of the surface of life, of the foibles and eccentricities of the *beau monde*, of the manners and oddities of Regency England, and of the France of Louis XVIII, Louis-Philippe and Napoleon III, he is unsurpassed. 'My reminiscences', he himself confessed, 'are nothing more than miniature illustrations of contemporary history.' But this verdict contains only part of the truth. The illustrations, miniature though they are, combine to give an impression of his times as vivid as any that have come down to us. Moreover, they are not all froth. The descriptions of Waterloo, of the revolution of 1848 and the *coup d'état* of 1851 in Paris are brilliant first-hand accounts of

historical events of the greatest importance. 'The ground was completely covered with those brave men,' he writes in sombre mood of the
repulse of a charge of the Red Hussars of the Imperial Guard, 'who lay
in various positions, mutilated in every conceivable way. Among the
fallen we perceived the gallant colonel of the hussars lying under his
horse, which had been killed. All of a sudden two riflemen of the
Brunswickers left their battalion, and after taking from their helpless
victim his purse, watch and other articles of value, they deliberately put
the colonel's pistols to the poor fellow's head, and blew out his brains.
"Shame! Shame!" was heard from our ranks, and a feeling of
indignation ran through the whole line.'

Yet it is primarily as a highly gifted raconteur, with a memory at once
retentive and elastic, and as a master of the thumbnail sketch and the
anecdotal short story, that Gronow deserves to be remembered. His
sketches are, indeed, truly memorable. We are introduced to Dr Keate,
the fearsome headmaster of Eton, a short, thickset man with a red face
and stentorian voice, the very sight of whose cocked hat, placed on his
head like Napoleon's, struck terror into the heart of all offenders; and
later we come across Keate again in Paris, where, to the astonishment
of a group of his former pupils, he is discovered eating ice cream at
Tortoni's. They ask him to dine with them at Beauvilliers', where he
declares that if he has a regret in his life it is that he did not flog his hosts
a good deal more when they were young.

We meet the celebrated wit and extremely rich man of pleasure,
Lord Alvanley, whose lisp 'added piquancy and zest to his sayings'.
Although well-mannered and invariably good-natured, Alvanley's
method of putting out his light at night was not a very pleasant one for
his host. 'He always read in bed, and when he wanted to go to sleep, he
either extinguished his candle by throwing it on the floor in the middle
of the room, and taking a shot at it with the pillow, or else quietly placed
it, when still lighted, under the bolster. At Badminton, and other
country houses, his habits in this respect were so well known, that a
servant was ordered to sit up in the passage' outside his room to make
sure he did not set the whole place on fire.

Gronow introduces us also to the 'exceedingly agreeable' Mrs Clarke,
who tells scandalous stories of the Royal Family and describes her lover,
the Duke of York, commander-in-chief of the army, as 'a big baby, not
out of his leading strings'; to the ninety-eight-year-old Madame
Rothschild, who asks her doctor to do something for her and, when he
replies there is nothing he can do, he can't make her young again, says,
'No, doctor, I don't want to be young again, but I want to continue to

grow old'; and to Townshend, the famous Bow Street Runner, 'a little fat man with a flaxen wig, kerseymere breeches, a blue straight-cut coat, and a broad-brimmed white hat'. We encounter Colonel Mackinnon, who amuses his friends by 'creeping over the furniture of a room like a monkey'; and P. B. Shelley, sitting on the seashore at Genoa, 'very carelessly dressed', eating bread and fruit, 'his long brown hair, already streaked with grey', presenting a 'wild and strange appearance' as it flows in tangled masses from under the wide brim of a large straw hat. And in Paris, amongst a host of other characters, we come across both Honoré de Balzac, squalid and slovenly, with a cascade of double chins and straight, greasy hair, 'dressed in the worst possible taste, [with] sparkling jewels on a dirty shirt-front, and diamond rings on unwashed fingers', and Madame de Staël, 'a large, masculine-looking woman, rather coarse, and with a thoracic development worthy of a wet nurse'. We are treated to frequent glimpses of Byron, at one moment protesting that he does not like to see women eat 'from a wish to believe in their more ethereal nature', at another averring that his real dislike to their presence at the dinner table arises from their being helped first and consequently getting all the best bits of the chickens, at yet another begging his friend, Scrope Davies, who has caught him in bed with his hair in curlers, not to let the cat out of the bag, 'for, says he, "I am as vain of my curls as a girl of sixteen."'

We are offered vignettes of Marshal Blücher roaring like a lion and swearing like one of his own troopers after losing all his money at the gaming table; and of Henry Fox, Secretary of the British Embassy in Paris, breaking the bank at the Salon des Étrangers, spending his winnings on cashmere shawls, Chantilly veils, ladies' bonnets, gloves and dresses, and, in his delightfully good-humoured way, answering the question what on earth he wanted with all this millinery: 'Why, my dear Gronow, it was the only means to prevent those rascals at the salon winning back my money'. We catch sight of Queen Charlotte taking such immense quantities of snuff out of her gold box on the terrace at Windsor that 'the royal nose was covered with snuff both within and without'; of poor King George III, his mind deranged by porphyria, and his beard grown to an unusual length, tottering beneath the castle windows with his doctors and keepers behind him; of the Duke of Wellington informing his startled guests at the breakfast table at Walmer Castle that he must imperatively leave for London imme-diately as he has discovered all his razors need setting and he cannot trust them to anyone other than a man he knows in Jermyn Street; of Colonel Disney, disgraced for having put the Queen's gold toilet vase 'to a use that cannot be named in ears polite', dying heartbroken in his Bury Street lodgings 'on the second anniversary of his thoughtless freak'; and Colonel Kelly of the 1st Foot Guards, 'a thin, emaciated-looking dandy', burned to death trying to save a favourite pair of boots.

Gronow's was an age rich in oddities, and in his recollections of it eccentrics make frequent and welcome appearances. Here, representatively, is Mr Blackburn, 'extremely absent and otherwise odd . . . one of the oldest members of the House of Commons', whose invariable habit at dinner it was to drink not only the wine from his own glass but also that from his neighbour's. Gronow gives him a letter to frank; he deliberately opens it, reads it in Gronow's presence and upon being asked rather testily whether or not it has amused him, replies that he is sorry to say he cannot make head or tail of it. Here, too, is Sir Lumley Skeffington, 'who used to paint his face, so that he looked like a French toy; he dressed *à la* Robespierre. . . . You always knew of his approach by an *avant-courier* of sweet smells; and when he advanced a little nearer, you might suppose yourself in the atmosphere of a perfumer's shop.' And here, most eccentrically of all, is Lord Dudley, who on a morning visit to a lady of his acquaintance, sits for an unconscionably long time in her drawing room until the lady, giving him some friendly hints in an effort to persuade him to leave, eventually takes up her needlework. 'A very pretty woman this,' Dudley mutters to himself after a prolonged silence, but 'She stays a devilish long time!'

It has to be admitted that Gronow is not – and never pretends to be – a commentator on human nature and social relations in the manner of Trollope. His England is the England of *Vanity Fair*, but he does not examine it with Thackeray's critical eye; his Paris is that of *L'Éducation sentimentale*, but his view of it remains that of the idle *habitué* of the Petit Cercle rather than that of the industrious, infinitely painstaking Gustave Flaubert who drew its political and social background with such fidelity. Rarely does Gronow allow himself a criticism or offer an opinion. His animadversions upon the drinking habits of the six-bottle men of his younger days are an unusual interpolation, as is his condemnation of the 'unspeakably odious' dandies of the Regency, who 'were generally not high-born, nor rich, nor very good looking, nor clever, nor agreeable . . . with large appetites and weak digestions. . . . They hated everybody and abused everybody, and would sit together in White's bay window or the pit-boxes at the Opera. . . . They swore a good deal, never laughed, had their own particular slang and looked hazy after dinner'.

For the most part Gronow is urbane and tolerant, a calm observer of men and manners, interested in the appearance of life rather than its meaning. And as such he is superb. Nor are his pages remarkable only for the unforgettable characters that crowd them, but also for their teeming minutiae of social history, their observations on women's fashions and the theatre, on the dressing and powdering of hair, on the tipping of the servants in gentlemen's houses, on London hotels and Parisian cafés, on the serving of meals and the taking of snuff, on anything, in fact, that took the fancy of his watchful, ever-curious eye.

Revealing as he is about the foibles of others, however, Gronow is remarkably reticent about his own. He was said to have 'committed the greatest follies without in the least disturbing the points of his shirt collar'; but there is no hint of what these follies might have been. He is known to have fought several duels. Indeed, Thomas Creevey refers to him as 'Member of Parliament and duellist', as though these were his only two claims to fame. Yet, while other men's duels are described in detail, Gronow does not refer to his own. He was reputed to be, with the exception of one Captain Ross, the best pistol shot of his day; but as evidence of this expertise he is content merely to recount his extraordinary feat, while on guard duty at the Tower of London, of shooting at the sparrows in the trees from the windows of Lady Jane Grey's room and bagging eleven without missing a single one. 'This I may say, without flattering myself, was considered the best pistol shooting ever heard of.'

He appears but fleetingly in the other memoirs and diaries of his time. Creevey, in a letter to Miss Ord, in which he is identified by the brief description mentioned above, gives him credit for having negotiated the terms – '£2,000 down and £800 a year!' – upon which an opera dancer was willing to become the mistress of a 'very aspiring young man of fashion', grandson of the first Earl Grey. Charles Greville refers to Gronow only once and then in a list of 'some very bad characters' elected to Parliament in 1832. Croker does not mention him at all; nor does he appear in any of the eight thick volumes which Professor Aspinall devoted to the correspondence of George, Prince of Wales, whose corpulent presence is noted in so many of Gronow's stories.

Perhaps this is how Gronow would have had it be. He is one of those memoirists who divulge only what they care to have known. His little face peers out at us from the engraving of his portrait by J. C. Armytage, extremely well groomed, handsome, quizzical, strangely prim and utterly enigmatic. We can imagine him in London, a neat, well-turned-out figure, tripping in and out of the Guards' Club and White's; and later, an equally familiar sight in Paris, sitting in the window of the Petit

Cercle, a small, smart club that he had helped to found on the Boulevard des Italiens, with the head of his cane pressed to his lips as he surveys the world he was to describe with such felicity. But what sort of man he was it is impossible to say for sure.

A French journalist who knew him in the days when he lived in Paris gave this sketch of him:

Mr Gronow, when I knew him, was small, spare and about fifty years of age; his hair was thinning, and he wore a small moustache of which the edge was daily shaved, which did not disguise the circumstance that the Captain's latent vanity had recourse to a brown dye. He always wore a blue tight-fitting coat closely buttoned, just allowing a white line of waistcoat to be visible. . . .

He was very 'good form', had a great respect for everything that was proper and convenient, and a strong propensity to become eccentric. . . . He had married a lady of the *corps de ballet*, and would rather have blown out his brains than gone to the opera in morning costume.

This little man, with his hair well arranged, scented, cold and phlegmatic, knew the best people in Paris, visited all the diplomats and was evidently intimate with everybody of note in Europe.

Further information about Rees Howell Gronow is difficult to come by. His short entry in the *Dictionary of National Biography*, where he was deemed worthy of space as a 'writer of reminiscences', answers few of the questions we would like to ask about him. But this much at least is known: he was born in 1794, the son of a prosperous Welsh landowner who claimed descent from Sir Tudor ap Gronow, great-great-grandfather of King Henry VII. He was sent to Eton, where he was a contemporary of Shelley, 'a boy of studious and meditative habits, averse to all games and sports, and a great reader of novels and romances. . . . a thin, slight lad, with remarkably lustrous eyes, fine hair, and a very peculiar shrill voice and laugh.'

After leaving Eton and the tutelage of Dr Keate – who having been 'subjected to such indignities as the screwing up and smashing of his desk, the singing of songs in chorus during schooltime, and an occasional fusillade of rotten eggs', restored discipline by flogging more than eighty boys on the same day – Gronow obtained a commission as an ensign in the 1st Foot Guards in December 1812. This was the year in which the waltz was first danced in England's ballrooms; the main streets of London were first lit by gas; the steamship *Comet* reached a speed of seven knots on the Clyde; Humphry Davy published his *Elements of*

Chemical Philosophy, Lord Byron his *Childe Harold's Pilgrimage* and the Grimm Brothers their *Fairy Tales*. It was the year in which Beethoven's Seventh and Eighth Symphonies were first performed, and Mrs Siddons made her last appearance on the stage; in which Spencer Perceval was assassinated in the House of Commons and was succeeded as Prime Minister by Lord Liverpool; in which frame-breaking was made a capital offence by Act of Parliament; Napoleon invaded Russia and was forced to retreat from Moscow; the United States declared war on Britain; and Arthur Wellesley, later Duke of Wellington, achieved a series of victories over the French in Spain.

Gronow himself, astonished by the limitations and imperfections of the instruction which an officer then received, was sent to Spain with a detachment of his regiment, having spent a few months on guard duty at St James's Palace. He marched down to Portsmouth where transports were waiting to convey him and his men to Lord Wellesley, who 'was making his arrangements, after taking St Sebastian, for a yet more important event in the history of the Peninsular War'. Within a few weeks the eighteen-year-old ensign had come under fire and, for the first time, had witnessed a death – that of a Spanish soldier cut in half by a cannon ball. He was not in action for long, however; and in 1814 his battalion was once more in its old quarters in Portman Street. Gronow now became one of those very few privileged young officers who were permitted access to Almack's Assembly Rooms, 'that exclusive temple of the *beau monde*', entrance to which was strictly regulated by its various patronesses, *grandes dames* of the formidable quality of Lady Jersey, Madame de Lieven, Lady Castlereagh and Princess Esterhazy, whose minions denied entry one evening to Wellington, by then a duke and a field marshal, because he was wearing trousers. A voucher of admission to the weekly ball held at Almack's on a Wednesday night was deemed to be the 'seventh heaven of the fashionable world' and to be struck off the patronesses' list the most dreaded of social ostracisms.

Belonging to Almack's and mixing with its rich and aristocratic members proved too expensive for Ensign Gronow; and when in 1815 an opportunity presented itself for him to go on active service again as aide-de-camp to a fellow Welshman, General Sir Thomas Picton, he had no money to buy the necessary equipment. He accordingly borrowed £200 (which would now be the equivalent of about £12,000) from his agents, Cox and Greenwood, and went to a gambling house in St James's Square where he won about £600 (around £36,000). Flush with this money, he bought two horses at Tattersall's and the other necessaries with which an aide-de-camp was then required to supply himself. Then, without bothering to obtain permission from his regiment, he embarked for Ostend with a groom and made his way to Brussels, where he booked rooms for himself and General Picton at the Hôtel d'Angleterre. Picton's division was already engaged when they arrived at Quatre Bras; and Gronow, as he admitted with regret, had no more to do than act as a mere spectator of the battle. One of the general's other aides-de-camp suggested that, as he had 'really nothing to do with Picton', he ought to go and see whether he could be of any use to the Guards, whose losses had been very severe. His reception there was not of the friendliest. 'What the deuce brought you here?' he was asked. 'Why are you not with your battalion in London? Get off your horse and explain how you came here!' He was allowed to remain with them, however, and so was able to witness the battle of Waterloo and to provide one of the best first-hand accounts of it that has survived.

At the end of the day he found that a grape shot had passed through the top of his shako and one of his coat tails had been shot off; but he had escaped without a wound and entered Paris in good spirits. After a fortnight there he obtained leave to return to his own battalion of the Grenadier Guards in London and never forgot the reception he was given as he dashed up in a chaise and four to the door of Fenton's Hotel in St James's Street. Very few men from the army had yet arrived in London after Wellington's great victory, and a crowd of some thousand people gathered round the door of Fenton's as he got out in his torn and weather-beaten uniform, cheering loudly and offering to shake his hand. 'I also recollect,' he added characteristically, 'the capital English dinner old James, the well-known waiter, had provided to celebrate my return.'

He remained in the army for a further six years, obtaining no higher rank than captain in a regiment in which majorities and colonelcies were sold for extremely high sums. Official prices of commissions were printed in the Army List: in Gronow's day a majority in the Foot Guards was listed at £8,300 (about £50,000 in today's terms), and almost twice as much as a lieutenant-colonelcy in a regiment of the line. But vacancies were not common and the prices fetched were often far in excess of those set out in the Army List. The Earl of Lucan, for example, paid £25,000 (£1,500,000) for the command of the 17th Lancers in 1826.

Such sums were far beyond Gronow's reach. Indeed, after his retirement from the army in October 1821 he seems to have found the life of a man about town in London more than he could afford, for in

June 1823 he became insolvent and was for a short time in prison before his discharge under the Insolvent Debtors Act.

In 1830 his father died; and the next year – his finances in a far more healthy condition – he was comfortably established in Chesterfield Street, Mayfair, in a house that had belonged to George ('Beau') Brummell. He was now able to stand as a parliamentary candidate at Grimsby. He was asked to do so by Lord Yarborough, who had once been Member for Grimsby, and who promised Gronow his 'utmost support and interest but with one proviso that [he] would give [his] word not to bribe'. According to Gronow's own account, he stood by his promise, despite warnings that he would certainly not be elected if he did so, and consequently received few of the electors' votes. The next year he stood as a Whig candidate at Stafford, determined, as he readily confessed, not to repeat his mistake. He rode to Stafford and put up at the Star Inn, where several hundred electors assembled under his bedroom window and received his appearance with cheers.

'Now, Gronow, my old boy,' their leader declared, 'we like what we have heard about you, your principles and all that sort of thing. We will therefore all vote for you if . . .' Here he paused and all the men in the crowd struck their breeches pockets with open hands. 'You know what we mean, old fellow? If not – you understand – you won't do for Stafford.' 'His comrades loudly cheered their leader,' Gronow continued, 'and I made them a speech of some length setting forth the principles upon which I presented myself to their notice, and solicited their suffrages, concluding by significantly assuring them that they should all have reason to be well satisfied with me.'

He accordingly set to work 'to bribe every man, woman and child in the ancient borough of Stafford. . . . I engaged numerous agents, opened all the public houses which were not already taken by my opponents, gave suppers every night to my supporters, kissed all their wives and children, drank their health in every sort of abominable mixture, and secured my return against great local interest.' Even so the electors of Stafford were apparently not satisfied; and a petition was presented to the House complaining of Gronow's parsimony.

I forget the exact wording of this precious document [Gronow wrote], but the purport of it was, that I ought to be unseated because I had not bribed the electors sufficiently. When Mr Lee, the clerk, read out this humble petition roars of laughter were heard from all sides of the House, and the Speaker, very much scandalised, ruled that it could not be received.

On leaving the House, I met the late Lord Campbell, then Solicitor-General, who had been M.P. for Stafford in the last Parliament. He immediately called out, 'Here comes the immaculate Gronow, who did not bribe the electors of Stafford to their hearts' content.' I replied that I supposed they expected me to give all the wives of electors pianofortes, as he was reported to have done; but that he had been quite right to bribe, as his election had made him Solicitor-General. Sir John Campbell laughed, and said I must not talk of bribery to one of his Majesty's principal law-officers; but added, 'There is nothing like leather' – a cant expression which was, and I believe is still, used by the worthy and independent electors of Stafford, who are mostly shoemakers, and who take care to sell their leather at election time at a highly remunerative price.

At the next election in 1835, when Lord Melbourne became Prime Minister for the second time, Gronow was defeated. He still had 'plenty of money in those days'; but evidently did not spend as much as his opponent, F. L. Holyoake Goodricke, who distributed bribes on a scale described as 'profligate' and who, as a reward for his victory, was created a baronet on the recommendation of Sir Robert Peel.

Abandoning hope of a further political career, although remaining a member of the Reform Club – and no doubt enjoying there the meals of its great chef, Alexis Soyer – Gronow devoted the next thirty years to a life of idleness and fashionable pursuits in London and Paris. His first wife, the former Mademoiselle Didier of the Paris Opera, whom he had married in 1825, bore him a daughter, Mathilde, who, according to her father's obituary in the *Gentleman's Magazine*, married 'M. Coursier, a gentleman of French parentage'. After his first wife's death, Gronow married Mademoiselle de St Pol, 'a lady belonging to an old and noble family of Brittany'. By this wife he had four more children and, so the *Morning Post* reported upon Gronow's own death, these 'infant children' were left 'wholly unprovided for'. 'Some friends in Paris,' the *Post* added, 'are endeavouring to get up a subscription on their behalf.'

So, we are led to suppose, the 'plenty of money' which he had had in his parliamentary days had at last been dissipated, and the sums he had received from his memoirs had gone with it. There were four volumes of these memoirs. The first, entitled *Reminiscences of Captain Gronow, formerly of the Grenadier Guards and Member of Parliament for Stafford, being Anecdotes of the Camp, the Court, and the Clubs, at the close of the Last War with France, related by himself*, was published in 1861. A second revised edition of this appeared the following year. In 1863 he published his *Recollections*

and Anecdotes, being a Second Series of Reminiscences by Captain R. H. Gronow;
in 1865 his *Celebrities of London and Paris, being a Third Series of Reminiscences
and Anecdotes*; and in 1866, the year after his death, *Captain Gronow's Last
Recollections, being the Fourth and Final Series of his Reminiscences and
Anecdotes.* In 1889 a new edition of the four volumes appeared as *The
Reminiscences and Recollections of Captain Gronow* with 'illustrations from
contemporary sources' by Joseph Grego.

By the time Gronow came to write his last volume, it has to be
confessed that he was scraping the barrel of his memory. Indeed, he
confessed as much himself. 'I cannot help feeling', he wrote, 'that
amongst my anecdotal progeny there may be some abortions.' I have
excluded these from this edition, which contains the cream skimmed
from the four volumes mentioned above. I have also completely
rearranged the order in which the material originally appeared, since
Gronow keeps returning in later volumes to people and events
mentioned in earlier ones, frequently repeating himself and jumping
disconcertingly from France to England and from the days of the Prince
Regent to those of Queen Victoria. This reorganisation of Gronow's
material makes, I hope, for easier reading while preserving the
idiosyncrasies of style and discursive presentation of his vivid,
kaleidoscopic picture of his times.

CHRISTOPHER HIBBERT
July 1990

1

Etonians

SHELLEY

Shelley, the poet, cut off at so early an age, just when his great poetical talents had been matured by study and reflection, and when he probably would have produced some great work, was my friend and associate at Eton. He was a boy of studious and meditative habits, averse to all games and sports, and a great reader of novels and romances. He was a thin, slight lad, with remarkably lustrous eyes, fine hair, and a very peculiar shrill voice and laugh. His most intimate friend at Eton was a boy named Price, who was considered one of the best classical scholars amongst us. At his tutor, Bethell's, where he lodged, he attempted many mechanical and scientific experiments.[1] By the aid of a common tinker, he contrived to make something like a steam-engine, which, unfortunately, one day suddenly exploded, to the great consternation of the neighbourhood and to the imminent danger of a severe flogging from Dr Goodall.[2]

Soon after leaving school, and about the year 1810, he came, in a state of great distress and difficulty, to Swansea, when we had an opportunity

[1] George Bethell, who had entered Eton at Election in 1790, aged ten, was an assistant master from 1802 to 1818. He was Vice-Provost from 1851 until his death in 1857.

[2] Joseph Goodall (1760–1840) was appointed headmaster of Eton in 1801. In marked contrast to that of his successor Thomas Keate, of whom Gronow writes below, his rule was benevolent rather than strict. It was said of him that 'his countenance was illuminated with an almost perpetual smile'. Severe floggings were not nearly so common in his day as they were later to become.

of rendering him a service; but we could never ascertain what had brought him to Wales, though we had reason to suppose it was some mysterious *affaire du cœur*.

The last time I saw Shelley was at Genoa, in 1822, sitting on the sea-shore, and, when I came upon him, making a true poet's meal of bread and fruit. He at once recognised me, jumped up, and appearing greatly delighted, exclaimed, 'Here you see me at my old Eton habits; but instead of the green fields for a couch, I have here the shores of the Mediterranean. It is very grand, and very romantic. I only wish I had some of the excellent brown bread and butter we used to get at Spiers's:[1] but I was never very fastidious in my diet.' Then he continued, in a wild and eccentric manner: 'Gronow, do you remember the beautiful Martha, the Hebe of Spiers's?[2] She was the loveliest girl I ever saw, and I loved her to distraction.'

Shelley was looking careworn and ill; and, as usual, was very carelessly dressed. He had on a large and wide straw hat, his long brown hair, already streaked with grey, flowing in large masses from under it, and presented a wild and strange appearance.

During the time I sat by his side he asked many questions about myself and many of our schoolfellows; but on my questioning him in turn about himself, his way of life, and his future plans, he avoided entering into any explanation: indeed, he gave such short and evasive answers, that, thinking my inquisitiveness displeased him, I rose to take my leave. I observed that I had not been lucky enough to see Lord Byron in any of my rambles, to which he replied, 'Byron is living at his villa, surrounded by his court of sycophants; but I shall shortly see him at Leghorn.' We then shook hands. I never saw him again; for he was drowned shortly afterwards and his body was washed ashore near Via Reggio. Every one is familiar with the romantic scene which took place on the sea-shore, when the remains of my poor friend were burnt, in the presence of Byron and Trelawny,[3] in the Roman fashion. His ashes were gathered into an urn, and buried in the Protestant cemetery at Rome. He was but twenty-nine years of age at his death.

---

[1] Spiers's was a popular 'sock shop' in Eton, or tuck shop as it would have been known at other schools.
[2] Hebe was the daughter of Zeus and Hera. Cup-bearer to the gods, she was herself a goddess of youth.
[3] Edward John Trelawny (1792–1881) had deserted from the Royal Navy and thereafter lived an adventurous life. He met Shelley at Pisa in 1821. His *Records of Shelley, Byron, and the Author* were published in 1858.

SHELLEY'S FIGHT AT ETON

In the year 1809 an incident occurred at Eton which caused no small sensation and merriment throughout the school. It was announced one morning that Shelley, the future poet, had actually accepted wager of battle from Sir Thomas Styles. Whether he had received an insult, and that vast disparity in size gave him confidence, or that, over-full of the warlike descriptions of Homer's heroes, he was fired to imitate their exploits against some one or other, remains a secret. Meet, however, they did, after twelve, in the playing-fields. The usual preliminaries were arranged – a ring was formed, seconds and bottle-holders were all in readiness, and the combatants stood face to face. The tall, lank figure of the poet towered above the diminutive, thick-set little Baronet, by nearly a head and shoulders. In the first round no mischief was done; Sir Thomas seemed to be feeling his way, being naturally desirous of ascertaining what his gigantic adversary was made of; and Shelley, though brandishing his long arms, had evidently no idea of their use in a pugilistic point of view. After a certain amount of sparring without effect, the combatants were invited by their seconds to take breath. The Baronet did not hesitate to accept the offer to sit upon the knee of his second: but Shelley disdainfully declined to rest, and, calculating upon finishing the fight by a single blow, stalked round the ring, looking defiance at his little adversary.

Time was called, and the battle was renewed in earnest. The Baronet, somewhat cautious, planted his first blow upon the chest of Shelley, who did not appear to relish it. However, though not a proficient in the art of self-defence, he nevertheless went in, and knocked the little Baronet off his legs, who lay sprawling upon the grass more dead than alive. Shelley's confidence increased; he stalked round the ring as before, and spouted one of the defiant addresses usual with Homer's heroes when about to commence a single combat; the young poet, being a first-rate classical scholar, actually delivered the speech in the original Greek, to the no small amusement of the boys. In the third and last round, Styles went to work like a first-rate artist, and, after several slighter blows, delivered what is called in the prize-ring 'a heavy slogger' on Shelley's bread-basket; this seemed positively to electrify the bard, for, I blush to say, he broke through the ring, and took to his heels with a speed that defied pursuit. His seconds, backers, and all who had witnessed the fight, joined in full cry after him, but he outran them all, and got safe to the house of his tutor, Mr Bethel.

This incident naturally excited much merriment at Eton at the time, and Shelley never more, during his stay at college, ventured to enter the pugilistic arena, but passed his leisure hours in making various experiments in chemistry and natural science. He even went so far as to employ a travelling tinker to assist him in making a miniature steam-engine, which burst, and very nearly blew the bard and the Bethel family into the air.

SIR THOMAS STYLES

Poor Sir Thomas Styles received a commission in the 1st Foot Guards. Had it been in the time of peace, poor Styles would have shone to advantage on parade and at the mess-table; but the active life of a soldier proved too fatiguing for him, as will be seen by the following anecdote. In course of time he was sent with a detachment of his regiment to Portugal; but on his arrival at Lisbon, the Guards had left to join the army in the neighbourhood of the Pyrenees; accordingly, our young Guardsman received orders to march through Portugal and Spain until he came up with his regiment. The heat was excessive; and on his falling in with the brigade, poor Styles was more dead than alive. All his brother officers hastened to congratulate him on his safe arrival after so long a march; but he spoke little, saying, that, ever since he had left Lisbon, he had not closed his eyes for half-an-hour, and that his health was in such a state that he feared he could not long survive. Observing that something extraordinary had happened, he was pressed to be more explicit, and to tell what had occurred to make him so miserable. He replied, with a very grave countenance, that the fleas and vermin on the march had nearly driven him mad; and that when the peasant girls observed him scratching himself, they would laugh, and shaking their petticoats over pails full of water, tell him how much more they were to be pitied than he. Our doctor, a very kind fellow, anticipating brain fever, placed Styles in his camp bed, covered his head with wet towels, and desired his batman to watch over his master, and not to leave him for an instant. However, the servant fell asleep, and during the night poor Styles got out of bed, unlocked his trunk where his razors were kept, and with one of them deliberately cut his throat from ear to ear.

BALL HUGHES

I was at Eton with my late friend Ball Hughes, whose recent death was so much lamented in Paris.[1] He was known at Eton by the name of Ball only; but the year before he came of age, he took the additional name of Hughes, his uncle [in fact, stepfather], Admiral Hughes, having left him the fortune he had amassed during his command of the fleet on the Indian seas, and which was supposed to be not less than forty thousand a year. But Hughes entered the army early in life, his uncle having bought him a commission in the 7th Hussars, and made him a handsome allowance. He was a great imitator of the Colonel of his regiment, the Earl of Uxbridge, afterwards Marquis of Anglesea,[2] whom he took as a model for his coats, hats, and boots; indeed, everything that his noble commander said or did was law to him. Hughes was a remarkably handsome man, and made a considerable figure in the best society; his manners were excellent; he was a thoroughly amiable, agreeable fellow, and universally popular.

When he came into his fortune, he was considered a great match by all the women in London. He fell desperately in love with Lady Jane Paget,[3] the daughter of his Colonel, and the marriage-settlements were all arranged; but, unluckily for the disappointed lover, Lady Jane, at the last moment, gave a most decided negative, and the match was broken off. Ball was not long disconsolate, but looking around him, fixed his attention upon the lovely Miss Floyd, who afterwards married Sir Robert Peel.[4] This, however, did not prevent him from being considered an eligible match by a great many mothers, who diligently sought his society. He was courted, followed, and admired by every one who had daughters to dispose of; but, unfortunately for him, the young ladies, having heard of his numerous disappointments, were not ready to unite their fate with a man whose rejected addresses were so well known. 'The Golden Ball,' as he was called, continued, nevertheless, to make his appearance everywhere. He was devoted to female society; no dinner, ball, pic-nic, or party, was complete unless the popular millionaire formed one of the social circle.

[1] Edward Hughes Ball Hughes (d. 1863) was the son of a captain in the Royal Navy named Ball whose widow married Admiral Sir Edward Hughes from whom he inherited his fortune. He took the additional name of Hughes in 1819.
[2] Henry William Paget, second Earl of Uxbridge and first Marquess of Anglesey (1768–1854), commanded the British cavalry and horse artillery at Waterloo, where he lost a leg.
[3] Lady Jane Paget was the Marquess of Anglesey's second daughter by his first wife. She married the second Marquess Conyngham in 1824 and died in 1876.
[4] Julia Floyd, youngest daughter of General Sir John Floyd, married Peel in 1820.

Ball Hughes's first step, on entering into possession of his fortune, was to employ Mr Wyatt the architect to furnish a mansion for him in Brook Street.[1] No expense was spared to make it as near perfection as possible. Wyatt had *carte-blanche*, and bought for him buhl furniture, rich hangings, statues, bronzes, and works of art to an extent that made an inroad even upon his wealth.

A beautiful Spanish *danseuse*, named Mercandotti,[2] arrived in London, in the midst of the gay season of 1822, under the immediate patronage of Lord Fife.[3] She was then only fifteen years of age, and by some she was believed to be his daughter, by others only his *protégée*. At Barcelona she was considered inimitable; at Madrid she gained great applause; in Seville she acquired immense reputation; and by the time the lovely girl reached London, great curiosity was excited to see the new candidate for public favour at the King's Theatre, where she was engaged for the season at £800. The new *débutante* met with complete success, and was pronounced divine. All the dandies who had the *entrée* behind the scenes surrounded her and paid her homage, and more than one scion of the fashionable world offered to surrender his liberty for life to the fascinating dancer. Ebers, then manager of the theatre, was pestered from morning to night by young men of fashion anxious to obtain an introduction to Mademoiselle Mercandotti, but they were invariably referred by the *impresario* to Lord Fife.

One night, March 8, 1823, the house was enormously crowded by an audience eager to see the favourite in the then popular ballet by Auber,[4] 'Alfred;' when, just before the curtain drew up, the manager came forward and expressed his regret that Mademoiselle Mercandotti had disappeared, and that he had been unable to discover where she had gone. Knowing ones, however, guessed that she had been carried off by the 'Golden Ball,' whose advances had been very favourably received, and who had evidently made a strong impression upon the damsel; and a few days after, the *Morning Post* announced that a marriage had taken place between a young man of large fortune and one of the most remarkable dancers of the age. The honeymoon was passed at

[1] Philip William Wyatt, the fourth and youngest son of James Wyatt and younger brother of the more celebrated Benjamin Dean Wyatt, redecorated 40 Upper Brook Street for Ball Hughes in 1819.

[2] Maria Mercandotti (b. *c.* 1801). Known as the 'Andalusian Venus', she came to London in 1814 and appeared at the King's Theatre. She danced at the Paris Opera in 1821-2.

[3] James Duff, fourth Earl of Fife (1776-1857).

[4] Daniel-François-Esprit Auber (1782-1871) was appointed director of the Paris Conservatoire in 1842. His opera *La Muette de Portici* (1828) was much admired by Wagner.

Oatlands, which the happy bridegroom had shortly before purchased from the Duke of York.[1]

Ball Hughes died at St Germains two years ago. His fortune had dwindled down to a fourth of its original amount, for he was perhaps the greatest gambler of his day. His love of play was such, that at one period of his life he would rather play at pitch and toss than be without his favourite excitement. He told me that at one time he had lost considerable sums at battledore and shuttlecock. On one occasion, immediately after dinner, he and the eccentric Lord Petersham[2] commenced playing with these toys, and continued hard at work during the whole of the night; next morning he was found by his valet lying on the ground, fast asleep, but ready for any other species of speculation. His purchase of Oatlands, which at the time was considered a foolish one, proved a very good speculation; for it was sold, for building villas, for so large a sum, that Hughes, whose fortune had dwindled to a mere pittance, became in his latter days very well off again; and though he lived in retirement, kept a large establishment, and was in the enjoyment of every luxury.

Dr Goodall, of Eton

This gentleman was proverbially fond of punning. About the same time that he was made Provost of Eton [in 1809] he received, also, a stall at Windsor. A young lady of his acquaintance, while congratulating him on his elevation, and requesting him to give the young ladies of Eton and Windsor a ball during the vacation, happened to touch his wig with her fan, and caused the powder to fly about. Upon which the doctor exclaimed, 'My dear, you see you can get the powder out of the *canon*, but not the ball.'

Eton College in 1810

When Dr Keate,[3] the head master of the Lower School, was elevated to the Upper, he did not bring with him a popular name; his abrupt,

[1] Oatlands House, Weybridge, Surrey, was built by Henry Holland for Frederick, Duke of York, in 1794–1800.

[2] Charles Stanhope, Viscount Petersham, later fourth Earl of Harrington (1780–1851).

[3] The Rev. John Keate (1773–1852) was appointed headmaster of Eton in 1809. He was celebrated for the stern manner in which he established the school's discipline. 'He was little more (if more at all) than five feet in height, and was not very great in girth,' Alexander Kinglake wrote of him, 'but in this space was concentrated the pluck of ten battalions.' He was a respected master; and, after the famous flogging mentioned by Gronow below, the boys cheered him. He retired in 1834 to a rectory in Hampshire.

blunt, and somewhat rude manner, which contrasted strongly with the mild and polished bearing of his predecessor, Dr Goodall, did not tend to remove the unfavourable impression his antecedents had produced. The consequence was a good deal of disaffection, which showed itself in various ways. The most remarkable and successful trick which was played off on him, by some bold and skilful boy whose name to this day remains undisclosed, I will endeavour to describe. The head master, when he came from his private chambers to the upper schoolroom, had to pass through the old library by a private door, the key of which Keate always carried in his pocket. One morning coming to his accustomed duties, on reaching the door he tried in vain to insert the key into the lock; the key could not be forced into it: and no wonder, for it was afterwards discovered that a small bullet had been dexterously inserted into the wards of the lock. The little autocrat (for Keate was diminutive in stature), thus compelled to sound a retreat, descended the private stairs, and after making a long detour under the colonnade, entered the upper schoolroom: he strode along full of ire and breathing vengeance; which, however, was never gratified. But the game was not yet played out; for when the Doctor got to the upper end of the school, and ascended the steps which led to the pulpit, he found the door which led into it was screwed up. Keate was considered to be a sort of pocket Hercules, but nevertheless all his efforts to force open the door proved ineffectual. Foiled here, he rushed to the other side; but the same result awaited him. The well-known Eton cry, 'Boo, boo,' was now reiterated from one end of the schoolroom to the other, which naturally added fuel to the flame of the Doctor's wrath. Plucky to the last, with one bound he vaulted over the doorway into his sanctum, his face glowing with rage like a fiery meteor. Off flew his three-corner cocked-hat, and down he sat; but his seat being smeared all over with cobbler's wax, the little man found that he could not rise without an awkward rent in his silk breeches. I leave it to the reader's imagination to picture the result of this species of practical joking: it certainly did not improve the Doctor's temper, for he grew more unpopular with the school, and he avenged himself upon the persons of delinquent boys.

FLOGGING AT ETON, UNDER DR KEATE

Eton under Dr Keate was conducted on a system of brutal severity, which never ought to have been permitted. I recollect that a row – or, as it was foolishly denominated, a rebellion – took place there in 1809, owing to the vexatious and tyrannical conduct of the head master, who had ordered an extra muster roll during the summer months, by which the boys were precluded from amusing themselves as before at cricket, boating, &c. On this occasion, no fewer than ninety grown-up boys were flogged for the crime of declining to comply with the irksome regulation. Though this affair occurred nearly sixty years ago, I really cannot think of it without indignation; for I remember that the fear of the birch was so strong at the time that no boy went up with his lesson without trembling with apprehension of being put in the bill for a flogging.

Keate, however, paid the penalty for his excessive severity, for he never got on in the Church; while the late excellent Archbishop Sumner, who was a tutor under Keate, and never got a boy flogged, owed his position to his kindness towards those who afterwards became public men.[1]

DR KEATE IN PARIS

Every one has heard of the famous Dr Busby, head-master of Westminster, who, while showing Charles II over the school, apologised to that merry monarch for keeping his hat on in the presence of royalty; 'For,' said he, 'it would not do for my boys to suppose that there existed in the world a greater man than Dr Busby.'[2] He was notorious for his Spartan discipline, and constantly acted up to the old adage of not sparing the rod and spoiling the boy. He was once invited, during a residence at Deal, by an old Westminster – who, from being a very idle, well-flogged boy, had, after a course of distinguished service, being named to the command of a fine frigate in the Downs – to visit him on board his ship. The Doctor accepted the invitation; and, after he had got up the ship's side, the captain piped all hands for punishment, and said to the astonished Doctor, 'You d——d old scoundrel, I am delighted to have the opportunity of paying you off at last. Here, boatswain, give him three dozen.'

The old pupils of Dr Keate in Paris, soon after Waterloo, many of

---

[1] John Bird Sumner (1780–1862) was the brother of Charles Richard Sumner, Bishop of Winchester and former tutor to the sons of George IV's mistress, Lady Conyngham (see note, p. 26). Having been educated there between 1791 and 1798, he returned to Eton as an assistant master in 1802. He was consecrated Bishop of Chester in 1828 and Archbishop of Canterbury in 1848.

[2] Richard Busby (1606–1695) was appointed headmaster of Westminster School in 1638.

whom had suffered at least as much at his hands as the rancorous sea-captain had at Dr Busby's, received their former pedagogue in a far different manner. He had been seen, to our great astonishment, eating an ice at Tortoni's on the Boulevards, and we determined to give him a dinner at Beauvilliers', the best dining-place in Paris, and far superior to anything of the kind in the present day.

We had ordered a most excellent dinner, and I never witnessed a more jovial banquet. The Doctor evinced his appreciation of the dinner and wines in a manner most gratifying to his hosts; ate as if he had never eaten before, and paid his addresses, in large bumpers, to every description of wine; and, towards the end of the dinner, expressed his delight at finding that his old friends and pupils had not forgotten him; concluding 'a neat and appropriate speech' with 'Floreat Etona.'

After drinking his health, as the bottle passed gaily round, we took the opportunity of giving him a little innocent 'chaff,' reminding him of his heavy hand and arbitrary manner of proceeding. The Doctor took our jokes in good part, and in his turn told us that, if he had a regret, it was that he had not flogged us a good deal more; but he felt certain that the discipline had done us a great deal of good: he then concluded by paying us all compliments in a few well-turned phrases. We heartily cheered his address, and parted on excellent terms.

Keate was a very short, thickset man, with a red face and a stentorian voice. The very sight of the cocked hat he always wore, placed frontways on his head, like that of the Emperor Napoleon, struck terror into the hearts of all offenders. However, in spite of his severity, he was generally liked by the boys at Eton, and was a thoroughly honourable and upright man. He had been in his youth a capital fighter, was an excellent scholar, and an admirable writer of Latin verse. Every old Etonian of his time must have felt hurt that the Whig government should not have thought fit to name Keate provost of Eton, in the room of Dr Goodall; and we all thought it very hard that he should have left the school without any recognition or acknowledgment of his long and arduous services.

SUMNER, AND OTHER ETON MASTERS

When I was a boy at Eton, now, alas! many, many years ago, by far the most popular tutor was Dr Sumner, whose loss as Archbishop of Canterbury we have lately had to deplore. This most able and excellent man went by the name of 'Crumpety Sumner,' whether from some fancied resemblance in his fine open countenance to that farinaceous esculent, or from some episode of his more youthful days, I was never able to discover; but I can safely say that no one was more universally beloved throughout the precincts of the venerable college of Henry VI than he was.

This respected Eton tutor, after passing through many intermediary posts of great utility and importance, became primate of England, with the applause of all who had at any time been brought within the sphere of his beneficent influence. He was at once the most learned, able, and at the same time the most modest and unpretending of men. Though he lived to a great age, his mind was vigorous to the last, and he preserved all the fire and energy which distinguished him in youth, and which was always exercised for some useful and benevolent purpose. Peace to his ashes! I feel proud to have known him and regret to think that so much of his advice and example should not have brought better fruit in me.

SCROPE DAVIES

The name of Scrope Davies is now but little known,[1] except in connection with Brummell's[2] exit from the fashionable world of London, and from his being occasionally mentioned by Lord Byron and by Moore;[3] yet few men were better received in society, or more the fashion than he once was. He was educated at Eton, and from thence he migrated in due time to King's College, Cambridge, of which he became a fellow; there he formed those acquaintances that at a later period served as an introduction into that world of which he soon became a distinguished ornament. His manners and appearance were of the true Brummell type: there was nothing showy in his exterior. He was quiet and reserved in ordinary company, but he was the life and soul of those who relished learning and wit; being a ripe scholar, and well read, he was always ready with an apt quotation.

As was the case with many of the foremost men of that day, the greater number of his hours were passed at the gambling-table, where for a length of time he was eminently successful; for he was a first-rate

[1] Scrope Berdmore Davies (1782–1852), Fellow of King's College, Cambridge. Byron's intimate friend, wit, gambler, womaniser, dandy and radical politician. His papers were discovered in 1976 in a bank vault where they had been deposited when Davies fled to France in 1820 to escape his creditors.
[2] George Bryan ('Beau') Brummell (1778–1840), the great arbiter of fashion of the Regency.
[3] Thomas Moore (1779–1852), the Irish poet, of whom Gronow has more to say below (see pp. 192–3).

calculator. He seldom played against individuals; he preferred going to the regular establishments. But on one occasion he had, by a remarkable run of good luck, completely ruined a young man who had just reached his majority and come into the possession of a considerable fortune. The poor youth sank down upon a sofa in abject misery, when he reflected that he was a beggar; for he was on the point of marriage. Scrope Davies, touched by his despair, entered into conversation with him, and ended by giving him back the whole of his losses, upon a solemn promise that he never would play again. The only thing that Scrope retained of his winnings was one of the little carriages of that day, called a dormeuse, from its being fitted up with a bed, for he said, 'When I travel in it I shall sleep the better for having acted rightly.' The youth kept his promise; but when his benefactor wanted money, he forgot that he owed all he possessed to Scrope's generosity, and refused to assist him.[1]

For a long time Scrope Davies was a lucky player; but the time arrived when Fortune deserted her old favourite; and, shortly after the Dandy dynasty was overthrown, he found himself unable to mingle with the rich, the giddy, and the gay. With the wreck of his fortune, and indeed but little to live upon beyond the amount of his own Cambridge fellowship, he sought repose in Paris, and there, indulging in literary leisure, bade the world farewell. He had but few intimates, and those only whom he had formerly known in his days of affluence.

Scrope Davies bore with perfect resignation the loss of the wealth he had once possessed; and though his annual income was very limited, he made no complaint of poverty. He daily sat himself down on a bench in the garden of the Tuileries, where he received those whose acquaintance he desired, and then returned to his study, where he wrote notes upon the men of his day, which have unfortunately disappeared: that they existed there can be no doubt, as he occasionally read extracts from his diary to those in whom he placed confidence. Ball Hughes was about the last of his visitors. Scrope found the former gay young man very much improved in mind by adversity, and was wont to say, 'He is no longer "Golden Ball;" but since the gilt is off, he rolls on much more smoothly than he did.' Having heard that Brummell had obtained a

---

[1] Scrope Davies's biographer suggests that 'this story is quite obviously too good to be true. And yet, on more than one occasion [John Cam] Hobhouse makes mention of Scrope's *dormeuse*' (T. A. J. Burnett, *The Rise and Fall of a Regency Dandy: The Life and Times of Scrope Berdmore Davies*, John Murray, 1981, p. 54).

consulship[1] when Lord Melbourne came into office,[2] Scrope went over to London and had an interview with the noble Lord; but he told his friends, 'Lamb looked so sheepish when I was ushered into his presence, that I asked him for nothing; indeed, there were so many nibbling at his grass, that I felt I ought not to jump over the fence into the meadow upon which such animals were feeding.'

'TEAPOT' CRAWFURD

Crawfurd [Craufurd] was brought up at Eton, and subsequently entered the 10th Hussars.[3] He possessed immense strength, was a handsome fellow, and his bravery was proverbial. His riding to hounds particularly, when a boy at Melton Mowbray and Belvoir Castle,[4] was plucky in the extreme. He was called 'Teapot,' because of his predilection when at Eton for brewing tea in a black pot, which he kept and cherished when a soldier; though some would have it that his handsome head looked like those on old-fashioned teapots. He was noble-looking to the last day of his life, though worn down by disease. As a companion, he was charming; his bewitching manner found him friends everywhere, and he was courted by the dandies and men of fashion. He married Lady Barbara Coventry, a very beautiful woman, with whom he lived happily many years. The Prince Regent was very partial to him; and on the occasion of the 10th Hussars being paraded before their departure for Spain,[5] the Prince said to him. 'Go, my boy, show the world what stuff you are made of. You possess strength, youth, and courage; go, and conquer.' Crawfurd arrived in Spain, and his first rencontre with the enemy was at Orthes, where he was foremost in the charge, and behaved splendidly. A brother of his, equally brave, was killed at Waterloo, whilst defending the château of Huguemont.

[1] Brummell was appointed British Consul at Caen in 1830.
[2] William Lamb, second Viscount Melbourne (1779–1848). He became Home Secretary in 1830 and Prime Minister in 1834.
[3] Alexander Charles Craufurd (not Crawfurd), son of Sir James Gregan-Craufurd, second baronet. He married Barbara, second daughter of the seventh Earl of Coventry, in 1818. He rose to the rank of lieutenant-colonel. Both he and his wife died in 1838.
[4] Belvoir Castle, seat of the Dukes of Rutland, was reconstructed by John Webb after being slighted by Parliamentary troops in the Civil War. It was remodelled in 1800–13 by James Wyatt for the fifth Duke.
[5] The Peninsular War (1808–13) was fought between French and British armies for control of Spain and Portugal, after a Spanish rebellion against Napoleon's attempt to establish his brother, Joseph Bonaparte, as King of Spain. Wellington's army, supported by Spanish and Portuguese guerillas, eventually drove the French army out of Spain.

An Englishman's Visit to St Petersburg

I recollect among others, an adventure of which a friend of mine, a Mr Kington, the son of a rich Bristol merchant, was the hero. My old school-fellow took it into his head to visit the Continent, but being above following in the tracks of other tourists, who did the grand tour in a mechanical way that was perfectly ludicrous, he determined on visiting St Petersburg, then a *terra incognita* to the ordinary run of British travellers. Fully equipped with purse, portmanteaus, and the usual supply of stiffly-starched neckcloths, he left his friends at Bristol, after receiving the usual cautions respecting damp sheets, wet feet, and the neglect of flannel, and in due course of time arrived at St Petersburg. There he had some difficulty in making himself understood as to the hotel he wished to put up at, for he could not speak a single word of any Continental language; he was on the point of being consigned to the care of the police as a madman, when one of the officials, who could speak English, came to the rescue and conducted him to one of the best hotels, where, according to the notice appended to its cards, English was spoken. After recovering from the fatigues of his journey, my friend hired a guide and proceeded to view the lions of the Russian metropolis, and also to visit our vice-consul (the only diplomatic agent England could boast of at that time), for the purpose of having the necessary forms gone through with regard to his passport.

In the course of conversation, Mr Kington inquired whether he could see the Emperor, and was told in reply that possibly an interview might be obtained, if he called at the palace and left his name. Off started our ambitious tourist, and on arriving at the porter's lodge, instead of writing his name down, he gave in his card, on which was inscribed in large characters, 'MR KINGTON, *Carlton House.*' The following day, one of the equerries of the Emperor dashed up to the hotel where my friend was staying, bearing an invitation for him to dine with the Emperor that evening. Kington, although surprised at the deference with which he was treated by the officer, and the honour conferred upon him, bade one of the servants at the hotel to interpret his thanks to the bearer of the invitation, and his grateful acceptance of it. At the appointed hour, Kington, rigged out in best suit, presented himself at the palace, and was ushered into the Imperial presence. The Emperor received him very graciously; and speaking English perfectly, asked him a thousand questions about London, which city he had visited the year before: in short, he appeared to treat him as an equal.

At dinner, there were many ladies, personages of the highest rank, and officers in uniform, and the conversation became general. But what puzzled Kington was the constant allusions made to 'Carlton House' and the Prince of Wales;[1] and his answers to the questions put to him on these subjects were naturally vague and unsatisfactory. To crown all, the Emperor observed to one of the ladies, in French, 'He is evidently a natural son of the Prince of Wales, or he would not be so shy.' On retiring from the dining-table, Kington was called aside by the lady, who spoke English, and asked what mystery it was that surrounded him and made him so diffident. He replied that he himself did not know why the allusions to Carlton House and the Prince Regent were made, but that they were no doubt intended as compliments to his country. 'No doubt you wish to preserve your incognito,' observed the lady; 'but I must tell you frankly the opinion of the Emperor, in which I fully coincide – viz., that you are a natural son of the Prince of Wales: is it not so?'

The truth instantly flashed across Kington's mind that he had come to the palace under false colours; a discovery which was succeeded by a terrific vision of what was usually the fate of impostors: he rushed from the palace, haunted by the idea that he was pursued by Cossacks, lance in hand, for the purpose of being consigned, first to the knout, and then to Siberia.

The card given by Kington to the porter had been handed to an equerry, and by him laid before the Emperor; who, seeing 'Carlton House' on it (which was the name of the country residence of the father of our hero), fell into the mistake of supposing that Kington was in some way or other connected with the Prince Regent; and hence the invitation.

Fearing to be arrested by the police, Kington bribed the landlord of the hotel to hide him in a garret while the necessary forms were being gone through to facilitate his departure; and after passing two days without sleep, he succeeded in providing himself with a berth in a vessel

---

[1] George Augustus Frederick, Prince of Wales (1762-1830), was King George III's eldest son. He became Prince Regent in 1810 when his father, suffering from the rare metabolic disorder known as porphyria, exhibited signs of madness. On his father's death in 1820, the Prince succeeded to the throne as King George IV.

Carlton House, his palatial London house in Pall Mall, was reconstructed from 1783 by Henry Holland at a cost which even the Regent himself admitted was 'enormous'. The scene of several extraordinarily grand receptions and balls, it was demolished when the Regent came to the throne as George IV and decided that an even more splendid palace was required. Work began, therefore, on the transformation of Buckingham House. Carlton House Terrace was built on the site of the Pall Mall house and in its gardens, which had been laid out by William Kent.

bound for England. When on board he exclaimed, 'Thank God, I am saved! Never, never will I trust myself in a foreign country again.' Poor Kington was so overcome with anxiety and fright that he arrived in London more dead than alive; for I was among the first persons who saw him on his arrival, when he recounted his adventures in such a doleful manner, that for the life of me I could not contain my laughter. But the climax was reached when he said, 'It is all very well for you to quiz me, but how would you have acted, sir, if you were in a strange country, among a horde of barbarians, and were called virtually a bastard, without being able to revenge yourself? Confound it! my father and mother were honest people, and this insult affects me more than all.' Poor Kington found his way back to his anxious family; but, either from 'funk,' or some disease contracted on his voyage, he died a very short time after his return. He was considered, when at Eton, to be an extremely well-built and powerful boy; he was a famous cricketer, and one of the 'cocks of the school.'

BEAU BRUMMELL

Amongst the curious freaks of fortune there is none more remarkable in my memory than the sudden appearance, in the highest and best society in London, of a young man whose antecedents warranted a much less conspicuous career: I refer to the famous Beau Brummell. We have innumerable instances of soldiers, lawyers, and men of letters elevating themselves from the most humble stations, and becoming the companions of princes and lawgivers; but there are comparatively few examples of men obtaining a similarly elevated position simply from their attractive personal appearance and fascinating manners. Brummell's father, who was a steward to one or two large estates, sent his son George to Eton.[1] He was endowed with a handsome person, and distinguished himself at Eton as the best scholar, the best boatman, and the best cricketer; and, more than all, he was supposed to possess the comprehensive excellences that are represented by the familiar term of 'good fellow.' He made many friends amongst the scions of good families. He immediately became a great favourite with the ladies, and was asked by all the dowagers to as many balls and soirées as he could attend.

---

[1] Brummell's father, William Brummell, had been Private Secretary to Lord North, who procured for him various profitable appointments. He left a fortune of £65,000. His own father had been a gentleman's gentleman.

At last the Prince of Wales sent for Brummell, and was so much
pleased with his manner and appearance, that he gave him a commission in his own regiment, the 10th Hussars. Unluckily, Brummell,
soon after joining his regiment, was thrown from his horse at a grand
review at Brighton, when he broke his classical Roman nose. This
misfortune, however, did not affect the fame of the beau; and although
his nasal organ had undergone a slight transformation, it was forgiven
by his admirers, since the rest of his person remained intact. When we
are prepossessed by the attractions of a favourite, it is not a trifle that
will dispel the illusion; and Brummell continued to govern society, in
conjunction with the Prince of Wales. He was remarkable for his dress,
which was generally conceived by himself; the execution of his sublime
imagination being carried out by that superior genius, Mr Weston,
tailor, of Old Bond Street. The Regent sympathised deeply with
Brummell's labours to arrive at the most attractive and gentlemanly
mode of dressing the male form, at a period when fashion had placed at
the disposal of the tailor the most hideous material that could possibly
tax his art. The coat may have a long tail or a short tail, a high collar
or a low collar, but it will always be an ugly garment. The modern hat
may be spread out at the top, or narrowed, whilst the brim may be
turned up or turned down, made a little wider or a little more narrow;
still it is inconceivably hideous. Pantaloons and Hessian boots were the
least objectionable features of the costume which the imagination of a
Brummell and the genius of a Royal Prince were called upon to modify
or change. The hours of meditative agony which each dedicated to the
odious fashions of the day have left no monument save the coloured
caricatures in which these illustrious persons have appeared.

In the zenith of his popularity Brummell might be seen at the bay
window of White's Club,[1] surrounded by the lions of the day, laying
down the law, and occasionally indulging in those witty remarks for
which he was famous. His house corresponded with his personal 'get
up;' the furniture was in excellent taste, and the library contained the
best works of the best authors of every period and of every country. His
canes, his snuff-boxes, his Sèvres china, were exquisite; his horses and

[1] White's, the oldest and grandest of London's gentlemen's clubs, was founded at
White's Chocolate House which had been established in 1693 on the site of what is now
Boodle's by an Italian, Francis White, whose real name was presumably Francesco Bianco.
The earliest records of the club date from 1736. It is still in existence - with an extremely
long waiting-list - at 37-8 St James's Street. When pressed for the repayment of a debt of
£500, Brummell was said to have replied airily, 'I paid you when I was standing at the
window of White's and said as you passed, "How do you do?" '

carriage were conspicuous for their excellence; and, in fact, the superior taste of a Brummell was discoverable in everything that belonged to him.

But the reign of the king of fashion, like all other reigns, was not destined to continue for ever. Brummell warmly espoused the cause of Mrs Fitzherbert,[1] and this of course offended the Prince of Wales. I refer to the period when his Royal Highness had abandoned that beautiful woman for another favourite.[2] A coldness then ensued between the Prince and his *protégé*; and finally, the mirror of fashion was excluded from the royal presence.

A curious accident brought Brummell again to the dinner-table of his royal patron; he was asked one night at White's to take a hand at whist, when he won £20,000. This circumstance having been related by the Duke of York[3] to the Prince of Wales, the beau was again invited to Carlton House. At the commencement of the dinner, matters went off smoothly; but Brummell, in his joy at finding himself with his old friend, became excited, and drank too much wine. His Royal Highness – who wanted to pay off Brummell for an insult he had received at Lady Cholmondeley's ball, when the beau, turning towards the Prince, said to Lady Worcester, 'Who is your fat friend?' – had invited him to dinner merely out of a desire for revenge. The Prince therefore pretended to be affronted with Brummell's hilarity, and said to his brother, the Duke of York, who was present, 'I think we had better order Mr Brummell's carriage before he gets drunk.' Whereupon he rang the bell, and Brummell left the royal presence. This circumstance originated the story about the beau having told the Prince to ring the bell. I received these details from the late General Sir Arthur Upton, who was present at the dinner.

---

[1] Maria Anne Fitzherbert, née Smythe (1756–1837), a charming and graceful Roman Catholic widow, six years older than the Prince. They were married in a secret ceremony in her drawing room in 1785. The marriage, contracted without the King's consent, was invalid under the Royal Marriage Act of 1772. After the Prince's marriage to Princess Caroline, his relationship with Mrs Fitzherbert, broken off for a time, was resumed; but by 1803 other mistresses had taken her place. When the King was buried it was discovered by the Duke of Wellington that he was wearing a miniature of her on a black ribbon round his neck.

[2] This was Frances, Countess of Jersey (1753–1821), a clever, ambitious, sensual and rather heartless woman. Gronow elsewhere described her manner as being that of a 'theatrical tragedy Queen; and whilst attempting the sublime, she frequently made herself simply ridiculous, being inconceivably rude, and in her manner often ill-bred'.

[3] Frederick, Duke of York and Albany (1763–1827), George III's second son. Gronow has much to say of him below.

The latter days of Brummell were clouded with mortifications and penury. He retired to Calais, where he kept up a ludicrous imitation of his past habits. At last he got himself named consul at Caen; but he afterwards lost the appointment, and eventually died insane, and in abject poverty, at Calais.[1]

JACK TALBOT OF THE GUARDS

Poor Jack Talbot,[2] after leaving Eton, entered the Coldstream Guards, and accompanied his regiment to Spain, where he evinced great courage, and was foremost in every fight. Though he possessed many imperfections, he was the manliest and kindest of human beings, and was the idol of the women; and their champion, also, for he was one of the few men who would never hear improper epithets applied to them under any circumstances, or allow their failings to be criticised by those who were in all probability the cause of them. There was a charm in Talbot's conversation that I never found in that of any other man; his brave good heart, and love of punch, made him an agreeable companion, and many friends. When in his cups, or rather bowls, he would talk facetiously about his rich father in Ireland, Lord Malahide, spending that nobleman's money all the time. He was foolishly generous. I have often seen him, at a club or in a coffee-house, pay for the whole of his friends present; and his liberality to women of all classes was profuse. He used to say, 'I would rather disoblige my father or my best friend than a pretty woman.'

Whether in the Guards' Club or at private assemblies, you were always sure to find Jack surrounded by a circle of friends, amused with his witty conversation and charmed with his good-humour. He had always a smile on his face; in fact, everybody acknowledged him as their friend.

During his last illness, [Lord] Alvanley[3] asked the doctor of the regiment what he thought of it. The doctor replied, 'My Lord, he is in a bad way, for I was obliged to make use of the lancet this morning.' 'You should have tapped him, doctor,' said Lord Alvanley; 'for I am sure he has more claret than blood in his veins.' The late Duke of Beaufort one day called upon him at his lodgings in Mount Street, and found him drinking sherry at breakfast: the Duke remonstrated with

---

[1] In fact, in the Asylum of the Bon Sauveur, Caen.
[2] John Malpas Talbot (d. 1828), elder son of the second Baron Talbot of Malahide.
[3] See chapter 14.

him, saying, 'It will be the death of you.' Talbot replied, 'I get drunk every night, and find myself the better for it next morning.' Talbot was a great favourite of the late Duke of Cambridge,[1] who frequently called to inquire after his health. Upon one occasion, the Captain's servant, in answer to the Duke's interrogations, told his Royal Highness that his master did not want to see either doctor or parson, but only wished to be left to die in peace. The Duke, with sad forebodings, sent Dr Keate to see him; the doctor, on his arrival, found Talbot seated in his arm-chair dead, with a bottle of sherry half-empty on the table beside him. He was only twenty-seven.

---

[1] Adolphus Frederick, Duke of Cambridge (1774–1850), the seventh son of King George III and father of George, Duke of Cambridge, who was commander-in-chief of the army for thirty-nine years.

2

The Prince Regent, His Family and Friends

THE PRINCE REGENT

When the eldest son of George the Third assumed the Regency [in 1810], England was in a state of political transition. The convulsions of the Continent were felt amongst us; the very foundations of European society were shaking, and the social relations of men were rapidly changing. The Regent's natural leanings were towards the Tories; therefore, as soon as he undertook the responsibility of power, he abruptly abandoned the Whigs, and retained in office the admirers and partisans of his father's policy. This resolution caused him to have innumerable and inveterate enemies, who never lost an opportunity of attacking his public acts and interfering with his domestic relations.

The Regent was singularly imbued with petty royal pride. He would rather be amiable and familiar with his tailor than agreeable and friendly with the most illustrious of the aristocracy of Great Britain; he would rather joke with a Brummell than admit to his confidence a Norfolk or a Somerset. The Regent was always particularly well-bred in public, and showed, if he chose, decidedly good manners; but he very often preferred to address those whom he felt he could patronise. His Royal Highness was as much the victim of circumstances and the child of thoughtless imprudence as the most humble subject of the Crown. His unfortunate marriage with a Princess of Brunswick originated in his debts; as he married that unhappy lady for one million sterling.[1]

The Princess of Wales married nothing but an association with the Crown of England. If the Prince ever seriously loved any woman, it was Mrs Fitzherbert, with whom he had appeared at the altar.

Public opinion in England, under the inspiration of the Whigs, raised a cry of indignation against the Prince. It was imagined, I presume, that a royal personage should be born without heart or feeling; that he should have been able to live only for the good of the state and for the convenience of his creditors. The Princess of Wales was one of the most unattractive and almost repulsive women for an elegant-minded man that could well have been found amongst German royalty. It is not my intention to recall the events of the Regency. It is well known that the Prince became eventually so unpopular as to exclude himself as much as possible from public gaze.

THE PRINCESS CHARLOTTE OF WALES AT A FÊTE IN THE YEAR 1813 AT CARLTON HOUSE

Carlton House, at the period to which I refer, was a centre for all the great politicians and wits who were the favourites of the Regent. The principal entrance of this palace in Pall Mall, with its screen of columns, will be remembered by many.[2] In the rear of the mansion was an extensive garden – greensward, stately trees (probably two hundred years old), and beds of the choicest flowers, gave to the grounds a picturesque attraction perhaps unequalled. It was here that the heir to the throne of England gave, in 1813, an open-air *fête*, in honour of the battle of Vittoria. About three o'clock p.m. the *élite* of London society, who had been honoured with an invitation, began to arrive, all in full dress; the ladies particularly displaying their diamonds and pearls, as if

[1] Princess Caroline Amelia Elizabeth of Brunswick-Wolfenbüttel (1768–1821) was the daughter of the Duchess of Brunswick, King George III's eldest sister. A good-natured, *gauche*, indiscreet and impulsive woman, none too clean in her person, she married the Prince of Wales in 1795. He was extremely drunk during the ceremony, which he had undergone on condition that the government paid his debts. These had then reached the astonishing figure of £630,000, the equivalent today of not much less than £18,000,000. It was agreed that his income should be increased to £138,000 a year (about £8,000,000) and that £65,000 a year should be deducted from this for the payment of his debts. He and his wife separated soon after the marriage and she went to live abroad (see note, p. 79). She returned when he became King and died soon afterwards.

[2] When Carlton House was demolished (see note, p. 15), these columns were preserved and later used for the portico of the National Gallery.

they were going to a drawing-room, the men, of course, in full dress, wearing knee-breeches and buckles.

This was the first day that her Royal Highness the Princess Charlotte appeared in public. She was a young lady of more than ordinary personal attractions; her features were regular, and her complexion fair, with the rich bloom of youthful beauty; her eyes were blue and very expressive, and her hair was abundant, and of that peculiar light brown which merges into the golden: in fact, such hair as the Middle-Age Italian painters associate with their conceptions of the Madonna. In figure her Royal Highness was somewhat over the ordinary height of women, but finely proportioned and well developed. Her manners were remarkable for a simplicity and good-nature which would have won admiration and invited affection in the most humble walks of life. She created universal admiration, and I may say a feeling of national pride, amongst all who attended the ball.[1]

The Prince Regent entered the gardens giving his arm to the Queen,[2] the rest of the royal family following. Tents had been erected in various parts of the grounds, where the bands of the Guards were stationed. The weather was magnificent, a circumstance which contributed to show off the admirable arrangements of Sir Benjamin Bloomfield, to whom had been deputed the organisation of the *fête*, which commenced by dancing on the lawn.[3]

A year afterwards, the Duke of York said to his royal niece, 'Tell me, my dear, have you seen any one among the foreign princes whom you would like to have for a husband?' The Princess naïvely replied, 'No one so much prepossesses me as Prince Leopold of Coburg. I have heard much of his bravery in the field, and I must say he is personally

---

[1] Princess Charlotte Augusta (1796-1817), the only child of the Regent and Princess Caroline, was conceived on the morning after her parents' ill-fated marriage. Her father had fallen drunkenly into the grate the night before and her mother had left him there. In 1816 she married Prince Leopold of Saxe-Coburg-Saalfeld and died the next year at Claremont. Prince Leopold was elected King of the Belgians in 1831. Gronow's portrait of Princess Charlotte is a flattering one. Before her marriage she was an excitable, hot-tempered, acquisitive and pert young woman, renowned for her hoydenish behaviour and loud and ready laugh.

[2] Queen Charlotte (1744-1818), the Prince Regent's mother, was the niece of the third Duke of Mecklenburg-Strelitz. She married George III in 1761 and bore him fifteen children.

[3] Sir Benjamin Bloomfield (1768-1846), later first Baron Bloomfield, the Regent's Gentleman Attendant since 1808. He became his Private Secretary in 1817 and Keeper of the Privy Purse. Irritated by his sulky moods and bossy, petulant manner, George IV – as the Prince Regent had then become – relieved him of his office in 1822, much to the satisfaction of the King's then mistress, Lady Conyngham (see p. 26).

agreeable to me. I have particularly heard of his famous cavalry charge at the battle of Leipsic [Leipzig], where he took several thousand prisoners, for which he was rewarded with the Order of Maria Theresa.' In a few months afterwards she became the wife of the man whom she so much admired, and from whom she was torn away not long after by the cruel hand of death. It will be remembered that she died in childbirth, and her offspring expired at the same time. The accoucheur who attended her was so much affected by the calamity that he committed suicide some short time afterwards.[1]

CAPTAIN HESSE, FORMERLY OF THE 18TH HUSSARS

One of my most intimate friends was the late Captain Hesse, generally believed to be a son of the Duke of York, by a German lady of rank. Though it is not my intention to disclose certain family secrets of which I am in possession, I may, nevertheless, record some circumstances connected with the life of my friend, which were familiar to a large circle with whom I mixed. Hesse, in early youth, lived with the Duke and Duchess of York; he was treated in such a manner by them as to indicate an interest in him by their Royal Highnesses which could scarcely be attributed to ordinary regard, and was gazetted a cornet in the 18th Hussars at seventeen years of age. Shortly afterwards he went to Spain, and was present in all the battles in which his regiment was engaged; receiving a severe wound in the wrist at the battle of Vittoria. When this became known in England, a royal lady wrote to Lord Wellington, requesting that he might be carefully attended to; and, at the same time, a watch, with her portrait, was forwarded, which was delivered to the wounded hussar by Lord Wellington himself. When he had sufficiently recovered, Hesse returned to England, and passed much of his time at Oatlands, the residence of the Duchess of York; he was also honoured with the confidence of the Princess Charlotte and her mother, Queen Caroline.

Many delicate and important transactions were conducted through the medium of Captain Hesse; in fact, it was perfectly well known that he played a striking part in many scenes of domestic life which I do not

---

[1] This was Sir Richard Croft (1762–1818), the tall, elegant and most fashionable *accoucheur* who had taken upon himself the sole responsibility of his patient's care. The Regent did his best to shield him from the attacks made after Princess Charlotte's death, thanking him publicly for the 'zealous care' he had taken of his patient. In 1818 while attending a woman whose difficulties in labour resembled those he had witnessed at Claremont, he shot himself in her house.

wish to reveal[1] . . . I may, however, observe that the Prince Regent sent the late Admiral Lord Keith[2] to Hesse's lodgings, who demanded, in his Royal Highness's name, the restitution of the watch and letters which had been sent him when in Spain. After a considerable amount of hesitation, the admiral obtained what he wanted the following day; whereupon Lord Keith assured him that the Prince Regent would never forget so great a mark of confidence, and that the heir to the throne would ever afterwards be his friend. I regret to say, from personal knowledge, that upon this occasion the prince behaved most ungratefully and unfeelingly; for, after having obtained all he wanted, he positively refused to receive Hesse at Carlton House.

Hesse's life was full of singular incidents. He was a great friend of the Queen of Naples, grandmother of the ex-Sovereign of the Two Sicilies; in fact, so notorious was that *liaison*, that Hesse was eventually expelled from Naples under an escort of gendarmes. He was engaged in several affairs of honour, in which he always displayed the utmost courage; and his romantic career terminated by his being killed in a duel.

The late Lord Bloomfield

The late Lord Bloomfield likewise owed his elevation to the Peerage to his musical talents. When the Prince of Wales was living at the Pavilion at Brighton, he wanted some one who could accompany him on the violoncello, and having ascertained that Captain Bloomfield, of the Royal Artillery, who was then at Brighton with his troop, was an accomplished violoncello player, the captain was accordingly summoned to appear before the prince at the Pavilion. From that night commenced an intimacy which for many years existed between the prince and Captain Bloomfield, who for a considerable length of time was well known in fashionable circles under the title of Sir Benjamin

---

[1] For better reasons than all but a few people knew, the Regent had good cause not to receive Captain Charles Hesse, whose attentions to the sixteen-year-old Princess Charlotte had been encouraged by her mother. Princess Charlotte confessed all to her father in the presence of his sister, Princess Mary, who recorded: 'The Princess Charlotte . . . always met [Captain Hesse] at her mother's at Kensington, and had private interviews with him . . . with the Princess of Wales's knowledge and connivance. . . . The Princess of Wales used to let him into her own apartments by a door that opens into Kensington Gardens, and then left them together in her own bedroom, and turned the key upon them saying, "À present je vous laisse, amusez vous."'

[2] Admiral George Keith Elphinstone, Viscount Keith (1746–1823) married as his second wife Hester Maria, daughter of Samuel Johnson's friend, Mrs Thrale. He was the father, by his first wife, of Margaret Mercer Elphinstone, Princess Charlotte's best friend.

Bloomfield. A court intrigue, headed by a fascinating marchioness [Elizabeth, Marchioness Conyngham],[1] caused him to be sent into splendid exile: this lady attributing to Sir Benjamin Bloomfield her being compelled to send back some jewels which had been presented to her by the Prince Regent, but which, it was discovered, belonged to the Crown, and could not be alienated. Sir Benjamin was created a peer, and sent to Stockholm as ambassador,[2] where his affable manners and his unostentatious hospitality rendered him exceedingly popular; and he became as great a favourite with Bernadotte[3] as he had been with the Prince Regent. The name of Bloomfield is to this day respected in Sweden.

PARTY AT MANCHESTER HOUSE IN 1816, AND THE REGENT'S ETIQUETTE

In 1816, when I was residing in Paris, I used to have all my clothes made by Staub, in the Rue Richelieu.

As I went out a great deal into the world, and was every night at some ball or party, I found that knee-breeches were only worn by a few old fogies; trousers and shoes being the usual costume of all the young men of the day. I returned to London towards the end of the year, and we put up at Fenton's in St James's Street.

I mention the following somewhat trivial circumstance to give some notion of the absurd severity in matters of dress and etiquette of Brummell's worthy pupil, the Prince Regent. A few days after my arrival, I received an invitation to a party at Manchester House, from Lady Hertford, 'to have the honour of meeting the Prince.'[4]

[1] Elizabeth, Marchioness Conyngham (d. 1861), a stout, kindly, rich and rapacious woman. She had been married for twenty-seven years and had four grown-up children when she became the King's mistress. Their relationship seems to have been warmly domestic rather than hotly passionate.

[2] While in Sweden, Bloomfield became a Wesleyan. After his death a minister of that faith issued a tract entitled 'A Coronet laid at Jesus's Feet in the Conversion of the late Lord Bloomfield'.

[3] Jean-Baptiste Bernadotte (1753-1844) was one of Napoleon's marshals. He was elected Crown Prince of Sweden in 1810, taking the name Charles John. He became King of Sweden and Norway on the death of Charles XIII in 1818.

[4] Manchester House, Manchester Square, later known as Hertford House, was built in about 1777 by the fourth Duke of Manchester largely because of the good duck shooting to be enjoyed nearby. It was purchased in 1797 by the second Marquess of Hertford. Both the third and fourth Marquesses were great collectors; and by the time of his death the fourth Marquess was the owner of one of Europe's finest private collections, being particularly remarkable for French eighteenth-century furniture, paintings and *objets d'art*. His illegitimate son, Richard Wallace, inherited the collection and left it at his death in 1890 to his widow, who, in her turn, left it to the nation as the Wallace Collection.

I went there dressed *à la Française*, and quite correctly, as I imagined, with white neckcloth and waistcoat, and black trousers, shoes, and silk stockings. The Prince had dined there, and I found him in the octagon-room, surrounded by all the great ladies of the Court. After making my bow, and retiring to the further part of the room, I sat down by the beautiful Lady Heathcote, and had been engaged in conversation with her for some time, when Horace Seymour[1] tapped me on the shoulder and said, 'The "great man,"' meaning the Prince, 'is very much surprised that you should have ventured to appear in his presence without knee-breeches. He considers it as a want of proper respect for him.'

This very disagreeable hint drove me away from Manchester House in a moment, in no very pleasant mood, as may be imagined; and I much fear that I went to bed devoting my royal master to all the infernal gods.

In the morning, being on guard, I mentioned what had occurred, with some chagrin, to my colonel, who good-naturedly told me not to take the matter to heart, as it was really of no consequence; and he added – 'Depend upon it, Gronow, the Prince, who is a lover of novelty, will wear trousers himself before the year is out, and then you may laugh at him.'

[The Colonel] proved a true prophet, for in less than a month I had the satisfaction of seeing 'the finest gentleman in Europe' at a ball at Lady Cholmondeley's, dressed exactly as I had been at Lady Hertford's, when I incurred his displeasure, in black trousers and shoes; and Lord Fife, who was in attendance upon the Prince, congratulated me upon the fact that his royal master had deigned to take example by the young Welshman.

GEORGE IV WHEN PRINCE OF WALES

When everybody took snuff, the Prince of Wales followed the fashion; or rather led it, for he was known to possess the finest collection of snuff-boxes that were to be had for love or money; but it appeared to me as if [His Royal Highness] took snuff for fashion's sake. He would take the box in his left hand, and, opening it with his right thumb and fore-finger, introduce them into this costly reservoir of snuff, and with a consequential air convey the same to the nose; indeed, those who were

---

[1] Horace Beauchamp Seymour (1781–1851), a nephew of the second Marquess of Hertford.

well acquainted with [him] frequently told me he took snuff for effect, but never liked it, and allowed all of it to escape from his finger and thumb before it reached the nose. His Royal Highness never permitted his friends or acquaintances the liberty to take a pinch out of his box, so that every one had his own particular *tabatière*. How different this was to times gone by, when a great man delighted in nothing so much as to offer any one he was acquainted with a pinch of snuff: for instance, the greatest dandy of the time to which I am referring, thought it an honour to take a *prise* from the poet Dryden's box; but there was unfortunately a wide difference between the Prince and the poet.

Mrs Fitzherbert lived in a magnificent house in Tilney Street, Hyde Park, in great state, her carriages and servants being the same as those HRH made use of. Brummell, who was then on good terms with the Prince, called on this lady one day and found the Prince seated on a sofa. The Prince, according to the Beau's statement, appeared sullen and evidently annoyed at the visit of the two gentlemen, and on Brummell's taking a pinch of snuff and carelessly placing his box on a small table nearly opposite HRH, the Prince observed, 'Mr Brummell, the place for your box is in your pocket, and not on the table.' Another specimen of HRH's rudeness may be cited. Lord Barrymore called at Carlton House one day, and was ushered into the Prince's private room;[1] on entering he placed his hat on a chair, when HRH observed, in a sarcastic manner, 'My Lord, a well-bred man places his hat under his arm on entering a room, and on his head when out of doors.'

BEAU BRUMMELL'S AUNT, MRS SEARLE

At the small entrance of the Green Park, opposite Clarges Street, and close to the reservoir, there stood some years back a neat cottage, surrounded by a courtyard, with stables for cows. The exterior of the cottage betokened no small degree of comfort and modest affluence; nor did the interior disappoint those who formed that opinion. Its inmates were two old ladies, dressed in the style of Louis XV, with high lace caps and dresses of brocaded silk.

In the autumn of 1814 I happened to stroll into the Park to see these cows, which were famed for their colour and symmetry. It was the hour for milking them, and one of the old ladies, observing my curiosity to see that operation performed, came up to the palings and begged me to walk in. I readily complied, and remained some time, then, thanking

---

[1] Richard Barry, seventh Earl of Barrymore (1769-93), known as 'Hellgate'.

her for the honour she had done me, I took my leave, having accepted her invitation to pay her a visit the next evening; which I did. After saluting Mrs Searle and inquiring after her health, I led her on to talk on divers matters. She had an excellent memory, was replete with *esprit*, and appeared to possess a knowledge of everything and everybody. I soon discovered that the old lady was proud of her blood, and she told me that she was aunt to George Brummell, the Beau; that George III had placed her as gate-keeper of the Green Park, and that the Princess Mary had kindly furnished her little cottage.[1] Her description of the royal family was somewhat interesting. She said, that one day the Prince of Wales called upon her, and as it was a beautiful summer's evening, stopped to see her cows milked. Her nephew George Brummell, who had only a day or two before left Eton, happened to be present. The Prince, attracted by his nice manners, entered into conversation with him, and before he left said, 'As I find you intend to be a soldier, I will give you a commission in my own regiment.' Tears of gratitude filled the youth's eyes, and he fell on his knees and kissed the royal hand. Shortly after, George Brummell's commission in the 10th Hussars was made out, and he was soon quartered with his regiment at Brighton. Mrs Searle added, 'But what is most singular, a striking change took place in my nephew's behaviour; for so soon as he began to mix in society with the Prince, his visits to me became less and less frequent, and now he hardly ever calls to see his old aunt.'

LORD HAY AND THE PRINCE REGENT

At the Prince Regent's first levee, in 1815, Lord Hay, eldest son of the Earl of Errol, was presented with other officers of the Guards to have the honour of kissing hands.[2] When the Prince gave his hand to be kissed, the young nobleman, unversed in court etiquette, caught hold of it and shook it with all his might. The Prince, though a very proud and formal personage, seeing the youth of the young soldier, took the salute in good part, and inquired how the Earl of Errol was. Lord James Murray,[3] observing that something had occurred which was creating a laugh at the expense of his young countryman, good-naturedly took him by the

---

[1] Princess Mary, later Duchess of Gloucester (1776–1857), George IV's fourth and favourite sister.

[2] James, Lord Hay, ensign in the 1st Foot Guards, eldest son of James, seventeenth Earl of Errol.

[3] Lord James Murray, later Baron Glenlyon (1782–1837), second son of the fourth Duke of Atholl, was lord-in-waiting to the Prince Regent.

arm and removed him from the royal presence. 'What have you been doing, Lord Hay,' inquired Lord James Murray, 'to be the cause of so much mirth?' 'I don't know, unless it was that I shook the Prince's hand with all my might.' 'Only that, my Lord!' replied Lord James; 'why, you have committed a flagrant breach of etiquette.' 'How so?' inquired Lord Hay. 'Why, you ought only to have placed the royal hand to your mouth, instead of shaking it.' 'Oh, my Lord, I will make amends. I will return and apologise to his Royal Highness.' 'No, no, Lord Hay; that will make matters worse.' The same evening Lord James Murray dined with the Prince, and mentioned to his Royal Highness what Lord Hay proposed doing, by way of making amends for his *gaucherie*. The Prince was extremely amused, and observed, he never had seen so handsome a young soldier in the uniform of the Guards.

Lord Hay, a few days subsequently, left England for Brussels, to join his regiment, the 1st Foot Guards; and at the battle of Quatre Bras, whilst gallantly leading his company in a charge against the French sharpshooters, this young nobleman received a musket ball in the heart, which, of course, caused instant death.

In those days the 1st Foot Guards were officered by some of the handsomest young men that England could boast of. But as nothing is perfect in this world, I must in justice state, that notwithstanding the noble list I have particularised, there were in the regiment one or two of the ugliest men, perhaps, that the world ever beheld.

THE PRINCE REGENT AND CARLTON HOUSE

One of the meanest and most ugly edifices that ever disfigured London, notwithstanding it was screened by a row of columns, was Carlton House, the residence of the Prince Regent. It was condemned by everybody who possessed taste; and Canova the sculptor, on being asked his opinion of it, said, 'There are at Rome a thousand buildings more beautiful, and whose architecture is in comparison faultless, any one of which would be more suitable for a princely residence than that ugly barn.' This building was constantly under repair, but never improved, for no material alterations were made in its appearance. The first step towards improvement should have been to give it a coat of 'lime-wash,' for it was blackened with dust and soot. *A propos* of the alterations: the workmen engaged therein were a great source of annoyance to the Prince, who, pretending that he did not like to be stared at, objected to their entering by the gateway. It is certain that the Prince Regent kept himself as much aloof as possible from the lower class of his subjects, and was annoyed by the natural curiosity of those who hold that as 'a cat may look at a king,' permission for that luxury should not be denied to bipeds.

I recollect that, having called, when on guard, upon Sir Benjamin Bloomfield about the sale of a cob, which he gave me to understand he wanted for the Prince Regent, while conversing we were interrupted by the entrance of the Prince, attended by M'Mahon[1] and the eccentric 'Tommy Tit.'[2] His Royal Highness was in an angry humour, and blurted out in his rage, 'I will not allow those maid-servants to look at me when I go in and out; and if I find they do so again, I will have them discharged.' I could hardly believe my ears, that a man born to the highest rank could take umbrage at such pardonable curiosity.

LORD BARRYMORE

This nobleman came of a very old family, and when of age succeeded to a fine estate. He acquired no small degree of notoriety from his love of pugilism and cock-fighting; but his *forte* lay in driving, and few coachmen on the northern road could 'tool' a four-in-hand like him. His Lordship was one of the founders of the 'Whip Club.' The first time I ever saw Lord Barrymore was one fine evening while taking a stroll in Hyde Park. The weather was charming, and a great number of the *bon ton* had assembled to witness the departure of the 'Four-in-hand Club.' Conspicuous among all the 'turns-out' was that of his Lordship, who drove four splendid greys, unmatched in symmetry, action, and power. Lord Barrymore was, like Byron and Sir Walter Scott, club-footed. I discovered this defect the moment he got off his box to arrange something wrong in the harness. If there had been a competitive examination, the prize of which would be given to the most proficient in slang and vulgar phraseology, it would have been safe to back his Lordship as the winner against the most foul-mouthed of coster-mongers; for the way he blackguarded his servants for the misadjust-ment of a strap was horrifying. On returning home, I dressed and went to the Club to dine, where I alluded to the choice morsels of English

[1] Colonel Sir John McMahon (d. 1817), said to be the illegitimate child of a chambermaid and a butler who had later kept an oyster shop in Dublin. He had been a clerk, then an actor, before becoming a soldier. He became Keeper of the Prince of Wales's Privy Purse in 1804 and his Private Secretary in 1806.

[2] Sir Thomas Tyrwhitt (c. 1763–1833), for several years the Prince of Wales's Private Secretary. He was dismissed from his office for taking the Princess of Wales's side in her quarrel with her husband's mistress, Lady Jersey. The Prince and he were later reconciled.

vernacular that had fallen from the noble whip's mouth in addressing his servants, and was assured that such was his usual language when out of temper.

In addition to his 'drag' in the 'Four-in-hand Club,' Lord Barrymore sported a very pretty 'Stanhope,'[1] in which he used to drive about town, accompanied by a little boy, whom the world denominated his tiger. It was reported that Lord Barrymore had, in his younger days, been taken much notice of by the Prince Regent; in fact, he had been the boon companion of his Royal Highness, and had assisted at the orgies that used to take place at Carlton House, where he was a constant visitor. Notwithstanding this, Lord Barrymore was considered by those intimately acquainted with him to be a man of literary talents. He certainly was an accomplished musician and a patron of the drama, yet I have heard a host of crimes attributed to his Lordship. This, if not a libel, showed that the connection existing between the Prince Regent and this nobleman could not have been productive of good results, and tends to confirm the impression that the profligate life led by his Royal Highness and those admitted to his intimacy was such, as to make it a matter of wonder that such scandalous scenes of debauchery could be permitted in a country like ours. Indeed, his acquaintance with the Prince ruined Lord Barrymore both in mind, body, and estate. While participating in the Regent's excesses, he had bound himself to do his bidding, however palpably iniquitous it might be; and when he was discarded, in accordance with that Prince's habit of treating his favourites, he left Carlton House ruined in health and reputation.

Lord Barrymore during his last years was a martyr to the gout and other diseases; and on his deathbed he was haunted by the recollection of what he had been, and the thought of what he might have become: indeed, the last scene of his profligate life, when tortured by the inward reproaches of his accusing conscience, was harrowing in the extreme.

ADMIRAL NAGLE

Admiral Nagle[2] was a great favourite of George the Fourth, and passed much of his time with his Majesty. He was a bold, weatherbeaten tar, but nevertheless a perfect gentleman, with exceedingly pleasing

---

[1] A light one-seated carriage originally constructed for the Rev. the Hon. Fitzroy Stanhope (1787–1864).

[2] Admiral Sir Edmund Nagle (1757–1830), saw little service at sea after his marriage to a rich widow and became a Groom of the Bedchamber to George IV in 1820. His rollicking good nature made him a favourite butt for such practical jokes as Gronow describes.

manners, and possessed of much good-nature and agreeability. The late Duke of Cambridge on one occasion sent his brother a cream-coloured horse, from the royal stud at Hanover, and the king gave the animal to Colonel Peters, the riding-master. Admiral Nagle ventured to express a hope, that if his Majesty received a similar present from Hanover, he would graciously make him a present of it, upon which the king replied, 'Certainly, Nagle, you shall have one.'

The admiral was shortly afterwards sent to Portsmouth, to superintend the building of the royal yacht, during which time Strohling, the fashionable painter of the day, was summoned, and ordered to paint over the admiral's favourite hack, to make it appear like one of the Hanoverian breed. The horse was accordingly placed in the riding-school, and, in an incredibly short period, the metamorphosis was successfully completed. In due time the admiral returned from Portsmouth, and, as usual, went to the royal stables, and was charmed to see that his Majesty had fulfilled his promise. He lost no time in going to Carlton House to return thanks, when the King said, 'Well, Nagle, how do you like the horse I sent you?' 'Very much,' was the reply; 'but I should like to try his paces before I can give your Majesty a decided opinion about him.' 'Well, then, let him be saddled, though it does rain, and gallop him round the park and return here, and let me know what you think of him.' It rained cats and dogs; the paint was gradually washed off the horse, to the admiral's great astonishment, and he returned to Carlton House, where the King and his friends had watched his departure and arrival with the greatest delight. The admiral was welcomed with roars of laughter, which he took with great good-humour; and, about a month afterwards, the King presented him with a real Hanoverian horse of great value.

Snuff-taking

Snuff-taking became generally the fashion in France in the early part of the reign of Louis XV. In the unfortunate reign of Louis XVI, the beautiful Marie-Antoinette preferred bon-bons to snuff, and prided herself on her *bonbonnières*; while the old ladies of her court carried snuff-boxes of immense dimensions, with the miniatures of their lovers and children on the lid.

In England, Queen Charlotte, the grandmother of our gracious Queen, was so fond of snuff, that she was the principal cause of making it fashionable. I recollect having seen her Majesty on the terrace at Windsor walking with the King, George III, when, to the great delight of the Eton boys, she applied her finger and thumb to her gold box, out of which her Majesty appeared to have fished a considerable quantity, for the royal nose was covered with snuff both within and without.

All the old ladies in London took a prodigious quantity. I once called upon the old Duchess of Manchester[1] in Berkeley Square, when she did me the honour to offer me a pinch of her best snuff. I was then young, but nevertheless accepted the Duchess's offer, and snuffled up a decent quantity; which made me sneeze for at least an hour afterwards, creating much mirth in the drawing-room, where many persons were assembled. The Duchess observed how happy she would be if snuff could have the same effect upon her nose as it had upon mine.

I should say that the majority of men of fashion at the period I am speaking of carried snuff-boxes. If you knew a man intimately, he would offer you a pinch out of his own box; but if others, not so well acquainted, wished for a pinch, it was actually refused. In those days of snuff-taking, at the tables of great people, and the messes of regiments, snuff-boxes of large proportions followed the bottle, and everybody was at liberty to help himself.

It was reported that Brummell, who was celebrated for the beauty of his snuff-boxes and the quality of his snuff, was once dining at the Pavilion with the Prince, and incurred his master's heavy displeasure in the following manner. The then Bishop of Winchester,[2] perceiving Brummell's snuff-box within his reach, very naturally took it up and supplied himself with a pinch; upon which Brummell told his servant, who was standing behind his chair, to throw the rest of the snuff into the fire or on the floor. The Prince all the while looked daggers: he gave Master Brummell a good wigging the following day, and never forgot the insult offered to the Bishop. Brummell was then apparently in great favour, but the Prince from that period began to show his dislike for the Beau on several occasions; and shortly afterwards quarrelled with him, and kept him at arm's length for the remainder of his life.

THE PRINCESS CHARLOTTE OF WALES

A few months after the death of the lamented Princess Charlotte of Wales, Prince Leopold, now the King of the Belgians, went to Paris,

---

[1] Elizabeth, widow of the fourth Duke of Manchester (see note, page 26). She was the eldest daughter of Sir James Dashwood. She died in 1832.

[2] Brownlow North, elder son of Francis North, first Earl of Guilford, by his second wife. He was half-brother to Lord North, George III's Prime Minister. He was Bishop of Winchester from 1781 until 1820.

where he lived at the Hotel des Princes, Rue Richelieu; but for a length of time he remained incognito. I was on one occasion dining in the company of his Royal Highness, who interrogated me about a shooting party at St Germain, which had taken place a day or two before. When I mentioned the number of hares we had shot, the Prince observed, 'I never intend again to shoot a hare, because at Claremont, one day, when walking with my beloved wife, we heard the cries of one that had been wounded by one of the shooting party; and so affected was she by its pitiful screams, that she begged I would not be the cause of pain to one of these animals in future.'

The Duchess of Leeds used to tell an anecdote of her Royal Highness and her love of fishing.[1] When engaged in this sport, on catching a fish the Princess used to tie a piece of ribbon round its tail and throw it back again into the water, noticing with delight that those which had not been caught attacked those decorated by her. Once, having been very successful in catching a great many, and having exhausted all her ribbon, she unpicked her bonnet and made use of its trimmings to decorate the fish she caught.

THE DUKE OF CLARENCE

At the commencement of 1817, the Duke of Clarence, bent upon improving his pecuniary means, decided on marrying a rich heiress.[2] The report was circulated all over England (where it produced the most intense sensation), that the Duke had, with the consent of his brother, the Prince Regent, actually proposed to Miss Wykeham, whose estates in Oxfordshire were large and of immense value. When the event was communicated to Queen Charlotte, his royal mother was outrageous; she flew into a violent rage, and with vehement asseverations (either in English or German), declared that her consent should never be given to the match. The law officers of the Crown were consulted, cabinet councils met daily, and after much discussion, ministers determined on opposing the Duke's project; notwithstanding the opinion of one of the

[1] Catherine, Duchess of Leeds (d. 1837), second wife of the fifth Duke, was appointed Princess Charlotte's governess in 1812.
[2] William, Duke of Clarence (1765-1837), one of George IV's younger brothers. He separated from the actress Dorothea Jordan, mother of his ten illegitimate children, and unsuccessfully sought the hand of various rich young ladies, in addition to Miss Wyckham (not Wykeham), heiress to the Oxfordshire estates of Lord Wenman, whom Gronow mentions. In 1818 he married Princess Adelaide, eldest daughter of the Duke of Saxe-Coburg Meiningen. He became King William IV in 1830.

best lawyers that 'a prince of the blood-royal, being of age, and notifying his intended marriage previous to its taking place, was at liberty to marry without the consent of the King, unless the two Houses of Parliament should address the Crown against it.'

The excitement among all classes was at its height, when the *Morning Post* informed the world one morning that the Duke's intended marriage was entirely 'off;' HRH having been prevailed upon by the Queen to forego his intentions. In this course Queen Charlotte was evidently supported by the rest of the royal family; and it was whispered that, as an inducement to the Prince to behave like a good boy, the Queen, the Prince Regent, and his royal sisters had subscribed a sufficient sum among themselves to pay off all HRH's debts, and to provide him with an increase of income for the future. Much amusement was caused at the clubs by a caricature of an old sailor, called 'the love-sick youth.'

The Duke of Clarence, together with his brothers, were in the habit of frequently dining at the table prepared for the officers who mount guard at St James's, and it was the custom for their Royal Highnesses to send in their names when they intended to honour the Colonel with their presence. Although I was at the time very young, I recollect being present on several occasions when the Duke of Clarence honoured our mess with his presence, and the amusing anecdotes he used to relate. He astonished Colonel Archibald Macdonald one day at table by putting the following question to him: 'Colonel, are you ever under the necessity of giving "chocolate" to your young officers?' The Colonel replied that he did not understand what HRH meant by 'giving chocolate.' The Duke replied, 'Oh, I can see, Colonel, that you have not breakfasted with Sir David Dundas,[1] for it was his invariable custom to ask such officers as had fallen under his displeasure for breaches of military discipline to breakfast with him, in order that during the repast, where some excellent chocolate invariably formed one of the comestibles, the culprit should be severely lectured, and sometimes recommended to leave the service.' Ensign 'Bacchus' Lascelles, who was present, a plain-spoken fellow, sang out from the end of the table, 'Your Royal Highness, if the Colonel does not understand the meaning of "chocolate" I do; for only this morning I received "goose" from the adjutant for not having sufficient powder on my hair: it is quite immaterial

---

[1] General Sir David Dundas (1735–1820), the son of an Edinburgh merchant, a tall, curmudgeonly officer who was appointed quartermaster-general in 1796.

whether a rowing be denominated "chocolate" or "goose," for it is one and the same thing.' The royal Duke laughed heartily at the *sang froid* of the young ensign, and ever after evinced great partiality for him.

Talking of military despotism, my old friend [General Sir Arthur] Upton, though an excellent man, was extremely rigorous in enforcing attention to military regulations. Having discovered that I shirked morning parade, he sent for me, intending to administer a due amount of 'goose.' On my arriving at the Queen's Lodge, where he lived as one of the equerries, and entering his apartments, I was horrified at finding this excellent fellow lying on the floor bleeding. It appeared that he had, in a temporary absence of mind, made use of a pair of razors to pull on his boots with! Fortunately, Dr Heberden,[1] who was on duty in attendance upon the King, was immediately sent for, and succeeded in stopping the hæmorrhage; but he at the same time expressed his fears that lock-jaw would ensue. Luckily, Upton's strong constitution carried him through the disaster, and in a few weeks he was able to resume command of the battalion: and ready to administer a plentiful allowance of 'goose' to the first unlucky wight who fell under his displeasure.

WINDSOR CASTLE IN 1819

While on duty with my regiment at Windsor in the summer of 1819, I received an invitation to dine at the Equerries' table at the castle, or the 'Queen's House,' as it was then called,[2] on which occasion I met Lord Liverpool,[3] the Prime Minister, the Archbishop of York,[4] Dr Baillie,[5]

---

[1] Dr William Heberden (1710-1801) was described by Samuel Johnson as 'the last of our learned physicians'.

[2] At the time of George III's accession, Windsor Castle was much neglected and several parts of it were occupied by families with real or pretended claims upon royal favour. Rather than turn these occupants out, the King chose to build a new house on Castle Hill when his own family had grown to such an extent that a country house larger than any at his disposal was required. He moved into Upper Lodge, or Queen's Lodge as it was generally known, in the summer of 1778. The house was demolished by George IV in 1823.

[3] Robert Banks Jenkinson, second Earl of Liverpool (1770-1828), became Prime Minister in 1812 and remained in that office for almost fifteen years.

[4] Edward Venables Vernon Harcourt (1757-1847) was Archbishop of York from 1807 to 1847.

[5] Dr Matthew Baillie (1761-1823), the Scottish anatomist, was physician to St George's Hospital from 1787 to 1799 when he set up in private practice in Grosvenor Street and became physician extraordinary to George III.

Sir H. Halford,[1] Dr Heberden, and the 'mad Doctor' Willis.[2] These personages had come from London, in virtue of their office, to inquire after the health of the King. I must confess to a feeling of aversion, and even horror, at being placed next the 'mad Doctor' at table. He was sallow, ill-looking, and indeed had a most forbidding countenance. He was dressed in black, with silk breeches, white neckcloth, and frill. However, my feelings were soon calmed; for although he never spoke, he seemed to enjoy his dinner, eating and drinking as much as any two persons at table. Dr Baillie was evidently a great favourite with the Prime Minister and the Archbishop.

I once saw George III walking with his favourite son, the Duke of York, with whom he talked incessantly, repeating his, 'Yes, yes, yes, Frederick,' in his usual loud voice. His beard was of unusual length, and he stooped very much. He wore the Windsor uniform,[3] with a large cocked hat, something like that with which Frederick the Great is usually represented. The doctors walked behind the King, which seemed greatly to annoy him, as he was constantly looking round. It was said, and I believe with truth, that the poor King could not hear Dr Willis's name spoken without shuddering. HRH the Duke of Cumberland frequently visited his Royal parents, with his beautiful wife, whose figure at that time was such as few women could boast of.[4]

I cannot pass by an event which caused some scandal at the time. The Duke of Cumberland, on his visits to Windsor, was generally accompanied by his aide-de-camp, Colonel Disney. One day, on the occasion of the Duke's recovery from the wounds received in resisting the

[1] Sir Henry Halford (1766-1844) was born Henry Vaughan, the son of a physician practising in Leicester. He was appointed physician extraordinary to George III in 1793. He changed his name to Halford upon inheriting the large estate of a cousin of that name.

[2] Dr Francis Willis (1718-1807), an elderly clergyman who had been granted a medical degree by Oxford University and was celebrated for his skill in the treatment of symptoms of madness. He had a lunatic asylum in Lincolnshire. His method, he said, was to 'break in' his patients as horses were broken. He put the King in a straitjacket when he became excessively agitated.

[3] In 1778, perhaps in imitation of Frederick the Great, George III designed a uniform to be worn at Windsor. It was blue with scarlet and gold accessories. It was abandoned by William IV but revived by Queen Victoria. It is still occasionally worn at Windsor in the evenings by the Duke of Edinburgh and other members of the Royal Family and Household.

[4] Ernest Augustus, Duke of Cumberland (1771-1851), George III's fifth son. An unpleasant, mysterious man, he became King of Hanover in 1837. His beautiful wife was his cousin, Frederica, daughter of the Duke of Mecklenburg-Strelitz. She had been married twice before, first to Prince Frederick of Prussia and then, having become engaged to Cumberland's brother, the Duke of Cambridge, hurriedly to Prince Frederick of Solms-Braunfels by whom she had discovered herself pregnant.

murderous attack of his valet,[1] HRH arrived at the Castle to pay his respects to his Royal parents, when, finding that the Queen was walking on the terrace, he hastened to join her Majesty, desiring Colonel Disney to remain in waiting. The Colonel, who was a hare-brained, half-cracked sort of a fellow, finding waiting rather irksome, commenced making a tour through the apartments, and in his peregrinations entered her Majesty's bed-chamber, which was rightly held to be sacred ground. Curiosity led him to inspect the various toilet articles of the Queen, and still further to examine a golden vase, which he put to a use that cannot be named to ears polite. This breach of good manners was detected by the royal housekeeper, who, with tears in her eyes, reported to the Duke of Cumberland the gross impropriety. His Royal Highness, a proud overbearing man, sought out Disney, and attempted to inflict summary chastisement for the insult he had perpetrated; however, the Colonel evaded the punishment so richly deserved, but he was almost immediately placed on the shelf, and died at his lodgings, in Bury Street, St James's, heart-broken, on the second anniversary of his thoughtless freak.

A SHOULDER OF MUTTON À LA SOUBISE

When George IV passed through Carmarthenshire on his return from Ireland,[2] he remained a day and night at Dynevor Castle, the seat of the nobleman of that name.[3] His Lordship, desirous of entertaining his Majesty in a befitting manner, asked Sir Benjamin Bloomfield what particular dish the King preferred. Sir Benjamin replied, that his Majesty was very fond of a shoulder of mutton boiled with 'sauce soubise.'[4] Lord D. sent word to that effect to the cook, who, full of vanity and self-conceit, like the majority of Welshmen, did not deign to make

[1] On 31 May 1810 the Duke's Corsican valet, Joseph Sellis, was found dead in his blood-splashed room at St James's Palace. It was immediately rumoured that Cumberland – who was supposed either to have been caught in bed with Sellis's wife or to have been blackmailed after making homosexual advances to the valet himself – had murdered him. At the subsequent inquiry the Duke claimed that he had been attacked in bed by a man wielding a sabre which he had attempted to grab, almost severing his right thumb. He jumped out of bed and ran for help, his assailant pursuing him and cutting him on his buttocks and thigh, and, more seriously, on his head. The Duke's cries for help aroused other servants and the assailant escaped. Shortly afterwards 'a gurgling noise' was heard coming from Sellis's room where the valet was found with his throat cut.

[2] George IV paid a visit to Ireland in August 1821.

[3] George Talbot, third Baron Dynevor (1765–1852).

[4] Soubise sauce, a white sauce containing boiled onions.

the inquiry as to what a '*sauce soubise*' meant. The consequence was that Taffy got into a scrape, for when the shoulder appeared on the dinner-table, the King observing it, said that he had never seen a shoulder of mutton covered with currant-jelly, instead of onion sauce. The Welsh cook was called, and Lord Dynevor asked him what could have induced him to make such an egregious mistake. He replied, that he thought the gentleman (meaning the King) would prefer sweet sauce to that ordered by his Lordship.

ATTEMPT TO ASSASSINATE THE PRINCE REGENT

An attempt was made to assassinate the Prince Regent when on his way home from the Houses of Parliament in 1819; but it happily failed. In the park, opposite Marlborough House, a bullet was fired from an air-gun by a man concealed in one of the trees, who escaped. This occurred when I was on duty at the Horse Guards, marching across the park with what was commonly called the 'Tilt Guard,' and I remember it was anything but pleasant to get through the mob of blackguards who were ripe for mischief. The Life Guards, who escorted the Prince Regent, evinced great want of energy on the occasion. The officer commanding the troop, when he saw the danger, should have commanded his men to charge and clear the way. Such was my opinion then; and I am persuaded, from all that I have witnessed abroad since, that the wisest plan upon such occasions, is to take the initiative and act promptly. The fact of this attempt having been made, was doubted at the time by the public at large, but I can speak from my personal knowledge that a shot was fired, and it was aimed at the royal carriage.

CORONATION OF GEORGE IV

At this gorgeous solemnity it fell to my lot to be on guard on the platform along which the royal procession had to pass, in order to reach the Abbey.[1] The crowd that had congregated in this locality exceeded anything I had ever before seen; struggling, fighting, shrieking, and laughing, were the order of the day among this motley assemblage. Little Townsend, the chief police officer of Bow Street,[2] with his flaxen

---

[1] The King's coronation in Westminster Abbey on 19 July 1821 cost no less than £243,000.

[2] The services of James Townsend, an amusing man with the tastes of a dandy, were much in demand as a private detective. He left £20,000 when he died.

wig and broad-brimmed hat, was to be seen hurrying from one end of the platform to the other, assuming immense importance. On the approach of the *cortège* you heard this officious person, 'dressed with a little brief authority,' hallooing with all his might, 'Gentlemen and ladies, take care of your pockets, for you are surrounded by thieves;' and hearty laughter responded to Mr Townsend's salutary advice.

When the procession was seen to approach, and the royal canopy came in sight, those below the platform were straining with all their might to get a peep at the Sovereign, and the confusion at this moment can be better imagined than described. The pick-pockets, of course, had availed themselves of the confusion, and in the twinkling of an eye there were more watches and purses snatched from the pockets of his Majesty's loyal subjects than perhaps on any previous occasion.

Amidst the crowd a respectable gentleman from the Principality hallooed out in his provincial tongue, 'Mr Townsend, Mr Townsend, I have been robbed of my gold watch and purse, containing all my money. What am I to do? what am I to do to get home? I have come two hundred miles to see this sight, and instead of receiving satisfaction or hospitality, I am robbed by those cut-throats called "the swell mob."' This eloquent speech had a very different effect upon the mob than the poor Welshman had reason to expect; for all of a sudden the refrain of the song of 'Sweet Home' was shouted by a thousand voices; and the mob bawled out, 'Go back to your goats, my good fellow.' The indignities that were heaped upon this unfortunate gentleman during the royal procession, and his appearance after the King had passed, created pity in the minds of all honest persons who witnessed this disgusting scene: his hat was beaten over his eyes, and his coat, neckcloth, &c., were torn off his body. For there were no police in those days;[1] and with the exception of a few constables and some soldiers, there was no force to prevent the metropolis from being burnt to the ground, if it had pleased the mob to have set it on fire.

---

[1] It was not until 1829 that the Metropolitan Police Act provided for a properly organised professional police force in London. Its headquarters were at 4 Whitehall Place, the back of which opened on to a courtyard known as Scotland Yard. Only in 1856 did another Police Act oblige all counties in England to raise and maintain a constabulary.

GEORGE IV AND BISHOP PORTEOUS

Lord Brougham,[1] the late lamented Thackeray,[2] and others, have been very severe in their censures on the character of George IV. My readers will perhaps be interested in hearing the following: – Some few years before the death of the King, Dr Porteous,[3] then Bishop of London, having heard that his Majesty had appointed a review of the Household Troops to take place on a Sunday, ordered his carriage, though he was in a precarious state of health, and waited upon his Majesty at Carlton House. The Bishop was most graciously received, and proceeded to say, 'I am come to warn your Majesty of the awful consequences of your breaking the Sabbath, by holding a review on that day which the Almighty has hallowed and set apart for Himself.' The King upon this burst into tears, and fell on his knees before the Bishop, who bestowed upon his Majesty his blessing. The King then assured Dr Porteous that no review should take place on the Sabbath during his life. Bishop Porteous then left the royal presence never more to return; for on arriving at his residence he took to his bed, and died shortly afterwards. The King was so deeply afflicted at the news that, on hearing it, he retired into his own apartments and was heard to sob as one in deep affliction.

DEATH AND FUNERAL OF THE DUKE OF YORK

I perfectly recollect the sorrow felt in London at the death of the Duke of York, and the splendid funeral honours paid to him. The royal Duke died after three or four weeks' suffering from dropsy, in his sixty-fourth year. His administration at the Horse Guards will long be held in

[1] Henry Peter Brougham, Baron Brougham and Vaux (1778–1868) came to London from Scotland in 1805 and was called to the English bar in 1808. An active Member of Parliament, he became Lord Chancellor in 1830. He was an outspoken supporter of Queen Caroline and was consequently much disliked by George IV. He was, indeed, much disliked generally as an over self-confident know-all and orotund chatterbox. The Irish politician Daniel O'Connell said of him that if he had known a little law he would have known a little of everything. He spent much of his time at Cannes, which he saw transformed from a fishing village into a fashionable resort. The one-horsed closed carriage was named after him.

[2] William Makepeace Thackeray (1811–63), whose vituperative *Four Georges* was published in 1860.

[3] Beilby Porteous (1731–1808) was Bishop of London from 1787. His parents were born in America. Although he was certainly given to tears in his cups, the Regent's behaviour on this occasion, as related by Gronow, seems rather unlikely.

remembrance, as beneficial in the highest degree to the British soldier; and such was his popularity, that ministers, statesmen, and general officers followed his remains to the grave. I recollect my late lamented friend, John Scott,[1] telling me that his father, Lord Eldon, spoilt a new hat by placing it on the ground and putting his feet into it to keep them warm; for it was intensely cold weather at the time, and the funeral took place at night. It is certain that a great many persons who took part in the procession caught severe colds from their not having sufficiently wrapped themselves up; and among them was Mr Canning,[2] who never entirely recovered: he died the same year, in the room at Chiswick where Charles James Fox breathed his last.[3]

LATTER DAYS OF GEORGE IV

For some months prior to his death, the King abstained from eating animal food, and lived on vegetables and pastry, for which he had a great liking.[4] His conduct, from being that of a sensual, greedy old man, became that of a spoilt child; and the way he spent his time was frivolous in the extreme. He was very fond of punch, made from a recipe by his *maître d'hôtel*, and which he drank after dinner; this was the only time he was agreeable, and on these occasions he would sing songs, relate anecdotes of his youth, and play on the violoncello: afterwards going to bed in a 'comfortable' state. But a nervous disorder which affected him prevented his sleeping well, and he invariably rose in the morning in the most unamiable of tempers. Poor man, he was greatly to be pitied; for he was surrounded by a set of harpies, only intent on what they could get out of him, among the most prominent of whom was Lady C [onyngham], the 'English Pompadour.'

[1] John Scott, second Earl of Eldon (1805-54). His father, the first Earl (1751-1838), was Lord Chancellor.

[2] George Canning (1770-1827) succeeded Lord Castlereagh as Foreign Secretary and became Prime Minister in 1827.

[3] Chiswick House, modelled on villas by Palladio and Scamozzi, was built by the third Earl of Burlington in 1725-9. It was inherited by the fourth Duke of Devonshire in 1753. Charles James Fox died there in 1806.

[4] It is not true that the King 'abstained from eating animal food' for 'some months prior to his death'. One evening in April, two months before he died, he called in his page and said to him, 'Go downstairs and cut me off just such a piece of beef as you would like to have yourself, cut from the part you like best yourself, and bring it me up.' According to Mrs Arbuthnot, 'the page accordingly went and fetched an enormous quantity of roast beef, all of which he ate.' That same month, Wellington reported, after taking a dose of laudanum, the King consumed two pigeons and three beef steaks for breakfast as well as 'three parts of a bottle of Mozelle [*sic*], a glass of dry champagne, two glasses of port and a glass of brandy!'

3

War in the Peninsula

My Entrance into the Army

After leaving Eton, I received an Ensign's commission in the First Guards, during the month of December 1812.[1] Though many years have elapsed, I still remember my boyish delight at being named to so distinguished a regiment, and at the prospect of soon taking a part in the glorious deeds of our army in Spain. I joined in February 1813, and cannot but recollect with astonishment how limited and imperfect was the instruction which an officer received at that time; he absolutely entered the army without any military education whatever. We were so defective in our drill, even after we had passed out of the hands of the sergeant, that the excellence of our non-commissioned officers alone prevented us from meeting with the most fatal disasters in the face of the enemy. Physical force and our bull-dog energy carried many a hard-fought field. Luckily, *nous avons changé tout cela*, and our officers may now vie with those of any other army in an age when the great improvements in musketry, in artillery practice, and in the greater rapidity of manœuvring, have entirely changed the art of war, and rendered the individual education of those in every grade of command an absolute necessity.

---

[1] In 1661 the soldiers who had guarded King Charles II in exile were formed into two regiments of foot guards and two troops of horse guards. In 1665 the foot guards were amalgamated into a single regiment, the 1st Foot Guards, later more commonly known as the Grenadier Guards.

After passing through the hands of the drill sergeant and mounting guard at St James's[1] for a few months, we were hurried off, one fine morning, in charge of a splendid detachment of five hundred men to join Lord Wellington in Spain.[2] Macadam[3] had just begun to do for England what Marshal Wade[4] did in Scotland seventy years before; and we were able to march twenty miles a day with ease until we reached Portsmouth. There we found transports ready to convey a large reinforcement, of which we formed part, to Lord Wellington, who was now making his arrangements, after taking St Sebastian, for a yet more important event in the history of the Peninsular War – the invasion of France.

DEPARTURE FOR AND ARRIVAL IN SPAIN

We sailed under convoy of the *Madagascar* frigate and were ordered to join the army without loss of time. In three hours we got fairly into camp, where we were received with loud cheers by our brothers in arms.

The whole British army was here under canvas; our allies, the Spaniards and Portuguese, being in the rear. About the middle of October, to our great delight, the army received orders to cross the Bidassoa. At three o'clock on the morning of the 15th our regiment advanced through a difficult country, and, after a harassing march, reached the top of a hill as the grey light of morning began to dawn. We marched in profound silence, but with a pleasurable feeling of excitement amongst all ranks at the thought of meeting the enemy, and perhaps with not an equally agreeable idea that we might be in the next world before the day was over.

As we ascended the rugged side of the hill, I saw, for the first time, the immortal Wellington. He was accompanied by the Spanish General,

---

[1] St James's Palace was then being restored after a large part of it had been destroyed in a fire. The Prince Regent, who had been born there, no longer lived in the Palace, having moved to Carlton House, but his brothers had apartments here.

[2] The Hon. Arthur Wellesley (1769–1852) had been created Marquess of Wellington in August 1812 after forcing the French to withdraw from Madrid. On 21 June 1813 he defeated the French again at Vittoria, and the next month laid siege to San Sebastian as a preliminary to his invasion of France.

[3] John Loudon McAdam (1756–1836), inventor of a new system of road construction whereby layers of broken stone are successively subjected to pressure.

[4] George Wade (1673–1748) was appointed commander-in-chief in Scotland in 1724. He superintended the construction of a system of roads which brought even the remote Highlands under military control.

Alava,[1] and Lord Fitzroy Somerset.[2] He was very stern and grave-looking; he was in deep meditation, so long as I kept him in view, and spoke to no one. His features were bold, and I saw much decision of character in his expression. He rode a knowing-looking, thoroughbred horse, and wore a grey overcoat, Hessian boots, and a large cocked hat.

We commenced the passage of the Bidassoa about five in the morning, and in a short time infantry, cavalry, and artillery found themselves upon French ground. The stream at the point we forded was nearly four feet deep, and had Soult[3] been aware of what we were about, we should have found the passage of the river a very arduous undertaking.

Three miles above, we discovered the French army, and ere long found ourselves under fire. The sensation of being made a target to a large body of men is at first not particularly pleasant, but, 'in a trice, the ear becomes more Irish, and less nice.' The first man I ever saw killed was a Spanish soldier, who was cut in two by a cannon ball. The French army, not long after we began to return their fire, was in full retreat; and after a little sharp, but desultory fighting, in which our Division met with some loss, we took possession of the camp and strong position of Soult's army. We found the soldiers' huts very comfortable; they were built of branches of trees and furze, and formed squares and streets, which had names placarded up, such as Rue de Paris, Rue de Versailles, &c. We were not sorry to find ourselves in such commodious quarters, as well as being well housed. The scenery surrounding the camp was picturesque and grand. From our elevated position, immediately in front, we commanded a wide and extensive plain, intersected by two important rivers, the Nive and the Nivelle. On the right, the lofty Pyrenees, with their grand and varied outline, stood forth conspicuously in a blue, cloudless sky; on our left was the Bay of Biscay, with our cruisers perpetually on the move.

[1] Miguel Ricardo de Alava y Esquivel (1771–1843), Spanish commissary at Welling-ton's headquarters. He became President of the Spanish Cortes in 1822 and later served as Spanish Ambassador in London.

[2] Lord Fitzroy Somerset (1788–1855), later first Baron Raglan, youngest son of the fifth Duke of Beaufort, was Wellington's military secretary. A lieutenant-colonel in Gronow's regiment, the 1st Foot Guards, he was to lose an arm at Waterloo. In 1854 he was appointed commander-in-chief in the Crimea. Bearing much of the blame for the government's incompetence, he died before the still untaken Sebastopol.

[3] Nicolas-Jean de Dieu Soult (1769–1851), the French commander-in-chief, was appointed a Marshal of France in 1804. Having distinguished himself at Austerlitz and Jena, he was created duc de Dalmatie and sent to Spain in 1808. Although he served as Napoleon's chief of staff at Waterloo and was thereafter banished, he was restored to favour in 1819.

THE UNIFORM AND BEARING OF THE FRENCH SOLDIER

The French infantry soldier averaged about five feet five or six in height; in build they were much about what they are now, perhaps a little broader over the shoulder. They were smart, active, handy fellows, and much more able to look after their personal comforts than British soldiers, as their camps indicated. The uniform of those days consisted in a shako, which spread out at the top;[1] a short-waisted, swallow-tailed coat; and large, baggy trousers and gaiters. The clothing of the French soldier was roomy, and enabled him to march and move about at ease: no pipeclay accessories occupied their attention; in a word, their uniforms and accoutrements were infinitely superior to our own, taking into consideration the practical necessities of warfare. Their muskets were inferior to ours, and their firing less deadly. The French cavalry we thought badly horsed; but their uniforms, though showy, were, like those of the infantry, comfortably large and roomy.

I have frequently remarked that firearms are of little use to the mounted soldier, and often an incumbrance to man and horse. Cavalry want only one arm - the sabre. Let the men be well mounted, and at home in the saddle. It requires great knowledge in a Commander-in-Chief to know when and how to use his cavalry. It has been my misfortune to witness oft-repeated blunders in the employment of the best-mounted regiments in the world. I consider the French generals had more knowledge of the use of cavalry than our own when a great battle was to be fought.

MAJOR-GENERAL STEWART AND LORD WELLINGTON

If the present generation of Englishmen would take the trouble of looking at the newspaper which fifty years ago informed the British public of passing events both at home and abroad, they would, doubtless, marvel at the very limited and imperfect amount of intelligence which the best journals were enabled to place before their readers. The progress of the Peninsular campaign was very imperfectly chronicled; it will, therefore, be easily imagined what interest was attached to certain letters that appeared in the *Morning Chronicle*[2] which criticised with much severity, and frequently with considerable injus-

---

[1] A military hat shaped like a truncated cone and having a peak.
[2] A Whig newspaper founded by William Woodfall in 1769. Richard Brinsley Sheridan, Thomas Moore and Henry Brougham were among its contributors. It ceased publication in 1862.

tice, the military movements of Lord Wellington's Spanish campaigns.

The attention of the Commander-in-Chief being drawn to these periodical and personal comments on his conduct of the war, his lordship at once perceived, from the information which they contained, that they must have been written by an officer holding a high command under him. Determined to ascertain the author – who, in addressing a public journal, was violating the Articles of War, and, it might be, assisting the enemy – means were employed in London to identify the writer. The result was that Lord Wellington discovered the author of the letters to be no other than Sir Charles Stewart, the late Lord Londonderry.[1] As soon as Lord Wellington had made himself master of this fact, he summoned Sir Charles Stewart to headquarters at Torres Vedras; and, on his appearance, he, without the least preface, addressed him thus:

'Charles Stewart, I have ascertained with deep regret that you are the author of the letters which appeared in the *Morning Chronicle*, abusing me and finding fault with my military plans.'

Lord Wellington here paused for a moment, and then continued:

'Now, Stewart, you know your brother Castlereagh is my best friend, to whom I owe everything; nevertheless, if you continue to write letters to the *Chronicle*, or any other newspaper, by God, I will send you home.'

Sir Charles Stewart was so affected at this rebuke that he shed tears, and expressed himself deeply penitent for the breach of confidence and want of respect for the Articles of War. They immediately shook hands and parted friends. It happened, however, that Sir Charles Stewart did not remain long in the cavalry, of which he was Adjutant-General. Within a few weeks he was named one of the Commissioners deputed to proceed to the Allied Armies, where the Sovereigns were then completing their plans to crush Napoleon.

St Jean de Luz

During the winter of 1813, the Guards were stationed with headquarters at St Jean de Luz, and most comfortable we managed to make them.

---

[1] Charles Stewart, third Marquess of Londonderry (1778–1854), was half-brother to Lord Castlereagh, then Foreign Secretary. A gallant cavalry officer, though both short-sighted and rather deaf, he had been appointed adjutant-general in 1809. Despite his carping criticisms of the commander-in-chief, the two men remained on friendly terms. Before Stewart left for England, Wellington bought from him the charger, Copenhagen, which carried the Duke for over sixteen hours at Waterloo.

For some short time previously we had been on scanty commons, and had undergone considerable privation. I had no cause to complain personally; for my servant, a Sicilian, was one of the most accomplished foragers (ill-natured persons might give him a worse name) in the whole army; and when others were nearly starving, he always managed to provide meat or poultry. He rode on his mule sometimes from twenty to thirty miles, often running the greatest dangers, to procure me a good meal; of which he took care to have, very justly, a large share for himself.

At St Jean de Luz, we were more attentive to our devotions than we had been for some time. Divine service was performed punctually every Sunday on the sand-hills near the town; Lord Wellington and his numerous Staff placed themselves in the midst of our square, and his lordship's chaplain read the service, to which Lord Wellington always appeared to listen with great attention.

The mayor of the town, thinking to please 'the great English lord,' gave a ball at the Hôtel de Ville: our Commander-in-Chief did not go, but was represented by Waters.[1] I was there, and expected to see some of the young ladies of the country, so famed for their beauty; they were, however, far too patriotic to appear.

The ball was a dead failure, in spite of the efforts of the mayor, who danced, to our intense amusement, an English hornpipe, which he had learnt in not a very agreeable manner, viz., when a prisoner of war in the hulks at Plymouth.

Shortly before we left St Jean de Luz, we took our turn of outposts in the neighbourhood of Bidart, a large village, about ten miles from Bayonne. Early one frosty morning in December, an order came, that if we saw the enemy advancing, we were not to fire or give the alarm. About five, we perceived two battalions wearing grenadier caps coming on. They turned out to belong to a Nassau regiment which had occupied the advanced post of the enemy, and hearing that Napoleon had met with great reverses in Germany, signified to us their intention to desert. They were a fine-looking body of men, and appeared, I thought, rather ashamed of the step they had taken. On the same day, we were relieved, and on our way back met Lord Wellington with his hounds. He was dressed in a light-blue frock-coat which had been sent

[1] Sir John Waters (1774–1842) was appointed aide-de-camp to Charles Stewart in 1808. Wellington, who frequently employed him on intelligence duties, appointed him assistant adjutant-general in 1811. He was promoted lieutenant-general in 1841. Gronow writes more about him below.

out to him as a present from Lady Salisbury,[1] then one of the leaders of the fashionable world, and an enthusiastic admirer of his lordship.

Here I remember seeing for the first time a very remarkable character, the Hon. W. Dawson,[2] of my regiment. He was surrounded by muleteers, with whom he was bargaining to provide carriage for innumerable hampers of wine, liqueurs, hams, potted meat, and other good things which he had brought from England. He was a particularly gentlemanly and amiable man, much beloved by the regiment: no one was so hospitable or lived so magnificently. His cooks were the best in the army, and he, besides, had a host of servants of all nations – Spaniards, French, Portuguese, Italians – who were employed in scouring the country for provisions. Lord Wellington once honoured him with his company; and on entering the ensign's tent, found him alone at table, with a dinner fit for a king, his plate and linen in good keeping, and his wines perfect. Lord Wellington was accompanied on this occasion by Sir Edward Pakenham[3] and Colonel du Burgh, afterwards Lord Downes.[4] It fell to my lot to partake of his princely hospitality, and dine with him at his quarters, a farmhouse in a village on the Bidassoa, and I never saw a better dinner put upon table. The career of this amiable Amphitryon, to our great regret, was cut short, after exercising for about a year a splendid but not very wise hospitality. He had only a younger brother's fortune; his debts became very considerable, and he was obliged to quit the Guards. He and his friends had literally eaten up his little fortune.

FOOLHARDINESS

I may here recount an instance of the folly and foolhardiness of youth, and the recklessness to which a long course of exposure to danger produces. When Bayonne was invested, I was one night on duty on the outer picket. The ground inside the breastwork which had been thrown

[1] Emily Mary, daughter of the first Marquess of Downshire. She married the first Marquess of Salisbury in 1773. She was burned to death with the west wing of Hatfield House in 1835. Her daughter-in-law, Frances, wife of the second Marquess, was also a friend of Wellington.

[2] The son of John Dawson, second Viscount Carlow.

[3] The Hon. Sir Edward Pakenham (1778–1815), son of the second Baron Longford, was Wellington's brother-in-law. Appointed deputy adjutant-general in 1810, he commanded the 3rd Division at Salamanca in 1812. He was killed in action in America in 1815.

[4] Sir Ulysses Bagenal Burgh, second Baron Downes (1788–1863), an Irishman, the son of an old friend of Wellington, was one of the Duke's aides-de-camp. He was promoted general shortly before his death, after which the peerage became extinct.

up for our protection by Burgoyne was in a most disagreeable state for any one who wished to repose after the fatigues of the day, being knee-deep in mud of a remarkably plastic nature. I was dead tired, and determined to get a little rest in some more agreeable spot; so calling my sergeant, I told him to give me his knapsack for a pillow; I would make a comfortable night of it on the top of the breastwork, as it was an invitingly dry place. 'For heaven's sake, take care, sir,' said he; 'you'll have fifty bullets in you: you will be killed to a certainty.' 'Pooh, nonsense,' said I, and climbing up, I wrapt myself in my cloak, laid my head on the knapsack, and soon fell into a sound sleep.

By the mercy of Providence I remained in a whole skin, either from the French immediately underneath not perceiving me or not thinking me worth a shot; but I received a severe wigging, and was told to consider myself lucky that I was not put under arrest for exposing my life in so foolish a manner.

Among the many officers of the Guards who were taken prisoners in the unfortunate sortie from Bayonne, was the Hon. H. Townshend, commonly called Bull Townshend.[1] He was celebrated as a *bon vivant*, and in consequence of his too great indulgence in the pleasures of the table, had become very unwieldy, and could not move quick enough to please his nimble captors, so he received many prods in the back from a sharp bayonet. After repeated threats, however, he was dismissed with what our American friends would be pleased to designate 'a severe booting.' The late Sir Willoughby Cotton was also a prisoner.[2] It really seemed as if the enemy had made choice of our fattest officers. Sir Willoughby escaped by giving up his watch and all the money which he had in his pockets; but this consisting of a Spanish dollar only, the smallness of the sum subjected him to the same ignominious treatment as had been experienced by Townshend.

Among the numerous bad characters in our ranks, several were coiners, or utterers of bad money. In the second brigade of Guards, just before we arrived at St Jean de Luz, a soldier was convicted of this offence, and was sentenced to receive 800 lashes. This man made sham Spanish dollars out of the pewter spoons of the regiment. As he had

[1] The Hon. Horatio George Powys Townshend, third son of the second Viscount Sydney. He died unmarried in 1843.
[2] Sir Willoughby Cotton (1783-1860), 'one of the dandies of the brigade of guards', had led a rebellion at Rugby School where he burned the headmaster's desk and books in the close. In 1821 he obtained a lieutenant-colonelcy in the 47th Foot in India and spent most of the rest of his life there. Fatter than ever, he returned home a general, having unsuccessfully sought service in the Crimean War.

before been convicted and flogged, he received this terrible sentence, and died under the lash.

DISCIPLINE

When the headquarters of the army were at St Jean de Luz, Soult made a movement in front of our right centre, which the English general took for a reconnaissance. As the French general perceived that we had ordered preparations to receive him, he sent a flag of truce to demand a cessation of hostilities, saying that he wanted to shoot an officer and several men for acts of robbery committed by them, with every sort of atrocity, on the farmers and peasantry of the country. The execution took place in view of both armies, and a terrible lesson it was. I cannot specify the date of this event, but think it must have been the latter end of November 1813. About the same time General Harispe,[1] who commanded a corps of Basques, issued a proclamation forbidding the peasantry to supply the English with provisions or forage, on pain of death; it stated that we were savages, and, as a proof of this, our horses were born with short tails. I saw this absurd proclamation, which was published in French and in the Basque languages, and distributed all over the country.

Before we left the neighbourhood of Bayonne for Bordeaux, a soldier was hanged for robbery, on the sands of the Adour. This sort of punishment astonished the French almost as much as it did the soldier. On a march we were very severe; and if any of our men were caught committing an act of violence or brigandage, the offender was tried by a drum-head court-martial, and hanged in a very short time.

I knew an officer of the 18th Hussars, young, rich, and a fine-looking fellow, who joined the army not far from St Sebastian. His stud of horses was remarkable for their blood; his grooms were English, and three in number. He brought with him a light cart to carry forage, and a fourgon[2] for his own baggage. All went on well till he came to go on outpost duty; but not finding there any of the comforts to which he had been accustomed, he quietly mounted his charger, told his astonished sergeant that campaigning was not intended for a gentleman, and instantly galloped off to his quarters, ordering his servants to pack up everything immediately, as he had hired a transport to take him off to

---

[1] Jean Isidore, comte Harispe, Marshal of France (1769–1855).
[2] A baggage-wagon. The word is French: it did not come into common use in English until the 1840s.

England. He left us before any one had time to stop him; and though despatches were sent off to the Commander-in-Chief, requesting that a court-martial might sit to try the young deserter, he arrived home long enough before the despatches to enable him to sell out of his regiment. He deserved to have been shot.

SIR JOHN WATERS

Amongst the distinguished men in the Peninsular war whom my memory brings occasionally before me, is the well-known and highly popular Quartermaster-General Sir John Waters, who was born at Margam, a Welsh village in Glamorganshire.[1] He was one of those extraordinary persons that seem created by kind nature for particular purposes; and without using the word in an offensive sense, he was the most admirable spy that was ever attached to an army. One would almost have thought that the Spanish war was entered upon and carried on in order to display his remarkable qualities. He could assume the character of Spaniards of every degree and station, so as to deceive the most acute of those whom he delighted to imitate. In the posada [inn] of the village he was hailed by the contrabandist or the muleteer as one of their own race; in the gay assemblies he was an accomplished hidalgo; at the bull-fight the torreador received his congratulations as from one who had encountered the toro in the arena; in the church he would converse with the friar upon the number of Ave Marias and Paternosters which could lay a ghost, or tell him the history of every one who had perished by the flame of the Inquisition, relating his crime, whether carnal or anti-Catholic; and he could join in the seguadilla or in the guaracha [Spanish dances in ¾- or ⅜-time].

But what rendered him more efficient than all was his wonderful power of observation and accurate description, which made the information he gave so reliable and valuable to the Duke of Wellington. Nothing escaped him. When amidst a group of persons, he would minutely watch the movement, attitude, and expression of every individual that composed it; in the scenery by which he was surrounded he would carefully mark every object: – not a tree, not a bush, not a

---

[1] John Waters was, in fact, born at Tyfry, near Welsh St Donats, Glamorganshire. His grandfather, Edward Waters, was High Sheriff of the county. His father died soon after John's birth. Wellington wrote of him, 'His knowledge of the [Spanish] language and customs of the country has induced me to send him generally with the patrols employed to ascertain the position of the enemy. . . . I have employed him in several important affairs.'

large stone, escaped his observation; and it was said that in a cottage he noted every piece of crockery on the shelf, every domestic utensil, and even the number of knives and forks that were got ready for use at dinner.

His acquaintance with the Spanish language was marvellous; from the finest works of Calderon[1] to the ballads in the *patois* of every province he could quote, to the infinite delight of those with whom he associated. He could assume any character that he pleased: he could be the Castilian, haughty and reserved; the Asturian, stupid and plodding; the Catalonian, intriguing and cunning; the Andalusian, laughing and merry; – in short, he was all things to all men. Nor was he incapable of passing off, when occasion required, for a Frenchman; but as he spoke the language with a strong German accent, he called himself an Alsatian. He maintained that character with the utmost nicety; and as there is a strong feeling of fellowship, almost equal to that which exists in Scotland, amongst all those who are born in the departments of France bordering on the Rhine, and who maintain their Teutonic originality, he always found friends and supporters in every regiment in the French service.

He was on one occasion intrusted with a very difficult mission by the Duke of Wellington, which he undertook effectually to perform, and to return on a particular day with the information that was required.

Great was the disappointment when it was ascertained beyond a doubt that just after leaving the camp he had been taken prisoner, before he had time to exchange his uniform. Such, however, was the case: a troop of dragoons had intercepted him, and carried him off; and the commanding officer desired two soldiers to keep a strict watch over him and carry him to headquarters. He was of course disarmed, and being placed on a horse, was, after a short time, galloped off by his guards. He slept one night under durance vile at a small inn, where he was allowed to remain in the kitchen; conversation flowed on very glibly, and as he appeared a stupid Englishman, who could not understand a word of French or Spanish, he was allowed to listen, and thus obtained precisely the intelligence that he was in search of. The following morning, being again mounted, he overheard a conversation between his guards, who deliberately agreed to rob him, and to shoot him at a mill where they were to stop, and to report to their officer that

[1] Pedro Calderón de la Barca (1600–81), Spanish poet and dramatist, author of *La hija del aire* (1653).

they had been compelled to fire at him in consequence of his attempt to escape.

Shortly before they arrived at the mill, for fear that they might meet with some one who would insist on having a portion of the spoil, the dragoons took from their prisoner his watch and his purse, which he surrendered with a good grace. On their arrival at the mill they dismounted, and in order to give some appearance of truth to their story, they went into the house, leaving their prisoner outside, in the hope that he would make some attempt to escape. In an instant Waters threw his cloak upon a neighbouring olive bush, and mounted his cocked hat on the top. Some empty flour sacks lay upon the ground, and a horse laden with well-filled flour sacks stood at the door. Sir John contrived to enter one of the empty sacks and throw himself across the horse. When the soldiers came out of the house they fired their carbines at the supposed prisoner, and galloped off at the utmost speed.

A short time after the miller came out and mounted his steed; the general contrived to rid himself of the encumbrance of the sack, and sat up, riding behind the man, who, suddenly turning round, saw a ghost, as he believed, for the flour that still remained in the sack had completely whitened his fellow-traveller and given him a most unearthly appearance. The frightened miller was 'putrified,' as Mrs Malaprop would say, at the sight, and a push from the white spectre brought the unfortunate man to the ground, when away rode the gallant quartermaster with his sacks of flour, which, at length bursting, made a ludicrous spectacle of man and horse.

On reaching the English camp, where Lord Wellington was anxiously deploring his fate, a sudden shout from the soldiers made his lordship turn round, when a figure, resembling the statue in 'Don Juan,' galloped up to him. The duke, affectionately shaking him by the hand, said –

'Waters, you never yet deceived me; and though you have come in a most questionable shape, I must congratulate you and myself.'

THE BATTLE OF THE NIVELLE

We expected to remain quietly in our winter quarters at St Jean de Luz; but, to our surprise, early one morning, we were aroused from sleep by the beating of the drum calling us to arms. We were soon in marching order. It appeared that our outposts had been severely pushed by the French, and we were called upon to support our companions in arms.

The whole of the British army, as well as the division of the Guards, had commenced a forward movement. Soult, seeing this, entirely changed his tactics, and from that time – viz., the 9th of December – a series of engagements took place. The fighting on the 9th was comparatively insignificant. When we were attacked on the 10th, the Guards held the mayor's house and the grounds and orchards attached: this was an important station.

Large bodies of the enemy's infantry approached, and, after desultory fighting, succeeded in penetrating our position, when many hand-to-hand combats ensued. Towards the afternoon, officers and men having displayed great gallantry, we drove the enemy from the ground which they courageously disputed with us, and from which they eventually retreated to Bayonne. Every day there was constant fighting along the whole of our line, which extended from the sea to the Lower Pyrenees – a distance probably not less than thirty miles.

On the 11th we only exchanged a few shots, but on the 12th Soult brought into action from fifteen to twenty thousand men, and attacked our left with a view of breaking our line. One of the most remarkable incidents of the 12th was the fact of an English battalion being surrounded by a division of French in the neighbourhood of the mayor's house, which, as before observed, was one of our principal strategical positions. The French commanding officer, believing that no attempt would be made to resist, galloped up to the officer of the British regiment and demanded his sword. Upon this, without the least hesitation, the British officer shouted out, 'This fellow wants us to surrender: charge, my boys! and show them what stuff we are made of.' Instantaneously a hearty cheer rang out, and our men rushed forward impetuously, drove off the enemy at the point of the bayonet, and soon disposed of the surrounding masses. In a few minutes, they had taken prisoners, or killed, the whole of the infantry regiment opposed to them.

On the 13th was fought the bloody battle of the Nivelle. Soult had determined to make a gigantic effort to drive us back into Spain. During the night of the 12th, he rapidly concentrated about sixty thousand troops in front of Sir Rowland Hill's *corps d'armée*, consisting of 15,000 men, who occupied a very strong position, which was defended by some of the best artillery in the world. At daybreak Sir Rowland Hill[1] was astonished to find himself threatened by masses of infantry advancing over a country luckily intersected by rivulets, hedges, and woods, which

---

[1] Sir Rowland Hill, first Viscount Hill (1772–1842), known as 'Daddy' Hill, the stout and florid, genial General who was to be appointed commander-in-chief of the army when Wellington became Prime Minister in 1828. He commanded the right of the British army at the battle of the Nivelle.

prevented the enemy from making a rapid advance; whilst, at the same time, it was impossible on such ground to employ cavalry. Sir Rowland, availing himself of an elevated position, hurriedly surveyed his ground, and concentrated his men at such points as he knew the nature of the field would induce the enemy to attack. The French, confident of success from their superior numbers, came gallantly up, using the bayonet for the first time in a premeditated attack. Our men stood their ground, and for hours acted purely on the defensive; being sustained by the admirable practice of our artillery, whose movements no difficulty of ground could, on this occasion, impede, so efficiently were the guns horsed, and so perfect was the training of the officers. It was not until mid-day that the enemy became discouraged at finding that they were unable to make any serious impression on our position; they then retired in good order, Sir Rowland Hill not daring to follow them.

Lord Wellington arrived just in time to witness the end of the battle; and while going over the field with Sir Rowland Hill, he remarked that he had never seen so many men *hors de combat* in so small a space.

Whilst these operations were going on, Soult was organising his discouraged army, in order to make, as early as possible, another convenient stand. The enemy fell back on Orthes, and there took up a strong position; Soult was, nevertheless, destined to be beaten again at Orthes. It so happened that, for the first time since the battle of Vittoria, our cavalry were engaged: the nature of the ground at Nive and Nivelle was such as to prevent the possibility of employing the mounted soldier.

I must here record an incident which created a considerable sensation in military circles in connection with the battle of Orthes. The 10th Hussars, officered exclusively by men belonging to the noblest families of Great Britain, showed a desire to take a more active part in the contest than their colonel (Quintin) thought prudent. They pressed hard to be permitted to charge the French cavalry on more than one occasion, but in vain. This so disgusted every officer in the regiment, that they eventually signed a *round robin*, by which they agreed never again to speak to their colonel. When the regiment returned to England, a court of inquiry was held, which resulted, through the protection of the Prince Regent, in the colonel's exoneration from all blame, and at the same time the exchange of the rebellious officers into other regiments.

It was at the battle of Orthes that the late Duke of Richmond was shot through the body, gallantly fighting with the 7th Fusiliers.[1]

---

[1] Charles Gordon-Lennox, fifth Duke of Richmond and Lennox (1791-1860).

Lord Wellington had determined to cross the Adour, and Sir John Hope[1] was intrusted with a *corps d'armée*, which was the first to perform this difficult operation. It was necessary to provide Sir John Hope with a number of small boats; these were accordingly brought on the backs of mules from various Spanish ports, it being impossible, on account of the surf at the entrance of the Adour, as well as the command which the French held of that river, for Lord Wellington to avail himself of water carriage. Soult had given orders to dispute the passage.

The first operation of our corps was to throw over the 3d Guards. This was not accomplished without much difficulty: but it was imperatively necessary, in order to protect the point where the construction of the bridge of boats would terminate. They had not been long on the French side of the river before a considerable body of men were seen issuing from Bayonne. Sir John Hope ordered our artillery, and rockets, then for the first time employed, to support our small band. Three or four regiments of French infantry were approaching rapidly, when a well-directed fire of rockets fell amongst them. The consternation of the Frenchmen was such, when these hissing, serpent-like projectiles descended, that a panic ensued, and they retreated upon Bayonne. The next day the bridge of boats was completed, and the whole army crossed.

Bayonne was eventually invested after a contest, in which it was supposed our loss exceeded 500 or 600 men. Here we remained in camp about six weeks, expecting to besiege the citadel; but this event never came off: we, however, met with a severe disaster and a reverse. The enemy made an unexpected sortie, and surrounded General Sir John Hope, when he and the whole of his staff were taken prisoners.[2] The French killed and wounded about 1000 men on this occasion.

The hardly-contested battle of Toulouse was fought about this period, but the Guards were not present to share the honours of a contest which closed the eventful war of the Spanish Peninsula.[3]

---

[1] Sir John Hope (1765-1823) succeeded to the command of the army at Corunna on the death of Sir John Moore in 1809. He commanded the 1st Division at the battle of the Nivelle and the battles of the Nive where he was wounded. On his recovery he was appointed to command the left wing of the army in the crossing of the Adour. In Wellington's opinion the ablest man in the Peninsular army, he succeeded his brother as fourth Earl of Hopetoun in 1816.

[2] Hope, wounded again during this sortie, was soon released.

[3] The battle of Toulouse, which brought the Peninsular War to an end in April 1814, resulted in heavy losses to the Allies – about 4500 men compared with French casualties of some 3200.

Arrival of the Guards at Bordeaux

When we reached Bordeaux, which had now become a stronghold of the Royalists, we were received by the inhabitants with a welcome which resembled what would be shown to friends and deliverers, rather than to a foreign soldiery. Nothing could be more gratifying and more acceptable to our feelings, since it was the first time after our arrival on the Continent that we met with cordiality and an apparent desire to make our quarters as comfortable as possible. The Duc d'Angoulême had reached Bordeaux before us, and no doubt his presence had prepared the way for all the friends of the Bourbons.[1] Everywhere some description of white rag was doing duty for a Royalist banner. I lived at M. Devigné's, a rich wine-merchant, who had a family of two sons and two beautiful daughters; the latter, as I thought, taken remarkable care of by their maternal parent. Here I had evidently fallen upon my legs, for not only was the family a most agreeable one, but their hospitality was of the most generous kind.

Here I had an opportunity of meeting some of the prettiest women of a city famed all over Europe for its female beauty. The young ladies were remarkable for their taste in dress, which in those days consisted of a mantilla *à l'Espagnole*, and silken shawls of varied hues, so admirably blended, that the eye was charmed with their richness of colour. The *grisettes* [young French women of the working class], who were as much admired by the soldiers as were the high dames by the officers, were remarkable for a coquettish species of apron of a red dye, which was only to be obtained from the neighbourhood.

Of course we were all very anxious to taste the Bordeaux wines; but our palates, accustomed to the stronger vintages of Spain, I suspect were not in a condition to appreciate the more delicate and refined bouquets which ought to characterise claret. A *vin ordinaire*, which now at a restaurateur's would cost three francs, was then furnished at the hotels for fifteen sous: a Larose, Lafitte, Margaux, such as we are now paying eight or ten francs a bottle for, did not cost a third. I must not, however, forget that greater attention and care is now employed in the preparation of French wines. The exportation to England of the light red wines of France was not sufficiently profitable, as I learnt from my host, at that time to attract the cupidity of commerce.

---

[1] Louis-Antoine de Bourbon, duc d'Angoulême (1775–1844), son of the Comte d'Artois, later King Charles X, had raised the Royalist standard at Bordeaux. When his father was forced to abdicate in the revolution of 1830, Angoulême went into exile and died at Gorizia in Austrian-occupied Venezia.

In the Guards, Bordeaux was more affectionately remembered in connection with its women than its wine. We left it with regret, and the more youthful and imaginative amongst us said that we were wafted across the Channel by the gentle sighs of 'the girls we left behind us.'

THE LIGHT COMPANY'S POODLE AND SIR F. PONSONBY[1]

Every regiment has a pet of some sort or another. One distinguished Highland regiment possesses a deer; the Welsh Fusiliers a goat, which is the object of their peculiar affection, and which generally marches with the band. The light company of my battalion of the 1st Guards, in 1813, rejoiced in a very handsome poodle, which had, if I mistake not, been made prisoner at Vittoria. At the commencement of the battle of the 9th of December 1813, near the mayor's house, not far from Bidart, we observed the gallant Frederick Ponsonby well in front with the skirmishers, and by the side of his horse the soldiers' poodle. The colonel was encouraging our men to advance; and the poodle, in great glee, was jumping and barking at the bullets, as they flew round him like hail. On a sudden, we observed Ponsonby struggling with a French mounted officer, whom he had already disarmed, and was endeavouring to lead off to our lines; when the French skirmishers, whose numbers had increased, fired several shots, and wounded Ponsonby, forcing him to relinquish his prisoner and to retire. At the same time a bullet broke one of the poor dog's legs. For his gallant conduct in this affair, the poodle became, if possible, a still greater favourite than he was before; and his friends, the men of the light company, took him to England, where I saw my three-legged friend for several years afterwards, the most prosperous of poodles, and the happiest of the canine race.

THE GUARDS AND THE UMBRELLAS

During the action of the 10th of December 1813, the Grenadier Guards occupied an unfinished redoubt on the right of the high road. The Duke of Wellington happened to pass by on his return to headquarters, having satisfied himself that the fighting was merely a feint on the part of Soult. His Grace on looking around saw, to his surprise, a great many

[1] Colonel the Hon. Sir Frederick Cavendish Ponsonby (1783-1837), second son of the third Earl of Bessborough. He commanded the 12th Light Dragoons. Promoted major-general in 1835, he was appointed Governor of Malta the following year. His son, Sir Henry Frederick Ponsonby (1825-95), became Queen Victoria's Private Secretary.

umbrellas, with which the officers protected themselves from the rain that was then falling. Arthur Hill came galloping up to us saying, 'Lord Wellington does not approve of the use of umbrellas during the enemy's firing, and will not allow [officers] to make themselves ridiculous in the eyes of the army.' [Their Colonel], a few days afterwards, received a wigging from Lord Wellington for suffering his officers to carry umbrellas in the face of the enemy; his lordship observing, 'The guards may in uniform, when on duty at St James's, carry them if they please; but in the field it is not only ridiculous but unmilitary.'

A WORD FOR BROWN BESS[1]

When the British army invested Bayonne, it fell to my lot to be on outpost duty, and I then and there saw a long shot fired from one of our old muskets which showed that Brown Bess, though not equalling our modern weapons, had yet some good solid merits of her own, and when held straight was not to be despised even at a long range. Several shots had been fired from the French pickets, when Captain Grant of the 1st Foot Guards, being the senior officer on duty, came to me to inquire the cause of the firing, and desired me to make my way to the front and endeavour to ascertain what had occurred. Having arrived near the ravine which separated us from the French, I stumbled upon an advanced sentry, a German, who was coolly smoking his pipe. I asked him whether the shots that had been heard came from his neighbourhood, upon which he replied in broken English, 'Yes, zir, that feelow you see yonder has fired nine times at mine target' (meaning his body), 'but has missed. I hopes you, Capitaine, will let me have one shot at him.' The distance between the French picket and ours could not have been less than 400 yards; so, without giving myself time to think, I said, 'Yes, you can have one shot at him.' He levelled his musket, fired, and killed his man; whereupon a sergeant and two or three French soldiers who had seen him fall, ran down to the front and removed the body.

I have been informed that the Duke of Wellington, during the Peninsular War, visited Lisbon only once, remaining three days at that town, at the Palace of Necessidades;[2] and on this occasion he was

---

[1] The smooth-bore flintlock musket was known as the Brown Bess. It was a counterpart of the Brown Bill, the halberd used by infantry before muskets came into use.

[2] The Palácio das Necessidades was a royal palace built between 1745 and 1750 to the design of Caetano Tomás de Sousa on the site of a chapel dedicated to Nossa Senhora das Necessidades. It became the Foreign Office in 1916.

received in the most enthusiastic manner by the Portuguese and English. Unfortunately, Marshal Beresford[1] and our Minister, Sir Charles Stuart, afterwards Lord Stuart de Rothsay,[2] were at this time at variance, and hated each other most cordially. The Marshal wanted to lodge our great commander at his own house, and thereby monopolise his society; but to no purpose, as the Duke went to the palace. The Duke did not disguise his displeasure at the inefficiency exhibited by many of the superior officers in the British army then at Lisbon, and sent several of them back to England, saying, 'It is not my fault that they are sent home, but the fault of those who sent them out.'

Whilst the Duke was insisting on Sir Warren Peacocke's acting with severity against the skulkers from the army, these gentlemen were complaining bitterly of the Governor for not allowing them to shirk their duties, alleging that, on account of 'ill health' (unfortunately a common excuse in the service), they ought to be allowed to remain at Lisbon to recruit it: this 'recruiting of health,' be it understood, generally consisting of a minimum of work, combined with a maximum of dissipation. Sir Warren was so disgusted with the amount of extra work and anxiety entailed upon him by these useless officers, that he several times requested the Duke to find some one to supply his place as Governor; but the answer he generally received was, 'You are too valuable here to be replaced by any one. I cannot possibly spare you.'

One of the heroes of [the battles of the Pyrenees, 25 July–2 August 1813] was Frank Russell,[3] 'the Pride of Woburn Abbey,' whose character it would be as difficult to over-estimate as it would be to give an idea of his chivalrous bearing in presence of the enemy. He possessed all the requisites for a good soldier. Of noble birth, good-looking, and with a splendid figure, he was valiant in the extreme. He was gazetted in the 7th Fusiliers at the age of sixteen, and forthwith sent with them to Spain, where he followed the fortunes of his corps up to the time of the battle of the Pyrenees. One of the most furious attacks made by Soult on our position at this celebrated conflict was directed on the left wing of the British army. The Fusiliers were posted on the right, and ordered to maintain themselves against all odds, and not to budge a foot. The

[1] William Carr Beresford, first Viscount Beresford (1768-1854), was appointed to command the Portuguese army in 1809 and given the rank of marshal in it.

[2] Sir Charles Stuart, later Baron Stuart de Rothesay (1779-1845), was Ambassador in Paris from 1815 to 1830. In 1841 he was appointed Ambassador in St Petersburg. His daughter, Charlotte, married Lord Canning, first Viceroy of India.

[3] Francis Russell (1793-1832) was a nephew of the fifth and sixth Dukes of Bedford. He reached the rank of lieutenant-colonel and died unmarried at the age of thirty-nine.

French General being determined to turn our right, sent an overwhelming force against Frank's regiment, which was posted against a mountain wall. The Fusiliers defended themselves with obstinate courage, but their Colonel, for some reason which was never explained, declared it prudent to order a retreat, though his line was unbroken. Frank Russell, however, shouted out, 'Not yet, Colonel,' and with the colours of his regiment mounted the wall and cheered our men on; the French meanwhile renewing their attack with redoubled vigour. During this fierce struggle, however, our hero kept his position, till the fierce energy with which the French had been fighting began to cool: for Wellington had meanwhile broken Soult's centre, and the retreat of the French forces was ordered. Before Russell quitted his post of honour, Lord Wellington with his staff happened to pass by the wall, and saw Russell standing on the wall, holding the colours of his regiment, which were riddled with bullet holes. On the following day, when the gallant young officer's conduct was reported to our great commander, he exclaimed, 'Ah! there's nothing like blood.'

The chivalrous bearing of Frank Russell affords a memorable example of the feeling which actuated young officers at the time of which I am now speaking. As a man of the world, Frank was a great favourite with the fair sex, and enjoyed in a remarkable degree the confidence of his friends; for his temper and disposition were eminently sociable, and he was noted for his kindness of heart. He died at an early age, holding a company of the Guards, and was universally regretted. A pretty compliment was paid to him by the Duchess of York,[1] who presented him with a ring, made by Lawrier, the jeweller in St James's Street, having for a motto, 'None but the brave deserve the fair.'

HUNTING IN THE PYRENEES, 1813, 1814

The Commissary-General succeeded in collecting from England a kennel of splendid hounds. On the Marquis of Worcester's (the late Duke of Beaufort) leaving the army, he promised to send some of his father's dogs; other gentlemen followed this nobleman's example, and before we crossed the Bidassoa the pack was complete, and in fine condition. The hunting in the Pyrenees reminded me of my native Wales; it was all up hill and down dale, and for that reason, when a fox

---

[1] Princess Frederica, Duchess of York (1767-1820). She was the eldest daughter of Frederick William III of Prussia. She was 'very small, not at all pretty and had poor teeth', but Lord Malmesbury thought her 'lively, sensible and very tractable'.

was found he was seldom if ever killed. The best riders belonging to the hunt were the officers of the 14th and 16th Dragoons, who were, as a rule, well mounted. I have seen at a meet in the Pyrenees about two hundred officers assembled, some (as I have said) well mounted, but the majority on 'screws,' ponies, or even mules – a strange contrast to the Quorn and Pytchley gatherings. The greatest character of all was Lascelles, on his immense horse, on which he used to delight to race up hill for a lark; and many were the scrapes he got into with the whipper-in for riding over the hounds.

One fine morning in October 1813, Reynard took it into his head to cross the Bidassoa, and the dogs and huntsman, heedless of danger, followed. The notes of the hounds and the cheering of the huntsman alarmed a French drum-major and some twenty boys whom he was instructing in a secluded spot on the banks of the river. Instead of showing fight, the drum-major with his young pupils scampered off; the dogs meanwhile, accompanied by the huntsman, were in full cry, and shortly afterwards killed a fine dog fox. The field had remained on our side of the river, enjoying the sport without incurring any danger; when all of a sudden the enemy, wondering what the deuce we were about, came down in force, with a battery of field-pieces, and opened fire, which made us all scamper off as if old Nick had been at our heels. [The Commissary-General], however, advanced to the water's edge, and with his white pocket-handkerchief as a flag of truce, asked permission of the French officer in command to cross and explain what we were doing. This request was acceded to, and when our gallant foe had heard the reasons why we had advanced out of bounds, he very graciously permitted the huntsman and dogs to recross the river and join us.

DYSENTERY IN THE PENINSULA

Early in the year 1812 the Duke of York despatched to the seat of war the 3d Battalion of my old regiment. It was considered by military men to have been the finest in his Majesty's service. All the men, with the exception of the grenadier company, were strong, active young fellows, but had not seen active service. They were conveyed to Cadiz in men-of-war, and arrived there without any accident; but owing to change of diet, and the substituting the horrid wine of the country for the porter they had been accustomed to at home, before the expiration of a few weeks, five hundred of these fine fellows died in the hospital at Vizu, and were buried in the churchyard there. I mention this to show how careful commanding-officers ought to be to prevent similar consequences from decimating bodies of fresh troops: although warnings of this sort have occurred all over the globe.

On joining my regiment in the Peninsula, one of the grenadiers, a tall and well-built man, was recommended to me as the best person to employ for pitching my tent. This man had been brought up as a carpenter, but through some misunderstanding with his relations had enlisted. While cutting the trench he entered into conversation with me, and said he hoped, as I appeared very young and unaccustomed to bivouacking, that I would forgive him for being so bold as to offer a little salutary advice: which was to drink every morning on rising a small glass of brandy or rum, as by so doing rheumatism, dysentery, and many other camp disorders, would be prevented. He added, with tears in his eyes, that he had lost his brother at Vizu, owing to his not following the advice he was now giving me. I was so struck with the earnest manner of the man that I adopted his panacea, and during the whole time that I was in camp I never had a day's illness.

A Daring Exploit

Among the incidents that occurred in the war in Spain, the following will no doubt surprise the reader: – In Picton's[1] division in the Pyrenees there was an Irishman of extraordinary courage, by name O'Keefe, who was addicted to all sorts of irregularities, which brought him more than once to the halberds,[2] but who performed a feat worthy of the heroes of antiquity. Near the pass of Roncesvalles the French occupied a peak or impregnable mountain called the Boar's Head, at the top of which a company of the enemy was posted. To drive them away appeared impossible; Picton thought so, and determined to invest this natural fort, to prevent useless bloodshed. During a reconnaissance, the General said, in a loud voice, which was overheard by the men below, that the French could, if they pleased, pelt us away with stones from the top of the mountain. O'Keefe stepped up, touched his cap, and addressed Sir T. Picton thus: 'If your honour chooses, I will take the hill alone.' This speech astonished all who heard it; but not the General, who had frequently witnessed the daring and intrepidity of O'Keefe. 'If you do so,' replied Sir Thomas, 'I will report it to Lord Wellington, and

---

[1] Sir Thomas Picton (1758–1815), commanded the 3rd Division in the Peninsula. Something of a martinet, he was a man of brusque manner and blunt speech. He was celebrated for the top hat which he wore in battle to protect his eyes. He was shot through this hat and killed at Waterloo. See also pp. 125–7.

[2] Miscreants were tied to halberds before being subjected to the lash.

I promise you your discharge, with a shilling a day for life.' O'Keefe stole away, having whispered to the commanding-officer of his company to follow him, and climbed up the goat-path, the English sentinels firing at him, thinking he was deserting to the enemy. O'Keefe having entered the stronghold of the French, was received with open arms, as a deserter. He then began to play his part, by showing signs of imbecility, laughing, dancing, singing, &c.; so that the enemy thought that they had actually received a madman instead of a deserter, and told him to decamp, as there was not food enough there to feed him. During this farce, our men quickly got up to the summit, where they found O'Keefe occupying the attention of the enemy. They rushed in and took possession of this stronghold without losing a man. O'Keefe (I believe that was his name) received for this act of daring the nomination of one of the warders of the Tower from the Duke of Wellington.

My Soldier-Servant

My Sicilian soldier-servant, Proyd, was an excellent servant and caterer, but he possessed one fault – a too great admiration, unqualified with respect, for the charms of the fair sex, and he seldom lost an opportunity of stealing a kiss from any pretty girl that came in his way.

On our return from the Peninsula, I took this Figaro with me to White Knights, the seat of the Duke of Marlborough, where I was invited to spend some days. At this charming house I found a great number of visitors, among whom were Lord and Lady Macclesfield.[1] It happened on the day of my arrival that my servant met the maid of Lady Macclesfield on the staircase, and without the slightest ceremony he attempted to kiss her. The maid, unaccustomed to such behaviour, screamed, ran downstairs, and then up again, with Proyd close at her heels; he even followed her into her lady's room, where she flew to take refuge. Her ladyship, alarmed at seeing a strange man in her room, shrieked loudly; many persons ran to her assistance; and her noble husband, more dead than alive, thinking some sad disaster had befallen the Countess, inquired with caution, 'What is the matter?' Her ladyship replied in a faint voice, 'The man is under the bed.' Pokers and tongs were seized, and the noble Lord made use of his weapons to such purpose that the delinquent quietly surrendered. This incident, which created great confusion, rendered it necessary that the Sicilian should be

---

[1] The fourth Earl of Macclesfield (1755–1842). His wife was Mary Frances, daughter of the Rev. Thomas Drake.

sent to rejoin his regiment. Poor Proyd soon after applied for his discharge, and returned to his native land to make love to his own countrywomen.

SIR JOHN ELLEY OF THE 'BLUES'[1]

I have received a letter from a gentleman who knew [Elley] personally, giving me the following information respecting this dashing hero: – 'I spent some time at Harrogate with this gallant soldier, whom I admired not only for his bravery, but for his talents; he was replete with wit and fun, and full of the most interesting anecdotes. On my leaving him, he said that he had an old acquaintance residing not far from my father's place, whither I was going, and he would feel obliged if I would ride over some day to a certain toll-bar in the west of Cumberland, and deliver a message to his old friend, the sergeant who had enlisted him in the Blues. I did not forget a promise which might lead to some anecdotes respecting Sir John's early life; and shortly after arriving at home, I mounted my nag, rode to the toll-bar, and saw the old sergeant, who kept the turnpike and appeared to be seventy-five years of age. When he came to take the toll he appeared much astonished at receiving the message from Sir John, and asking after his health, said that it was true that he had enlisted him into the Blues, and he related the circumstance: – "The sergeant, having charge of a recruiting party at Barnet, one fine day a tall and respectable-looking young fellow addressed him, stating he wanted to enlist; the shilling was therefore given, and on the following day the recruit was sent to headquarters, where he was passed and duly enlisted in the Royal Guards." '

The old man being asked what he knew of Sir John's antecedents said, that the appearance and manner of the recruit proved him to have been a gentleman. He declined affirming as to the truth of what he had heard; but added that the report current in the regiment after his entering it, was that the new recruit had held a cornet's commission in the Scots Greys, then quartered at Doncaster; but owing to a misunderstanding with an officer about a lady, he had thrown up his commission in disgust, and having spent all his money, enlisted as a

[1] Sir John Elley (d. 1839), the son of a man who kept a chop-house in Holborn, enlisted in the Royal Horse Guards in 1789, purchasing a cornetcy with his father's help in 1794 and a lieutenant-colonelcy in 1808. He was adjutant-general of cavalry at Waterloo. Elsewhere Gronow describes him as 'one of the most powerful men in the Army'. Neither helmet nor cuirass could stand against a sword wielded by his strong arm.

private in the manner described. In the barrack-room he was 'hail fellow well met' with all his comrades, who nevertheless treated him as their superior. As a swordsman and rider, he was considered the best in the regiment; and in consequence of his gentlemanly deportment, and being a good penman, he was taken into the adjutant's office, whence he was promoted to a commission in the regiment.

Perhaps the most distinguished service ever performed by Sir John Elley was in the cavalry engagement at the battle of Vittoria, when he was assistant adjutant-general to the cavalry. [The 3rd Light Dragoons were given orders to] charge a superior force of the enemy, which proved disastrous; for the regiment was almost entirely cut to pieces. Sir John Elley, observing this disaster, got together as many of the 14th and 16th Dragoons as he could, and charged at the head of them through the enemy; thereby saving many of the fine fellows, who were dispersed and unable to act. In the charge he was knocked down, together with his horse, the fall breaking his leg; and although continually ridden over by friend and foe in the *mêlée*, Elley, nothing daunted, cheered on his men to fight for the honour of old England, and at last, catching hold of [a sergeant's] stirrup, was dragged to the rear.

THE HEROIC LADY WALDEGRAVE

When the British army was about to enter France, I was struck with the beauty and attainments of the chivalrous Lady Waldegrave,[1] who accompanied her lord throughout the war. Her conduct was the theme of the army, and she won universal praise and admiration. She was a perfect heroine.

Since the peace, I have had the honour to receive invitations to her house in the Champs-Elysées. She used to speak of her campaigns with the same energy that an old soldier would talk of battles wherein he had distinguished himself, and would tell you of the innumerable risks she had been exposed to in the several charges of cavalry which her husband had led. She felt much, she used to say, for those poor fellows who were left wounded on the ground, and her description of their sufferings was so natural and touching that it frequently brought tears into the eyes of those who heard her. The heroine was nearly taken prisoner upon one occasion; but, upon presenting her pocket-pistol at the breast of the

---

[1] Anne, Lady Waldegrave, was the wife of John James, sixth Earl Waldegrave, a lieutenant-colonel in the 54th Foot. She was a daughter of John William King of Hastings.

French cavalry soldier who menaced her, he dropped his sword, and suffered her to escape.

The Countess of Waldegrave was not only young but beautiful; she had a splendid figure, and was one of the best riders I ever saw. She was not at all masculine in her style; her voice and manner of speaking were remarkable for sweetness and grace. I cannot hope to see her like again.

THE BRITISH IN BORDEAUX

Towards the close of the Continental war, viz., in 1814, the militia of that epoch were full of military ardour. The Marquis of Buckingham, who was enormously fat, and not unlike the pictures which are represented of Falstaff, volunteered, in conjunction with his friend Sir Watkin Williams Wynne, to take their regiments, the Buckinghamshire and Flintshire Militia, to the seat of war.[1] Permission was granted them to join the Duke of Wellington's army, and off they started for Bordeaux. But they arrived 'a day after the fair,' for the treaty of peace had been signed by the allied sovereigns; so, as the King of France with forty thousand men

Marched up a hill, and then marched down again,[2]

our patriotic warriors were obliged to retrace their steps without having fired a shot at the enemy.

Before they re-embarked for their native land, however, they took good care to impress upon the inhabitants of Bordeaux their value as soldiers, by parading their battalions with all the pomp and circumstance of war, both in the morning and at noon. Those for whose benefit this spectacle was intended never failed attending these military parades; not with the idea of gaining any hints as to evolutions, &c., but to gaze on the commanding officers, whom they denominated, 'Les bœufs-gras anglais.' The militia regiments appeared but a sorry sight in comparison with British veterans who had marched through Portugal

---

[1] Sir Charles Watkin Williams Wynn (1775-1850), an active politician and member of the Cabinet. George Canning thought him the 'worst man of business' he had ever come across. He was elder brother of the diplomat, Sir Henry Watkin Williams Wynn (1783-1856), and commanded the Montgomeryshire Yeomanry from 1803-44. The two brothers appear in the James Gillray caricature 'The Bear and his Leader' (BM 10566, 19 May 1806) as 'Bubble' and 'Squeak', nicknames bestowed upon them because of their respective manners of speaking.

[2] In Arthur Rackham's *Mother Goose* (1917) it becomes 'the noble Duke of York' who 'had ten thousand men' and 'marched them up to the top of the hill, and marched them down again.'

and Spain, fighting a hundred battles, and afterwards remained some time at Bordeaux, where they gained the respect of the inhabitants by their orderly conduct and manly bearing. Unfortunately, too, our militiamen did not conduct themselves in a becoming manner; for, delighted at the cheapness of the wine and brandy, and happening to be officered by men incapable of looking after them properly, when off duty they were constantly tipsy, and getting into all sorts of scrapes and broils with the inhabitants; so much so, that their conduct was reported to the Commander-in-Chief, who ordered them home without delay.

The wine-merchants, who had not done badly during the stay of our warlike friends in Bordeaux, persuaded the Marquis and the Welsh baronet, on the eve of their departure, into buying a quantity of stuff they designated claret. Proud of their purchase, they had it carefully shipped; and when it arrived in due course at London, it was stowed away in the cellars of Stowe[1] and Wynstay.[2] Orders were eventually given to have the precious liquid bottled; but when the casks were tapped it was found that an acetous fermentation had taken place, converting the 'delicate Bordeaux wine' into very bad vinegar. The two heroes, doubly disappointed of the wine they had bought and the honours they hoped to win, commenced legal proceedings against the vendors of the liquor; but they were non-suited, and had to pay costs, amounting to a considerable sum.

[1] The estate of the Temple family, Dukes of Buckingham. It was begun in 1697 and reconstructed in 1775. Vanbrugh, Robert Adam, William Kent and Grinling Gibbons all worked here, and James Gibbs designed several temples in the gardens. George Nugent-Temple-Grenville, first Marquess of Buckingham, died here in 1813. His son became first Duke of Buckingham in 1822. The title is now extinct. The public school here was opened in 1923.

[2] Wynnstay (Gronow misspells it), the Denbighshire house of the Williams Wynns. Designed by Francis and William Smith in 1736-9, remodelled by James Wyatt in 1785 and altered again for Sir Watkin Williams Wynn in 1825 (probably by Benjamin Gummow), it was burned down in 1858.

4

London in the Days of the Regency

SOCIETY IN LONDON IN 1814

In the year 1814, my battalion of the Guards was once more in its old quarters in Portman Street barracks, enjoying the fame of our Spanish campaign. Good society at the period to which I refer was, to use a familiar expression, wonderfully 'select.' At the present time one can hardly conceive the importance which was attached to getting admission to Almack's, the seventh heaven of the fashionable world.[1] Of the three hundred officers of the Foot Guards, not more than half-a-dozen were honoured with vouchers of admission to this exclusive temple of the *beau monde*; the gates of which were guarded by lady

---

[1] Almack's Assembly Rooms were in King Street, St James's. Named after their first proprietor, William Almack, they were designed by Robert Mylne and opened in the 1760s. Henry Luttrell wrote of the guest lists controlled by seven ladies of high rank:

> All on that magic list depends:
> Fame, fortune, fashion, lovers, friends.
> 'Tis that which gratifies or vexes
> All ranks, all ages, and both sexes.
> If once to Almack's you belong,
> Like monarchs, you can do no wrong;
> But banished thence on Wednesday night
> By jove you can do nothing right.

The lady patronesses were: Lady Jersey, Lady Castlereagh, Lady Cowper (later Lady Palmerston), Lady Sefton, Mrs Drummond Burrell (later Lady Willoughby), Princess Esterhazy and Countess Lieven.

patronesses, whose smiles or frowns consigned men and women to happiness or despair.

Many diplomatic arts, much finesse, and a host of intrigues, were set in motion to get an invitation to Almack's. Very often persons whose rank and fortunes entitled them to the *entrée* anywhere, were excluded by the cliqueism of the lady patronesses; for the female government of Almack's was a pure despotism, and subject to all the caprices of despotic rule: it is needless to add that, like every other despotism, it was not innocent of abuses. The fair ladies who ruled supreme over this little dancing and gossiping world, issued a solemn proclamation that no gentleman should appear at the assemblies without being dressed in knee-breeches, white cravat, and *chapeau bras*.[1] On one occasion, the Duke of Wellington was about to ascend the staircase of the ball-room, dressed in black trousers, when the vigilant Mr Willis, the guardian of the establishment, stepped forward and said, 'Your Grace cannot be admitted in trousers,' whereupon the Duke, who had a great respect for orders and regulations, quietly walked away.

In 1814, the dances at Almack's were Scotch reels and the old English country-dance; and the orchestra, being from Edinburgh, was conducted by the then celebrated Neil Gow.[2] It was not until 1815 that Lady Jersey introduced from Paris the favourite quadrille, which has so long remained popular. In course of time, the waltzing mania, having turned the heads of society generally, descended to their feet, and the waltz was practised in the morning in certain noble mansions in London with unparalleled assiduity.[3]

Drinking and play were more universally indulged in then than at the present time, and many men still living must remember the couple of bottles of port at least which accompanied his dinner in those days. Indeed, female society amongst the upper classes was most notoriously neglected; except, perhaps, by romantic foreigners, who were the heroes of many a fashionable adventure that fed the clubs with ever-acceptable scandal. How could it be otherwise, when husbands spent their days in the hunting-field, or were entirely occupied with politics, and always away from home during the day; whilst the dinner-party, commencing

---

[1] A small, three-cornered flat silk hat which could be carried under the arm.
[2] Niel Gow (1727–1807), Scottish violinist and composer, the son of a plaid weaver. He lived and worked mostly in Scotland but was often summoned to London to play music for Scottish dances.
[3] The waltz – from the German *walzen*, to revolve – was derived from the lively Bavarian dance, the *Ländler*. It was popular in Vienna in the 1770s and came to London in 1791.

at seven or eight, frequently did not break up before one in the morning. There were then four, and even five bottlemen; and the only thing that saved them was drinking very slowly, and out of very small glasses. I really think that if the good society of 1815 could appear before their more moderate descendants in the state they were generally reduced to after dinner, the moderns would pronounce their ancestors fit for nothing but bed.

A MISHAP AT ALMACK'S

Among the many droll incidents which occurred at those elegant balls at Almack's I recollect one which created much amusement among those who witnessed it, at the expense of the person whose name I am about to mention. The late Lord Graves,[1] who was extremely fat, but who danced well for his size, engaged the beautiful Lady Harriet Butler[2] one evening as his partner in a quadrille. Her Ladyship had just arrived from Paris, where she had been brought up under the auspices of Joséphine, and having received lessons in dancing from the celebrated Vestris,[3] she electrified the English with the graceful ease with which she made her *entrechats*; so much so, that a circle was generally formed to admire her dancing. Lord Graves, desirous of doing his utmost to please his fair partner, ventured on imitating the lady's *entrechat*; but in making the attempt, he unluckily fell heavily on the floor. Nothing daunted, however, he got on his legs again and finished the quadrille as well as he could; when his friends hastened to sympathise with him. But Sir John Burke,[4] in a sarcastic manner, said, 'What could have induced you, at your age and in your state, to make so great a fool of yourself as to attempt an *entrechat*?' Lord Graves, not relishing the manner in which the Baronet had addressed him, replied, 'If you think I am too old to dance, I consider myself not too old to blow your brains out for your impertinence; so the sooner you find a second the better.' Lord Sefton,[5] who overheard the conversation, said, 'Tut tut tut, man, the sooner you

[1] Thomas North, second Baron Graves (1775-1830).
[2] Lady Harriet Eleanor Butler, daughter of the first Marquess and nineteenth Earl of Ormonde (d. 1885).
[3] Vestris, the stage name of the opera singer and actress Lucia Elizabeth Bartolozzi (1797-1856). She married the ballet dancer Auguste-Armand Vestris, ballet-master at the King's Theatre, in 1813 and left him in 1817. She later married the actor Charles James Matthews, with whom she managed various London theatres.
[4] Sir John Burke, second baronet (1782-1847).
[5] William Philip, second Earl of Sefton (1772-1838).

shake hands the better; for the fact is, the world will condemn you both
if you fight on such slight grounds: and you, Graves, won't have a leg to
stand on.' This sensible remark led to the parties shaking hands, and
thus the matter dropped.

HYDE PARK AFTER THE PENINSULAR WAR[1]

That extensive district of park land, the entrances of which are in
Piccadilly and Oxford Street, was far more rural in appearance in 1814
than at the present day. Under the trees cows and deer were grazing; the
paths were fewer, and none told of that perpetual tread of human feet
which now destroys all idea of country charms and illusions. As you
gazed from an eminence, no rows of monotonous houses reminded you
of the vicinity of a large city, and the atmosphere of Hyde Park was then
much more like what God had made it than the hazy, grey, coal-
darkened, half-twilight of the London of to-day. The company which
then congregated daily about five was composed of dandies and women
in the best society; the men mounted on such horses as England alone
could then produce. The dandy's dress consisted of a blue coat with
brass buttons, leather breeches, and top boots; and it was the fashion to
wear a deep, stiff white cravat, which prevented you from seeing your
boots while standing. All the world watched [Beau] Brummell to
imitate him, and ordered their clothes of the tradesman who dressed
that sublime dandy. One day a youthful beau approached Brummell
and said, 'Permit me to ask you where you get your blacking?' 'Ah!'
replied Brummell, gazing complacently at his boots, 'my blacking
positively ruins me. I will tell you in confidence; it is made with the finest
champagne!'

Many of the ladies used to drive into the park in a carriage called a
vis-à-vis, which held only two persons. The hammer-cloth, rich in
heraldic designs, the powdered footmen in smart liveries, and a
coachman who assumed all the gaiety and appearance of a wigged
archbishop, were indispensable. The equipages were generally much
more gorgeous than at a later period, when democracy invaded the
parks, and introduced what may be termed a 'Brummagem society,'
with shabby-genteel carriages and servants. The carriage company

---

[1] Hyde Park had become fashionable soon after being opened to the public at the
beginning of the seventeenth century. After the Civil War it had been sold by Parliament.
It was taken back into royal hands in 1660 by Charles II, who had it enclosed by a brick
wall.

consisted of the most celebrated beauties [; and in those earlier days, you never saw] any of the lower or middle classes of London intruding themselves in regions which, with a sort of tacit understanding, were then given up exclusively to persons of rank and fashion.

LONDON HOTELS IN 1814

There was a class of men, of very high rank, - such as Lords Wellington, Nelson, and Collingwood, Sir John Moore,[1] and some few others, - who never frequented the clubs. The persons to whom I refer, and amongst whom were many members of the sporting world, used to congregate at a few hotels. The Clarendon, Limmer's, Ibbetson's, Fladong's, Stephens's, and Grillon's, were the fashionable hotels.[2] The Clarendon was then kept by a French cook, Jacquiers, who contrived to amass a large sum of money. This was the only public hotel where you could get a genuine French dinner, and for which you seldom paid less than three or four pounds; your bottle of champagne or of claret, in the year 1814, costing you a guinea.

Limmer's was an evening resort for the sporting world; in fact, it was a midnight Tattersall's,[3] where you heard nothing but the language of the turf, and where men with not very clean hands used to make up their books. Limmer's was the most dirty hotel in London; but in the gloomy, comfortless coffee-room might be seen many members of the rich squirearchy who visited London during the sporting season. This hotel was frequently so crowded, that a bed could not be obtained for any amount of money; but you could always get a very good plain English dinner, an excellent bottle of port, and some famous gin-punch.

Ibbetson's hotel was chiefly patronised by the clergy and young men from the universities. The charges there were more economical than at similar establishments. Fladong's, in Oxford Street, was chiefly frequented by naval men; for in those days there was no club for sailors.[4] Stephens's, in Bond Street, was a fashionable hotel, supported by

---

[1] Vice-Admiral Horatio, Viscount Nelson (1758-1805); Vice-Admiral Cuthbert, Lord Collingwood (1750-1810); Lieutenant-General Sir John Moore (1761-1809).

[2] Of these hotels, Grillon's was perhaps the most fashionable of all. It was at 7 Albemarle Street. Louis XVIII stayed here in great pomp in 1814 on his way back to France.

[3] Tattersall's was established by Richard Tattersall, an auctioneer, in the 1760s near Hyde Park Turnpike. There were two subscription rooms for members of the Jockey Club. The premises were demolished in the 1860s and the site covered by a new wing for St George's Hospital.

[4] The Army and Navy Club was founded in 1837, the Naval and Military in 1864.

officers of the army and men about town. If a stranger asked to dine there, he was stared at by the servants, and very solemnly assured that there was no table vacant. It was not an uncommon thing to see thirty or forty saddle-horses and tilburies waiting outside this hotel. I recollect two of my old Welsh friends, who used each of them to dispose of five bottles of wine daily, residing here in 1815, when the familiar joints, boiled fish, and fried soles, were the only eatables you could order.

THE CLUBS OF LONDON IN 1814

The members of the clubs in London, many years since, were persons, almost without exception, belonging exclusively to the aristocratic world. Bankers and merchants, had not then invaded White's, Boodle's, Brookes's, or Wattiers's, in Bolton Street, Piccadilly; which, with the Guards', Arthur's, and Graham's, were the only clubs at the West End of the town. White's was decidedly the most difficult of entry: its list of members comprised nearly all the noble names of Great Britain.[1]

The politics of White's Club were then decidedly Tory. It was here that play was carried on to an extent which made many ravages in large fortunes, the traces of which have not disappeared at the present day. General Scott,[2] the father-in-law of George Canning and the Duke of Portland, was known to have won at White's £200,000, thanks to his notorious sobriety and knowledge of the game of whist. The general possessed a great advantage over his companions by avoiding those indulgences at the table which used to muddle other men's brains. He confined himself to dining off something like a boiled chicken, with toast-and-water; by such a regimen he came to the whist-table with a clear head, and possessing as he did a remarkable memory, with great coolness and judgment, he was able honestly to win the enormous sum of £200,000.

At Brookes's, for nearly half a century, the play was of a more gambling character than at White's. Faro and macao[3] were indulged in

---

[1] Of these clubs, Boodles (founded 1762) and Brooks's (1764), as well as White's, still exist in St James's Street. The Guards Club was merged with the Cavalry Club (1890) in 1976. It is in Piccadilly. Arthur's Club, which was founded in about 1811, was a descendant of Arthur's Chocolate House of 69 St James's Street. Robert Arthur was a son of John Arthur, assistant to Francis White. When the club closed several of its members were admitted into the Carlton Club (1832) in St James's Street.

[2] Major-General John Scott's daughter Joan brought £100,000 to Canning upon their marriage. Her sister, Henrietta, married William Henry Cavendish Scott Bentinck, Marquess of Titchfield, who became fourth Duke of Portland in 1809 and died in 1854.

[3] In faro the players bet on the order in which cards will appear when taken from the top of the pack. Macao resembles *vingt-et-un*.

to an extent which enabled a man to win or to lose a considerable fortune in one night.

On one occasion, Lord Robert Spencer[1] contrived to lose the last shilling of his considerable fortune, given him by his brother, the Duke of Marlborough; General Fitzpatrick[2] being much in the same condition, they agreed to raise a sum of money in order that they might keep a faro bank. The members of the club made no objection, and ere long they carried out their design. As is generally the case, the bank was a winner, and Lord Robert bagged, as his share of the proceeds, £100,000. He retired, strange to say, from the fœtid atmosphere of play, with the money in his pocket, and never again gambled. George Harley Drummond,[3] of the famous banking-house, Charing Cross, only played once in his whole life at White's Club at whist, on which occasion he lost £20,000 to Brummell. This event caused him to retire from the banking-house of which he was a partner.

Lord Carlisle[4] was one of the most remarkable victims amongst the players at Brookes's, and Charles Fox,[5] his friend, was not more fortunate, being subsequently always in pecuniary difficulties. Many a time, after a long night of hard play, the loser found himself at the Israelitish establishment of Howard and Gibbs, then the fashionable and patronised money-lenders. These gentlemen never failed to make

[1] Brother of the fourth Duke of Marlborough. He died in 1831.

[2] General Richard Fitzpatrick (1747–1813), the second son of the first Earl of Upper Ossory, was a close friend of Charles James Fox, with whom he once shared lodgings in Piccadilly. A talented amateur actor and devoted gambler, he was Member of Parliament for Tavistock in 1774–1807 and became Secretary at War in 1783. Renowned for his wit and polite manners, he was left a large legacy specifically for these qualities by the Duke of Queensberry.

[3] Drummond's Bank was founded at the sign of the Golden Eagle in Charing Cross in 1717 by Andrew Drummond, goldsmith. In 1760 he moved to the bank's present site on the west side of Charing Cross, where George III was one of his customers. The business was acquired by the Royal Bank of Scotland in 1924.

[4] Frederick Howard, fifth Earl of Carlisle (1748–1825), a contemporary at Eton of Charles James Fox (see note below), for whose gambling debts he became surety, an act of generosity which obliged him to abandon the gaming tables of London for a less extravagant life at Castle Howard. He was appointed Lord Privy Seal in 1783 and in 1798 very reluctantly accepted the post of guardian of Lord Byron, to whom he was related.

[5] According to Horace Walpole, Charles James Fox (1749–1806) would arrive to speak in the House of Commons after playing hazard at Almack's for more than twenty-four hours at a stretch. For the whole of the night before one important debate he sat up gambling, and by five o'clock the next afternoon, a Wednesday, he had lost £11,000. 'On the Thursday he spoke [again in the House of Commons]; went to dinner at past eleven at night; from thence to White's where he drank until seven the next morning; thence to Almack's where he won £6,000.' Later, in three consecutive nights, he and his brother lost £32,000 between them. Their father had made an immense fortune as Paymaster General.

hard terms with the borrower, although ample security was invariably demanded.

The Guards' Club was established for the three regiments of Foot Guards, and was conducted upon a military system. Billiards and low whist were the only games indulged in. The dinner was, perhaps, better than at most clubs, and considerably cheaper. I had the honour of being a member for several years, during which time I have nothing to remember but the most agreeable incidents. Arthur's and Graham's were less aristocratic than those I have mentioned.

Upon one occasion, some gentlemen of both White's and Brookes's had the honour to dine with the Prince Regent, and during the conversation, the prince inquired what sort of dinners they got at their clubs; upon which Sir Thomas Stepney, one of the guests, observed that their dinners were always the same, 'the eternal joints, or beef-steaks, the boiled fowl with oyster sauce, and an apple-tart – this is what we have, sir, at our clubs, and very monotonous fare it is.' The prince, without further remark, rang the bell for his cook, Wattier [Jean Baptiste Watier] and, in the presence of those who dined at the royal table, asked him whether he would take a house and organise a dinner club. Wattier assented, and named Madison, the prince's page, manager, and Labourie, the cook, from the royal kitchen. The club flourished only a few years, owing to the high play that was carried on there. The Duke of York patronised it, and was a member. I was a member in 1816, and frequently saw his Royal Highness there. The dinners were exquisite; the best Parisian cooks could not beat Labourie.

THE GUARDS' CLUB

In order that my readers may understand what I am about to relate, it is desirable for me to advert to the causes which induced the officers of the Foot Guards to form their Club. Circumstances which it is unnecessary to enter into had for a long time prevented those gallant sons of Mars from carrying out the object they had in view. Unseemly broils and quarrels often took place in the room at the St James's Coffee-house, at the bottom of St James's Street, where the officers of the Guards used to congregate, and these were caused mainly by the admission of (or rather the impossibility of excluding) Irish bullies and persons of fashionable exterior but not of good birth or breeding. Consequently the officers were obliged, on the return of their regiments from the Peninsula, after the disaster at Corunna, to establish a club of their own. Arrangements were made, and the Guards' Club was formed, the subscription to which was at first only £5 per annum for each member.

Among those who first patronised this new institution were the Dukes of York, Cambridge, and Gloucester,[1] and nearly all the general and field officers then in London. The room where the meetings of the officers of the Guards used to be held at St James's Coffee-house was a miserable little den, the floor sanded over like a tap-room now-a-days: a strange contrast to the luxurious apartments now occupied by the officers in Pall Mall; but notwithstanding this, among the people who used to assemble might be found all the wits of the day whose choice sayings over their punch and pipes would fill a volume. The rules of the new Club excluded gambling; and from 1812 till 1821, when I left it, I cannot recollect any serious quarrel occurring among the members, who were composed of the best men England could boast of. So great was the loyalty that pervaded them, that when the trial of Queen Caroline[2] took place, and the *Times* made use of disrespectful language towards her, that paper was, at a meeting of the Club convened by Sir Henry Hardinge,[3] later Lord Hardinge, expelled. *Tempora mutantur et nos mutamur in illis* [Times change and we change with them].

CROCKFORD'S CLUB

I have alluded to the high play which took place at White's and Brookes's in the olden time. In the reign of George IV, a new star rose

---

[1] For Dukes of York and Cambridge, see notes, pp. 18 and 20 respectively. William Frederick, Duke of Gloucester (1776–1834), great-grandson of George II, described by Baron Stockmar as being 'large and stout but with weak, helpless legs ... prominent meaningless eyes ... [and] an animal expression'. He married George IV's favourite sister, Mary, and went to live at Bagshot Park in Surrey.

[2] Queen Caroline, consort of George IV (see note, p. 22), lived on the Continent while her husband was Regent and was supposed to have had an adulterous relationship there with her major-domo, Bartolommeo Pergami. In 1820 she returned to England whereupon a Bill of Pains and Penalties – a parliamentary method of punishing a person without resort to a trial in a court of law – was introduced to dissolve the marriage and deprive her of the title of Queen. Because of the King's unpopularity, the Bill aroused widespread protest. It was eventually abandoned. Next year the Queen was forcibly prevented from entering Westminster Abbey for her husband's coronation. She died a few days later.

[3] Henry Hardinge, first Viscount Hardinge of Lahore (1785–1856). After distinguished service in the Napoleonic Wars, he was appointed Secretary at War. He became Governor-General of India in 1844 and in 1852 succeeded Wellington as commander-in-chief.

upon the horizon in the person of Mr William Crockford;[1] and the old-fashioned games of faro, macao, and lansquenet[2] gave place to the all-devouring thirst for the game of hazard.[3] Crockey, when still a young man, had relinquished the peaceful trade of a fishmonger for a share in a 'hell,' where, with his partner Gye, he managed to win, after a sitting of twenty-four hours, the enormous sum of one hundred thousand pounds. With this capital added to his former gains, he built the well-known palace in St James's Street, where a club was established and play organised on a scale of magnificence and liberality hitherto unknown in Europe.

One may safely say, without exaggeration, that Crockford won the whole of the ready money of the then existing generation. As is often the case at Lords' Cricket-ground, the great match of the gentlemen of England against the professional players was won by the latter.[4] It was a very hollow thing, and in a few years twelve hundred thousand pounds were swept away by the fortunate fishmonger. He did not, however, die worth more than a sixth part of this vast sum; the difference being swallowed up in various unlucky speculations.

No one can describe the splendour and excitement of the early days of Crockey. A supper of the most exquisite kind, prepared by the famous Ude,[5] and accompanied by the best wines in the world, together with every luxury of the season, was furnished gratis. The members of the club included all the celebrities of England, from the Duke of Wellington to the youngest Ensign of the Guards; and at the gay and festive board, which was constantly replenished from midnight to early dawn, the most brilliant sallies of wit, the most agreeable conversation, the most interesting anecdotes, interspersed with grave political discussions and acute logical reasoning on every conceivable subject,

---

[1] William Crockford (1775–1844) ran his fishmonger's business from a shop at Temple Bar. A writer in the *Edinburgh Review* told a different story about the foundation of his gambling club from that related by Gronow. According to this other account, Crockford and a partner named Taylor set up a hazard bank at Watier's old clubhouse, where they were immediately successful. After a quarrel they separated, and Crockford subsequently started business on his own account at 50 St James's Street in a clubhouse designed by Benjamin and Philip Wyatt, which, in 1874, became the home of the Devonshire Club. Crockford retired, a millionaire, in 1840.

[2] Lansquenet, also known as 'lambskinit', was a gambling game of German origin played in England since the end of the seventeenth century.

[3] A game with complicated chances played with two dice.

[4] The first Gentlemen versus Players cricket match was played at Lord's in 1806, the last in 1962.

[5] Crockford's chef, Eustace Ude, was paid the then huge sum of £1200 a year.

proceeded from the soldiers, scholars, statesmen, poets, and men of pleasure, who, when the 'house was up' and balls and parties at an end, delighted to finish their evening with a little supper and a good deal of hazard at old Crockey's. The tone of the club was excellent. A most gentlemanlike feeling prevailed, and none of the rudeness, familiarity, and ill-breeding which disgrace some of the minor clubs of the present day, would have been tolerated for a moment.

Though not many years have elapsed since the time of which I write, the supper table had a very different appearance from what it would present did the club now exist. Beards were completely unknown, and the rare mustachios were only worn by officers of the Household Brigade or hussar regiments. Stiff white neckcloths, blue coats and brass buttons, rather short-waisted white waistcoats, and tremendously embroidered shirt-fronts with gorgeous studs of great value, were considered the right thing. A late deservedly popular Colonel in the Guards used to give Storr & Mortimer £25 a year to furnish him with a new set of studs every Saturday night during the London season.

The great foreign diplomatists and all persons of distinction and eminence who arrived in England, belonged to Crockford's as a matter of course; but many rued the day when they became members of that fascinating but dangerous coterie. The great Duke himself, always rather a friend of the dandies, did not disdain to appear now and then at this charming club; whilst many more of our Peninsula and Waterloo heroes, were constant visitors. The two great novelists of the day, who have since become great statesmen, Disraeli and Bulwer Lytton,[1, 2] displayed at that brilliant supper-table the one his sable, the other his auburn curls. The old fishmonger himself, seated snug and sly at his desk in the corner of the room, watchful as the dragon that guarded the golden apples of the Hesperides, would only give credit to sure and approved signatures. Who that ever entered that dangerous little room can ever forget the large green table with the croupiers with their suave manners, sleek appearance, stiff white neckcloths, and the almost miraculous quickness and dexterity with which they swept away the money of the unfortunate punters. But the brightest medal has its reverse, and after all the wit and gaiety and excitement of the night, how disagreeable the waking up, and how very unpleasant the sight of the

---

[1] Benjamin Disraeli, first Earl of Beaconsfield (1804-81), succeeded Lord Derby as Prime Minister in 1868.

[2] Edward George Lytton Bulwer-Lytton, first Baron Lytton (1803-73), novelist. His *Last Days of Pompeii* was published in 1834.

little card, with its numerous figures marked down on the debtor side in
the fine bold hand of Mr Page [one of the croupiers]. Alas, poor
Crockey's! shorn of its former glory, has become a sort of refuge for the
destitute, a cheap dining-house. How are the mighty fallen! Irish
buckeens, spring captains, 'welchers' from Newmarket, and suspicious-
looking foreigners, may be seen swaggering, after dinner, through the
marble halls and up that gorgeous staircase where once the chivalry of
England loved to congregate; and those who remember Crockford's in
all its glory, cast, as they pass, a look of unavailing regret at its dingy
walls, with many a sigh to the memory of the pleasant days they passed
there, and the gay companions and noble gentlemen who have long
since gone to their last home.

RAGGETT, OF WHITE'S CLUB

Raggett, the well-known club proprietor of White's,[1] and the Roxburgh
Club in St James's Square,[2] was a notable character in his way. He
began life as a poor man, and died extremely rich. It was his custom to
wait upon the members of these clubs whenever play was going on.
Upon one occasion, at the Roxburgh, [several gamblers, including
Hervey Combe and Sir John Malcolm] played at high stakes at whist;
they sat during that night, viz., Monday, the following day and night,
and only separated on Wednesday morning at eleven o'clock; indeed,
the party only broke up then owing to Hervey Combe being obliged to
attend the funeral of one of his partners who was buried on that day.
Hervey Combe, on looking over his card, found that he was a winner of
thirty thousand pounds from Sir John Malcolm, and he jocularly said,
'Well, Sir John, you shall have your revenge whenever you like.' Sir
John replied, 'Thank you; another sitting of the kind will oblige me to

---

[1] George Raggett took over White's in 1812, the year after the famous bow window was
placed in the middle of the façade. Having made a fortune from the club, Raggett put it
up for auction. The members bid £38,000 for it; but it went for £46,000 to Henry William
Eaton, afterwards first Baron Cheylesmore, who was said to have been an omnibus driver
before making his fortune in a city firm. He had been put up for membership but had been
blackballed. His son, an old Etonian Guards officer, was elected; but, out of loyalty to his
father, declined to take up membership.
[2] The Roxburgh Club was founded by a number of bibliophiles in 1813 on the
anniversary of the sale of the contents of 13 St James's Square by the fifth Duke of
Roxburgh. Among the items sold was the Valdarfer Boccaccio which was bought by the
Marquess of Blandford for £2260, the highest price ever paid for a single volume up to that
time. The club was founded at the St Alban's Tavern, St Alban's Street, now Waterloo
Place.

return again to India.' Hervey Combe, on settling with Raggett, pulled out of his pocket a handful of counters, which amounted to several hundred pounds, over and above the thirty thousand he had won of the baronet, and he gave them to Raggett, saying, 'I give them to you for sitting so long with us, and providing us with all required.' Raggett was overjoyed, and in mentioning what had occurred to one of his friends a few days afterwards, he added, 'I make it a rule never to allow any of my servants to be present when gentlemen play at my clubs, for it is my invariable custom to sweep the carpet after the gambling is over, and I generally find on the floor a few counters, which pays me for the trouble of sitting up. By this means I have made a decent fortune.'

The Pig-faced Lady

Among the many absurd reports and ridiculous stories current in former days, I know of none more absurd or more ridiculous than the general belief of everybody in London, during the winter of 1814, in the existence of a lady with a pig's face. This interesting specimen of porcine physiognomy was said to be the daughter of a great lady residing in Grosvenor Square.

It was rumoured that during the illuminations which took place to celebrate the peace, when a great crowd had assembled in Piccadilly and St James's Street, and when carriages could not move on very rapidly, *horresco referens!* an enormous pig's snout had been seen protruding from a fashionable-looking bonnet in one of the landaus which were passing. The mob cried out, 'The pig-faced lady! – the pig-faced lady! Stop the carriage – stop the carriage!' The coachman, wishing to save his bacon, whipped his horses, and drove through the crowd at a tremendous pace; but it was said that the coach had been seen to set down its monstrous load in Grosvenor Square.

Another report was also current. Sir William Elliot, a youthful baronet, calling one day to pay his respects to the great lady in Grosvenor Square, was ushered into a drawing-room, where he found a person fashionably dressed, who, on turning towards him, displayed a hideous pig's face. Sir William, a timid young gentleman, could not refrain from uttering a shout of horror, and rushed to the door in a manner the reverse of polite; when the infuriated lady or animal, uttering a series of grunts, rushed at the unfortunate baronet as he was retreating, and inflicted a severe wound on the back of his neck. This highly probable story concluded by stating that Sir William's wound was a severe one, and had been dressed by Hawkins the surgeon, in South Audley Street.

I am really almost ashamed to repeat this absurd story; but many persons now alive can remember the strong belief in the existence of the pig-faced lady which prevailed in the public mind at the time of which I speak. The shops were full of caricatures of the pig-faced lady, in a poke bonnet and large veil, with 'A pig in a poke' written underneath the print. Another sketch represented Sir William Elliot's misadventure, and was entitled, 'Beware the pig-sty!'[1]

LADY HOLLAND AND 'THE BRIDGE'[2]

When Holland House was a rendezvous of all that was great and illustrious, a gentleman, well known on account of his literary attainments, requested permission from its noble hostess to introduce a friend of his, who had just written a novel which had been well received by the public. Lady Holland, ever happy to do a good-natured act, said, 'You may bring him here to-night.' The gentleman and his friend accordingly made their appearance that very evening, and were graciously received. On the following day, the introducer called on her ladyship to thank her for the honour she had conferred upon his friend, when she observed, 'I can't say much for his good looks, for it was impossible for me to get over the bridge.' 'What bridge, my Lady?' 'Why, the broken bridge of his nose, which has made him the ugliest man I ever saw.' 'Oh, madam, allow me to state that he was born with that unfortunate defect.' 'More's the pity, sir; and I conjure you never bring any more of your friends to Holland House who are not blessed with bridges to their noses.'

EQUIPAGES IN LONDON AND PARIS – THE FOUR-IN-HAND CLUB

When lately in London, on driving through the parks, I was struck with the inferiority of the equipages, to those which I remember fifty years

---

[1] *The Pig Faced Lady of Manchester Square* is the title of a caricature by George Cruikshank (BM 12508, 21 March 1815). 'This extraordinary Female is about 18 years of age – of High rank and great fortune. Her body limbs are of the most perfect and Beautiful Shape, but, her head & Face resembles that of a Pig – she eats her victuals out of a Silver Trough in the same manner as Pigs do, & when spoken to she can only answer by grunting! Her chief amusement is the Piano which she plays most delightfully.'

[2] Elizabeth Vassall Fox, Lady Holland (1770–1845), the beautiful, clever and bossy chatelaine of Holland House, Kensington, was the daughter of a rich West Indian planter. Her marriage to Sir Godfrey Webster was dissolved because of her adultery with Lord Holland.

ago. Paris now quite equals London in external display; indeed, the horses are, generally speaking, even superior. The Emperor, whose long residence in England gave him an opportunity of forming an idea of the care and attention necessary to produce a fine breed of horses, has been indefatigable in selecting a stud; and introduced into France a love of sport which seemed almost peculiar to England.

I look back upon the time when the most magnificent parade of horses and carriages attracted attention in London, and when the famous Four-in-hand Club was the theme of general admiration. The spectacle of a grand turn-out of the members of that distinguished body was one of the glories of the days of the Regent. There was a perfection in the minutest detail that made a well-appointed four-in-hand appear like a choice work of art. The symmetry of the horses, the arrangement of the harness, the plain but well-appointed carriage, the good taste of the liveries, the healthy, sturdy appearance of the coachmen and grooms, formed altogether one of those remarkable spectacles that make a lasting impression upon the memory.

The list of the members will show that some of the most distinguished scions of the aristocracy were the persons who vied with each other in producing this effect. They assembled in George Street, Hanover Square, and drove in regular order to Salt Hill, to the well-known house, named the Windmill, kept by Botham, where a sumptuous dinner awaited them; after which they returned to London, in high spirits,[1] and not unfrequently somewhat overcome by the quantity of sound port wine, for which that inn was celebrated.

The driving was never of such a character as to cause any accident; it was steady, and well regulated; one of the rules of the club being that no coach should pass another, and that the pace should never exceed a trot.

This club lasted in full vigour for upwards of twenty years, when it was broken up, in consequence of the death of many of the members, and the advanced age of several others. The love of coaching still existed amongst many distinguished leaders of fashion, and at a meeting held

[1] Salt Hill, about a mile west of where Slough railway station now stands. The hillock here known as the Mons was the goal of the old Eton Montem, a fancy-dress procession formerly held every third year when the scholars marched from the college to the Mons, where the spectators were 'salted', or levied for contributions. The ceremony was abolished in 1846. Before the coming of the railway put an end to the posting business, there were three hotels here; the most celebrated, the Windmill (more generally known as Botham's), was very popular with Etonians, old Etonians and their families.

at the house of Lord Chesterfield, in Stanhope Street,[1] it was determined to revive, in its former splendour, this national institution, which has served as an encouragement to the breeding of the finest cattle in the universe. Amongst my papers I found a list of the original members of this club, which met at Richmond on Saturday, June 2, 1838, and passed a series of resolutions, that formed the basis of the regulations which were observed during its existence.

SALLY LUNN CAKES – THE ETYMOLOGY OF THE WORD 'BUN'

Some fifty years back or thereabouts, Albinia, Countess of Buckinghamshire, lived in her charming villa in Pimlico, surrounded by a large and beautiful garden.[2] It was here she used to entertain the *élite* of London society with magnificent *fêtes*, *bals champêtres*, and public breakfasts. After one of those *fêtes*, I called one morning to pay my respects; and, on ringing the bell, the servant ushered me into the conservatory, where I found Lady Harrington,[3] the celebrated cantatrice Mrs Billington,[4] and the Duke of Sussex;[5] who was said to be very much *épris* with the English 'Catalani,' as she was called.[6]

Mrs Billington was extremely beautiful, though it was absurd to compare her to Catalani as a singer; but she was the favourite of the Duke of Sussex, which made her many friends. During my visit, chocolate and tea-cakes were served to our party, when Lady Harrington related a curious anecdote about those cakes. She said her friend Madame de Narbonne,[7] during the emigration, determined not to live upon the bounty of foreigners, found means to amass money

---

[1] Lord Chesterfield's house in Stanhope Gate was built by Philip Dormer Stanhope, fourth Earl of Chesterfield, in 1744–50. The sixth Earl, who succeeded to the title when he was ten years old, died in 1866.

[2] Albinia, Countess of Buckinghamshire, was the daughter of Lord Vere Bertie. She married the third Earl of Buckinghamshire in 1757 and died in 1816.

[3] See note, p. 109.

[4] Elizabeth Billington (*c.* 1768–1818). Her German father was principal oboist at the King's Theatre. Her husband, James Billington, a double-bass player at Drury Lane, gave her singing lessons. Singing at both Covent Garden and Drury Lane for very high salaries, she made a fortune and lived in splendid style at Fulham.

[5] Augustus Frederick, Duke of Sussex (1773–1843), sixth son of George III, from whom he was estranged on account of his liberal views. His tastes were more intellectual than those of most of his family.

[6] See note, p. 197.

[7] Louis, Comte de Narbonne-Lara, was one of Louis XV's many illegitimate sons.

enough to enable her to open a shop in Chelsea, not far from the then fashionable balls of Ranelagh.

It had been the custom in France, before the Revolution, for young ladies in some noble families to learn the art of making preserves and pastry; accordingly, Madame de Narbonne commenced her operations under the auspices of some of her acquaintances; and all those who went to Ranelagh made a point of stopping and buying some of her cakes. Their fame spread like lightning throughout the West End, and orders were given to have them sent for breakfast and tea in many great houses in the neighbourhood of St James's. Madame de Narbonne employed a Scotch maid-servant to execute her orders. The name of this woman was 'Sally Lunn,' and ever since a particular kind of tea-cake has gone by that name.[1]

Madame de Narbonne, not speaking English, replied to her customers (when they inquired the name of her *brioches*), 'bon;' hence the etymology of 'bun,' according to Lady Harrington: but I confess that I do not feel quite satisfied with her derivation.

Sir Robert Peel's Hat

A Welsh Baronet and MP entered the shop of Lock & Lincoln, in St James's Street, to purchase a hat.[2] The foreman could not find one sufficiently large for the Baronet's head, and stated that he only knew one person whose head was so large. 'Who is that person?' asked the indignant Welshman. The foreman replied, 'It is no other than the great minister, Sir Robert Peel.' 'Oh! oh!' exclaimed Taffy, 'you make hats for that Radical, do you? Well, then, it shall never be said that you have sold me a hat. I have a horror of such men as your great ministers.' And the Baronet left the shop in dudgeon, much to the wonder and astonishment of the hatter.

Hoby, the Bootmaker, of St James's Street

Hoby was not only the greatest and most fashionable bootmaker in London, but, in spite of the old adage, '*ne sutor ultra crepidam*,'[3] he employed his spare time with considerable success as a Methodist

---

[1] It is more commonly supposed that these tea-cakes took their name from Sally Lunn, a pastry cook who used to cry them about the streets of Bath in the 1790s.

[2] James Lock & Co. are now at 6 St James's Street.

[3] *Ne supra crepidam sutor iudicaret*: 'The cobbler should not judge above his last' (Pliny).

preacher at Islington. He was said to have in his employment three hundred workmen; and he was so great a man in his own estimation that he was apt to take rather an insolent tone with his customers. He was, however, tolerated as a sort of privileged person, and his impertinence was not only overlooked, but was considered as rather a good joke. He was a pompous fellow, with a considerable vein of sarcastic humour.

I remember Horace Churchill (afterwards killed in India with the rank of major-general), who was then an ensign in the Guards, entering Hoby's shop in a great passion, saying that his boots were so ill made that he should never employ Hoby for the future. Hoby, putting on a pathetic cast of countenance, called to his shopman –

'John, close the shutters. It is all over with us. I must shut up shop; Ensign Churchill withdraws his custom from me.'

Churchill's fury can be better imagined than described.

On another occasion the late Sir John Shelley came into Hoby's shop to complain that his top-boots had split in several places. Hoby quietly said,

'How did that happen, Sir John?'

'Why, in walking to my stable.'

'Walking to your stable!' said Hoby, with a sneer. 'I made the boots for riding, not walking.'

One may well say that there is nothing like leather; for Hoby died worth a hundred and twenty thousand pounds.

Hoby was bootmaker to George III, the Prince of Wales, the royal dukes, and many officers in the army and navy. His shop was situated at the top of St James's Street, at the corner of Piccadilly, next to the old Guards' Club.[1] He was bootmaker to the Duke of Wellington from his boyhood, and received innumerable orders in the Duke's handwriting, both from the Peninsula and France, which he always religiously preserved. Hoby was the first man who drove about London in a tilbury.[2] It was painted black, and drawn by a beautiful black cob. This vehicle was built by the inventor, Mr Tilbury, whose manufactory was, fifty years back, in a street leading from South Audley Street into Park Street.

---

[1] At that time the Guards' Club was in premises opposite White's.

[2] Tilburies were light, open, two-wheeled carriages. They were fashionable in the early nineteenth century, though in use by 1796. Mr Tilbury, the coach-builder who invented them, lived at Old Dove House, Hatch End.

5

Rakes, Dandies and Men About Town

THE LATE LORD DUDLEY

The English have, as we all know, the reputation among foreigners of being *des originaux*; and I am inclined to believe that we are a queer race of people, and that there are more 'characters' among us than are to be found abroad.

One of the most conspicuous of the eccentric oddities who flourished forty years ago was Lord Dudley and Ward.[1] I need not speak of his powers of conversation, which were most brilliant when he chose to exert them, of his sarcastic wit, and cultivated intellect. These great gifts were obscured by a singular absence of mind, which he carried to such a pitch, that some persons maintained that much of this peculiarity was assumed. Rather an amusing anecdote is related of him, in which the 'biter was bit;' that is, supposing it to have been true that his 'distractions' were not altogether genuine.

It happened one day that, coming out of the House of Lords, Lord Dudley's carriage was not to be found. It was late at night, and Lord Dudley, who was extremely nervous about catching cold, was in a

---

[1] William Ward, fourth Viscount Dudley and Ward and first Earl of Dudley (1781–1833), became Foreign Secretary in Canning's administration in 1827. Shy and eccentric, he rehearsed to himself in very audible whispers the sentences he was about to address to his companions, first talking in a deep voice, then a high-pitched one. It was, they said, Dudley talking to Ward. Undistinguished as a statesman, he was an excellent scholar and a good writer.

frantic state of excitement. Lord H—— kindly offered to set him down at Dudley House, which proposal was thankfully accepted. During the drive, Lord Dudley began, according to his usual custom, to talk to himself in an audible tone, and the burden of his song was as follows: - 'A deuce of a bore! This tiresome man has taken me home, and will expect me to ask him to dinner. I suppose I must do so, but it is a horrid nuisance.'

Lord H—— closed his eyes, and, assuming the same sleepy monotonous voice, muttered forth, 'What a dreadful bore! This good-natured fellow Dudley will think himself obliged to invite me to dinner, and I shall be forced to go. I hope he won't ask me, for he gives d——d bad dinners.'

Lord Dudley started, looked very much confused, but said nothing. He, however, never forgave his friend; for he prided himself upon being a good hater.

Another time, when dining with Lord W——, who particularly piqued himself upon his dinners, he began apologising to the company for the badness of the *entrées*, and excused himself for their execrable quality on account of the illness of his cook.

He was once paying a morning visit to [a beautiful lady]. He sat an unconscionably long time, and the lady, after giving him some friendly hints, took up her work and tried to make conversation. Lord Dudley broke a long fit of silence by muttering, 'A very pretty woman this. She stays a devilish long time - I wish she'd go.'

At a dinner some thirty years ago at Sir George Warrender's,[1] Lord Dudley took out a beautiful young married lady, who was extremely shy. Sir George was a singular mixture of extravagance and economy, and though (for he was a renowned epicure, and commonly known by the name of Sir George Provender) he fed his guests plentifully, the warming department was neglected, and the atmosphere of the dining-room resembled that of Nova Zembla.[2]

Lord Dudley asked the young lady where she would like to sit, and, out of pure shyness, she pointed to the nearest chair, which happened to be in the corner furthest from the fire. After they had sat down, she could hear Lord Dudley muttering angry sentences, in which she could almost fancy she heard herself consigned to the depths of an unmention-

---

[1] Sir George Warrender, Bt (1782–1849). He was a Lord of the Admiralty from 1812 to 1822 and a highly inefficient Commissioner of the Board of Control in 1822–8. In 1834 he cited his wife before an ecclesiastical court for adultery.

[2] Novaya Zemlya, a group of Russian islands in the Arctic Ocean.

able place. But what was her horror, when, after shivering and shaking for some time without speaking a word except to himself, Lord Dudley turned round, and in an angry voice asked for his cloak. It was one of that large sort of cloaks such as coachmen sometimes wore in England, with a gradation of capes; and in this he wrapped himself, and remained during the whole of dinner without speaking a word to his fair neighbour.

Lord Dudley was for a short time Secretary of State for Foreign Affairs, but became more and more eccentric, and, not very long after his resignation, was obliged to be placed under restraint. He eventually, I believe, entirely lost his reason, and died in 1833.

ROMEO COATES

This singular man, more than forty years ago, occupied a large portion of public attention; his eccentricities were the theme of general wonder, and great was the curiosity to catch a glance at as strange a being as any that ever appeared in English society.[1] This extraordinary individual was a native of one of the West India Islands, and was represented as a man of extraordinary wealth; to which, however, he had no claim.

About the year 1808, there arrived at the York Hotel, at Bath, a person about the age of fifty, somewhat gentlemanlike, but so different from the usual men of the day that considerable attention was directed to him. He was of a good figure; but his face was sallow, seamed with wrinkles, and more expressive of cunning than of any other quality. His dress was remarkable: in the daytime he was covered at all seasons with enormous quantities of fur; but the evening costume in which he went to the balls made a great impression, from its gaudy appearance; for his buttons, as well as his knee-buckles, were of diamonds. There was of course great curiosity to know who this stranger was; and this curiosity was heightened by an announcement that he proposed to appear at the theatre in the character of Romeo. There was something so unlike the impassioned lover in his appearance – so much that indicated a man with few intellectual gifts – that everybody was prepared for a failure. No one, however, anticipated the reality.

On the night fixed for his appearance, the house was crowded to

---

[1] Robert Coates (1772–1848). Born at Antigua, his father was a rich sugar-planter. Gronow was wrong about his wealth. In fact, he inherited a large fortune from his father – none of whose eight other children survived – as well as a splendid collection of diamonds.

suffocation. The playbills had given out that 'an amateur of fashion' would for that night only perform in the character of Romeo; besides, it was generally whispered that the rehearsals gave indication of comedy rather than tragedy, and that his readings were of a perfectly novel character.

The very first appearance of Romeo convulsed the house with laughter. Benvolio prepares the audience for the stealthy visit of the lover to the object of his admiration; and fully did the amateur give expression to one sense of the words uttered, for he was indeed the true representative of a thief stealing onwards in the night, 'with Tarquin's ravishing strides,' and disguising his face as if he were thoroughly ashamed of it. The darkness of the scene did not, however, show his real character so much as the masquerade, when he came forward with a hideous grin, and made what he considered his bow – which consisted in thrusting his head forward, and bobbing it up and down several times, his body remaining perfectly upright and stiff, like a toy mandarin with movable head.

His dress was *outré* in the extreme: whether Spanish, Italian, or English, no one could say; it was like nothing ever worn. In a cloak of sky-blue silk, profusely spangled, red pantaloons, a vest of white muslin, surmounted by an enormously thick cravat, and a wig *à la* Charles the Second, capped by an opera hat, he presented one of the most grotesque spectacles ever witnessed upon the stage. The whole of his garments were evidently too tight for him; and his movements appeared so incongruous, that every time he raised his arm, or moved a limb, it was impossible to refrain from laughter: but what chiefly convulsed the audience was the bursting of a seam in an inexpressible part of his dress, and the sudden extrusion through the red rent of a quantity of white linen sufficient to make a Bourbon flag, which was visible whenever he turned round. This was at first supposed to be a wilful offence against common decency, and some disapprobation was evinced; but the utter unconsciousness of the odd creature was soon apparent, and then unrestrained mirth reigned throughout the boxes, pit, and gallery. The total want of flexibility of limb, the awkwardness of his gait, and the idiotic manner in which he stood still, all produced a most ludicrous effect; but when his guttural voice was heard, and his total misapprehension of every passage in the play, especially the vulgarity of his address to Juliet, were perceived, every one was satisfied that Shakspeare's Romeo was burlesqued on that occasion.

The balcony scene was interrupted by shrieks of laughter, for in the midst of one of Juliet's impassioned exclamations, Romeo quietly took out his snuff-box and applied a pinch to his nose; on this a wag in the gallery bawled out, 'I say, Romeo, give us a pinch,' when the impassioned lover, in the most affected manner, walked to the side boxes and offered the contents of his box first to the gentlemen, and then, with great gallantry, to the ladies. This new interpretation of Shakspeare was hailed with loud bravos, which the actor acknowledged with his usual grin and nod. Romeo then returned to the balcony, and was seen to extend his arms; but all passed in dumb show, so incessant were the shouts of laughter. All that went on upon the stage was for a time quite inaudible, but previous to the soliloquy 'I do remember an apothecary,' there was for a moment a dead silence; for in rushed the hero with a precipitate step until he reached the stage lamps, when he commenced his speech in the lowest possible whisper, as if he had something to communicate to the pit that ought not to be generally known; and this tone was kept up throughout the whole of the soliloquy, so that not a sound could be heard.

The amateur actor showed many indications of aberration of mind, and seemed rather the object of pity than of amusement; he, however, appeared delighted with himself, and also with his audience, for at the conclusion he walked first to the left of the stage and bobbed his head in his usual grotesque manner at the side boxes; then to the right, performing the same feat; after which, going to the centre of the stage with the usual bob, and placing his hand upon his left breast, he exclaimed, 'Haven't I done it well?' To this inquiry the house, convulsed as it was with shouts of laughter, responded in such a way as delighted the heart of Kean on one great occasion, when he said, 'The pit rose at me.' The whole audience started up as if with one accord, giving a yell of derision, whilst pocket-handkerchiefs waved from all parts of the theatre.

The dying scene was irresistibly comic, [for Romeo] dragged the unfortunate Juliet from the tomb, much in the same manner as a washerwoman thrusts into her cart the bag of foul linen. But how shall I describe his death? Out came a dirty silk handkerchief from his pocket, with which he carefully swept the ground; then his opera hat was carefully placed for a pillow, and down he laid himself. After various tossings about, he seemed reconciled to the position; but the house vociferously bawled out, 'Die again, Romeo!' and, obedient to the command, he rose up, and went through the ceremony again. Scarcely had he lain quietly down, when the call was again heard, and the well-pleased amateur was evidently prepared to enact a third death; but Juliet now rose up from her tomb, and gracefully put an end to this ludicrous scene by advancing to the front of the stage and aptly applying a quotation from Shakspeare –

> Dying is such sweet sorrow,
> That he will die again until to-morrow.

Thus ended an extravaganza such as has seldom been witnessed; for although Coates repeated the play at the Haymarket, amidst shouts of laughter from the playgoers, there never was so ludicrous a performance as that which took place at Bath on the first night of his appearance. Eventually he was driven from the stage with much contumely, in consequence of its having been discovered that, under pretence of acting for a charitable purpose, he had obtained a sum of money for his performances. His love of notoriety led him to have a most singular shell-shaped carriage built, in which, drawn by two fine white horses, he was wont to parade in the park; the harness, and every available part of the vehicle (which was really handsome), were blazoned over with his heraldic device – a cock crowing; and his appearance was heralded by the *gamins* of London shrieking out, 'Cock-a-doodle-doo!' Coates eventually quitted London and settled at Boulogne, where a fair lady was induced to become the partner of his existence notwithstanding the ridicule of the whole world.[1]

MICHAEL ANGELO TAYLOR

It appears to be a law of natural history that every generation produces and throws out from the mob of society a few conspicuous men, that pass under the general appellation of 'men about town.' Michael Angelo Taylor was one of those remarkable individuals whom every one was glad to know;[2] and those who had not that privilege were ever talking about him, although he was considered by many a bit of a bore. Michael Angelo was a member of Parliament for many years, and generally sat in one of the most important committees of the House of

---

[1] This 'fair lady' was Emma Anne, who subsequently married the author Mark Boyd. Coates dissipated his fortune and, like Brummell, was obliged to retreat to France for a time. On his return he was badly injured in a carriage accident and died soon afterwards.

[2] Michael Angelo Taylor (1757–1834), the diminutive lawyer and politician, was a favourite butt of the caricaturists. His house in Whitehall Gardens was a rendezvous of the Whigs. Once a close friend of the Prince Regent, the two men quarrelled in 1811 when the Prince, so it was said, tried to seduce Mrs Taylor, the attractive daughter of the Rev. Sir Harry Vane. Taylor discovered the Prince in his attempted seduction and knocked him down.

Commons; for he was a man of authority and an attractive speaker. In appearance he was one of that sort of persons whom you could not pass in the streets without exclaiming, 'Who can that be?' His face blushed with port wine, the purple tints of which, by contrast, caused his white hair to glitter with silvery brightness; he wore leather breeches, top boots, blue coat, white waistcoat, and an unstarched and exquisitely white neckcloth, the whole surmounted by a very broad-brimmed beaver. If you met him in society, or at the clubs, he was never known to salute you but with the invariable phrase, 'What news have you?' Upon one occasion, riding through St James's Park, he met the great Minister, Mr Pitt, coming from Wimbledon, where he resided.[1] He asked Mr Pitt the usual question, upon which the Premier replied, 'I have not yet seen the morning papers.'

'Oh, that won't do, Mr Pitt. I am sure that you know something, and will not tell me.'

Mr Pitt good-humouredly replied: 'Well, then, I am going to a Cabinet Council, and I will consult my colleagues whether I can divulge state secrets to you or not.'

Upon another occasion, on entering Boodle's, of which he was a member, he observed the celebrated Lord Westmoreland at table, where the noble lord was doing justice to a roast fowl.[2] Taylor, of course, asked him the news of the day, and Lord Westmoreland coolly told the little newsmonger to go into the other room and leave him to finish his dinner, promising to join him after he had done. The noble lord kept his word, and the first thing he heard from Mr Taylor was, 'Well, my lord, what news? what had you for dinner?'

His lordship replied, 'A Welsh leg of mutton.'

'What then – what then?'

'Don't you think a leg of mutton enough for any man?'

'Yes, my lord, but you did not eat it all?'

'Yes, Taylor, I did.'

'Well, I think you have placed the leg of mutton in some mysterious place, for I see no trace of it in your lean person.'

Lord Westmoreland was remarkable for an appetite which made nothing of a respectable joint, or a couple of fowls.

---

[1] William Pitt (1759–1806), second son of the Earl of Chatham, became Prime Minister in 1783.
[2] John Fane, tenth Earl of Westmorland (1759–1841), a close friend of Pitt, was Lord Privy Seal for almost thirty years.

COLONEL MACKINNON[1]

Colonel Mackinnon, commonly called 'Dan,' was an exceedingly well-made man, and remarkable for his physical powers in running, jumping, climbing, and such bodily exercises as demanded agility and muscular strength. He used to amuse his friends by creeping over the furniture of a room like a monkey. It was very common for his companions to make bets with him: for example, that he would not be able to climb up the ceiling of a room, or scramble over a certain house-top. Grimaldi, the famous clown,[2] used to say, 'Colonel Mackinnon has only to put on the motley costume, and he would totally eclipse me.'

Mackinnon was famous for practical jokes; which were, however, always played in a gentlemanly way. Before landing at St Andero's, with some other officers who had been on leave in England, he agreed to personate the Duke of York, and made the Spaniards believe that his Royal Highness was amongst them. On nearing the shore, a royal standard was hoisted at the mast-head, and Mackinnon disembarked, wearing the star of his shako on his left breast, and accompanied by his friends, who agreed to play the part of aide-de-camp to royalty. The Spanish authorities were soon informed of the arrival of the Royal Commander-in-Chief of the British army; so they received Mackinnon with the usual pomp and circumstance attending such occasions. The mayor of the place, in honour of the illustrious arrival, gave a grand banquet, which terminated with the appearance of a huge bowl of punch. Whereupon Dan, thinking that the joke had gone far enough, suddenly dived his head into the porcelain vase, and threw his heels into the air. The surprise and indignation of the solemn Spaniards were such, that they made a most intemperate report of the hoax that had been played on them to Lord Wellington; Dan, however, was ultimately forgiven, after severe reprimand.

Another of his freaks very nearly brought him to a court-martial. Lord Wellington was curious about visiting a convent near Lisbon, and the lady abbess made no difficulty; Mackinnon, hearing this, contrived to get clandestinely within the sacred walls, and it was generally supposed that it was neither his first nor his second visit. At all events, when Lord Wellington arrived, Dan Mackinnon was to be seen among

---

[1] Colonel Daniel Mackinnon (1791–1836) was in the Coldstream Guards, of which he wrote an excellent two-volume history, published in 1832.

[2] Joseph Grimaldi (1779–1837), the great clown, was born in London into a family of Italian actors and pantomimists. He was a regular performer at Sadler's Wells Theatre. His memoirs were edited by Charles Dickens (1838).

the nuns, dressed out in their sacred costume, with his head and whiskers shaved; and as he possessed good features, he was declared to be one of the best-looking amongst those chaste dames. It was supposed that this adventure, which was known to Lord Byron, suggested a similar episode in *Don Juan*, the scene being laid in the East. I might say more about Dan's adventures in the convent, but have no wish to be scandalous.

SIR LUMLEY SKEFFINGTON

Another dandy of the day was Sir Lumley Skeffington,[1] who used to paint his face, so that he looked like a French toy; he dressed *à la* Robespierre, and practised other follies, although the consummate old fop was a man of literary attainments, and a great admirer and patron of the drama. Skeffington was remarkable for his politeness and courtly manners; in fact, he was invited everywhere, and was very popular with the ladies. You always knew of his approach by an *avant-courier* of sweet smells; and when he advanced a little nearer, you might suppose yourself in the atmosphere of a perfumer's shop.

LONG WELLESLEY POLE

Long Wellesley Pole[2] was a fashionable who distinguished himself by giving sumptuous dinners at Wanstead,[3] where he owned one of the finest mansions in England. He used to ask his friends to dine with him after the opera at midnight; the drive from London being considered *appétisant*. Every luxury that money could command was placed before his guests at this unusual hour of the night. He married Miss Tylney Pole, an heiress of fifty thousand a year, yet died quite a beggar: in fact, he would have starved, had it not been for the charity of his cousin, the present Duke of Wellington, who allowed him three hundred a year.

[1] Sir Lumley St George Skeffington (1771–1850). The son of Sir William, first Baronet. An extravagantly dressed dandy and writer of indifferent plays, he was a favourite butt of the caricaturists. In his old age he was celebrated for his false hair, painted cheeks and ancient, perfumed clothes.
[2] William Pole Tylney-Long-Wellesley, fourth Earl of Mornington (1788–1857), assumed the additional names of Tylney-Long on his marriage to Catherine Tylney-Long, a 'lovely nice little angel' of an heiress, whom George IV's brother, the Duke of Clarence, had wanted to marry.
[3] Wanstead House, Essex, was built in *c.* 1714–20 for Sir Richard Child, later Earl of Tylney, by Colen Cambell. The Prince of Condé lived here during the reign of Napoleon I. It was demolished in 1824. The original manor house, which came to the crown in the reign of Henry VIII, was rebuilt by Lord Chancellor Rich in the 1550s.

General Palmer

This excellent man had the last days of his life embittered by the money-lenders. He had commenced his career surrounded by every circumstance that could render existence agreeable; fortune, in his early days, having smiled most benignantly on him. His father was a man of considerable ability, and was to the past generation what Rowland Hill [originator of the penny postage] is in the present day – the great benefactor of correspondents.[1] He first proposed and carried out the mail-coach system; and letters, instead of being at the mercy of postboys, and a private speculation in many instances, became the care of Government, and were transmitted under its immediate direction.

During the lifetime of Mr Palmer, the reward due to him for his suggestions and his practical knowledge was denied; he accordingly went to Bath, and became the manager and proprietor of the theatre. He occasionally trod the boards himself, for which his elegant deportment and good taste eminently qualified him; and he has often been mistaken for Gentleman Palmer.

Mr Palmer was successful in his undertaking, and at his death his son found himself the inheritor of a handsome fortune, and became a universal favourite in Bath.

The corporation of that city, consisting of thirty apothecaries, were, in those borough-mongering days, the sole electors to the House of Commons, and finding young Palmer hospitable, and intimate with the Marquis of Bath and Lord Camden, and likewise desiring for themselves and their families free access to the most agreeable theatre in England, they returned him to Parliament. He entered the army, and became a conspicuous officer in the 10th Hussars, which regiment being commanded by the Prince Regent, Palmer was at once introduced at Carlton House, the Pavilion at Brighton, and consequently into the highest society of the country; for which his agreeable manners, his amiable disposition, and his attainments, admirably qualified him. His fortune was sufficiently large for all his wants; but, unfortunately, as it

---

[1] John Palmer (1742–1818), the projector of mail-coaches, was the son of a proprietor of theatres in Bath. He took over these theatres and it was in the course of journeys he made looking for talented actors that he had observed how slow and inefficient the existing state post was. He was Mayor of Bath and Member for the city in 1801–2 and 1806–7. His son, Charles, the 'young Palmer' of whom Gronow writes, succeeded him as Member for Bath in 1808. He served in the army throughout the Peninsular War and was promoted major-general in 1825. In saying that his father 'occasionally trod the boards himself', Gronow seems to be confusing John Palmer with John Palmer, the actor (1742?–98), who is, indeed, often mistaken for his namesake John ('Gentleman') Palmer (d. 1768).

turned out, the House of Commons voted to him, as the representative of his father, £100,000, which he was desirous of laying out to advantage.

A fine opportunity, as he imagined, had presented itself to him; for, in travelling in the diligence from Lyons to Paris – a journey then requiring three days – he met a charming widow, who told a tale that had not only a wonderful effect upon his susceptible heart, but upon his amply-filled purse. She said her husband, who had been the proprietor of one of the finest estates in the neighbourhood of Bordeaux, was just dead, and that she was on her way to Paris to sell the property, that it might be divided, according to the laws of France, amongst the family. Owing, however, to the absolute necessity of forcing a sale, that which was worth an enormous sum would realise one quarter only of its value. She described the property as one admirably fitted for the production of wine; that it was, in fact, the next estate to the Château Lafitte, and would prove a fortune to any capitalist. The fascinations of this lady, and the temptation of enormous gain to the speculator, impelled the gallant colonel to offer his services to relieve her from her embarrassment; so by the time the diligence arrived in Paris he had become the proprietor of a fine domain, which was soon irrevocably fixed on him by the lady's notary, in return for a large sum of money: and, had the colonel proved a man of business, he would no doubt have been amply repaid, and his investment might have become the source of great wealth.

Palmer, however, conscious of his inaptitude for business, looked around him for an active agent, and believed he had found one in a Mr Gray, a man of captivating manners and good connections, but almost as useless a person as the general himself. Fully confident in his own abilities, Gray had already been concerned in many speculations; but not one of them had ever succeeded, and all had led to the demolition of large fortunes. Plausible in his address, and possessing many of those superficial qualities that please the multitude, he appeared to be able to secure for the claret – which was the production of the estate – a large clientèle. Palmer's claret, under his auspices, began to be talked of in the clubs; and the bon vivant was anxious to secure a quantity of this highly-prized wine.

The patronage of the Prince Regent being considered essential, was solicited, and the prince, with his egotistical good-nature, and from a kindly feeling for Palmer, gave a dinner at Carlton House, when a fair trial was to be given to his claret. A select circle of gastronomes was to be present, amongst whom was Lord Yarmouth, well known in those days by the appellation of 'Red-herrings,' from his rubicund whiskers, hair, and face, and from the town of Yarmouth deriving its principal support from the importation from Holland of that fish.[1] The wine was produced, and was found excellent, and the spirits of the party ran high; the light wine animating them without intoxication. The Prince was delighted, and, as usual upon such occasions, told some of his best stories, quoted Shakspeare, and was particularly happy upon the bouquet of the wine as suited 'to the holy Palmer's kiss.'

Lord Yarmouth alone sat in moody silence, and, on being questioned as to the cause, replied that whenever he dined at his Royal Highness's table, he drank a claret which he much preferred – that which was furnished by Carbonell. The prince immediately ordered a bottle of this wine; and to give them an opportunity of testing the difference, he desired that some anchovy sandwiches should be served up. Carbonell's wine was placed upon the table: it was a claret made expressly for the London market, well dashed with Hermitage,[2] and infinitely more to the taste of the Englishmen than the delicately-flavoured wine they had been drinking. The banquet terminated in the prince declaring his own wine superior to that of Palmer's, and suggesting that he should try some experiments on his estate to obtain a better wine. Palmer came from Carlton House much mortified. On Sir Thomas Tyrwhitt attempting to console him, and saying that it was the anchovies that had spoiled the taste of the connoisseurs, the general said, loudly enough to be heard by Lord Yarmouth, 'No; it was the confounded red herrings.' A duel was very nearly the consequence.

General Palmer, feeling it his duty to follow the advice of the prince, rooted out his old vines, planted new ones, and tried all sorts of experiments at an immense cost, but with little or no result. He and his agent, in consequence, got themselves into all sorts of difficulties, mortgaged the property, borrowed largely, and were at last obliged to have recourse to usurers, to life assurances, and every sort of expedient, to raise money. The theatre at Bath was sold, the Reform in Parliament robbed him of his seat, and at last he and his agent became ruined men. A subscription would have been raised to relieve him, but he preferred

---

[1] Francis, Earl of Yarmouth, later third Marquess of Hertford (1777–1842), said to be the model for the Marquess of Steyne in Thackeray's *Vanity Fair*. He married the heiress, Maria Fagniani, daughter of the Marchesa Fagniani and of either George Selwyn or the Duke of Queensberry, each of whom, claiming the honour of paternity, left her large sums of money. Yarmouth's mother, Isabella, Lady Hertford, was the Prince Regent's mistress. Yarmouth had a passion for French furniture and advised the Regent on acquisitions for the royal collections.

[2] A French wine produced from vineyards near Valence.

ending his days in poverty to living upon the bounty of his friends. He sold his commission, and was plunged in the deepest distress; while the accumulation of debt to the userers became so heavy, that he was compelled to pass through the Insolvent Court.

Thus ended the career of a man who had been courted in society, idolised in the army, and figured as a legislator for many years. His friends, of course, fell off, and he was to be seen a mendicant in the streets of London - shunned where he once was courted. Gray, his agent, became equally involved; but, marrying a widow with some money, he was enabled to make a better fight. Eventually, however, he became a prey to the money-lenders, and his life ended under circumstances distressing to those who had known him in early days.

'MONK' LEWIS

One of the most agreeable men of the day was 'Monk' Lewis.[1] As the author of The Monk and Tales of Wonder, he not only found his way into the best circles, but gained a high reputation in the literary world. His poetic talent was undoubted, and he was intimately connected with Walter Scott in his ballad researches:[2] his Alonzo the Brave and the Fair Imogene was recited at the theatres. Wherever he went he found a welcome reception; his West Indian fortune and connections, and his seat in Parliament, giving him access to all the aristocratic circles. From these, however, he was banished upon the appearance of the fourth and last dialogue of the Pursuits of Literature. Had a thunderbolt fallen upon him, he could not have been more astonished than he was by the onslaught of Mr Matthias, which led to his ostracism from fashionable society.[3]

It is not for me to appreciate the value of this satirical poem, which created such an extraordinary sensation, not only in the fashionable, but in the political world; I, however, remember that whilst [in some houses] it was pronounced the most classical and spirited production

[1] Matthew Gregory Lewis (1775-1818), known as 'Monk' because of his Gothic novel of that name written while he was attaché to the British Embassy at The Hague and published in 1796. The book's indecent passages, the most objectionable of which were omitted from later editions, provoked many protests. He also wrote plays and humorous poems which influenced the earlier verse of Sir Walter Scott. Given a most generous allowance by his father, owner of extensive estates in Jamaica, he was a frequent guest in the houses of the nobility of whose company, so Scott said, he was over-fond.

[2] Sir Walter Scott (1771-1832), Scottish novelist and poet.

[3] Thomas James Mathias (c. 1754-1835), the satirist, was the author of Pursuits of Literature, which attacked various contemporary writers, in particular Lewis.

that had ever issued from the press, it was held up [in others] as one of
the most spiteful and ill-natured satires that had ever disgraced the
literary world, and one which no talent or classic lore could ever
redeem. Certain it is that Matthias fell foul of poor 'Monk' Lewis for his
romance: obscenity and blasphemy were the charges laid at his door; he
was acknowledged to be a man of genius and fancy, but this added only
to his crime, to which was superadded that of being a very young man.
The charges brought against him cooled his friends and heated his
enemies; the young ladies were forbidden to speak to him, matrons even
feared him, and from being one of the idols of the world, he became one
of the objects of its disdain. Even his father was led to believe that his son
had abandoned the paths of virtue, and was on the high road to ruin.[1]

'Monk' Lewis, unable to stand against the outcry thus raised against
him, determined to try the effects of absence, and took his departure for
the island in which his property was; but unfortunately for those who
dissented from the ferocious judgment that was passed upon him, and
for those who had discrimination enough to know that after all there
was nothing very objectionable in his romance, and felt assured that
posterity would do him justice, this amiable and kind-hearted man died
on his passage out; leaving a blank in one variety of literature which has
never been filled up.[2]

The denunciation was not followed by any other severe criticism; but
editors have, in compliance with the insinuations of Matthias, omitted
the passages which he pointed out as objectionable, so that the original
text is seldom met with.

'Monk' Lewis had a black servant, affectionately attached to his
master; but so ridiculously did this servant repeat his master's
expressions, that he became the laughing-stock of all his master's
friends. Brummell used often to raise a hearty laugh at Carlton House
by repeating witticisms which he pretended to have heard from Lewis's
servant: some of these were very stale; yet they were considered so good
as to be repeated at the clubs, and greatly added to the reputation of the
Beau as a teller of good things. 'On one occasion,' said Brummell, 'I
called to inquire after a young lady who had sprained her ankle; Lewis,
on being asked how she was, had said, in the black's presence, "The

---

[1] The differences between Lewis and his father arose largely through the parent's
association with a woman of whom the son, who was very fond of his mother, disapproved.

[2] Lewis died, in fact, of yellow fever on the way home. He had gone out to Jamaica to
ensure that the slaves he had inherited with his father's estates were being properly cared
for.

doctor has seen her, put her legs straight, and the poor chicken is doing well." The servant, therefore, told me, with a mysterious and knowing look, "Oh, sir, the doctor has been here; she has laid eggs, and she and the chickens are doing well." '

Such extravagances in those days were received as the essence of wit, and to such stories did the public give a willing ear, repeating them with unwearying zest. Even Sheridan's wit partook of this character,[1] making him the delight of the prince, who ruled over the fashionable world, and whose approbation was sufficient to give currency to anything, however ludicrous and absurd.

Visiting in the Country

When I returned to London from Paris, in 1815, upon promotion, I was accompanied by Colonel Brooke, who was good enough to invite me to pass some time at his brother's, Sir R[ichard] Brooke, in Cheshire, upon the occasion of the christening of his eldest son. The *fête* was truly magnificent, and worthy of our excellent host; and all the great people of the neighbouring counties were present.

Soon afterwards I went to the Hale, a country house near Liverpool, belonging to Mr Blackburn, one of the oldest members of the House of Commons, where many persons, who had been at Sir Richard Brooke's, met again. Mr Blackburn was extremely absent and otherwise odd: upon one occasion I gave him a letter to frank, which he deliberately opened and read in my presence; and on my asking him if it amused him, he replied that he did not understand what it meant. Upon another occasion, the Duke of Gloucester, accompanied by Mr Blackburn, went out to shoot pheasants in the preserves near the Hale; when all of a sudden, Mr B., observing that the duke's gun was cocked, asked his Royal Highness whether he always carried his gun cocked. 'Yes, Blackburn, always,' was the reply. 'Well then, good morning, your Royal Highness; I will no longer accompany you.'

At dinner Mr Blackburn was very eccentric: he would never surrender his place at table even to royalty; so the Duke was obliged to sit near him. Whenever the royal servant filled the duke's glass with wine-and-water, Mr B. invariably drank it off; until at length the duke asked his servant for more wine-and-water, and anticipating a repetition of the farce that had so often been played, drank it off, and

---

[1] Richard Brinsley Sheridan (1751–1816), politician, dramatist and author of *The Rivals*, *The School for Scandal* and *The Critic*.

said, 'Well, Blackburn, I have done you at last.' After dinner the duke
and the men went to join the ladies in the drawing-room, where the
servant in royal livery was waiting, holding a tray, upon which was a
cup of tea for the duke. Mr Blackburn, observing the servant in waiting,
and that nobody took the cup of tea, determined on drinking it; but the
domestic retired a little, to endeavour to prevent it. Mr Blackburn,
however, followed and persisted; upon which the servant said, 'Sir, it is
for his Royal Highness.' 'D—— his Royal Highness; I will have this
tea.' The duke exclaimed, 'That's right, Blackburn,' and ordered the
servant to hand it to him.

Colonel Kelly and his Blacking

Among the odd characters I have met with, I do not recollect any one
more eccentric than the late Lieutenant-Colonel Kelly, of the First Foot
Guards, who was the vainest man I ever encountered. He was a thin,
emaciated-looking dandy, but had all the bearing of the gentleman. He
was haughty in the extreme, and very fond of dress; his boots were so
well varnished that the polish now in use could not surpass Kelly's
blacking in brilliancy; his pantaloons were made of the finest leather,
and his coats were inimitable: in short, his dress was considered
perfect.

His sister held the place of housekeeper to the Custom-house, and
when it was burnt down, Kelly was burnt with it, in endeavouring to
save his favourite boots. When the news of his horrible death became
known, all the dandies were anxious to secure the services of his valet,
who possessed the mystery of the inimitable blacking. Brummell lost no
time in discovering his place of residence, and asked what wages he
required; the servant answered, his late master gave him £150 a year,
but it was not enough for his talents, and he should require £200; upon
which Brummell said, 'Well, if you will make it guineas, I shall be
happy to attend upon *you.*'

Twisleton Fiennes, the late Lord Saye and Sele

Twisleton Fiennes was a very eccentric man, and the greatest epicure
of his day.[1] His dinners were worthy of the days of Vitellius or

---

[1] William Thomas Eardley Twistleton Fiennes, fifteenth Baron Saye and Sele
(1798-1847).

Heliogabalus.[1] Every country, every sea, was searched and ransacked to find some new delicacy for our British Sybarite. I remember, at one of his breakfasts, an omelette being served which was composed entirely of golden pheasants' eggs! He had a very strong constitution, and would drink absinthe and curaçoa in quantities which were perfectly awful to behold. These stimulants produced no effect upon his brain; but his health gradually gave way under the excesses of all kinds in which he indulged. He was a kind, liberal, and good-natured man, but a very odd fellow. I never shall forget the astonishment of a servant I had recommended to him. On entering his service, John made his appearance as Fiennes was going out to dinner, and asked his new master if he had any orders. He received the following answer, – 'Place two bottles of sherry by my bed-side, and call me the day after to-morrow.'

THE LATE LORD HENRY SEYMOUR

I knew Lord Henry perhaps better than any other Englishman, having lived with him on terms of great intimacy.[2] He was famous for his racing stud and good taste in his carriages and riding horses. It was said, by persons who were little acquainted with him, that he was fond of masquerades, fighting, and was also the terror of pugilists, from his great strength and science in boxing; on the contrary, he was a gentle, retiring, and humane man, and never was known to have been present at a masquerade, or any place of the sort. But it unfortunately happened that a man named 'Franconi,' of the Circus, – a low-born and vulgar fellow, – resembled him in looks and stature, and having been mistaken for my noble friend, gave himself out as Lord Seymour, in those dens of infamy where the noble lord was unknown.

Lord Henry Seymour was a man of fine taste, and fond of the arts, and, at his death, his paintings, library, and plate fetched a considerable sum at public auction. During his lifetime he patronised young artists: often advancing them money, and assisting them in every possible way.

---

[1] Roman emperors notorious for their gluttony. Vitellius was emperor in AD 69, Elagabalus in 218-22.
[2] Lord Henry Seymour (1805-59), son of the third Marquess of Hertford. He founded the French Jockey Club in Paris, where he died a bachelor, leaving money for the maintenance of his favourite horses and almost £40,000 a year to the hospitals of the city. His niece, Mary Seymour, was brought up by Mrs Fitzherbert after her parents' death.

COUNT D'ORSAY

Count d'Orsay had many disciples among our men of fashion, but none of them succeeded in copying the original.[1] His death produced, both in London and in Paris, a deep and universal regret. The count's life has been so well delineated in the public prints, that nothing I could say would add to the praise that has been bestowed upon him. Perfectly natural in manners and language, highly accomplished, and never betraying the slightest affectation or pretension, he had formed friendships with some of the noblest and most accomplished men in England. He was also a great favourite in Paris, where he had begun to exercise his talent as an artist, when death prematurely removed him from society.

In speaking of this gifted and accomplished man, I shall strictly confine myself, as I have done in other instances, to his public character, and not enter into the details of his private life; which are, perhaps, better left in the shade. I first saw him at an evening party given in 1816, by his grandmother in the Rue d'Anjou Saint Honoré. He was then sixteen years old, and he appeared to be a general favourite, owing to his remarkable beauty and pleasing manners. His father and mother were both present, and did me the honour to invite me to their house in the Rue du Mont Blanc, now called the Rue de la Chaussée d'Antin. They occupied the apartment in which the celebrated composer Rossini now lives.[2] d'Orsay's father, justly surnamed 'Le Beau d'Orsay,' was one of the handsomest men in the French army; he was one of Napoleon's generals, and distinguished himself in Spain, particularly at the battle of Salamanca.

I believe, and I like to think, that had Count d'Orsay fallen into good hands, he might have been a great many things that he was not. Unfortunate circumstances, which entangled him as with a fatal web

[1] Alfred-Guillaume-Gabriel, Count d'Orsay (1801-52), the son of a general in the Grande Armée, came to England in 1831 with the recently widowed Lady Blessington. He had been travelling on the Continent with Lord and Lady Blessington and in Naples had married the fifteen-year-old daughter of Lord Blessington by his first marriage. D'Orsay and Lady Blessington lived in nearby houses at first in Mayfair, then in Kensington. An artist as well as a man of fashion, d'Orsay became one of the leading arbiters of taste. In 1849 debts forced him to return to France, whence Lady Blessington soon followed him. She died in Paris soon afterwards. D'Orsay, who had long been separated from her stepdaughter, outlived her by only a few years, having supported himself by making busts and statues of the Parisian beau monde.

[2] Gioacchino Antonio Rossini (1792-1868). His Barbiere di Seviglia was first performed in 1816. (See note, pp. 207-9.)

from his early youth, dragged him downwards and led him step by step to his ruin. On these peculiar circumstances, I shall not dwell. They are known to all, and cannot be palliated. But he was a grand creature in spite of all this; beautiful as the Apollo Belvidere in his outward form, full of health, life, spirits, wit, and gaiety, radiant and joyous, the admired of all admirers: – such was d'Orsay when I first knew him. If the Count had been born with a fortune of a hundred thousand pounds a year, he would have been a great man. He loved money, not for money's sake, but for what it could procure. He was generous even to ostentation, and he had a real pleasure in giving even what he himself had borrowed. He was born with princely tastes and ideas, and would have heartily despised a man who could have sat down contented in a simple dwelling-place, with a bad cook and a small competence.

He possessed in a great degree the faculty of pleasing those whom he wished to attract. His smile was bright and genial, his manner full of charm, his conversation original and amusing, and his artistic taste undeniable. It might have been objected that this taste was somewhat too gaudy; but the brilliant tints with which he liked to surround himself suited his style of beauty, his dress, and manner. When I used to see him driving in his tilbury some thirty years ago, I fancied that he looked like some gorgeous dragon-fly skimming through the air; and though all was dazzling and showy, yet there was a kind of harmony which precluded any idea or accusation of bad taste. All his imitators fell between the Scylla and Charybdis of tigerism and charlatanism; but he escaped those quicksands, though, perhaps, somewhat narrowly, and in spite of a gaudy and almost eccentric style of dress.

Many of his *bons mots* and clever sayings have been cited by his numerous friends and admirers; but perhaps there was more humour and *à propos* in the majority of them than actual wit. There was also much in his charming manner, and the very successful mixture of French and English which he had adopted in conversation. I call to mind a story of him not generally known. When he first came to England as a very young man, and was about twenty-two years of age, he was invited to dine at Holland House, where he was seated next to Lady Holland herself, who supposed that the handsome stranger was a shy young man, awe-struck by her majestic selfishness. Owing to a considerable abdominal development, her ladyship was continually letting her napkin slip from her lap to the ground, and as often as she did so, she smiled blandly, but authoritatively, on the French Count, and asked him to pick it up. He politely complied several times, but, at last, tired of this exercise, he said, to her great surprise, '*Ne ferais-je pas mieux,*

Madame, de m'asseoir sous la table, afin de pouvoir vous passer la serviette plus rapidement?[1]

On another occasion, the well-known Tom Raikes, whose letters and memoirs have been lately published,[2] and who was a tall, large man, very much marked with the small-pox, having one day written an anonymous letter to d'Orsay, containing some piece of impertinence or other, had closed it with a wafer, and stamped it with something resembling the top of a thimble. The Count soon discovered who was the writer, and in a room full of company thus addressed him – 'Ha! ha! my good Raikes, the next time you write an anonymous letter, you must not seal it with your nose!'

I cannot conclude without giving some description of the personal appearance of one who reigned pre-eminent in the fashionable circles of London and Paris. He was rather above six feet in height, and when I first knew him, he might have served as a model for a statuary. His neck was long, his shoulders broad, and his waist narrow, and though he was, perhaps, somewhat underlimbed, nothing could surpass the beauty of his feet and ankles. His dark chestnut hair hung naturally in long waving curls; his forehead was high and wide, his features regular, and his complexion glowed with radiant health. His eyes were large and of a light hazel colour, he had full lips and very white teeth, but a little apart; which sometimes gave to the generally amiable expression of his countenance a rather cruel and sneering look, such as one sees in the heads of some of the old Roman emperors. He was wonderfully strong and active, and excelled in manly exercises. He was a fine horseman, a good swordsman, and a fair shot. I knew him intimately, and saw a great deal of him. He had an amusing *naïveté* in speaking of his own personal advantages.

I remember on one occasion, when about to fight a duel, he said to his second who was making the preliminary arrangements, 'You know, my dear friend, I am not on a par with my antagonist: he is a very ugly fellow, and if I wound him in the face, he won't look much the worse for

[1] A very similar story is told, more convincingly, of Sydney Smith, who asked her ladyship if, while he was getting her napkin from under the table, she would like him to sweep the carpet as well.
[2] Thomas Raikes (1777–1848), dandy and diarist. Robert Raikes, the promoter of Sunday schools – who is commemorated by a bronze statue by Sir Thomas Brock in Victoria Embankment Gardens – was his uncle. Thomas was at Eton with Brummell and was a fellow member of White's. He was made a partner in his father's City firm but spent most of his life in the West End or in travelling abroad or in the country houses of his aristocratic friends.

it; but on my side it ought to be agreed that he should not aim higher than my chest, for if my face should be spoiled, "*ce serait vraiment dommage.*"' He said this with such a beaming smile, and looked so handsome and happy, that his friend fully agreed with him.

Though his tastes, pursuits, and habits were thoroughly manly, yet he took as much care of his beauty as a woman might have done. He was in the habit of taking perfumed baths, and his friends remember the enormous gold dressing-case, which it required two men to carry, and which used to be the companion of all his excursions.

HARRINGTON HOUSE AND LORD PETERSHAM

When our army returned to England in 1814, my young friend, Augustus Stanhope, took me one afternoon to Harrington House, in Stableyard, St James's, where I was introduced to Lord and Lady Harrington, and all the Stanhopes.[1] On entering a long gallery, I found the whole family engaged in their sempiternal occupation of tea-drinking. Neither in Nankin, Pekin, nor Canton was the teapot more assiduously and constantly replenished than at this hospitable mansion. I was made free of the corporation, if I may use the phrase, by a cup being handed to me; and I must say that I never tasted any tea so good before or since.

As an example of the undeviating tea-table habits of the house of Harrington, General Lincoln Stanhope[2] once told me, that after an absence of several years in India, he made his reappearance at Harrington House, and found the family, as he had left them on his departure, drinking tea in the long gallery. On his presenting himself, his father's only observation and speech of welcome to him was, 'Hallo, Linky, my dear boy! delighted to see you. Have a cup of tea?'

I was then taken to Lord Petersham's apartments,[3] where we found his lordship, one of the chief dandies of the day, employed in making a particular sort of blacking, which he said would eventually supersede every other. The room into which we were ushered was more like a shop

---

[1] Charles Stanhope, third Earl of Harrington (1753–1829), had served as aide-de-camp to General Burgoyne in America. He had been promoted general in 1802 after a not very active military career. His wife, Jane Seymour, was daughter and co-heiress of Sir John Flemming of Brompton Park. They had six sons and two daughters, both of whom married dukes.

[2] Major-General the Hon. Lincoln Edwin Robert Stanhope was Lord Harrington's second son. He died in 1840.

[3] See note, p. 7.

than a gentleman's sitting-room: all round the walls were shelves, upon which were placed tea-canisters, containing Congou, Pekoe, Souchong, Bohea, Gunpowder, Russian, and many other teas, all the best of the kind; on the other side of the room were beautiful jars, with names, in gilt letters, of innumerable kinds of snuff, and all the necessary apparatus for moistening and mixing. Lord Petersham's mixture is still well known to all tobacconists. Other shelves and many of the tables were covered with a great number of magnificent snuff-boxes; for Lord Petersham had perhaps the finest collection in England, and was supposed to have a fresh box for every day in the year. I heard him, on the occasion of a delightful old light-blue Sèvres box he was using being admired, say, in his lisping way – 'Yes, it is a nice summer box, but would not do for winter wear.'

In this museum there were also innumerable canes of very great value. The Viscount was likewise a great Mæcenas[1] among the tailors, and a particular kind of great-coat, when I was a young man, was called a Petersham.

In person, Lord Petersham was tall and handsome, and possessed a particularly winning smile. He very much resembled the pictures of Henry IV of France, and frequently wore a dress not unlike that of the celebrated monarch. His carriages were unique of their kind: they were entirely brown, with brown horses and harness. The groom, a tall youth, was dressed in a long brown coat reaching to his heels, and a glazed hat with a large cockade. It is said that Lord Petersham's devotion to brown was caused by his having been desperately in love with a very beautiful widow bearing that name.[2]

In addition to his other eccentricities, Lord Petersham never ventured out of doors till six p.m. His manners were decidedly affected, and he spoke with a kind of lisp; but in spite of his little foibles, Lord Petersham was a thorough gentleman, and was beloved by all who knew him.

TOWNSHEND, THE BOW-STREET OFFICER

Townshend, the famous Bow-Street officer, when I knew him, was a little fat man with a flaxen wig, kerseymere breeches, a blue straight-cut

[1] Strictly speaking a patron of literature or art. Gaius Maecinas (d. 8 BC) kept an open house for writers in the reign of Augustus.

[2] Petersham eventually married the actress Maria Foote (c. 1797–1867), daughter of the manager of the Plymouth theatre.

coat, and a broad-brimmed white hat. To the most daring courage he added great dexterity and cunning; and was said, *in propriâ personâ*, to have taken more thieves than all the other Bow-Street officers put together. He frequently accompanied mail-coaches when the Government required large sums of money to be conveyed to distant parts of the country.

Upon one occasion, when Townshend was to act as escort to a carriage going to Reading, he took with him the famous Joe Manton, the gunmaker, who was always ready for a lark, and was as brave as steel.[1] Soon after reaching Hounslow three footpads stopped the coach, and Joe Manton was preparing to try the effect of one of his deadly barrels upon them, when Townshend cried out - 'Stop, Joe, don't fire! - let me talk to the gentlemen.' The moment the robbers heard Townshend's voice they took to their heels; but he had been able to identify them, and a few months afterwards they were taken, tried, and upon Townshend's evidence, sent to Botany Bay.[2]

The short, corpulent police-officer was, for his daring exploits and general good conduct, selected by the Home Office to attend at drawing-rooms, levees, and all state occasions; and he became a kind of personage, and was much noticed by the Royal Family and the great people of the day: every one went up to speak to Townshend. He was eccentric and amusing, and somewhat inclined to take advantage of the familiarity with which he was treated; but he was a sort of privileged person, and could say what he liked.

On one occasion the Duke of Clarence recommended Townshend to publish his memoirs, which he thought would be very interesting. Townshend, who had become somewhat deaf, seemed rather surprised, but said he would obey HRH's commands. A few weeks afterwards, Townshend was on duty at Carlton House, when the Duke asked him if he had fulfilled his promise. His answer was –

---

[1] Joseph Manton (*c.* 1766–1835) was in business as a gunmaker at 25 Davies Street, Berkeley Square, before moving to 11 Hanover Square. Despite his fame and the high quality of his guns, he became bankrupt in 1826. His sons carried on the business in Holles Street. His brother, John, was also a gunmaker at 6 Dover Street.

[2] Botany Bay, an inlet of the Tasman Sea in New South Wales, was discovered by Captain James Cook in 1770. It was so called because of the many plants found there by Joseph Banks, the expedition's naturalist. A naval officer, Captain Arthur Phillip, was instructed to establish a convict settlement there. He set sail with 558 men and 192 women, but when he arrived over forty of his prisoners had died on the way; others had managed to escape; and two men had gone off in a French discovery ship. Phillip found Botany Bay a barren area of swamp and sand, unsuitable for a settlement, and took his charges on to an inlet which Cook had named Fort Jackson.

'O sir, you've got me into a devil of a scrape! I had begun to write my *amours*, as you desired, when Mrs Townshend caught me in the act of writing them, and swore she'd be revenged; for you know, your Royal Highness, I was obliged to divulge many secrets about women, for which she'll never forgive me.'

When the Duke of Clarence became king, and was going down to prorogue Parliament, the Master of the Horse had not got the state carriage ready in time; and the King, in a fit of anger against Lord Albemarle,[1] swore he would order a hackney-coach and go to the House in that humble vehicle. Upon which Townshend, to the amazement of every one, cried out from behind a screen –

'Well said, sir; I think your Majesty is d——d right.' The King, very much surprised and amused, called out –

'Is that you, Townshend?'

'Yes, sir; I am here to see that your Majesty has fair play!'

At one of Queen Charlotte's drawing-rooms – I think the last before her death, which was held at old Buckingham House[2] – an immense crowd assembled, and in going up the stairs much confusion arose among the ladies; for as no order was kept, and every one wished to get first into the presence of royalty, much rushing and squeezing took place, loud shrieks were heard, and several ladies fainted.

I was on guard on that day, and doing what I could to preserve order, when Townshend called out to me to conduct a foreign lady, who had fallen and nearly fainted on the staircase, to the top of the landing-place. I did so, and brought her into the presence of the Queen; when a gentleman, in very good English, thanked me for the courtesy I had shown to his wife, the Duchess of Orleans (afterwards Queen Marie Amélie).[3]

EXTRAVAGANCE – THE DUKE OF MARLBOROUGH, GRANDFATHER OF THE PRESENT DUKE

Lord Blandford, afterwards fifth Duke of Marlborough, with many good and amiable qualities, was by far the most extravagant man I ever

[1] William Charles Keppel, fourth Earl of Albemarle (1772–1849).

[2] Buckingham House, St James's Park, was built in 1702–5 for John Sheffield, first Duke of Buckingham and Normanby. King George III bought it in 1762 from the Duke's illegitimate son, Sir Charles Sheffield, and gradually enlarged it. George IV built Buckingham Palace on the site.

[3] Queen Marie-Amélie (1782–1866). She was the daughter of King Ferdinand IV of Naples. She married the duc d'Orléans, later King Louis-Philippe, at Palermo in 1809.

remember to have seen.[1] He lived in lodgings at Triphook's the bookseller in St James's Street, whilst his father and mother resided in great state at Marlborough House.[2] Although supporting himself upon money borrowed at an exorbitant interest, Lord Blandford would give Lee and Kennedy £500 for a curious plant or shrub; and I well remember his paying £1800 for a fine edition of Boccaccio; whilst his country-seat, Whiteknights, near Reading, was kept up with a splendour worthy of a royal residence.[3]

His mother, the Duchess of Marlborough[4] (of whom Queen Charlotte used to say, that she and Lady Carlisle,[5] grandmother of Lord Carlisle, were the two haughtiest and proudest women in England), had quarrelled with Lord Blandford for several years past. She persuaded the Duke to settle a large portion of the Blenheim estates, which were unentailed, upon his brother, Lord Francis Spencer, who was created Lord Churchill.[6] Lord Blandford's allowance during his father's lifetime was insufficient for a person in his position. He was, therefore, obliged to have recourse to the Jews, who eventually ruined him. He was always very kind to me, and I lived a good deal with him and his sons when I was a young man.

I remember, in 1816, going down with him to Whiteknights; which was afterwards sold, and has since been pulled down. During our journey, Lord Blandford opened a sort of cupboard, which was fixed on one side of the coach in which we travelled, and which contained a capital luncheon, with different kinds of wine and liqueurs. Another part of this roomy vehicle, on a spring being touched, displayed a sort of *secrétaire*, with writing materials, and a large pocket-book; the latter he opened, and showed me fifty Bank of England notes for £1000 each, which he told me he had borrowed the day before from a well-known

[1] George Spencer, fifth Duke of Marlborough (1766–1840). In 1791 he married Susan, daughter of the seventh Earl of Galloway. He obtained a Royal Licence to assume the additional surname of Churchill in 1807.

[2] Marlborough House was built in 1709–11 for Sarah, Duchess of Marlborough, probably to the designs of Christopher Wren, the Younger, under the supervision of his father. The house remained in the Marlborough family until 1817 when it reverted to the Crown. It was the home of Edward, Prince of Wales, later Edward VII, in whose time it was known as 'the best-kept house in London'. It now houses the Commonwealth Foundation.

[3] White Knights Park is now the site of the University of Reading.

[4] Lord Blandford's mother was Caroline, only daughter of the fourth Duke of Bedford. She died in 1811.

[5] Margaret Caroline, daughter of Granville Leveson, first Marquess of Stafford. She married the fifth Earl of Carlisle in 1770.

[6] Lord Francis Almeric Spencer (1779–1845) was created first Baron Churchill in 1815.

money-lender in the city, named Levy. He stated that he had given in return a post-obit on his father's death for £150,000; and added, 'You see, Gronow, how the immense fortune of my family will be frittered away: but I can't help it; I must live. My father inherited £500,000 in ready money, and £70,000 a year in land; and, in all probability, when it comes to my turn to live at Blenheim, I shall have nothing left but the annuity of £5000 a year on the Post-Office.'

Lord Blandford's prediction was verified; for when I went to see him at Blenheim some years later, and when he had become Duke of Marlborough, he told me that I should find a great difference between his magnificent way of living at Whiteknights, and his very reduced establishment at Blenheim. He said that he had from the estate, fish, game, venison, mutton, and poultry in abundance, and a good cellar of wine; but that he was so involved that he could obtain credit neither in Oxford nor in London, and that his sole revenue (and much of that forestalled) was the annuity on the Post-Office, which was inalienably secured to the great Duke.

Fortunately for his successors, the vast estates of the Marlborough family were strictly entailed, and the present possessor has ample revenues, and is a most worthy representative of one of the greatest names in English history.

6

Courtesans

MRS MARY ANNE CLARKE

Our army, despite its defects, was nevertheless infinitely better administered at home when I joined than it had been a few years before, owing principally to the inquiry that had taken place in the House of Commons, relative to the bribery and corruption which had crept in, and which had been laid open by the confessions of a female, who created no small sensation in those days, and who eventually terminated her extraordinary career, not very long since, in Paris.

The squibs fired off by Mrs Mary Anne Clarke[1] had a much greater influence, and produced more effect upon the English army, than all the artillery of the enemy directed against the Duke of York when commanding in Holland. This lady was remarkable for her beauty and her fascinations; and few came within the circle over which she presided who did not acknowledge her superior power. Her wit, which kept the House of Commons during her examination in a continued state of merriment, was piquant and saucy. Her answers on that occasion have been so often brought before the public, that I need not repeat them; but, in private life, her quick repartee, and her brilliant sallies, rendered her a lively, though not always an agreeable companion. As for prudence, she had none; her dearest friend, if she had any, was just as

---

[1] Mary Anne Clarke (1776–1852), a flamboyant and extravagant actress, was the mistress of Frederick, Duke of York, when he was commander-in-chief at the Horse Guards.

likely to be made the object of her ridicule as the most obnoxious person of her acquaintance.

Her narrative of her first introduction to the Duke of York has often been repeated; but, as all her stories were considered apocryphal, it is difficult to arrive at a real history of her career. Certain, however, is it that, about the age of sixteen, she was residing at Blackheath – a sweet, pretty, lively girl – when, in her daily walk across the heath, she was passed, on two or three occasions, by a handsome, well-dressed cavalier, who, finding that she recognised his salute, dismounted; pleased with her manner and wit, he begged to be allowed to introduce a friend. Accordingly, on her consenting, a person to whom the cavalier appeared to pay every sort of deference was presented to her, and the acquaintance ripened into something more than friendship. Not the slightest idea had the young lady of the position in society of her lover, until she accompanied him, on his invitation, to the theatre, where she occupied a private box, when she was surprised at the ceremony with which she was treated, and at observing that every eye and every lorgnette in the house were directed towards her in the course of the evening. She accepted this as a tribute to her beauty. Finding that she could go again to the theatre when she pleased, and occupy the same box, she availed herself of this opportunity with a female friend, and was not a little astonished at being addressed as her Royal Highness. She then discovered that the individual into whose affections she had insinuated herself was the son of the King, the Duke of York, who had not long before united himself to a lady, for whom she had been mistaken.

Mrs Mary Anne Clarke was soon reconciled to the thought of being the wife of a prince by the left hand, particularly as she found herself assiduously courted by persons of the highest rank, and more especially by military men. A large house in a fashionable street was taken for her, and an establishment on a magnificent scale gave her an opportunity of surrounding herself with persons of a sphere far beyond anything she could in her younger days have dreamt of;[1] her father having been in an honourable trade,[2] and her husband being only a captain in a marching regiment.[3] The duke, delighted to see his fair friend so well received,

---

[1] This was 62 Gloucester Place, where she lived in splendid style from 1803 to 1810, employing twenty servants and keeping ten horses for her several carriages.

[2] He was a bricklayer named Thompson living in Ball and Pin Alley, White's Alley, Chancery Lane.

[3] This is improbable. It seems more likely that Mr Clarke was a stonemason.

constantly honoured her dinner-table with his presence, and willingly gratified any wish that she expressed; and he must have known (and for this he was afterwards highly censured) that her style of living was upon a scale of great expense, and that he himself contributed little towards it. The consequence was that the hospitable lady eventually became embarrassed, and knew not which way to turn to meet her outlay. It was suggested to her that she might obtain from the duke commissions in the army, which she could easily dispose of at a good price. Individuals quickly came forward, ready to purchase anything that came within her grasp, which she extended not only to the army, but, as it afterwards appeared, to the Church; for there were reverend personages who availed themselves of her assistance, and thus obtained patronage, by which they advanced their worldly interests very rapidly.

Mrs Mary Anne Clarke and Col. Wardle

Amongst those who paid great attention to Mrs Mary Anne Clarke was Colonel Wardle, at that time a remarkable member of the House of Commons, and a bold leader of the Radical Opposition.[1] He got intimately acquainted with her, and was so great a personal favourite that it was believed he wormed out all her secret history, of which he availed himself to obtain a fleeting popularity.

Having obtained the names of some of the parties who had been fortunate enough, as they imagined, to secure the lady's favour, he loudly demanded an inquiry in the House of Commons as to the management of the army by the Commander-in-Chief, the Duke of York. The nation and the army were fond of his Royal Highness, and every attempt to screen him was made; but in vain. The House undertook the task of investigating the conduct of the duke, and witnesses were produced, amongst whom was the fair lady herself, who by no means attempted to screen her imprudent admirer. Her responses to the questions put to her were cleverly and archly given, and the whole mystery of her various intrigues came to light. The duke consequently resigned his place in the Horse-Guards, and at the same time repudiated the beautiful and dangerous cause of his humiliation.[2] The lady, incensed at the desertion of her royal swain, announced her

[1] Colonel Gwllym Lloyd Wardle (c. 1762–1833) was Radical Member of Parliament for Okehampton.
[2] Although the Duke resigned, Wardle's charges were not found proven against him. He was acquitted, after examination in the House of Commons, by a majority of eighty-two.

intention of publishing his love-letters, which were likely to expose the whole of the royal family to ridicule, as they formed the frequent themes of his correspondence. Sir Herbert Taylor was therefore commissioned to enter into a negotiation for the purchase of the letters;[1] this he effected at an enormous price, obtaining a written document at the same time by which Mrs Clarke was subjected to heavy penalties if she, by word or deed, implicated the honour of any of the branches of the royal family. A pension was secured to her, on condition that she should quit England, and reside wherever she chose on the Continent. To all this she consented, and, in the first instance, went to Brussels, where her previous history being scarcely known, she was well received; and she married her daughters without any inquiry as to the fathers to whom she might ascribe them.

Mrs Clarke afterwards settled quietly and comfortably in Paris, receiving occasionally visits from members of the aristocracy who had known her when mingling in a certain circle in London.

Her manners were exceedingly agreeable, and to the latest day she retained pleasing traces of past beauty. She was lively, sprightly, and full of fun, and indulged in innumerable anecdotes of the members of the royal family of England – some of them much too scandalous to be repeated. She regarded the Duke of York as a big baby, not out of his leading strings, and the Prince of Wales as an idle sensualist, with just enough of brains to be guided by any laughing, well-bred individual who would listen to stale jokes and impudent ribaldry. Of Queen Charlotte she used to speak with the utmost disrespect, attributing to her a love of domination and a hatred of every one who would not bow down before any idol that she chose to set up; and as being envious of the Princess Caroline and her daughter the Princess Charlotte of Wales, and jealous of their acquiring too much influence over the Prince of Wales. In short, Mary Anne Clarke had been so intimately let into every secret of the life of the royal family that, had she not been tied down, her revelations would have astonished the world, however willing people might have been to believe that they were tinged with scandal and exaggeration.[2]

The way in which Colonel Wardle first obtained information of the

[1] Colonel Sir Herbert Taylor (1775–1839) was Private Secretary to the Duke of York and afterwards to his father, King George III. He offered Mrs Clarke £7,000 for the letters (a sum which today would be worth about £400,000) and a pension of £400 a year.
[2] In 1813 Mrs Clarke was sentenced to nine months' imprisonment for libel. She died at Boulogne at the age of seventy-six.

sale of commissions was singular enough. He was paying a clandestine visit to Mrs Clarke, when a carriage with the royal livery drove up to the door, and the gallant officer was compelled to take refuge under the sofa; but instead of the royal duke, there appeared one of his aide-de-camps, who entered into conversation in so mysterious a manner as to excite the attention of the gentleman under the sofa, and led him to believe that the sale of a commission was authorised by the Commander-in-Chief; though it afterwards appeared that it was a private arrangement of the unwelcome visitor. At the Horse-Guards, it had often been suspected that there was a mystery connected with commissions that could not be fathomed; as it frequently happened that the list of promotions agreed on was surreptitiously increased by the addition of new names. This was the crafty handiwork of the accomplished dame; the duke having employed her as his amanuensis, and being accustomed to sign her autograph lists without examination.

Mademoiselle Duthé

This celebrated courtesan lived with great splendour and magnificence in Paris before the first French Revolution. The old Lord Egremont, a man of immense wealth, who had then lately come of age,[1] and the Count d'Artois, afterwards Charles X, were rivals in her affections, and vied with each other in the most reckless prodigality. Her splendid mansion, and her carriages, which were covered with gold, and drawn by eight cream-coloured horses, were the admiration of all Paris. When the Revolution broke out in France, this fair and frail beauty took example from her betters, and emigrated to England.

Mademoiselle Duthé was the idol of the young men of fashion; and from the pictures of her at this time, she must have been surpassingly beautiful. [Among her principal admirers in England were two brothers named Lee. The younger brother] acted the part of master of the ceremonies to the fair Frenchwoman, gave her his arm in all the public promenades, and escorted her to the play and opera on all occasions. The elder Lee, her favoured inamorato, though dotingly fond of her, would never appear with her in public.

---

[1] Sir George O'Brien Wyndham, third Earl of Egremont (1751–1837), philanthropist, supporter of the turf and patron of art. His horses won the Derby and the Oaks more frequently than those of any other owner. He spent the latter part of his life at Petworth, where Turner had a studio. In 1801 he married Elizabeth Iliffe, by whom he had already had six illegitimate children.

The Duke of Queensberry,[1] so well known by the name of old Q, and who was a great friend of Mademoiselle Duthé (as he was of all persons eminent in that lady's profession), asked her the meaning of her conduct with respect to the two brothers. She replied, with unblushing effrontery, 'The younger Lee is *"mon Lit de parade;"* the elder, *"mon Lit de repose."'*

On the restoration of the Bourbons, Mademoiselle Duthé, in possession of a considerable fortune, but no longer beautiful and young, returned to Paris, and resided at a fine house in the Rue Marbœuf, in the Champs Elysées. One of the famous gilt carriages given her by Lord Egremont again figured in the public promenades; but, instead of being admired, was much laughed at, as the style and shape were quite out of fashion. At her death it was sold to the elder Franconi, for theatrical performances.

Mademoiselle Duthé, in addition to a beautiful face, was supposed to have the finest figure in the world. A picture of her is extant, which I have seen. It was painted by one of the first artists in France. She is represented in all the glory of her youth and beauty, at full length, reclining on a couch, very much in the costume of our mother Eve. She is said to have been full of wit and cleverness, and possessed a fund of curious anecdotes about everything and everybody.

Mr Lee, whose fortune was much injured by her extravagance, bade her farewell in a single Latin line, which he told her her friend the Duke of Queensberry, of whom he was rather jealous, would translate; it was, '*Non possum te cum vivere, nec sine te* [I can live neither with you nor without you].'

KATE NORTH

Kate North[2] was the daughter of a discharged sergeant of the Guards, who had the appointment of suttler at Chatham. Her mother dying

---

[1] William Douglas, third Earl of March and fourth Duke of Queensberry (1724–1810), the rake, whoremonger and gambler, renowned for his escapades and wicked debaucheries. 'He was', wrote Raikes, 'a little sharp-looking man, very irritable and swore like ten thousand troopers.' Towards the end of his life he lived in a large house in Piccadilly where he spent most of his time in a large bow window overlooking the street watching the passersby and sending his groom with messages to friends and acquaintances.

[2] Kate North is mentioned in Harriette Wilson's *Memoirs* (see note, p. 244). According to these, she was at one time the mistress of Sir Harry Mildmay, who took her from Lord Reay.

after a long illness, Kate, though young, worked hard early and late, and managed her father's house for a length of time; and the entire garrison, from the commanding officer to the private soldier, were loud in their praise of this incomparable young girl, whose marvellous beauty was the theme of conversation.

Among the officers at Chatham there happened to be a young ensign, extremely good-looking, upon whom Kate's beauty made a strong impression; he succeeded in captivating the affections of the charming and innocent girl, and at last seduced her. The regiment to which the ensign belonged having received marching orders, Kate determined to follow her seducer, and she marched with the soldiers to London. The secret of her seduction was not long before it got known and reached the ears of the Commander-in-Chief, the Duke of York; who, being informed that the poor girl was in a state of destitution, sent an aide-de-camp to discover her retreat, which proved to be an unfurnished room in the worst part of Spitalfields. The aide-de-camp told her his errand, but at the same time bound her to secrecy.

Early robbed of her virtue, abandoned by her betrayer, and an utter stranger in London, she reproached herself with her sin, and in a paroxysm of remorse and despair, the wretched girl determined to poison herself. She had purchased some laudanum, and was on the point of swallowing it, when a gentle rap at the door was heard outside. She opened the door, and in walked the Duke of York. His Royal Highness was struck with her beauty, modest deportment, and the frankness with which she answered all his questions, and, on his taking leave, said that he would send her a few necessaries to make her comfortable; upon which the poor girl fell upon her knees, and, in a voice almost inarticulate with emotion, thanked her benefactor.

When the Duke again called, she expressed her gratitude for all she had received, but hinted to her royal visitor that her earnest desire was to live an honourable life. The Duke was astounded, but said nothing in reply. He was simply dressed in a plain riding costume, and was, without exception, one of the finest men England could boast of. He stood above six feet; was rather stout, but well proportioned; his chest broad, and his frame muscular; his face bore the stamp of authority, and every feature was handsome; his brow was full and prominent, the eye greyish, beaming with benevolence; and a noble forehead, with premature grey hairs, though the Prince was hardly in the vale of years, completed the picture which presented itself to the unhappy Kate. The poor girl, overawed by the royal presence, attempted to leave the room, but was prevented. Her thoughts were how to avoid the danger which she felt was awaiting her, if the Royal Duke should persist in his assiduities.

His Royal Highness, not knowing the girl's feelings, paid her frequent visits, and each succeeding day became more and more enamoured of her; though upon all occasions she evinced a desire to avoid his presence. The thoughts of her seducer, and the degrading situation in which she stood, contrasting with the benevolence, and apparent affection of the Royal Duke, overwhelmed her. She wept bitterly, and flung herself upon her bed in an agony of distress. Her first resolution was to tell the Duke that she could not bring herself to consent to his proposals; but scarcely was the resolution formed, when the royal visitor again made his appearance. He promised never to desert her; and at length, overcome by his kindness and his importunities, she exclaimed, 'If you really love me, Duke, I consent to be yours.' The Duke was made happy; a house, carriages, &c., were supplied to the fair Kate, who lived with him many years. As she had a love for reading, and a desire for knowledge, masters were engaged for her; and by dint of perseverance, and applying herself to study, she was enabled to dissipate that weight of sorrow which would have otherwise hastened her death.

One summer morning a friend of the Duke of York's called and told her that his Royal Highness would be under the necessity of giving up his connection with her, for he had promised the King, his father, that if his debts were paid, he would never more see the object of his affection. Poor Kate's heart was full; she could not reply to the messenger, but bursting into tears, hid her face, and flew out of the room. The sting which had been inflicted was more than she could bear, and she was seized with brain fever; but with much care and quiet, in course of time, the poor creature recovered her health and composure of mind.

There was no woman so much admired in London at the time as Kate North; her bewitching manners, the charm and grace of her conversation, brought to her pretty house in Green Street innumerable admirers. Among those anxious to woo her, a noble Scotch lord was most assiduous in his attentions, and he at length succeeded in prevailing upon her to accept the offer of his protection; she lived with him several years, and bore him a daughter, who is now the wife of a baronet and the mother of a numerous family. But the canker in Kate's mind was all this while corroding her life. She visited Paris for change of air and scene; but there her senses left her: she became raving mad, and died in a foreign land, without a friend to close her eyes.

SALLY BROOKE

There was a celebrated beauty who in my day made a conspicuous figure both in London and on the Continent. Miss Brooke, or, as she was more generally called, Sally Brooke, was the daughter of a beneficed clergyman; she had agreeable manners, her education had been highly finished, and she always mingled in the best men's circles. For some reason which never was known, she quitted her parents' roof and came to London, where she created a considerable impression; she was most particularly noticed by the Prince of Wales, and consequently well received by those who basked in princely favour. Nor a word, however, was ever breathed against her honour; and she was always looked upon as a model of unimpeachable veracity. Her beauty was such that she became the object of general admiration, and her portrait was taken by the first painters of the day. Her figure was perfection, and the sculptor would have been delighted to have obtained such a model. From whence she derived her income was always a mystery: a silly story was for a moment circulated that a person of the name of Bouverie, commonly called 'The Commissioner,' had succeeded in captivating her; this, however, soon died away. Whatever may have been her resources, she kept up a good establishment in Green Street, and lived always like a lady, but without much show. Her house was the rendezvous of the first men in London; but to her own sex she was distant and reserved, never admitting any female to her familiarity.

On one occasion, Miss Brooke dined at the house of a noble marquis, where some of the fashionable young men of the day were invited to meet her. Mr Christopher Nugent, a nephew of the celebrated Burke,[1] was most assiduous in his attentions, and begged permission to pay her a visit; the request was granted, and a day and an hour named. Some of the party present incidentally mentioned this engagement in the presence of the widow of a Mr Harrison, a lady who had access to the best circles in consequence of her remarkable beauty, and who had some right to place Mr Nugent on the list of her admirers. Jealous of her rival, the widow dressed herself as a boy, knocked at the door in Green Street, and was admitted into the presence of Miss Brooke, who was reclining on a sofa, whilst Nugent was on his knees before her; the distinguished lady, finding her lover in such a position, rushed upon

[1] Edmund Burke (1729-97), the statesman, married Jane Mary Nugent in 1757. She was the daughter of his doctor, Christopher Nugent, after whom Burke's son, like his cousin, was named.

him, seized a knife, and plunged it into his breast, fortunately without inflicting a mortal wound. Whatever might have been expected when this fact was generally known, it was soon believed that love had healed the wounds which jealousy inflicted; for Nugent and the lovely widow were soon seen walking together in familiar conversation in Hyde Park.

After being the admiration of the world of fashion for several seasons, Sally Brooke, seeing wrinkles coming into her once Hebe-like face, determined to leave scenes where she no longer reigned as the queen of beauty, but found other and fresher forms admired, and went to Baden. There some scoundrels having robbed her of all she possessed, she left the place, and arrived at the Hôtel du Palais Royal at Strasburg, where she remained some years, 'the world forgetting, by the world forgot.' A dropsical disease ravaged her once symmetrical form, and she died in a land of strangers. Her landlord nobly defrayed the expenses of her funeral, although she was already much indebted to him. Her family, however, liquidated her debts. Her remains repose in the city of Strasburg, and her tomb is one of the memorials of human vanity.

7

The Waterloo Campaign

THE GUARDS MARCHING FROM ENGHIEN ON THE 15TH OF JUNE

Two battalions of my regiment had started from Brussels; the other (the 2nd), to which I belonged, remained in London, and I saw no prospect of taking part in the great events which were about to take place on the Continent. Early in June I was introduced to Sir Thomas Picton.[1] He was very gracious, and, on his two aides-de-camp – Major Tyler and my friend Chambers, of the Guards – lamenting that I was obliged to remain at home, Sir Thomas said, 'Is the lad really anxious to go out?' Chambers answered that it was the height of my ambition. Sir Thomas inquired if all the appointments to his staff were filled up; and then added, with a grim smile, 'If Tyler is killed, which is not at all unlikely, I do not know why I should not take my young countryman: he may go over with me if he can get leave.' I was overjoyed at this, and, after thanking the general a thousand times, made my bow and retired.

I was much elated at the thoughts of being Picton's aide-de-camp, though that somewhat remote contingency depended upon my friends Tyler, or Chambers, or others, meeting with an untimely end; but at eighteen *on ne doute de rien.* So I set about thinking how I should manage to get my outfit, in order to appear at Brussels in a manner worthy of the aide-de-camp of the great general. As my funds were at a low ebb, I went

---

[1] See note, p. 65.

to Cox and Greenwood's,[1] those stanch friends of the hard-up soldier. Sailors may talk of the 'little cherub that sits up aloft,' but commend me for liberality, kindness, and generosity, to my old friends in Craig's Court. I there obtained £200, which I took with me to a gambling-house in St James's Square, where I managed, by some wonderful accident, to win £600; and, having thus obtained the sinews of war, I made numerous purchases, amongst others two first-rate horses at Tattersall's for a high figure, which were embarked for Ostend, along with my groom. I had not got leave; but I thought I should get back, after the great battle that appeared imminent, in time to mount guard at St James's.

On a Saturday I accompanied Chambers in his carriage to Ramsgate, where Sir Thomas Picton and Tyler had already arrived; we remained there for the Sunday, and embarked on Monday in a vessel which had been hired for the general and suite. On the same day we arrived at Ostend, and put up at a hotel in the square; where I was surprised to hear the general, in excellent French, get up a flirtation with our very pretty waiting-maid.

Sir Thomas Picton was a stern-looking, strong-built man, about the middle height. He generally wore a blue frock-coat, very tightly buttoned up to the throat; a very large black silk neckcloth, showing little or no shirt-collar; dark trousers, boots, and a round hat: it was in this very dress that he was attired at Quatre Bras, as he had hurried off to the scene of action before his uniform arrived. After sleeping at Ostend, the general and Tyler went the next morning to Ghent, and on Thursday to Brussels. I proceeded by boat to Ghent, and, without stopping, hired a carriage, and arrived in time to order rooms for Sir Thomas at the Hôtel d'Angleterre, Rue de la Madeleine, at Brussels: our horses followed us.

While we were at breakfast, Colonel Canning[2] came to inform the general that the Duke of Wellington wished to see him immediately. Sir Thomas lost not a moment in obeying the order of his chief, leaving the breakfast-table and proceeding to the park, where Wellington was walking with Fitzroy Somerset and the Duke of Richmond.[3] Picton's

---

[1] Army bankers. Richard Cox became regimental agent to the 1st Foot Guards in 1758.
[2] One of Wellington's aides-de-camp.
[3] Charles Lennox, fourth Duke of Richmond and Lennox (1764–1819). Commissioned into the 2nd Foot Guards, he had been promoted general by 1814. Before the battle of Waterloo he and the Duchess gave the celebrated ball at Brussels, where they then lived. At Waterloo he served on Wellington's staff. The year before his death in Canada, he was appointed Governor-General of British North America. He died from the effects of a bite from a fox. He had fourteen children. His son, the fifth Duke (see note, p. 57), was also on Wellington's staff.

manner was always more familiar than the duke liked in his lieutenants, and on this occasion he approached him in a careless sort of way, just as he might have met an equal. The duke bowed coldly to him, and said, 'I am glad you are come, Sir Thomas; the sooner you get on horseback the better: no time is to be lost. You will take the command of the troops in advance. The Prince of Orange knows by this time that you will go to his assistance.'[1] Picton appeared not to like the duke's manner; for when he bowed and left, he muttered a few words, which convinced those who were with him that he was not much pleased with his interview.

QUATRE BRAS

I got upon the best of my two horses, and followed Sir Thomas Picton and his staff to Quatre Bras at full speed. His division was already engaged in supporting the Prince of Orange, and had deployed itself in two lines in front of the road to Sombref when he arrived. Sir Thomas immediately took the command.

Ney[2] was very strong in cavalry, and our men were constantly formed into squares to receive them. The famous Kellerman, the hero of Marengo, tried a last charge, and was very nearly being taken or killed, as his horse was shot under him when very near us.[3] Wellington at last took the offensive; – a charge was made against the French, which succeeded, and we remained masters of the field. I acted as a mere spectator, and got, on one occasion, just within twenty or thirty yards of some of the cuirassiers; but my horse was too quick for them.

On the 17th, Wellington retreated upon Waterloo, about eleven o'clock. The infantry were masked by the cavalry in two lines, parallel to the Namur road. Our cavalry retired on the approach of the French

[1] Prince William of Orange, later William II, King of Holland (1792–1849). At the age of twenty-two he commanded the Dutch troops at Waterloo, where he did not distinguish himself. An unprepossessing young man, frail and sallow, he adopted an excessively hearty manner, drank too much and shook people by the hand with intemperate vigour. The Prince Regent hoped for a time that his daughter would marry him. He became King of The Netherlands on his father's abdication in 1840.

[2] Marshal Michel Ney, duc d'Elchingen and prince de la Moskowa (1769–1815). The son of a cooper, he was Napoleon's most celebrated though not always reliable marshal. He tried to escape from France after the restoration of the monarchy but was arrested and executed.

[3] This is not the great François-Christophe Kellerman, duc de Valmy, but his son François-Étienne Kellerman, one of Napoleon's best young cavalry officers. His charge at Marengo on 14 June 1800 was decisive: 'North Italy was recovered in that moment for the French Republic.'

cavalry, in three columns, on the Brussels road. A torrent of rain fell, upon the emperor's ordering the heavy cavalry to charge us; while the fire of sixty or eighty pieces of cannon showed that we had chosen our position at Waterloo. Chambers said to me, 'Now, Gronow, the loss has been very severe in the Guards, and I think you ought to go and see whether you are wanted; for, as you have really nothing to do with Picton, you had better join your regiment, or you may get into a scrape.' Taking his advice, I rode off to where the Guards were stationed. The officers expressed their astonishment and amazement on seeing me, and exclaimed, 'What the deuce brought you here? Why are you not with your battalion in London? Get off your horse, and explain how you came here?'

Things were beginning to look a little awkward, when the adjutant, a great friend of mine, took my part and said, 'As he is here, let us make the most of him: there's plenty of work for every one. Come, Gronow, you shall go with a detachment to the village of Waterloo, to take charge of the French prisoners.' 'What the deuce shall I do with my horse?' I asked. Upon which Captain Stopford, aide-de-camp to Sir John Byng, volunteered to buy him.[1] Having thus once more become a foot soldier, I started according to orders, and arrived at Waterloo.

GENERAL APPEARANCE OF THE FIELD OF WATERLOO

The day on which the battle of Waterloo was fought seemed to have been chosen by some providential accident for which human wisdom is unable to account. On the morning of the 18th the sun shone most gloriously, and so clear was the atmosphere that we could see the long, imposing lines of the enemy most distinctly. Immediately in front of the division to which I belonged, and, I should imagine, about half a mile from us, were posted cavalry and artillery; and to the right and left the French had already engaged us, attacking Huguemont and La Haye Sainte. We heard incessantly the measured boom of artillery, accompanied by the incessant rattling echoes of musketry.

The whole of the British infantry not actually engaged were at that time formed into squares; and as you looked along our lines, it seemed as if we formed a continuous wall of human beings. I recollect distinctly being able to see Bonaparte and his staff; and some of my brother officers using the glass, exclaimed, 'There he is on his white horse.' I should not

---

[1] Sir John Byng, Earl of Strafford (1772-1860), a grandson of Admiral Sir George Byng. He commanded the 2nd Brigade of Guards division at Waterloo.

forget to state that when the enemy's artillery began to play on us, we
had orders to lie down: we could hear the shot and shell whistling
around us, killing and wounding great numbers; then again we were
ordered on our knees to receive cavalry. The French artillery, which
consisted of three hundred guns, – we did not muster more than half
that number, – committed terrible havoc during the early part of the
battle, whilst we were acting on the defensive.

THE DUKE OF WELLINGTON IN OUR SQUARE

About four p.m. the enemy's artillery in front of us ceased firing all of a
sudden, and we saw large masses of cavalry advance: not a man present
who survived could have forgotten in after life the awful grandeur of
that charge. You perceived at a distance what appeared to be an
overwhelming, long moving line, which, ever advancing, glittered like
a stormy wave of the sea when it catches the sunlight. On came the
mounted host until they got near enough, whilst the very earth seemed
to vibrate beneath their thundering tramp. One might suppose that
nothing could have resisted the shock of this terrible moving mass. They
were the famous cuirassiers, almost all old soldiers, who had distinguished themselves on most of the battle-fields of Europe. In an almost
incredibly short period they were within twenty yards of us, shouting
'*Vive l'Empereur!*' The word of command, 'Prepare to receive cavalry,'
had been given, every man in the front ranks knelt, and a wall bristling
with steel, held together by steady hands, presented itself to the
infuriated cuirassiers.

I should observe that just before this charge the duke entered by one
of the angles of the square, accompanied only by one aide-de-camp; all
the rest of his staff being either killed or wounded. Our Commander-in-
Chief, as far as I could judge, appeared perfectly composed; but looked
very thoughtful and pale. He was dressed in a grey great-coat with a
cape, white cravat, leather pantaloons, Hessian boots, and a large
cocked hat *à la Russe.*

The charge of the French cavalry was gallantly executed; but our
well-directed fire brought men and horses down, and ere long the
utmost confusion arose in their ranks. The officers were exceedingly
brave, and by their gestures and fearless bearing did all in their power
to encourage their men to form again and renew the attack. The duke
sat unmoved, mounted on his favourite charger. I recollect his asking
Colonel [James] Stanhope [one of his aides-de-camp] what o'clock it
was, upon which Stanhope took out his watch, and said it was twenty

minutes past four. The Duke replied, 'The battle is mine; and if the Prussians arrive soon, there will be an end of the war.'

THE FRENCH CAVALRY CHARGING THE BRUNSWICKERS

Soon after the cuirassiers had retired, we observed to our right the red hussars of the Garde Impériale charging a square of Brunswick riflemen, who were about fifty yards from us. This charge was brilliantly executed, but the well-sustained fire from the square baffled the enemy, who were obliged to retire after suffering a severe loss in killed and wounded. The ground was completely covered with those brave men, who lay in various positions, mutilated in every conceivable way. Among the fallen we perceived the gallant colonel of the hussars lying under his horse, which had been killed. All of a sudden two riflemen of the Brunswickers left their battalion, and after taking from their helpless victim his purse, watch, and other articles of value, they deliberately put the colonel's pistols to the poor fellow's head, and blew out his brains. 'Shame! shame!' was heard from our ranks, and a feeling of indignation ran through the whole line; but the deed was done: this brave soldier lay a lifeless corpse in sight of his cruel foes, whose only excuse perhaps was that their sovereign, the Duke of Brunswick, had been killed two days before by the French.[1]

Again and again various cavalry regiments, heavy dragoons, lancers, hussars, carabineers of the Guard, endeavoured to break our walls of steel. The enemy's cavalry had to advance over ground which was so heavy that they could not reach us except at a trot; they therefore came upon us in a much more compact mass than they probably would have done if the ground had been more favourable. When they got within ten or fifteen yards they discharged their carbines, to the cry of 'Vive l'Empereur!' but their fire produced little effect, as is generally the case with the fire of cavalry. Our men had orders not to fire unless they could do so on a near mass; the object being to economise our ammunition, and not to waste it on scattered soldiers. The result was, that when the cavalry had discharged their carbines, and were still far off, we occasionally stood face to face, looking at each other inactively, not knowing what the next move might be.

The lancers were particularly troublesome, and approached us with the utmost daring. On one occasion I remember, the enemy's artillery

---

[1] Friedrich Wilhelm, Duke of Brunswick (1771–1815). He had come to England in 1809 after the battle of Wagram and entered the British service.

having made a gap in the square, the lancers were evidently waiting to avail themselves of it, to rush among us, when Colonel Staples, at once observing their intention, with the utmost promptness filled up the gap, and thus again completed our impregnable steel wall; but in this act he fell mortally wounded. The cavalry seeing this, made no attempt to carry out their original intentions, and observing that we had entirely regained our square, confined themselves to hovering round us. I must not forget to mention that the lancers in particular never failed to despatch our wounded, whenever they had an opportunity of doing so.

When we received cavalry, the order was to fire low; so that on the first discharge of musketry, the ground was strewed with the fallen horses and their riders, which impeded the advance of those behind them, and broke the shock of the charge. It was pitiable to witness the agony of the poor horses, which really seemed conscious of the dangers that surrounded them: we often saw a poor wounded animal raise its head, as if looking for its rider to afford him aid. There is nothing perhaps amongst the episodes of a great battle more striking than the *débris* of a cavalry charge, where men and horses are seen scattered and wounded on the ground in every variety of painful attitude. Many a time the heart sickened at the moaning tones of agony which came from man, and scarcely less intelligent horse, as they lay in fearful agony upon the field of battle.

THE LAST CHARGE AT WATERLOO

It was about five o'clock on that memorable day, that we suddenly received orders to retire behind an elevation in our rear. The enemy's artillery had come up *en masse* within a hundred yards of us. By the time they began to discharge their guns, however, we were lying down behind the rising ground, and protected by the ridge before referred to. The enemy's cavalry was in the rear of their artillery, in order to be ready to protect it if attacked; but no attempt was made on our part to do so. After they had pounded away at us for about half-an-hour, they deployed, and up came the whole mass of the Imperial infantry of the Guard, led on by the emperor in person. We had now before us probably about 20,000 of the best soldiers in France, the heroes of many memorable victories; we saw the bear-skin caps rising higher and higher, as they ascended the ridge of ground which separated us and advanced nearer and nearer to our lines.

It was at this moment that the Duke of Wellington gave his famous order for our bayonet charge, as he rode along the line: these are the precise words he made use of – 'Guards, get up and charge!'[1] We were instantly on our legs, and after so many hours of inaction and irritation at maintaining a purely defensive attitude, – all the time suffering the loss of comrades and friends, – the spirit which animated officers and men may easily be imagined. After firing a volley as soon as the enemy were within shot, we rushed on with fixed bayonets, and that hearty hurrah peculiar to British soldiers.

It appeared that our men, deliberately and with calculation, singled out their victims; for as they came upon the Imperial Guard our line broke, and the fighting became irregular. The impetuosity of our men seemed almost to paralyse their enemies: I witnessed several of the Imperial Guard who were run through the body apparently without any resistance on their parts. I observed a big Welshman of the name of Hughes, who was six feet seven inches in height, run through with his bayonet, and knock down with the butt-end of his firelock, I should think a dozen at least of his opponents. This terrible contest did not last more than ten minutes, for the Imperial Guard was soon in full retreat, leaving all their guns and many prisoners in our hands.

Hougoumont

Early on the morning after the battle of Waterloo, I visited Hougoumont, in order to witness with my own eyes the traces of one of the most hotly-contested spots of the field of battle. I came first upon the orchard, and there discovered heaps of dead men, in various uniforms: those of the Guards in their usual red jackets, the German Legion in green, and the French dressed in blue, mingled together. The dead and the wounded positively covered the whole area of the orchard; not less than two thousand men had there fallen. The apple-trees presented a singular appearance; shattered branches were seen hanging about their mother-trunks in such profusion, that one might almost suppose the stiff-growing and stunted tree had been converted into the willow: every tree was riddled and smashed in a manner which told that the showers of shot had been incessant. On this spot I lost some of my dearest and bravest friends, and the country had to mourn many of its most heroic sons slain here.

---

[1] Wellington is commonly supposed to have said, 'Up Guards and at them again!' When asked about this by J. W. Croker, the Duke replied, 'What I must have said and possibly did say was "Stand up Guards!" and then gave the commanding officers the orders to advance.'

I must observe that, according to the custom of commanding-officers, whose business it is after a great battle to report to the Commander-in-Chief, the muster-roll of fame always closes before the rank of captain. It has always appeared to me a great injustice that there should ever be any limit to the roll of gallantry of either officers or men. If a captain, lieutenant, an ensign, a sergeant, or a private, has distinguished himself for his bravery, his intelligence, or both, their deeds ought to be reported, in order that the sovereign and nation should know who really fight the great battles of England. Of the class of officers and men to which I have referred, there were many even of superior rank who were omitted to be mentioned in the public despatches.

AFTER QUATRE BRAS

I mentioned in a previous page that on my arrival to join my regiment, I was immediately sent to the village of Waterloo, with a detachment, under Captain [Robert] Clements, brother of Lord Leitrim, to take charge of some hundreds of French prisoners. They had been taken at Quatre Bras, and were confined in a barn and the courtyard of a large farm-house. As ill-luck would have it, Clements did not place sentinels on the other side of the wall, which overlooked the plain leading to the forest of Soignies; the consequence was, that with the aid of a large waggon, which had been left in the yard, several of the prisoners scaled the wall, and made their escape. As soon as it was night, some more poor fellows attempted to follow their example; but this time the alarm was given, and our men fired and killed or wounded a dozen of them.

This firing at so late an hour brought several officers of the staff from the neighbouring houses to ascertain the cause, and among them came my poor friend Chambers, who kindly invited me to Sir Thomas Picton's quarters to supper. I accompanied him thither, and after groping our way into the house, for it was very dark, we passed the door of a room in which Sir Thomas himself was lying. I heard him groan, from the pain of the wound he had received at Quatre Bras, but did not of course venture to disturb him, and we passed on into a small hall, where I got some cold meat and wine.

THE BATTLE OF WATERLOO

At daylight, on the 18th, we were agreeably surprised to see a detachment of the 3d Guards, commanded by Captain Wigston and Ensign George Anson, the lamented General who died in India, who had been sent to relieve us.[1] I took the opportunity of giving Anson, then a fine lad of seventeen, a silver watch, made by Barwise, which his mother, Lady Anson, had requested me to take over to him. Bob Clements and I then proceeded to join our regiment.

The road was ankle-deep in mud and slough; and we had not proceeded a quarter of a mile when we heard the trampling of horses' feet, and on looking round perceived a large cavalcade of officers coming at full speed. In a moment we recognised the Duke himself at the head. He was accompanied by the Duke of Richmond, and his son, Lord William Lennox.[2] The entire staff of the army was close at hand. They all seemed as gay and unconcerned as if they were riding to meet the hounds in some quiet English county.

In about half-an-hour we joined our comrades in camp, who were endeavouring to dry their accoutrements by the morning sun, after a night of rain and discomfort in their bivouac. I was now greeted by many of my old friends (whom I had not had time to speak to the day before, when I was sent off to the village of Waterloo) with loud cries of 'How are you, old fellow? Take a glass of wine and a bit of ham? it will perhaps be your last breakfast.' Then Burges called out, 'Come here, Gronow, and tell us some London news.'

He had made himself a sort of gipsy-tent, with the aid of some blankets, a sergeant's halberd, and a couple of muskets. My dear old friend was sitting upon a knapsack, with Colonel Stuart (who afterwards lost his arm), eating cold pie and drinking champagne, which his servant had just brought from Brussels. I was not sorry to partake of his hospitality, and after talking together some time, we were aroused by the drums beating to arms. We fell in, and the muster-roll having been called, the piling of arms followed; but we were not allowed to leave our places.

The position taken up by the British army was an excellent one: it was a sort of ridge, very favourable for artillery, and from which all the movements of the French could be discerned. In case of any disaster, Wellington had several roads in his rear by which a masterly retreat

[1] Hon. George Anson (1797–1857), second son of the first Viscount Anson, became commander-in-chief in India in 1856. He died of cholera shortly after the outbreak of the Indian Mutiny.
[2] Lord William Lennox (1799–1881), fourth son of the fourth Duke of Richmond and a cousin of Charles James Fox. After Waterloo he served as one of Wellington's aides-de-camp for three years. Disraeli portrayed him as Lord Prima Donna in *Vivian Gray*. He wrote a number of bad novels and various volumes of reminiscences.

could have been effected through the forest on Brussels; but our glorious commander thought little about retreating: on the contrary, he set all his energies to work, and determined to win the day.

We occupied the right centre of the British line, and had the château of Hougoumont at about a quarter of a mile's distance on our right. Picton was on the extreme left at La Haye Sainte, with his division of two British and one Hanoverian brigades. Hougoumont was garrisoned by the 2d and 3d regiments of the Guards, a battalion of Germans, and two battalions of artillery, who occupied the château and gardens. Between each regiment was a battery of guns, and nearly the whole of the cavalry was to the left of Sir Thomas Picton's division.

About half-past eleven the bands of several French regiments were distinctly heard, and soon after the French artillery opened fire. The rapid beating of the *pas de charge*, which I had often heard in Spain – and which few men, however brave they may be, can listen to without a somewhat unpleasant sensation – announced that the enemy's columns were fast approaching. On our side the most profound silence prevailed, whilst the French, on the contrary, raised loud shouts, and we heard the cry of '*Vive l'Empereur!*' from one end of their line to the other.

The battle commenced by the French throwing out clouds of skirmishers from Hougoumont to La Haye Sainte. Jérôme Bonaparte's division[1] attacked Hougoumont, the wood and garden of which were taken and retaken several times; but, after prodigies of valour performed on both sides, remained in the hands of the French: who, however, sustained immense loss, and the château still belonged to the invincible English Guards.

Whilst the battle was raging in the wood and orchard, eighty French guns, mostly twelve-pounders, opened upon us, and caused a heavy loss in our ranks. At the same moment, we could perceive from our elevated position that the enemy were attacking La Haye Sainte in great force. At about two o'clock, Ney, with the first corps formed in four columns, advanced *en échelon* the left wing forward. They completely defeated and put to flight a Dutch-Belgian brigade, and then attacked Picton's division. He, however, made a desperate resistance, and charged them several times, though they were four times his number. It was then that noble soldier was killed by a musket-ball. Things looked ill there; when

---

[1] Jérôme Bonaparte (1784–1860), Napoleon's youngest brother, was made King of Westphalia in 1807. He commanded a division on the French left. After Napoleon III's *coup d'état* he became a Marshal of France and President of the Senate.

the Duke ordered up Adam's brigade, which regained the ground, and pushed eagerly forward.[1]

At the same time Lord Uxbridge commanded the cavalry to charge.[2] This order was admirably executed by Somerset[3] on one side, and by Ponsonby on the other, and was for a time completely successful.

[Three] French infantry brigades were rolled up and almost annihilated; twenty guns were dismantled or spiked, and many hundred prisoners taken; several squadrons of cuirassiers were also charged and put to the rout. Unfortunately our cavalry went too far without proper supports, and were charged and driven back by heavy cavalry and lancers, and had to take refuge behind our own lines. Ney now received orders to attack La Haye Sainte, which was taken about four o'clock. At the same hour Bulow's first columns made their appearance, and attacked.[4]

The Guards had what in modern battues is called a hot corner of it, and the greatest 'gluttons' (and we had many such) must have allowed, when night came on, that they had had fighting enough. I confess that I am to this day astonished that any of us remained alive. From eleven o'clock till seven we were pounded with shot and shell at long and short range, were incessantly potted at by tirailleurs who kept up a most biting fire, constantly charged by immense masses of cavalry who seemed determined to go in and win, preceded as their visits were by a terrific fire of artillery; and, last of all, we were attacked by '*la Vieille Garde*' itself. But here we came to the end of our long and fiery ordeal. The French veterans, conspicuous by their high bearskin caps and lofty stature, on breasting the ridge behind which we were at that time, were met by a fearful fire of artillery and musketry, which swept away whole masses of those valiant soldiers; and, while in disorder, they were charged by us with complete success, and driven in utter rout and discomfiture down the ravine. The Prussians having now arrived in force on the French right, a general advance of the whole line was ordered, and the day was won.

During the battle our squares presented a shocking sight. Inside we

[1] Major-General Sir Frederick Adam (1781-1853). He commanded a brigade in Lord Hill's division.

[2] Henry William Paget (see note, p. 5).

[3] Lord (Robert) Edward Somerset (1776-1842), elder brother of Lord Fitzroy Somerset, commander of the household brigade of cavalry. He became inspector general of cavalry after the war and was promoted general in 1841.

[4] Friedrich Wilhelm, Freiherr von Bülow (1755-1816), commanded the Prussian IV Corps at Waterloo.

were nearly suffocated by the smoke and smell from burnt cartridges. It was impossible to move a yard without treading upon a wounded comrade, or upon the bodies of the dead; and the loud groans of the wounded and dying were most appalling.

At four o'clock our square was a perfect hospital, being full of dead, dying, and mutilated soldiers. The charges of cavalry were in appearance very formidable, but in reality a great relief, as the artillery could no longer fire on us; the very earth shook under the enormous mass of men and horses. I never shall forget the strange noise our bullets made against the breastplates of Kellermann's and Milhaud's cuirassiers, six or seven thousand in number, who attacked us with great fury. I can only compare it, with a somewhat homely simile, to the noise of a violent hail-storm beating upon panes of glass.

The artillery did great execution, but our musketry did not at first seem to kill many men; though it brought down a large number of horses, and created indescribable confusion. The horses of the first rank of cuirassiers, in spite of all the efforts of their riders, came to a stand-still, shaking and covered with foam, at about twenty yards' distance from our squares, and generally resisted all attempts to force them to charge the line of serried steel. Nothing could be more gallant than the behaviour of those veterans, many of whom had distinguished themselves on half the battle-fields of Europe.

In the midst of our terrible fire, their officers were seen as if on parade, keeping order in their ranks, and encouraging them. Unable to renew the charge, but unwilling to retreat, they brandished their swords with loud cries of '*Vive l'Empereur!*' and allowed themselves to be mowed down by hundreds rather than yield. Our men, who shot them down, could not help admiring the gallant bearing and heroic resignation of their enemies.

PERCIVAL, OF THE 1ST GUARDS

The wound which Captain Percival received was one of the most painful it ever fell to a soldier's lot to bear. He received a ball which carried away all his teeth and both his jaws, and left nothing on the mouth but the skin of the cheeks. Percival recovered sufficiently to join our regiment in the Tower, three years subsequent to the battle of Waterloo. He had to be fed with porridge and a few spoonfuls of broth; but notwithstanding all the care to preserve his life, he sunk from inanition, and died very shortly after, his body presenting the appearance of a skeleton.

Captain, afterwards Colonel [Edward] Kelly of the Life Guards, and our Cavalry Charges

This chivalrous man, of undaunted courage and very powerful frame, in the deadly encounter with the cuirassiers of the Imperial Guard, performed prodigies of valour.

In the gallant and, for a time, successful charge of the Household Brigade, he greatly distinguished himself; and when our gallant fellows, after sustaining a terrible fire of artillery, were attacked by an overwhelming force of French cavalry, and were forced to retreat behind our squares, Kelly was seen cutting his way through a host of enemies. Shaw, the famous prize-fighter, a private in his regiment, came to his assistance, and these two heroes fought side by side, killing or disabling many of their antagonists, till poor Shaw, after receiving several wounds, was killed from a thrust through the body by a French colonel of cuirassiers, who in his turn received a blow from Kelly's sword, which cut through his helmet and stretched him lifeless upon the ground.[1]

I recollect questioning my friend Kelly about this celebrated charge, at our mess at Windsor in 1816, when he said that he owed his life to the excellence of his charger, which was well bred, very well broke, and of immense power. He thought that with an ordinary horse he would have been killed a hundred times in the numerous encounters which he had to sustain.

Meeting of Wellington and Blücher[2]

After our final charge, and the retreat of the French army, we arrived and bivouacked about nine o'clock in the orchard of the farm of La Belle Alliance, about a hundred yards from the farmhouse where Napoleon had remained for some hours. We were presently disturbed by the sound of trumpets; I immediately hurried off, in company with several other officers, and found that the sound proceeded from a Prussian cavalry regiment with Blücher at its head. The Duke of Wellington, who had given rendezvous to Blücher at this spot, then rode up, and the two victorious Generals shook hands in the most cordial and hearty manner. After a short conversation, our chief rode off to Brussels, while

---

[1] Jack Shaw (1780–1815), a pugilist of enormous strength. He killed ten cuirassiers before being cut down himself.

[2] Gebhard Leberecht, Fürst Blücher von Wahlstatt (1742–1819), Prussian commander-in-chief.

Blücher and the Prussians joined their own army, which, under General Gneisenau, was already in hot pursuit of the French.[1] After this I entered the farmhouse where Napoleon had passed part of the day. The furniture had to all appearance been destroyed, but I found an immense fire made of a wooden bedstead and the legs of chairs, which appeared by the embers to have been burning for a considerable length of time.

SUFFERINGS OF THE WOUNDED

On the following morning, we had not advanced for many minutes before we met some of our gallant companions in arms who had been wounded. They were lying in waggons of the country, and had been abandoned by the drivers. Some of these poor fellows belonged to our regiment, and, on passing close to one of the waggons, a man cried out, 'For God's sake, Mr Gronow, give us some water or we shall go mad.' I did not hesitate for a moment, but jumped into the cart, and gave the poor fellow all the water my flask contained. The other wounded soldiers then entreated me to fill it with some muddy water which they had descried in a neighbouring ditch, half filled by the rain of the preceding day. As I thought a flask would be of little use among so many, I took off my shako, and having first stopped up with my belcher handkerchief[2] a hole which a musket ball had made in the top of it, filled it with water several times for these poor fellows, who were all too severely wounded to have got it for themselves, and who drank it off with tears of delight.

EXCESSES OF THE PRUSSIANS

We perceived, on entering France, that our allies the Prussians had committed fearful atrocities on the defenceless inhabitants of the villages and farms which lay in their line of march. Before we left La Belle Alliance, I had already seen the brutality of some of the Prussian infantry, who hacked and cut up, in a most savage manner, all the cows and pigs which were in the farmyards; placing upon their bayonets the still quivering flesh, and roasting it on the coals. On our line of march, whenever we arrived at towns or villages through which the Prussians

[1] August Wilhelm Anton, Graf Neithardt von Gneisenau (1760–1831), Marshal Blücher's chief of staff.

[2] A spotted handkerchief, usually one with white or yellow spots on a blue ground, worn around the neck. It was named after Jim Belcher, a well-known Regency pugilist who died in 1811.

had passed, we found that every article of furniture in the houses had been destroyed in the most wanton manner: looking-glasses, mahogany bedsteads, pictures, beds and mattresses, had been hacked, cut, half-burned, and scattered about in every direction; and, on the slightest remonstrance of the wretched inhabitants, they were beaten in a most shameful manner, and sometimes shot.

PÉRONNE LA PUCELLE

The fourth or fifth day after Waterloo, we arrived before Péronne la Pucelle, (the Virgin town), as the inhabitants delighted to call it; for they boasted that it had never been taken by an enemy. The Duke of Wellington suddenly made his appearance in our bivouac, and gave orders that we should, at all risks, take Péronne before night. We accordingly prepared for action, and commenced proceedings by battering the gates with a strong fire of artillery. The guns of the Virgin fortress returned the compliment, and the first shot from the town fell under the belly of the Duke's horse; but, beyond knocking the gravel and stones about in all directions, did no injury.

The garrison consisted of fifteen hundred National Guards, who had sworn never to surrender to mortal man; but when these ardent volunteers saw our red-coats coming in with a rush, and with a grim determination to take no denial, they wisely laid down their arms and capitulated. Our loss, on this occasion, amounted to nine killed and thirty wounded. Lord Saltoun had a narrow escape;[1] a ball struck him on his breeches-pocket, where half-a-dozen five-franc pieces broke the force of the blow: Saltoun, though not very Buonapartist in his opinions, retained the mark of the Emperor's effigy on his thigh for some time; and though not returned as wounded, suffered great pain for several days after.

SIR FREDERICK PONSONBY

This gallant and excellent cavalry officer,[2] who greatly distinguished himself at Talavera, and many other actions in Spain, was the son of

[1] Alexander George Fraser, sixteenth Baron Saltoun (1785–1853). He commanded the light companies of the 2nd brigade of Guards. He had four horses shot under him at Waterloo where his defence of the orchards and garden of Hougoumont became a legend of heroism. He later became commander-in-chief of the forces in China after the Opium War.

[2] See note, p. 60.

Lord Bessborough, and a distant cousin of Sir William Ponsonby who was killed. He commanded the 12th Light Dragoons and made a brilliant charge right through a French brigade and rolled up part of Jacquinot's Lancers, who were in pursuit of the remnant of the Union Brigade.[1] In this most gallant affair he was struck from his horse by several sabre cuts, run through the body by a lancer as he lay upon the ground, and trampled on by large bodies of cavalry. Ponsonby always considered that he owed his life to a French field-officer who had brought up some troops to the spot where he lay, had given him a draught of brandy from his flask, and directed one of his men to wrap him in a cloak, and place a knapsack under his head.

It is pleasant to think that Ponsonby became acquainted, many years afterwards, with his preserver. The Baron de Laussat, formerly deputy for his department, the Basses Pyrenées, and a gentleman universally respected and beloved by all who knew him, was at this time a major in the dragoons of the Imperial Guard. After he had quitted the army he travelled in the East for some years, and on his return, when at Malta, was introduced to Sir F. Ponsonby, then a Major-General and Governor of the island. In the course of conversation, the battle of Waterloo was discussed; and on Ponsonby recounting his many narrow escapes, and the kind treatment he had received from the French officer, M. de Laussat said, 'Was he not in such-and-such a uniform?' 'He was,' said Sir F. 'And did he not say so-and-so to you, and was not the cloak of such-and-such a colour?' 'I remember it perfectly,' was the answer. Several other details were entered into, which I now forget, but which left no doubt upon Ponsonby's mind that he saw before him the man to whom he owed his life.

Narrow Escapes – Reception in London

When we were lying down in square to present a rather less fair mark to the French artillery, which had got very near us, and had caused immense loss in our ranks, a cannon ball struck the ground close to Algernon Greville and myself, without injuring either of us.[2] At the end of the day, I found that a grapeshot had gone through the top of my

[1] The Union Brigade was so called because it comprised an English, a Scottish and an Irish regiment – the Royals, the Scots Greys and the Inniskillings. The Union of Great Britain and Ireland had been enacted on 7 August 1800.

[2] Algernon Frederick Greville (1798–1864), the brother of Charles Greville and Henry Greville, the diarists, then a young subaltern in Gronow's regiment, was aide-de-camp and in 1827 private secretary to the Duke of Wellington.

shako, and one of my coat-tails had been shot off. I got leave to go to England to join my battalion after we had been in Paris about a fortnight; and I never shall forget the reception I met with as I dashed up in a chaise and four to the door of Fenton's Hotel in St James's Street. Very few men from the army had yet arrived in London, and a mob of about a thousand people gathered round the door as I got out in my old, weather-beaten uniform, shaking hands with me, and uttering loud cheers. I also recollect the capital English dinner old James, the well-known waiter, had provided to celebrate my return. '*Ce sont les beaux jours de la vie,*' few and far between in our chequered existence, and I confess that my memory wanders back to them with pleasure, and some regret to think that they can never more return.

8

Paris After the War

APPEARANCE OF PARIS WHEN THE ALLIES ENTERED

I propose giving my own impression of the aspect of Paris and its vicinity when our regiment entered that city on the 25th of June 1815. I recollect we marched from the plain of St Denis, my battalion being about five hundred strong, the survivors of the heroic fight of the 18th of June. We approached near enough to be within fire of the batteries of Montmartre, and bivouacked for three weeks in the Bois de Boulogne. That now beautiful garden was at the period to which I refer a wild pathless wood, swampy, and entirely neglected. The Prussians, who were in bivouac near us, amused themselves by doing as much damage as they could, without any useful aim or object: they cut down the finest trees, and set the wood on fire at several points. There were about three thousand of the Guards then encamped in the wood, and I should think about ten thousand Prussians. Our camp was not remarkable for its courtesy towards them; in fact, our intercourse was confined to the most ordinary demands of duty, as allies in an enemy's country.

I believe I was one of the first of the British army who penetrated into the heart of Paris after Waterloo. I entered by the Porte Maillot, and passed the Arc de Triomphe, which was then building. In those days the Champs Elysées only contained a few scattered houses, and the roads and pathways were ankle-deep in mud. The only attempt at lighting was the suspension of a few lamps on cords, which crossed the roads.

Here I found the Scotch regiments bivouacking; their peculiar uniform created a considerable sensation amongst the Parisian women, who did not hesitate to declare that the want of *culottes* was most indecent. I passed through the camp, and proceeded on towards the gardens of the Tuileries. This ancient palace of the kings of France presented, so far as the old front is concerned, the same aspect that it does at the present day; but there were then no flower-gardens, although the same stately rows of trees which now ornament the grounds were then in their midsummer verdure.

Being in uniform, I created an immense amount of curiosity amongst the Parisians; who, by the way, I fancied regarded me with no loving looks. The first house I entered was a café in the garden of the Tuileries, called Legac's. I there met a man who told me he was by descent an Englishman, though he had been born in Paris, and had really never quitted France. He approached me, saying, 'Sir, I am delighted to see an English officer in Paris, and you are the first I have yet met with.' He talked about the battle of Waterloo, and gave me some useful directions concerning restaurants and cafés. Along the Boulevards were handsome houses, isolated, with gardens interspersed, and the roads were bordered on both sides with stately, spreading trees, some of them probably a hundred years old. There was but an imperfect pavement, the stepping-stones of which were adapted to display the Parisian female ankle and boot in all their calculated coquetry; and the road showed nothing but mother earth, in the middle of which a dirty gutter served to convey the impurities of the city to the river. The people in the streets appeared sulky and stupified: here and there I noticed groups of the higher classes evidently discussing the events of the moment.

How strange humanity would look in our day in the costume of the first empire. The ladies wore very scanty and short skirts, which left little or no waist; their bonnets were of exaggerated proportions, and protruded at least a foot from their faces; and they generally carried a fan. The men wore blue or black coats, which were baggily made, and reached down to their ankles; their hats were enormously large, and spread out at the top.

I dined the first day of my entrance into Paris at the Café Anglais, on the Boulevard des Italiens; where I found, to my surprise, several of my brother officers. I recollect the charge for the dinner was about one-third what it would be at the present day. I had a potage, fish – anything but fresh, and, according to English predilections and taste, of course I ordered a beef-steak and *pommes de terre*. The wine, I thought, was sour. The dinner cost about two francs.

The theatres at this time, as may easily be imagined, were not very well attended. I recollect going to the Française, where I saw for the first time the famous Talma.[1] There was but a scanty audience; in fact, all the best places in the house were empty.

It may easily be imagined that, at a moment like this, most of those who had a stake in the country were pondering over the great and real drama that was then taking place. Napoleon had fled to Rochfort; the wreck of his army had retreated beyond the Loire; no list of killed and wounded had appeared; and, strange to say, the official journal of Paris had made out that the great imperial army at Waterloo had gained a victory. There were, nevertheless, hundreds of people in Paris who knew to the contrary, and many were already aware that they had lost relations and friends in the great battle.

Louis XVIII arrived, as well as I can remember, at the Tuileries on the 26th of July 1815,[2] and his reception by the Parisians was a singular illustration of the versatile character of the French nation, and the sudden and often inexplicable changes which take place in the feeling of the populace. When the Bourbon, in his old lumbering state-carriage, drove down the Boulevards, accompanied by the Gardes du Corps, the people in the streets and at the windows displayed the wildest joy, enthusiastically shouting '*Vive le Roi!*' amidst the waving of hats and handkerchiefs, while white sheets or white rags were made to do the duty of a Bourbon banner. The king was dressed in a blue coat with a red collar, and wore also a white waistcoat, and a cocked hat with a white cockade in it. His portly and good-natured appearance seemed to be appreciated by the crowd, whom he saluted with a benevolent smile. I should here mention that two great devotees of the Church sat opposite to the King on this memorable occasion. The *cortège* proceeded slowly down the Rue de la Paix until the Tuileries was reached, where a company of the Guards, together with a certain number of the Garde Nationale of Paris, were stationed.

It fell to my lot to be on duty the day after, when the Duke of

---

[1] François-Joseph Talma (1763-1826), the most celebrated tragedian of his day. He had made his professional debut at the Comédie Française in 1787.

[2] Louis XVIII (1755-1824) was the fourth son of the Dauphin, Louis, son of Louis XV. He fled Paris when Napoleon returned from Elba, then re-entered the city on the 8 July 1815, 'in the baggage train of the Allied armies', as his enemies put it. He was, however, well received.

Wellington and Lord Castlereagh[1] arrived to pay their respects to the restored monarch. I happened to be in the Salle des Maréchaux when these illustrious personages passed through that magnificent apartment. The respect paid to the Duke of Wellington on this occasion may be easily imagined, from the fact that a number of ladies of the highest rank, and of course partisans of the legitimate dynasty, formed an avenue through which the hero of Waterloo passed, exchanging with them courteous recognitions. The king was waiting in the grand reception apartment to receive the great British captain. The interview, I have every reason to believe, was not confined to the courtesies of the palace.

The position of the duke was a difficult one. In the first place, he had to curb the vindictive vandalism of Blücher and his army, who would have levelled the city of Paris to the ground, if they could have done so; on the other hand, he had to practise a considerable amount of diplomacy towards the newly-restored king. At the same time, the duke's powers from his own Government were necessarily limited. A spirit of vindictiveness pervaded the restored Court against Napoleon and his adherents, which the duke constantly endeavoured to modify.

THE PALAIS ROYAL AFTER THE RESTORATION

France has often been called the centre of European fashion and gaiety; and the Palais Royal, at the period to which I refer, might be called the very heart of French dissipation. It was a theatre in which all the great actors of fashion of all nations met to play their parts: on this spot were congregated daily an immense multitude, for no other purpose than to watch the busy comedy of real life that animated the corridors, gardens, and saloons of that vast building. Mingled together, and moving about the area of this oblong-square block of buildings, might be seen, about seven o'clock p.m., a crowd of English, Russian, Prussian, Austrian, and

[1] Robert Stewart, Viscount Castlereagh, second Marquess of Londonderry (1769–1822). As War Minister in 1805–6 and 1807–9 and Foreign Secretary from 1812, he played a large part in the events that led to Napoleon's fall. He became deranged in 1822 and at his last audience with the King he had wept, accused himself of all sorts of crimes and told him that he was being accused of homosexual practices. As a precaution, all his razors and pistols were removed from his dressing room; but making use of a little nail-knife which he carried in his pocket book, he cut his carotid artery with 'anatomical accuracy'. He was much vilified in his lifetime; Shelley's comment upon him being characteristic of the vituperation with which he was pursued: 'I met Murder in the way/He had a mask like Castlereagh.'

other officers of the Allied armies, together with countless foreigners from all parts of the world.

A description of one of the houses of the Palais Royal will serve to portray the whole of this French pandemonium. On the ground-floor is a jeweller's shop, where may be purchased diamonds, pearls, emeralds, and every description of female ornament, such as only can be possessed by those who have very large sums of money at their command. It was here that the successful gambler often deposited a portion of his winnings, and took away some costly article of jewellery, which he presented to some female friend who had never appeared with him at the altar of marriage. Beside this shop was a staircase, generally very dirty, which communicated with the floors above. Immediately over the shop was a café, at the counter of which presided a lady, generally of more than ordinary female attractions, who was very much *décolletée*, and wore an amount of jewellery which would have made the eye of an Israelite twinkle with delight. And there *la crème de la crème* of male society used to meet, sip their ice and drink their cup of mocha, whilst holding long conversations, almost exclusively about gambling and women.

Men's thoughts, in this region, seemed to centre night and day upon the *tapis vert*, and at the entrance of this *salon* was that fatal chamber, over which might have been written the famous line of Dante, '*Voi che entrate lasciate ogni speranza.*'[1] The reader will at once understand that I am referring to the gambling-house, the so-called 'hell' of modern society. In one room was the *rouge-et-noir* table, which, from the hour of twelve in the morning, was surrounded by men in every stage of the gambling malady. There was the young pigeon, who, on losing his first feather, had experienced an exciting sensation which, if followed by a bit of good luck, gave him a confidence that the parasites around him, in order to flatter his vanity, would call pluck. There were others in a more advanced stage of the fever, who had long since lost the greater part of their incomes, having mortgaged their property, and been in too frequent correspondence with the Jews. These men had not got to the last stage of gambling despair, but they were so far advanced on the road to perdition that their days were clouded by perpetual anxiety, which reproduced itself in their very dreams. The gambler who has thus far advanced in his career, lives in an *inferno* of his own creation: the charms of society, the beauty of woman, the attractions of the fine arts,

---

[1] 'Abandon all hope, you who enter here' – *Divine Comedy, Inferno*, iii, 9.

and even the enjoyment of a good dinner, are to him rather a source of irritation than delight. The confirmed gamester is doing nothing less than perpetually digging a grave for his own happiness.

The third and most numerous group of men round the *tapis vert* consisted of a class most of whom had already spent their fortunes, exhausted their health, and lost their position in society, by the fatal and demoralising thirst for gold which still fascinated them. These became the hawks of the gambling table; their quick and wild-glancing eyes were constantly looking out for suitable game during the day, and leaving it where it might be bagged at night. Both at the *rouge-et-noir* table and *roulette* the same sort of company might be met with. These gambling-houses were the very fountains of immorality: they gathered together, under the most seductive circumstances, the swindler and the swindled. There were tables for all classes – the workman might play with 20 sous, or the gentleman with 10,000 francs. The law did not prevent any class from indulging in a vice that assisted to fill the coffers of the municipality of Paris.

The floor over the gambling-house was occupied by unmarried women. I will not attempt to picture some of the saddest evils of the society of large cities; but I may add that these Phrynes[1] lived in a style of splendour which can only be accounted for by the fact of their participating in the easily-earned gains of the gambling-house régime.

At that time the Palais Royal was externally the only well-lighted place in Paris. It was the rendezvous of all idlers, and especially of that particular class of ladies who lay out their attractions for the public at large. These were to be seen at all hours in full dress, their bare necks ornamented with mock diamonds and pearls; and thus decked out in all their finery, they paraded up and down, casting their eyes significantly on every side.

Some strange stories are told in connection with the gambling-houses of the Palais Royal. An officer of the Grenadier Guards came to Paris on leave of absence, took apartments here, and never left it until his time of absence had expired. On his arrival in London, one of his friends inquired whether this was true, to which he replied, 'Of course it is; for I found everything I wanted there, both for body and mind.'

---

[1] Nickname (*Greek*: toad) of an extremely rich Athenian courtesan of the fourth century BC. It is said that when she was tried on a capital charge, her defender, having failed to persuade the judges of her innocence, told her to uncover her breasts. When she did so they acquitted her without further ado.

THE ENGLISH IN PARIS AFTER THE RESTORATION OF THE BOURBONS

There is no more ordinary illusion belonging to humanity than that which enables us to discover, in the fashions of the day, an elegance and comeliness of dress which a few years after we ourselves regard as odious caricatures of costumes. Thousands of oddly-dressed English flocked to Paris immediately after the war: I remember that the burden of one of the popular songs of the day was, 'All the world's in Paris;' and our countrymen and women having so long been excluded from French modes, had adopted fashions of their own quite as remarkable and eccentric as those of the Parisians, and much less graceful. British beauties were dressed in long, straight pelisses of various colours; the body of the dress was never of the same colour as the skirt; and the bonnet was of the bee-hive shape, and very small. The characteristic of the dress of the gentleman was a coat of light blue, or snuff-colour, with brass buttons, the tail reaching nearly to the heels; a gigantic bunch of seals dangled from his fob, whilst his pantaloons were short and tight at the knees; and a spacious waistcoat, with a voluminous muslin cravat and a frilled shirt, completed the toilette. The dress of the British military, in its stiff and formal ugliness, was equally cumbrous and ludicrous.

Fox,[1] the secretary of the embassy, was an excellent man, but odd, indolent, and careless in the extreme; he was seldom seen in the daytime, unless it was either at the embassy in a state of *négligé*, or in bed. At night he used to go to the Salon des Étrangers; and, if he possessed a napoleon, it was sure to be thrown away at hazard, or *rouge et noir*. On one occasion, however, fortune favoured him in a most extraordinary manner. The late Henry Baring having recommended him to take the dicebox, Fox replied, 'I will do so for the last time, for all my money is thrown away upon this infernal table.' Fox staked all he had in his pockets; he threw in *eleven* times, breaking the bank, and taking home for his share 60,000 francs. After this, several days passed without any tidings being heard of him; but upon my calling at the embassy to get my passport *visé*, I went into his room, and saw it filled with Cashmere shawls, silk, Chantilly veils, bonnets, gloves, shoes, and other articles of ladies' dress. On my asking the purpose of all this millinery, Fox replied, in a good natured way, 'Why, my dear Gronow, it was the only means to prevent those rascals at the *salon* winning back my money.'

---

[1] Henry Stephen Fox (1791–1846), nephew of Charles James Fox and only son of General Henry Edward Fox, Charles James's younger brother.

Parisian Cafés in 1815

At the present day, Paris may be said to be a city of cafés and restaurants. The railroads and steamboats enable the rich of every quarter of the globe to reach the most attractive of all European cities with comparative economy and facility. All foreigners arriving in Paris seem by instinct to rush to the restaurateurs', where strangers may be counted by tens of thousands. It is not surprising that we find in every important street these gaudy modern *triclinia*,[1] which, I should observe, are as much frequented by a certain class of French people as by foreigners, for Paris is proverbially fond of dining out; in fact, the social intercourse may be said to take place more frequently in the public café than under the domestic roof.

In 1815, I need scarcely remark that the condition of the roads in Europe, and the enormous expense of travelling, made a visit to Paris a journey which could only be indulged in by a very limited and wealthy class of strangers. Hotels and cafés were then neither so numerous nor so splendid as at the present day. The most celebrated restaurant was that of Beauvilliers, in the Rue de Richelieu; mirrors and a little gilding were the decorative characteristics of this house, the *cuisine* was far superior to that of any restaurateur of our day, and the wines were first-rate. Beauvilliers was also celebrated for his *suprême de volaille*, and for his *côtelettes à la Soubise*. The company consisted of the most distinguished men of Paris.

Another famous dining-house was the Rocher de Cancale, in the Rue Mandar, kept by Borel, formerly one of the cooks of Napoleon. Here the *cuisine* was so refined that people were reported to have come over from England expressly for the purpose of enjoying it: indeed, Borel once showed me a list of his customers, amongst whom I found the names of Robespierre, Charles James Fox, and the Duke of Bedford. In the Palais Royal the still well-known Trois Frères Provençaux was in vogue, and frequented much by the French officers; being celebrated chiefly for its wines and its Provence dishes.

Review of the Allied Armies by the Allied Sovereigns in Paris

In July 1815, it was agreed by the sovereigns of Russia, Austria, Prussia, Bavaria, Wurtemberg, and a host of petty German powers, – who had

---

[1] From the Latin *triclinium*, a dining table with couches along three sides.

become wonderfully courageous and enthusiastically devoted to England, a few hours after the battle of Waterloo, – that a grand review
should be held on the plains of St Denis, where the whole of the allied
forces were to meet. Accordingly, at an early hour on a fine summer
morning, there were seen issuing from the various roads which centre
on the plains of St Denis, numerous English, Russian, Prussian, and
Austrian regiments of horse and foot, in heavy marching order, with
their bands playing; and finally, a mass of men, numbering not less than
two hundred thousand, took up their positions on the wide-spreading
field.

About twelve o'clock, the Duke of Wellington, commander-in-chief
of the allied army, approached, mounted on a favourite charger; and,
strange as it may appear, on his right was observed a lady in a plain
riding-habit, who was no other than Lady Shelley, the wife of the late
Sir John Shelley.[1] Immediately behind the duke followed the emperors
of Austria and Russia; the kings of Prussia, Holland, Bavaria, and
Wurtemberg; several German princes, and general officers – the whole
forming one of the most illustrious and numerous staffs ever brought
together. The Duke of Wellington, thus accompanied, took up his
position, and began manœuvring, with a facility and confidence which
elicited the admiration of all the experienced soldiers around him. Being
on duty near his grace, I had an opportunity of hearing Prince
Schwartzenberg say to the duke, 'You are the only man who can so well
play at this game.'[2] The review lasted two hours; then the men marched
home to their quarters, through a crowd of spectators which included
the whole population of Paris. The most mournful silence was observed
throughout on the part of the French.

THE BRITISH EMBASSY IN PARIS

England was represented at this period by Sir Charles Stuart,[3] who was
one of the most popular ambassadors Great Britain ever sent to Paris.
He made himself acceptable to his countrymen, and paid as much

---

[1] Frances, Lady Shelley, was one of Wellington's closest and most admiring friends. She
almost fainted with emotion on encountering him for the first time. 'He seldom speaks,' she
said, 'until he is well acquainted.' He himself feared that neither he nor his fellow
Conservative, Peel, would ever do as Prime Minister for the young Queen Victoria, who
had been so beguiled by Lord Melbourne. 'I have no small talk,' he confessed, 'and Peel
has no manners.'

[2] Karl Philipp, Fürst zu Schwartzenberg, the Austrian field marshal (1771–1820).

[3] See note, p. 62.

attention to individual interests as to the more weighty duties of State. His *attachés*, as is always the case, took their tone and manner from their chief, and were not only civil and agreeable to all those who went to the Embassy, but knew everything and everybody, and were of great use to the ambassador, keeping him well supplied with information on whatever event might be taking place. The British Embassy, in those days, was a centre where you were sure to find all the English gentlemen in Paris collected, from time to time. Dinners, balls, and receptions were given with profusion throughout the season: in fact, Sir Charles spent the whole of his private income in these noble hospitalities. England was then represented, as it always should be in France, by an ambassador who worthily expressed the intelligence, the amiability, and the wealth of the great country to which he belonged.

ESCAPE OF LAVALETTE FROM PRISON

Few circumstances created a greater sensation than the escape of Lavalette from the Conciergerie, after he had been destined by the French Government to give employment to the guillotine.[1] The means by which the prisoner avoided his fate and disappointed his enemies produced a deep respect for the English character, and led the French to believe that, however much the Governments of France and England might be disposed to foster feelings either of friendship or of enmity, individuals could entertain the deepest sense of regard for each other, and that a chivalrous feeling of honour would urge them on to the exercise of the noblest feelings of our nature. This incident likewise had a salutary influence in preventing acts of cruelty and bloodshed, which were doubtless contemplated by those in power.

Lavalette had been, under the Imperial Government, head of the Post-Office, which place he filled on the return of the Bourbons; and when the Emperor Napoleon arrived from Elba, he continued still to be thus employed. Doubtless, on every occasion when opportunity presented itself, he did all in his power to serve his great master; to whom, indeed, he was allied by domestic ties, having married into the Beauharnais family. When Louis the Eighteenth returned to Paris after the battle of Waterloo, Lavalette and the unfortunate Marshal Ney were singled out as traitors to the Bourbon cause, and tried, convicted, and sentenced to death.

[1] Antoine Marie Chamans, comte de Lavalette (1769–1830), Napoleon's Minister of Posts. His memoirs were published in 1831.

The 26th of December was the day fixed for the execution of Lavalette, a man of high respectability and of great connections, whose only fault was fidelity to his chief. On the evening of the 21st, Madame Lavalette, accompanied by her daughter and her governess, Madame Dutoit, a lady of seventy years of age, presented herself at the Conciergerie, to take a last farewell of her husband. She arrived at the prison in a sedan chair. On this very day the Procureur-Général had given an order that no one should be admitted without an order signed by himself; the *greffier* having, however, on previous occasions been accustomed to receive Madame Lavalette with the two ladies who now sought also to enter the cell, did not object to it; so these three ladies proposed to take coffee with Lavalette. The under-gaoler was sent to a neighbouring café to obtain it, and during his absence Lavalette exchanged dresses with his wife. He managed to pass undetected out of the prison, accompanied by his daughter, and entered the chair in which Madame Lavalette had arrived; which, owing to the management of a faithful valet, had been placed so that no observation could be made of the person entering it. The bearers found the chair somewhat heavier than usual, but were ignorant of the change that had taken place, and were glad to find, after proceeding a short distance, that the individual within preferred walking home, and giving up the sedan to the young lady. On the *greffier* entering the cell, he quickly discovered the *ruse*, and gave the alarm; the under-gaoler was despatched to stop the chair, but he was too late.

Lavalette had formed a friendship with a young Englishman of the name of [Robert] Bruce, to whom he immediately had recourse, throwing himself upon his generosity and kind feeling for protection, which was unhesitatingly afforded. But as Bruce could do nothing alone, he consulted two English friends who had shown considerable sympathy for the fate of Marshal Ney – men of liberal principles and undoubted honour, and both of them officers in the British service: these were Captain Hutchinson[1] and General Sir Robert Wilson.[2] To the latter was committed the most difficult task, that of conveying out of

[1] Captain John Hely-Hutchinson, afterwards third Earl of Donoughmore (1787-1851), had served at Waterloo in Gronow's regiment. He was deprived of his commission upon his imprisonment.
[2] General Sir Robert Wilson (1777-1849), son of the portrait painter Benjamin Wilson. Vain, outspoken and tactless, at some point in his varied career he exasperated almost everyone in power from the Prince Regent to Wellington and Castlereagh. He was British Military Commissioner at the Tsar's headquarters in 1812-14 and wrote an account of his experiences 'for the imitation', as he put it, of his thirteen children.

France the condemned prisoner; and for this achievement few men
were better fitted than Sir Robert Wilson, a man of fertile imagination,
ready courage, great assurance, and singular power of command over
others. He spoke French well, and was intimately acquainted with the
military habits of different nations.

Sir Robert undertook, in the midst of great dangers and difficulties,
to convey Lavalette out of France. Having dressed him in the uniform
of an English officer, and obtained a passport under a feigned name, he
took him in a cabriolet past the barriers as far as Compiègne, where a
carriage was waiting for them. They passed through sundry examinations at the fortified towns, but fortunately escaped; the great difficulty
being that, owing to Lavalette's having been the director of the posts, his
countenance was familiar to almost all the postmasters who supplied
relays of horses. At Cambray three hours were lost, from the gates being
shut, and at Valenciennes they underwent three examinations; but
eventually they got out of France.

The police, however, became acquainted with the fact that Lavalette
had been concealed in the Rue du Helder for three days, at the
apartments of Mr Bruce; and this enabled them to trace all the
circumstances, showing that it was at the apartments of Hutchinson
that Lavalette had changed his dress, and that he had remained there
the night before he quitted Paris. The consequence was that Sir Robert
Wilson, Bruce, and Hutchinson were tried for aiding the escape of a
prisoner; and each of them was condemned to three months' imprisonment: the under-gaoler, who had evidently been well paid for services
rendered, had two years' confinement allotted to him.

I went to see Sir Robert Wilson during his stay in the Conciergerie –
a punishment not very difficult to bear, but which marked him as a
popular hero for his life. A circumstance, I remember, made a strong
impression on me, proving that, however great may be the courage of
a man in trying circumstances, a trifling incident might severely shake
his nerves. I was accompanied by a favourite dog of the Countess of
Oxford's, which, being unaware of the high character of Sir Robert, or
dissatisfied with his physiognomy, or for some good canine reason, took
a sudden antipathy to him, and inserted his teeth into a somewhat fleshy
part, but without doing much injury. The effect, however, on the
general was extraordinary: he was most earnest to have the dog killed.
I, being certain that the animal was in no way diseased, avoided
obeying his wishes, and fear that I thus lost the good graces of the worthy
man.

Duelling in France in 1815

When the restoration of the Bourbons took place, a variety of circumstances combined to render duelling so common, that scarcely a day passed without one at least of these hostile meetings. Amongst the French themselves there were two parties always ready to distribute to each other '*des coups d'épée*' – the officers of Napoleon's army and the Bourbonist officers of the *Garde du Corps*. Then, again, there was the irritating presence of the English, Russian, Prussian, and Austrian officers in the French capital. In the duels between these soldiers and the French, the latter were always the aggressors.

At Tortoni's, on the Boulevards, there was a room set apart for such quarrelsome gentlemen, where, after these meetings, they indulged in riotous champagne breakfasts. At this café might be seen all the most notorious duellists, amongst whom I can call to mind an Irishman in the *Garde du Corps*, who was a most formidable fire-eater. The number of duels in which he had been engaged would seem incredible in the present day: he is said to have killed nine of his opponents in one year!

The meetings generally took place in the Bois de Boulogne, and the favourite weapon of the French was the small sword or the sabre; but foreigners, in fighting with the French, who were generally capital swordsmen, availed themselves of the use of pistols. The ground for a duel with pistols was marked out by indicating two spots, which were twenty-five paces apart; the seconds then generally proceeded to toss up who should have the first shot; the principals were then placed, and the word was given to fire.

The Café Foy, in the Palais Royal, was the principal place of rendezvous for the Prussian officers, and to this café the French officers on half-pay frequently proceeded in order to pick quarrels with their foreign invaders; swords were quickly drawn, and frequently the most bloody frays took place: these originated not in any personal hatred, but from national jealousy on the part of the French, who could not bear the sight of foreign soldiers in their capital; which, when ruled by the great captain of the age, had, like Rome, influenced the rest of the world. On one occasion, our Guards, who were on duty at the Palais Royal, were called out to put an end to one of these encounters, in which fourteen Prussians and ten Frenchmen were either killed or wounded.

The Faubourg St Germain

The distinguishing characteristics of the residents of the 'noble faubourg,' as it was called at the time I am speaking of, were indomitable pride and exclusiveness, with a narrow-minded ignorance of all beyond the circle in which its members moved. In our day of comparative equality and general civility, no one who has not arrived at my age, and lived in Paris, can form any idea of the insolence and hauteur of the higher classes of society in 1815. The glance of unutterable disdain which the painted old duchesse of the Restoration cast upon the youthful belles of the Chaussée d'Antin, or the handsome widows of Napoleon's army of heroes, defies description. Although often responded to by a sarcastic sneer at the antediluvian charms of the émigrée, yet the look of contempt and disgust often sank deep into the victim's heart, leaving there germs which showed themselves fifteen years later in the revolution of 1830.[1]

In those days, this privileged class was surrounded by a charmed circle, which no one could by any means break through. Neither personal attractions nor mental qualifications formed a passport into that exclusive society; to enter which the small nobility of the provinces, or the nouveau riche, sighed in vain. It would have been easier for a young Guardsman to make his way into the Convent des Oiseaux – the fashionable convent in Paris – than for any of these parvenus to force an entrance into the Faubourg St Germain.

One of the first acts which followed the Restoration of the Bourbons was the grant of a pecuniary indemnity, amounting to a milliard, or forty millions sterling, to be distributed amongst the émigrés who had lost fortunes or estates by their devotion to the royal family. They had now, therefore, the means of receiving their friends, political partisans, and foreigners, with more than usual splendour; and it must be admitted that those who were thought worthy to be received were treated like spoiled children, and petted and flattered to their hearts' content. In their own houses they were really des grands seigneurs, and quite incapable of treating their invited guests with the insolence that became the fashion among the Jewish parvenus during the reign of the 'citizen king.'

---

[1] In the revolution of 1830, Charles X, the younger brother of Louis XVIII, was forced to dismiss his reactionary minister, the prince de Polignac, and then to abdicate in favour of his cousin, Louis-Philippe, duc d'Orléans (1773-1850), who was proclaimed 'King of the French by the grace of God and the will of the nation'. He became known as 'the Citizen King', but was accused by his erstwhile radical supporters of 'confiscating' their revolution and was himself obliged to abdicate in 1848.

In their own houses, the inhabitants of the Faubourg St Germain were scrupulously polite: even if some enterprising foreigner should have got in surreptitiously, as long as he was under his host's roof he was treated with perfect courtesy; though ignominiously 'cut' for the remainder of his days. All this was not very amiable; but the inhabitants of the 'noble faubourg' were never distinguished for their amiability. Their best characteristics were the undaunted courage with which they met death upon the scaffold, and the cheerfulness and resignation with which they ate the bitter bread of exile.

In general, *les grandes dames* were not remarkable for their personal attractions, nor for the elegance of their appearance or dress. The galaxy of handsome women that formed the court of the emperor had perhaps sent beauty somewhat out of fashion; for the high-born ladies who took their place were what we should call dowdy, and had nothing distinguished in their appearance. Many of those who belonged to the most ancient families were almost vulgar in outward form and feature: their manner had a peculiar off-hand, easy style; and they particularly excelled in setting down any unlucky person who had happened to offend them.

The men of the aristocracy of the Revolution were less clever and satirical than the women; but on the other hand, they had far more of the distinguished bearing and graceful urbanity of the *grands seigneurs* of the olden time. The *émigré* nobles would have gazed with unutterable horror at their degenerate descendants of the present day; but these young, booted, bearded, cigar-smoking scions of *la jeune France* would have run round their courteous, though perhaps rather slow ancestors, in all the details of daily life.

Those who are now supposed to be the great people of the Faubourg St Germain are nothing more than actors, who put on a motley dress, and appear before the public with a view of attracting that attention to which they are not entitled; it is, therefore, an error to suppose that the modern faubourg is anything like what it was during the days of the Bourbons. At the present moment the only practical aid the inhabitants of this locality can accord to the legitimist cause in Europe, is by getting up subscriptions for the Papacy, and such exiled sovereigns as Francis II;[1] and, in order to do so, they generally address themselves to married

---

[1] The arch-conservative Francis II, last of the Holy Roman Emperors (1768–1835). Although finding it most distasteful to allow her to marry such a parvenu, for reasons of state he acquiesced in the marriage of his daughter, Marie-Louise, to Napoleon. He gave full encouragement to the repressive policies of his chief minister, Metternich.

women and widows: in fact, it is from the purses of susceptible females, many of whom are English, that donations are obtained for legitimacy and Popery in distress.

It is to be regretted that the most renowned and ancient families of France have, in society and politics, yielded their places to another class.[1] That refinement of perception, sensitiveness, and gentle bearing, which take three or four generations to produce, are no longer the characteristics of Parisian society. The gilded saloons of the Tuileries, and those magnificent hotels whose architects have not been geniuses of art, but the children of mammon, are occupied by the Jew speculator, the political parasite, the clever schemer, and those who - whilst following the fortune of the great man who rules France - are nothing better than harpies. Most of these pretended devotees of imperialism have, speaking figuratively, their portmanteaus perpetually packed, ready for flight.

The Salon des Étrangers, in Paris

When the allies entered Paris, after the battle of Waterloo, the English gentlemen sought, instinctively, something like a club. Paris, however, possessed nothing of the sort; but there was a much more dangerous establishment than the London clubs - namely, a rendezvous for confirmed gamblers. The Salon des Étrangers was most gorgeously furnished, provided with an excellent kitchen and wines, and was conducted by the celebrated Marquis de Livry, who received the guests and did the honours with a courtesy which made him famous throughout Europe. The Marquis presented an extraordinary likeness to the Prince Regent of England, who actually sent Lord Fife over to Paris to ascertain this momentous fact.

The Marquis de Livry had a charming villa at Romainville, near Paris, to which, on Sundays, he invited not only those gentlemen who were the most prodigal patrons of his *salon*, but a number of ladies, who were dancers and singers conspicuous at the opera; forming a society of the strangest character, the male portion of which were bent on losing their money, whilst the ladies were determined to get rid of whatever

---

[1] Gronow is speaking here of the Paris of the Third Empire. After the abdication of Louis-Philippe in 1848, France was proclaimed a republic once more. The proclamation was followed by a short though bloody civil war in Paris and then by the election as President of Louis-Napoleon Bonaparte (1808-73), Napoleon I's nephew, who, after a *coup d'état* in 1832, proclaimed himself Emperor as Napoleon III.

virtue they might still have left. The dinners on these occasions were supplied by the *chef* of the Salon des Étrangers, and were such as few *renommés* of the kitchens of France could place upon the table.

Hall Standish was always to be seen in this circle;[1] and his own hotel in the Rue Lepelletier was often lighted up, and *fêtes* given to the theatrical and *demi-monde*. Standish died in Spain, leaving his gallery of pictures to Louis Philippe.

As at Crockford's, a magnificent supper was provided every night [at the Salon des Étrangers] for all who thought proper to avail themselves of it. The games principally played were *rouge et noir* and hazard; the former producing an immense profit, for not only were the whole of the expenses of this costly establishment defrayed by the winnings of the bank, but a very large sum was paid annually to the municipality of Paris.

In calling up my recollections of the Salon des Étrangers, some forty years since, I see before me the noble form and face of the Hungarian Count Hunyady, the chief gambler of the day, who created considerable sensation in his time. He became *très à la mode*: his horses, carriage, and house were considered perfect, while his good looks were the theme of universal admiration; there were ladies' cloaks *à la Huniade*; and the illustrious Borel, of the Rocher de Cancale, named new dishes after the famous Hungarian. Hunyady's luck for a long time was prodigious: no bank could resist his attacks; and at one time he must have been a winner of nearly two millions of francs. His manners were particularly calm and gentlemanlike; he sat apparently unmoved, with his right hand in the breast of his coat, whilst thousands depended upon the turning of a card or the hazard of a die. His valet, however, confided to some indiscreet friend that his nerves were not of such iron temper as he would have made people believe, and that the count bore in the morning the bloody marks of his nails, which he had pressed into his chest in the agony of an unsuccessful turn of fortune. The streets of Paris were at that time not very safe; consequently, the count was usually attended to his residence by two gendarmes, in order to prevent his being attacked by robbers. Hunyady was not wise enough (what

[1] Frank Hall Standish (1799–1840) succeeded to the Lancashire estates of a cousin but lived mainly in Spain and France. He spent most of his fortune upon books and works of art. He left them in his will to King Louis-Philippe, intending that they should be held in trust for the French nation; but, after the Revolution of 1848, Louis-Philippe claimed them as his own. The pictures, including several Murillos, were accordingly brought back to England, where Louis-Philippe was living in exile, and sold at auction by Christie's. The books were sold in Paris.

gamblers are?) to leave Paris with his large winnings, but continued as usual to play day and night. A run of bad luck set in against him, and he lost not only the whole of the money he had won, but a very large portion of his own fortune.

LORD WESTMORELAND

When I was presented at the Court of Louis XVIII, Lord Westmoreland, the grandfather of the present lord, accompanied Sir Charles Stewart to the Tuileries. On our arrival in the room where the king was, we formed ourselves into a circle, when the king good-naturedly inquired after Lady Westmoreland, from whom his lordship was divorced, and whether she was in Paris. Upon this, the noble lord looked sullen, and refused to reply to the question put by the king. His majesty, however, repeated it, when Lord Westmoreland hallooed out, in bad French, '*Je ne sais pas, je ne sais pas, je ne sais pas.*' Louis, rising, said, '*Assez, milord; assez, milord.*'

On one occasion, Lord Westmoreland, who was Lord Privy Seal, being asked what office he held, replied, '*Le Chancelier est le grand sceau (sot); moi je suis le petit sceau d'Angleterre.*' On another occasion, he wished to say 'I would if I could, but I can't,' and rendered it, '*Je voudrais si je coudrais, mais je ne cannais pas.*'

ALDERMAN WOOD

Among the many English who then visited Paris was Alderman Wood, who had previously filled the office of Lord Major of London.[1] He ordered a hundred visiting cards, inscribing upon them, 'Alderman Wood, *feu Lord Maire de Londres*,' which he had largely distributed amongst people of rank – having translated the word 'late' into '*feu*,' which I need hardly state means 'dead.'

LORD THANET

The late Lord Thanet, celebrated for having been imprisoned in the Tower for his supposed predilection for republicanism,[2] passed much of

[1] Alderman, later Sir Matthew Wood (1768–1843), an extreme radical Member of Parliament for the City of London, was in a thriving way of business as chemist and hop merchant. He was one of Queen Caroline's leading supporters and consequently known to the Prince Regent as 'that beast Wood'.

[2] Sackville Tufton, ninth Earl of Thanet (1767–1825), was imprisoned in the Tower in 1799, having been found guilty of causing a riot in court during the trial of the Irish agitator Arthur O'Connor.

his time in Paris, particularly at the Salon des Étrangers. His lordship's infatuation for play was such, that when the gambling-tables were closed, he invited those who remained to play at chicken-hazard and écarté; the consequence was, that one night he left off a loser of £120,000. When told of his folly and the probability of his having been cheated, he exclaimed, 'Then I consider myself lucky in not having lost twice that sum!'

Lord Granville, the British Ambassador

Soon after Lord Granville's appointment,[1] a strange occurrence took place at one of the public gambling-houses. A colonel, on half-pay, in the British service, having lost every farthing that he possessed, determined to destroy himself, together with all those who were instrumental in his ruin. Accordingly, he placed a canister full of fulminating powder under the table, and set it on fire: it blew up, but fortunately no one was hurt. The police arrested the colonel, and placed him in prison; he was, however, through the humane interposition of our ambassador, sent out of France as a madman.

Marshal Blücher

Marshal Blücher, though a very fine fellow, was a very rough diamond, with the manners of a common soldier. On his arrival in Paris, he went every day to the *salon*, and played the highest stakes at *rouge et noir*. The *salon*, during the time that the marshal remained in Paris, was crowded by persons who came to see him play. His manner of playing was anything but gentlemanlike, and when he lost, he used to swear in German at everything that was French, looking daggers at the croupiers. He generally managed to lose all he had about him, also all the money his servant, who was waiting in the ante-chamber, carried. I recollect looking attentively at the manner in which he played; he would put his right hand into his pocket, and bring out several rouleaus of Napoleons, throwing them on the red or the black. If he won the first coup, he would allow it to remain; but when the croupier stated that the

---

[1] Lord Granville Leveson-Gower, first Earl Granville (1773-1846), succeeded Sir Charles Stuart as Ambassador in Paris in 1824. Known as 'the Wellington of gamblers', he was one of the most skilful whist players of his day. He once lost £23,000 in one session at Crockford's. His son became Foreign Secretary in Lord John Russell's administration.

table was not responsible for more than ten thousand francs, then Blucher would roar like a lion, and rap out oaths in his native language which would doubtless have met with great success at Billingsgate, if duly translated: fortunately, they were not heeded, as they were not understood by the lookers-on.

Conduct of the English and Prussian Armies during the Occupation of Paris

The Duke of Wellington's conduct to the Parisians was kind and considerate. He contented himself with occupying the Bois de Boulogne, the two faubourgs of La Villette and La Chapelle St Denis. Blücher was not so moderate in his conduct towards the French. His troops were billeted in every house; he obliged the inhabitants to feed and clothe them; and he issued an order (which I well recollect seeing) commanding the authorities to supply each soldier with a bedstead containing a bolster, a woollen mattress, two new blankets, and a pair of linen sheets. The rations per day, for each man, were two pounds of bread of good quality, one pound of butcher's meat, a bottle of wine, a quarter of a pound of butter, ditto rice, a glass of brandy, and some tobacco. The Prussian cavalry were not forgotten: each horse required ten pounds of oats, six of hay, ditto of straw, to be furnished early each day. Blücher's Generals occupied all the best hotels in the Faubourg St Germain; General Thielman[1] that of Marshal Ney, where he forcibly took possession of the plate, carriages, and horses. Other Prussian Generals acted in a similar manner.

The Russian and Austrian armies, with the two Emperors,[2] entered Paris soon after our arrival. The Emperors imitated Blucher in some respects; they refused to quarter their soldiers in the large and wholesome barracks which were in readiness to receive them: no; they preferred billeting them with peaceable merchants and tradespeople, whom they plundered and bullied in the most outrageous manner. Wellington, all this while, showed great moderation; and his army paid for everything they required. Blucher, on the other hand, threatened to take possession of the Bank of France and the Government offices: which threat was not carried into execution, owing to the wise and timely interposition of the Duke.

---

[1] Johann Adolf, Baron Thielmann (1765–1824).
[2] Tsar Alexander I of Russia (1777–1825) and Francis I, Emperor of Austria (1768–1835).

One day, I recollect, Paris was in a state of amazement and stupefaction. Muffling, the commander-in-chief in Paris of the Prussians,[1] installed at the Hôtel de Ville, demanded from the French prefect a very large sum of money, and sent an officer and a hundred soldiers to enforce his demand. The prefect had not the money: the consequence was, he was marched off to the Hôtel de Ville, where General Muffling kept him prisoner, intending, the following morning, to send him to Berlin as a hostage until the money was paid into the Prussian treasury.

THE DUKE AND MR CREEVEY

The late Mr Creevey, the well-known Whig M.P.,[2] stated in my presence, at a dinner in Berkeley Square, in 1816, that he was at the Duke of Wellington's quarters at Brussels the night of the battle of Waterloo. It was late when the Duke entered, and, perceiving Mr Creevey, shook him by the hand, and said, 'I have won the greatest battle of modern times, with twelve thousand of my old Peninsular troops.'

Creevey remarked that he was astonished at that, and asked, 'What, sir, with twelve thousand only?'

'Yes, Creevey,' replied the Duke; 'with twelve thousand of my old Spanish infantry. I knew I could depend upon them. They fought the battle, without flinching, against immense odds; but nearly all my staff, and some of my best friends, are killed. Good-night! I want rest, and must go to bed.'

Creevey called at an early hour on the following morning, in the hope of again seeing the Duke, but he had left Brussels before daylight, to join the army.

I do not pretend to say what the Duke meant in his conversation with Mr Creevey, - who was truth itself, - and I am equally certain that I am correctly relating what he said, for the statement made a great impression on me. He must have meant that the victory was mainly owing to the twelve thousand veterans; for, as near as I could make out,

---

[1] General Friedrich Carl Ferdinand Muffling (1775-1851).

[2] Thomas Creevey (1768-1838), son of a Liverpool merchant, was Member of Parliament for Thetford and afterwards for Appleby. 'He belonged to the Whigs,' Charles Greville wrote of him, 'displayed a good deal of shrewdness and humour, and was for some time very troublesome to the Tory government by continually attacking abuses. After some time he lost his seat and went to live at Brussels.' His correspondence and journals are an important source for the history of his time.

there were on our side at Waterloo about forty-five thousand English and Hanoverians, and twenty thousand Dutch, Belgian, and Nassau troops.

THE BRITISH EMBASSY – LORD AND LADY GRANVILLE

The announcement of the lamented death of Lady Granville in the papers the other day, brought to my mind vivid recollections of the palmy days of the British Embassy, and all the blooming happy faces that used to be constantly congregated there; but who are now grown old and careworn, or are lying in the grave, forgotten by those who loved them best, whilst others, fair, young, and happy, reign in their stead. England was never represented more worthily, or with greater magnificence, than by Lord and Lady Granville; though the high post of ambassador to Paris has been occupied by some of the greatest and proudest of our countrymen.

Lord Granville had been ambassador at St Petersburg in early life, and greatly distinguished himself as an able diplomatist on a most delicate and important mission. He was the *beau-idéal* of a high-bred English nobleman. He was considerably above the middle height, with a figure remarkable for symmetry and grace, which he preserved to an advanced age. His features were regular, and his countenance expressive of mildness and good-nature. He was one of those men who, once seen, leave an impression on the memory: he belonged to a race of gentlemen of the olden time, that seems almost extinct in our present free-and-easy days.

Lady Granville, though she did not possess the outward advantages of her husband, was considered his superior in conversational powers, and possessed, in a high degree, the charm of voice and manner which belongs to the Cavendish family.[1] She rather affected a remarkable simplicity in her dress, was generally attired in black, and would receive her guests in the plainest of caps, and wrapped up in a shawl. But, in spite of the homeliness of her costume, figure, and features, there was something in the *tout ensemble* which spoke of noble blood and ancient lineage; and her manner of receiving was perfect. Unlike most of our countrywomen, she was not subject to fits of caprice; she was perfectly independent, and could afford to form her own opinion, and act upon

---

[1] Lady Granville was the former Lady Harriet Elizabeth Cavendish, second daughter of William, fifth Duke of Devonshire. She died in 1862. Her eldest son, Granville George, the second Earl, became Foreign Secretary in 1851 and again in 1870 and 1880-5.

it; and if there was a kind and generous action to be performed, she was sure not to miss the opportunity of doing it. Through good report and evil report, she would cleave to those who had once won her affectionate regard, and without any appearance of patronising, she knew how to throw the mantle of her loving protection round those who needed it. At the same time, there was nothing *banal* in her manner or character. She had none of that excess of constrained politeness, which is, in reality, the height of incivility, but was courteous to all; by her perfect breeding, she constrained the presuming British Gogs and Magogs to keep at a respectful distance, without ever saying an unkind word, or showing any symptom of being ruffled or discomposed.

It was rather amusing, when Lady Granville first came to Paris, to see some of the *grandes dames* of the Faubourg St Germain feeling their way, and trying whether they could not dictate to and domineer over the quiet-looking English lady, who had more wit, and fun, and humour, and cleverness than a dozen of them put together. These arbiters of fashion soon discovered that they had found more than their match in Lady Granville, and that she would have her own list of guests, choose her own cap and shawl, and settle her armchairs and sofas in her own way, without taking the advice of a jury of noble matrons, who had hitherto considered themselves infallible.

The magnificent hospitality of Lord and Lady Granville, and the great liberality with which the Embassy was conducted in their time, were the constant theme of conversation and remark. Large dinners of the most *recherché* kind were constantly given. Small and intimate receptions were held every Monday, and large ones every Friday; whilst *déjeûners* and balls on a most magnificent scale electrified the whole of Parisian society.

When Lord and Lady Granville left Paris there was a general mourning in the gay world. Their place in Parisian society has never been filled up, and they themselves, personally, have never been forgotten.

PARIS AFTER THE PEACE

In 1815 and the following years there were gathered together in Paris all the flower of English society – men of fashion and distinction, beautiful matrons and their still lovelier daughters. A history of all that occurred in those days would afford amusing materials for the pen of the novelist, and tickle agreeably the ears of scandal-loving people. I shall, however, content myself with recording some of my own *souvenirs*.

Lord Castlereagh was the pre-eminent star of the autumn of 1815, –
'the observed of all observers.' He was here, there, and everywhere.
Indeed, the mass of business he had to transact was so immense, and the
fatigue he had to undergo so great, that he was compelled to spend
several hours each day in a bath; his nights being generally passed
without sleep. His bath was always taken at the Bains Chinois, at the
corner of the Rue de la Michodière. He was there shampooed by the
celebrated Fleury, and recruited his exhausted faculties by dozing for an
hour or two. His favourite promenade was the gallery of the Palais
Royal. In his walks he was almost always alone, and used to dress very
simply, never wearing any orders or decorations. On the other hand,
Lady Castlereagh astonished the French by the magnificence of her
diamonds.[1] At the balls and parties she used to be followed about by
envious women, affecting to admire, but looking daggers all the while.
On one occasion I heard a French lady exclaim, 'England is renowned
for beautiful women; but when they are ugly, *"elles ne le sont pas à demi."*'
But this remark was as false as it was ill-natured, for Lady Castlereagh
was rather handsome than otherwise.

The Duke of Devonshire,[2] then young, graceful, and distinguished,
was hunted down by mothers and daughters with an activity, zeal, and
perseverance – and, I am sorry to add, a vulgarity – which those only
can conceive who have beheld the British huntress in full cry after a
duke. It was amusing to see how the ambitious matrons watched every
movement, and how furious they became if any other girl was more
favoured than their own daughters by the attention of the monarch of
the Peak.[3] The young ladies, on their side, would not engage themselves
with any one until all hope of the Duke asking them to dance was at an
end. But as soon as he had selected a partner, the same young ladies
would go in search of those whom they had rejected, and endeavour to
get opposite or somewhere near him.

I remember seeing a serious quarrel between two great ladies, who
were only prevented from coming to extremities by the timely
intervention of our ambassadress, Lady Elizabeth Stuart.[4] There were

[1] Castlereagh's wife was Lady Emily Anne, youngest daughter and co-heiress of John
Hobart, second Earl of Buckinghamshire. They had no children.

[2] William Cavendish, sixth Duke of Devonshire (1790–1858) was born in Paris. His
tastes were literary rather than sensual.

[3] Chatsworth, the country house of the Dukes of Devonshire, is in the Peak District of
Derbyshire. The Devonshires also then owned Hardwick Hall in Derbyshire, where the
sixth Duke died.

[4] She was Elizabeth Margaret, third daughter of Philip Yorke, third Earl of Hardwicke.
Their daughter, Charlotte, married Earl Canning, first Viceroy of India.

at this time many men of rank and fortune among our countrymen. Some of these were particular in their attentions to Lady Elizabeth Conyngham,[1] but her mother, who was bent on securing a ducal coronet for her handsome daughter, discouraged all attempts that were made in less high quarters. Rumour had even then whispered that, owing to family secrets of a very peculiar nature, the Duke of Devonshire had entered into a solemn engagement never to marry; and though I have reason to believe that this was entirely false, it is certain that he lived and died a bachelor. Besides this, he was always considered by those who knew him well to be very unlikely to fall in love with anyone.

THE COUNTESS OF ALDBOROUGH

From the first years I remember Paris, I became acquainted with Lady Aldborough,[2] who had already acquired a kind of rather unenviable celebrity in the *beau monde*, for her *bons mots* and anecdotes of a peculiar kind. She spent many years of her long life in Paris, where she kept open house, and gave agreeable dinners, made up of pleasant men and good-looking women, not remarkable for any false modesty or affected prudery. Her sayings were quoted all over Europe, and she enjoyed a considerable share of popularity among a certain set, who admitted that her death (which occurred about twenty years ago) left a blank in Parisian society.

It behoves me in general to deal gently with the private characters of those who have gone to their last homes, but Lady Aldborough had no prejudices, and, far from being ashamed of the irregularities of her early life, continued in her old age to glory over them, and to speak of her past exploits with as much zest and ardour as some old veteran might recount his campaigns.

Lady Aldborough's language was plain and unvarnished, and many hardened men of the world have been known to blush and look aghast

---

[1] Lady Elizabeth Conyngham was daughter of King George IV's mistress, Marchioness Conyngham. The King paid her so much attention, it was said that it was she with whom he was in love rather than her mother. She later married the tenth Marquess of Huntly.

[2] Elizabeth, the daughter of the Rev. F. Hamilton, married John Stratford, third Earl of Aldborough, in 1777. Charles Greville encountered her at a dinner party in London in 1830 when she rushed up to Marshal Marmont, who had tried to hold Paris for Charles X, and cried out to him, ' "*Ah, mon cher Maréchal, embrassez moi!*" And so after escaping the cannon's mouth at Paris, he was obliged to face Lady Aldboro's mouth here.'

when this free-spoken old lady has attacked them at her dinner-table with sundry searching questions respecting their tastes and habits; in the presence perhaps of their wives and daughters, who could not easily avoid hearing the stage whisper in which her remarks were conveyed to the ears of the unwilling listeners.

With a kind of cynical *naïveté*, Lady Aldborough has often said she was perfectly aware that many persons objected to her style of conversation, but that, unfortunately, all the wit and humour for which she was celebrated lay in that kind of jesting which the over-particular considered offensive.

In appearance she did not give one (at least in her later years) the impression of having been as handsome as her full-length portrait by Cosway would have led one to suppose. She was rather under the middle height, but well formed; and to the last preserved a slight figure and a neat foot and ankle. Her features were regular in outline, but somewhat sharp; and the expression of her countenance was stern, hard, and restless. Her voice had none of those mellifluous tones so appreciated by Byron; it was harsh and loud, partly, perhaps, owing to her deafness; her manner was abrupt and unequal; and her wit, which was undeniable, fluctuated between levity and sarcasm.

She did not possess the French art of wrapping up a joke of doubtful propriety: her witticisms wore no mask, and left her hearer very little chance of appearing not to understand them. When an attempt has been made by a luckless wife to feign innocence in the presence of a jealous husband, the old lady would tap her victim sharply on the hand with her fan, saying, with a sardonic smile, and in her clear voice, audible from one end of the room to the other –

'You understand very well what I mean, my dear.'

Lady Aldborough had a very peculiar style of dress, which she continued to adopt till the latest period of her life. She wore habitually, when going out in the evening, a long white veil, which was fastened to her wig, and hung down to her feet; white satin shoes with diamond buckles, very short sleeves and petticoats, and an extremely *décolleté* gown.

Every one arrived at middle age has heard of innumerable *bons mots* attributed to Lady Aldborough; but, in newspaper phrase, they are generally 'unfit for publication.' It may, to a certain degree, be her excuse that the mode of speaking in the olden time was far plainer and coarser than anything which would be tolerated now-a-days; and even ladies of very good reputation were guilty of using queer language, and, as Pope says, of 'calling a spade a spade.'

En résumé, Lady Aldborough was a woman of good sense, and capable, if called upon seriously, of giving her opinion on important matters, and with great judgment and feeling. I have known of her doing many kind things to old friends, who had got into awkward scrapes; and if she spent a good deal of money on herself, she was very charitable, and always ready to extend a helping hand to the poor and needy.

THE MARQUIS D'ALIGRE

The Marquis d'Aligre, the richest and most avaricious man in France, and supposed to be worth three or four millions of money, was once seen entering a church during a charity sermon. He was accosted by a great lady of the Faubourg St Germain, who, holding a bag for charitable contributions, begged him to give her something for the poor. The Marquis did not appear to understand the request, but the lady returned to the charge; upon which the Marquis declined giving anything, stating that he had no money. The lady then placed the bag full of money under the nose of the Marquis, saying, 'Help yourself, Monsieur d'Aligre, for this bag contains money for the poor; and as you say you are penniless, pray help yourself.' Upon which the old miser, for once heartily ashamed of himself, pulled out of his pocket a purse full of gold, and threw it into the bag.

'HATS OFF'

At a party at the Vicomtesse de Noailles's soon after the Allied Armies had entered Paris, and at which I was present, some of the ladies expressed their surprise that Englishmen of high birth did not take off their hats when bowed to, as was the custom in France and other countries. Dupuytren, the celebrated surgeon,[1] happened to join the party, when some one observed that perhaps the Doctor could solve the riddle, and explain the real cause of such apparent rudeness on the part of the English. Dupuytren, in his coarse and blunt manner, said, 'The *teigne*, or scald-head, is a very common disease in Europe; it is therefore more than probable that those foreigners who keep their hats on in the presence of ladies are afflicted with that loathsome complaint.' Lady

---

[1] Guillaume, Baron Dupuytren (1777–1835), surgeon to Louis XVIII and Charles X.

Stafford, afterwards Duchess of Sutherland,[1] who had been quietly sitting on one of the sofas, and whose presence had escaped the notice of Dupuytren, rose, and, in a dignified manner, said, 'Doctor, that horrible disease is unknown in my country. My countrymen take off their hats to royalty, to ladies, and to none besides.' Whereupon Dupuytren rejoined, 'Surely, my lady, there is no law in England which precludes a well-bred gentleman from taking off his hat to his equals, and more especially to females.' Lady Stafford retorted with spirit, 'You can ridicule my countrymen if you think fit, Doctor; but with all their faults and apparent rudeness, they have never been guilty of cutting off the heads of beautiful and innocent women, as you have done in France.' This severe retort on the part of her ladyship was considered by all present as quite uncalled for; but the Vicomtesse apologised to her friends by saying that Lady Stafford should be pardoned, for she lived in Paris during the Revolution as ambassadress from England, and was a great favourite and friend of Queen Marie-Antoinette. She conveyed to the poor Queen when in prison many little comforts and necessaries; and when the embassy had left Paris, and Marie-Antoinette, after unheard-of barbarities, was guillotined, Lady Stafford regarded her execution as the most atrocious murder, and vowed the utmost detestation and abhorrence, not only of the ruffians who by their bloody deeds dishonoured France, but of the whole French nation.

[1] Elizabeth Sutherland, Countess of Sutherland in her own right, married the Marquess of Stafford in 1785. 'A leviathan of wealth,' in Charles Greville's words, he was created Duke of Sutherland in 1833. For two years during the Revolution he was British Ambassador in Paris.

9

Duels and Duellists

ENGLISHMEN IN PARIS IN 1817

In the year 1817 a certain young nobleman, his brother, and another friend, were staying in Paris. They had dined one day at Véry's, then the famous *restaurant* in the Palais Royal, and the conversation had turned upon the insults offered by the Parisians, particularly the military, to the English visitors. His Lordship was silent during this conversation, but took note of what had been said, while imbibing some potent Burgundy; and his indignation was none the weaker for having thus 'bottled it up.' On leaving the *restaurant* the first thing he did was to kick over a basket of toothpicks, which was presented to him for purchase; the next was to shove off the pavement a Frenchman, who proved to be an officer. Of course, there was a violent altercation; cards were exchanged, and each party went his way to make arrangements for the 'pistols and coffee for four.'

Our countrymen, when near home, picked up their friend Manners, who had been shut out of his lodgings, and promised to accommodate him with a sofa at their rooms. On their arrival, he partially uncased and wrapped himself up in a large Witney blanket[1] and great coat, and then 'turned in.' At an early hour the next morning, two gentlemen called on our countrymen, and were ushered into the saloon. The first who presented himself to receive them was his Lordship, who had

---

[1] Heavy woollen blanket made at Witney in Oxfordshire.

nothing on but a large pair of trousers, and a cotton nightcap full of holes: he being so particular about having it aired that it was constantly singed in the process. Not speaking French, he requested his servant to act as interpreter, and asked the strangers the object of their visit; the incidents of the preceding night having passed off from his memory with the fumes of the Chambertin. The discussion that ensued woke up Manners, who, wrapped in his blanket, rose from his couch, looking more like a white bear than anything else. It also drew from his dormitory Captain Meade, who made his appearance from a side door, clothed only in his night-shirt and a pair of expansive Russia duck trousers, whistling, as was his wont, and spitting occasionally through a hole that had been bored in one of his front teeth, in imitation of the stagecoachmen of the day. His Lordship's brother next appeared on the scene, in a costume little more complete than those of the others.

The visitors, although astonished at the appearance of the group, proceeded to business. Manners conducted it on the part of his friends, who could not speak French; and, with a view of discharging his office more comfortably, drew aside the folds of his Witney blanket and placed his back against the mantelpiece, to enjoy the warmth of the glowing wood-ashes in the grate below. The Frenchmen were refused an apology by our friends, coupled with the observation, that with Englishmen the case would be different; but that it was impossible on the present occasion to arrange matters in that way. They therefore requested the other party to name their weapons. Manners coolly informed them that they had decided on using *fusils*[1] at twelve paces! This seemed rather to astonish the Frenchmen: they exchanged glances, and then cast their eyes round the room, and on the strange figures before them. Meade was whistling through his teeth; his Lordship, whose coppers were rather hot,[2] had thrust his head out into the street through a pane of glass that had been smashed the night before; while the others were stalking about the room in their rather airy costumes. The gravity of the Frenchmen was overcome by the ludicrous aspect and *sang froid* of their opponents, and they burst out laughing. His Lordship, who was as full of fun as he was of pluck, stretching out his hand to the injured party, said, 'Come, I see you are good fellows, so shake hands. I had taken rather too much wine last night.' I need not say that the proffered hand was accepted, and the French officers retired. After their departure, Manners asked the servant what *fusil*

---

[1] Light muskets; also steels for sharpening knives.
[2] 'Hot coppers', a slang term for the hot, dry mouth associated with a hangover.

really meant, as, when naming the weapon to be used, he supposed it to be a kind of pistol.

COUNT MONTROND

This well-known personage belonged to a good family, and had already taken his place in the best French society before the first Revolution.[1] He was an inveterate gambler, rarely lost, and lived like a man possessed of a large fortune. When very young, at the court of Marie Antoinette, a certain Monsieur de Champagne, an officer of the Guards, who was playing at cards with him, said, '*Monsieur, vous trichez.*' Montrond answered, with the *sang-froid* which distinguished him through life under every circumstance, '*C'est possible; mais je n'aime pas qu'on me le dise,*' and threw the cards in Champagne's face.

They fought next morning with swords, and Montrond was run through the body. He was confined to his bed for two months, but when he got well again, called out Monsieur de Champagne, and, although he received another wound, succeeded in killing his adversary. This duel set him up in the world as a dangerous man to meddle with, and saved him from many insults, to which his very suspicious luck at play would have exposed him.

Montrond was thrown into prison during the reign of terror. For many days he expected every morning to be his last; and he used to relate that he had observed that those who showed themselves much at the windows, or talked to the sentry through the bars, were generally called for the next morning to be guillotined. He in consequence kept himself very much in the background, and remained at last with only one companion, an old lady, in his cell. One morning he heard so great a noise in the street, that he, with his usual caution, persuaded his companion to speak to the sentry, who said, 'Robespierre is dead – you will soon be free!'

He was released very shortly afterwards.

I knew Montrond well, but several years later; he had then no trace of having been the *charmant garçon* tradition represents him. He was rather above the middle height, and what the English novelists call *embonpoint*, and had the appearance of a *vieux bonhomme*. He was perfectly bald, had blue eyes, very small features, and a florid complexion. There was a peculiar twinkle in his eye, which boded no good to the victim he had selected for his prey.

[1] Casimir, comte de Montrond (1768–1843).

His countenance, as beheld by a casual observer, bore the stamp of an almost Pickwickian benevolence; but, on a closer inspection, there lurked behind this mask of mild philanthropy the stinging wit of Voltaire, mingled with the biting sarcasm of Rogers or Sir Philip Francis.[1,2] Montrond had none of the lively gestures or grimaces with which most foreigners adorn their conversation: his manner was singularly quiet. He was not a great talker, nor did he swagger, speak about himself, or laugh at his own *bons mots*. He was demure, sleek, sly, and dangerous. He would receive with a paternal air the silly quizzing of some feeble jester, but then would come the twinkle of that little pale blue eye, and then the poor moth or butterfly was ground to pieces on the wheel of his sharp sarcastic wit.

In the London clubs he went by the name of Old French, and managed to win very large sums of money off Lord Sefton (the only specimen I ever saw of a gigantic hunchback), who, with all his wit and cleverness, lost very largely on all occasions.

'Who the deuce is this Montrond?' said the Duke of York, one day to Arthur Upton.

'They say, sir,' replied Upton, 'that he is the most agreeable scoundrel and the greatest reprobate in France.'

'Is he, by Jove!' said HRH; 'then let us ask him to dinner immediately.'

The invitation was sent and accepted, and Montrond, as usual, made himself very agreeable, and became a constant guest at the dinner-table of HRH; and, unfortunately, at his whist-table also, by which the duke was a loser of many thousand pounds. Montrond lived in the best society both at Paris and in London, and was on terms, if not of intimacy, at all events of familiarity, with many of the greatest people in Europe. In the latter years of his life he resided in the Place Vendôme and was in the receipt of a pension of two thousand pounds a year from

[1] Samuel Rogers (1763-1855), the caustic poet. Having retired from his family's bank with a large income he went to live in a beautifully furnished house in St James's Place, where his breakfast parties became celebrated throughout the literary and artistic world. Thomas Carlyle described him as 'a most sorrowful, distressing, distracted old phenomenon, hovering over the rim of deep eternities with nothing but light babble, fatuity, vanity, and the frostiest London wit in his mouth.' Although he intimidated his guests with his spiteful sarcasm, he was quietly generous to writers in need.
[2] Sir Philip Francis (1740-1818) returned home to England in 1781 from India with a fortune made by gambling at cards and having fought a duel with Warren Hastings, the Governor-General. A friend of the Prince Regent, renowned for his sardonic humour and impatience with the long-winded, he was reputed to be the author of *The Letters of Junius*, bitterly scornful political diatribes which appeared in the *Public Advertiser* in 1769-72.

Louis Philippe; with some of whose secrets he was acquainted, and with whom he had been mixed up in various political intrigues, before the citizen-king came to the throne. He was universally considered to be one of the wittiest men of the age: but all his *bons mots* were in French, and the greater part of them lose by translation.

A DUEL BETWEEN TWO OLD FRIENDS

General A. de Girardin,[1] some forty years back, had a serious quarrel with one of his old friends, the Marquis de Briancourt, about a lady. A duel was the consequence. Pistols were chosen; but, prior to exchanging shots, de Girardin's second went (as was the custom) and felt the right side of his friend's antagonist, but found nothing there to indicate the existence of padding, &c. Accordingly, after measurement of the ground, pistols were handed to the combatants. The Marquis changed his pistol from his right into his left hand; both parties fired, and the Marquis fell. The seconds flew to the aid of the wounded man, but, to their astonishment, on opening his waistcoat several sheets of thick paper were found folded over the region of the heart. Notwithstanding this device, the blow from the bullet created a sore on the left side, which was never effectually cured. The Marquis died shortly afterwards.

THE GARDES DU CORPS

I knew several of those gentlemen who had succeeded in getting into the companies of the Gardes du Corps [including] Warren, an Irishman by birth, but whose father had married a French lady. Warren stood six feet four inches in height, and was an extremely powerful man. He was always in hot water with his comrades, and had fought duels with several of them, and his face and body showed marks of sabre cuts; indeed, fighting and drinking were his delights. I never saw a man so violent; when he had finished his bottle of champagne and a few glasses of brandy he became quite outrageous. He usually breakfasted, when off duty, at Tortoni's upon beefsteaks and broiled kidneys; and any one to whom he bore a grudge who entered the room at that moment was sure to be roughly handled.

It happened that a distinguished painter, had returned to Paris from

---

[1] Général comte Alexandre de Girardin (1776–1855). Émile de Girardin, who took his name upon the acceptance for publication of his first novel, was his illegitimate son.

England, where he had played a shameful and disgusting part. The
painter had been employed by the celebrated Mr Hope of Duchess
Street to paint the portrait of his wife, Mrs Hope, afterwards Lady
Beresford.[1] When the painting was finished, Mr Hope objected to pay
for it, stating that it was a daub. The enraged painter, determined to be
revenged, took the portrait home with him, and in a few days returned
it with the addition of a beast representing Mr Hope, in the presence of
his beautiful wife. A trial was the consequence, and the painter was cast
in damages. After this untoward event, London proved too hot for the
Frenchman, and he returned to Paris, where his imprudence in
speaking in no measured terms of the English got him into a scrape
which cost him his life.

The painter (unluckily for him) arrived at Tortoni's to breakfast at
the moment when Warren was in one of his dangerous fits, and
attempted to appease Warren by going up to him and begging him to
be more tranquil. This sort of impertinence Warren could not brook,
and exclaiming, 'You are the blackguard who laughs at the English,' he
seized hold of the artist, carried him as if he had been a bundle of straw,
and held him out of the window. By the interference of those gentlemen
present and the crowd below in the street, Warren was persuaded to
carry back the terrified painter into the room. A duel was the
consequence, in which the combatants were to fight with pistols until
one of them was killed: Warren won the first toss, he levelled and fired,
and his adversary fell mortally wounded. This duel was much talked of,
but no one lamented the result of the duel; for the painter was
overbearing, and generally disliked by his countrymen as well as by
foreigners.

I can scarcely look back to those days of duelling without shuddering.
If you looked at a man it was enough; for without having given the
slightest offence, cards were exchanged, and the odds were that you
stood a good chance of being shot, or run through the body, or maimed
for life.

LORD JERSEY AND AN OFFICER OF THE GUARDS

When duelling was at its height in England, the most absurd pretexts
were made for calling a man out. I recollect that at one of the dinners

---

[1] Thomas Hope, author of *Anastasius, or Memoirs of a Greek written at the Close of the
Eighteenth Century* (*c.* 1770–1831). He married the Hon. Louisa Beresford, his first cousin,
daughter of Lord Decies, Archbishop of Tuam. After his death, his widow married William
Carr, Viscount Beresford, the general.

at the Thatched House in St James's Street,[1] Mr Willis, the proprietor, in passing behind the chairs occupied by the company, was accosted by a Captain in the 3d Guards in a rather satirical manner. Mr Willis, smarting under the caustic remarks of the gallant Captain, said aloud, – 'Sir, I wrote to you at the request of Lady Jersey, saying that as her Ladyship was unacquainted with you, I had been instructed to reply to your letter by stating that the Lady Patronesses declined sending you a ticket for the ball.'[2] This statement, made in a public room, greatly irritated the Captain; his friends in vain endeavoured to calm his wrath, and he sent a cartel the following day to Lord Jersey, requesting he would name his second, &c. Lord Jersey replied in a very dignified manner, saying that if all persons who did not receive tickets from his wife were to call him to account for want of courtesy on her part, he should have to make up his mind to become a target for young officers, and he therefore declined the honour of the proposed meeting.

[1] The Thatched House Tavern, St James's Street, frequented by Swift and later by members of the Dilettanti Society, was demolished in 1814 and, having been rebuilt, was demolished again in 1843 when the Conservative Club was erected on the site. The Thatched House Club, known familiarly as 'The Ale House', of which Sheridan was a member, occupied premises next door.

[2] The Countess of Jersey was a Lady Patroness of Almack's (see page 71).

10

Artists and Men of Letters

A DINNER AT SIR JAMES BLAND BURGES'S, IN LOWER
BROOK STREET, AUTUMN, 1815

I was once invited to dinner by Sir James Burges, father of my friend,
Captain Burges of the Guards:[1] it was towards the end of the season
1815. I there met, to my great delight, Lord Byron and Sir Walter Scott.

Walter Scott was quite delightful; he appeared full of fire and
animation, and told some interesting anecdotes connected with his early
life in Scotland. I remember that he proved himself, what would have
been called in the olden times he delighted to portray, 'a stout trencher-
man;' nor were his attentions confined by any means to the eatables; on
the contrary, he showed himself worthy to have made a third in the
famous carousal in *Ivanhoe*, between the Black Knight and the Holy
Clerk of Copmanhurst.

Byron, whom I had before seen at the shooting-galleries and
elsewhere, was then a very handsome man, with remarkably fine eyes
and hair; but was, as usual, all show-off and affectation. I recollect his
saying that he disliked seeing women eat, or to have their company at
dinner, from a wish to believe, if possible, in their more ethereal nature;

---

[1] Sir James Bland Burges (1752–1824), a prominent Member of Parliament. He became
Under Secretary of State at the Foreign Office in 1789. He was also an occasional
playwright and author of an immenseley long poem, *Richard I*, which filled eighteen
volumes. He assumed the name of Lamb on coming into possession of the estate of his
friend, John Lamb.

but he was rallied into avowing that his chief dislike to their presence at the festive board arose from the fact of their being helped first, and consequently getting all the wings of the chickens, whilst men had to be content with the legs or other parts. Byron, on this occasion, was in great good-humour, and full of boyish and even boisterous mirth.

I never assisted at a more agreeable dinner. According to the custom of the day, we sat late; the poets, statesmen, and soldiers all drank an immense quantity of wine, and I for one felt the effects of it next day. Walter Scott gave one or two recitations, in a very animated manner, from the ballads that he had been collecting, which delighted his auditory.

LORD BYRON

I knew very little of Lord Byron personally, but lived much with two of his intimate friends, Scrope Davies[1] and Wedderburn Webster,[2] from whom I frequently heard many anecdotes of him. I regret that I remember so few; and wish that I had written down those told me by poor Scrope Davies, one of the most agreeable men I ever met.

When Byron was at Cambridge, he was introduced to Scrope Davies by their mutual friend, Matthews, who was afterwards drowned in the river Cam.[3] After Matthews's death, Davies became Byron's particular friend, and was admitted to his rooms at all hours. Upon one occasion he found the poet in bed with his hair *en papillote* [in curl-papers], upon which Scrope cried, 'Ha, ha! Byron, I have at last caught you acting the part of the Sleeping Beauty.'

Byron, in a rage, exclaimed, 'No, Scrope; the part of a d——d fool, you should have said.'

'Well, then, anything you please; but you have succeeded admirably in deceiving your friends, for it was my conviction that your hair curled naturally.'

[1] See note, p. 11.

[2] James (later Sir James) Wedderburn Webster (1789-1840). A Cambridge friend of Byron and a minor poet. He married Lady Frances Annesley. A notorious seducer, he once told Byron, 'I think any woman fair game, because I can depend upon Ly F's principles – she can't go wrong, and therefore I may.' In fact, she did go wrong, with Byron and Wellington amongst others.

[3] Charles Skinner Matthews (1782-1811). Byron's close friend at Trinity College, Cambridge. After his death by drowning, Byron wrote to Scrope Davies, 'In ability, who was like Matthews? How did we all shrink before him? You do me but justice in saying I would have risked my paltry existence to have preserved him . . . I am almost desolate'. He was a keen boxer as well as a swimmer. He was also an outspoken atheist and in politics radical.

'Yes, naturally every night,' returned the poet; 'but do not, my dear Scrope, let the cat out of the bag, for I am as vain of my curls as a girl of sixteen.'

When in London, Byron used to go to Manton's shooting-gallery, in Davies Street, to try his hand, as he said, at a wafer. Wedderburn Webster was present when the poet, intensely delighted with his own skill, boasted to Joe Manton that he considered himself the best shot in London. 'No, my lord,' replied Manton, 'not the best; but your shooting to-day was respectable.' Whereupon Byron waxed wroth, and left the shop in a violent passion.

Byron lived a great deal at Brighton, his house being opposite the Pavilion. He was fond of boating, and was generally accompanied by a lad, who was said to be a girl in boy's clothes. This report was confirmed to me by Webster, who was then living at Brighton. The vivid description of the page in *Lara*,[1] no doubt, gave some plausibility to this often-told tale. I myself witnessed the dexterous manner in which Byron used to get into his boat; for, while standing on the beach, I once saw him vault into it with the agility of a harlequin, in spite of his lame foot.

On one occasion, whilst his lordship was dining with a few of his friends in Charles Street, Pall Mall, a letter was delivered to Scrope Davies, which required an immediate answer. Scrope, after reading its contents, handed it to Lord Byron. It was thus worded:

'MY DEAR SCROPE, – Lend me £500 for a few days; the funds are shut for the dividends, or I would not have made this request.

G. BRUMMELL'

The reply was:

'MY DEAR BRUMMELL – All my money is locked in the funds.

SCROPE DAVIES.'

This was just before Brummell's escape to the Continent.

I have frequently asked Scrope Davies his private opinion of Lord Byron, and invariably received the same answer – that he considered Lord Byron very agreeable and clever, but vain, overbearing, conceited, suspicious, and jealous. Byron hated Palmerston, but liked Peel, and thought that the whole world ought to be constantly employed in admiring his poetry and himself; he never could write a poem or a drama without making himself its hero, and he was always the subject of his own conversation.

[1] Byron's poem in heroic couplets, published in 1814.

During one of Hobhouse's[1] visits to Byron, at his villa near Genoa, and whilst they were walking in the garden, his lordship suddenly turned upon his guest, and, *à propos* of nothing, exclaimed, 'Now, I know, Hobhouse, you are looking at my foot.' Upon which Hobhouse kindly replied, 'My dear Byron, nobody thinks of or looks at anything but your head.'[2]

LORD BYRON AND DAN MACKINNON

During Lord Byron's sojourn at Lisbon, he was much amused with Dan Mackinnon's various funny stories.[3] Upon one occasion Dan's time was entirely taken up by presenting women with toothbrushes, a supply of which he had received by the packet from London. Opposite his quarters there lived two very pretty Portuguese ladies, who, unmindful of Dan's proximity, and of the fact that his windows commanded a view of their chamber, dressed, undressed, and went through their morning ablutions and toilet. Dan's astonishment was great when he perceived that the fair ones never brushed their teeth; and he lost no time in sending his servant with two tooth-brushes in paper, well perfumed and sealed up. The ladies opened the packet, and appeared delighted with the present; but judge of Mackinnon's horror in beholding those dainty creatures perseveringly brushing their raven locks with the tiny brushes!

Lord Byron was a great admirer of well-formed hands: he preferred a pretty hand to a pretty face. He was asked whether he admired pretty feet: his answer was, 'that he never went so low;' 'and as for teeth,' said he, 'a blackamoor has as white a set of teeth as the fairest lady in the land.' His Lordship added, 'A Frenchman thinks very little of the teeth, face, or colour of the hair; provided a woman put on her cashmere veil in a graceful manner and is well shod, then he is in raptures with her.'

Dan Mackinnon was ever in good spirits and good humour, and he was a great swell both in Lisbon and London. His calm smile, black

---

[1] John Cam Hobhouse, later first Baron Broughton de Gyfford (1786–1869), Byron's friend from their days at Cambridge together. Member of Parliament for Westminster, he became Secretary at War in Earl Grey's ministry in 1832, his radical opinions having much mellowed with age. He was said to have been the first to use the term 'His Majesty's Opposition' to describe the anti-government side in Parliament.

[2] Byron was always extremely sensitive about the club foot which occasioned his pronounced limp. His right foot was bent inwards and he could walk only on the balls of his toes. Painful treatment undergone as a child had exacerbated the condition.

[3] See note, p. 175.

eyes, and splendid figure, when he strutted in uniform down St James's Street, struck every one with admiration. He was the most active man I ever saw: he would run, jump, and climb against the most expert professional gymnasts.

ROBERT SOUTHEY, THE POET

In the year 1803 my father received a letter of introduction from Mr Rees, of the well-known firm of Longman, Paternoster Row, presenting Robert Southey, the poet, to him.[1] He came into Wales with the hope of finding a cottage to reside in. Accordingly we rode up the Valley of Neath to look at a cottage about eight miles from the town. The poet, delighted with the scenery and situation, decided upon taking it; but the owner, unfortunately for the honour of Welshmen, actually declined to let it to Robert Southey, fearing that a poet could not find security for the small annual rent of twenty-five pounds. This circumstance led the man of letters, who eventually became one of the most distinguished men of his day, to seek a home elsewhere, and the Lakes were at length chosen as his residence. Probably the picturesque beauties of Cumberland compensated the Laureate for the indignity put upon him by the Welshman.

ROGERS AND LUTTRELL

I saw a good deal of the poet Rogers during his frequent visits to Paris; and often visited him in his apartments, which were always on the fourth or fifth storey of the hotel or private house in which he lived. He was rich, and by no means avaricious, and chose those lofty chambers partly from a poetic wish to see the sun rise with greater brilliancy, and partly from a fancy that the exercise he was obliged to take in going up and down stairs, would prove beneficial to his liver.

I could relate many unpublished anecdotes of Rogers, but they lose their piquancy when one attempts to narrate them. There was so much in his appearance, in that cadaverous, unchanging countenance, in the peculiar low drawling voice, and rather tremulous accents in which he spoke. His intonations were very much those one fancies a ghost would use if forced by some magic spell to give utterance to sounds. The mild venom of every word was a remarkable trait in his conversation. One

---

[1] Robert Southey (1774-1843) settled at Greta Hall, Keswick, in 1803. He was appointed Poet Laureate in 1813.

might have compared the old poet to one of those velvety caterpillars that crawl gently and quietly over the skin, but leave an irritating blister behind. To those, like myself, who were *sans* consequence, and with whom he feared no rivalry, he was very good-natured and amiable, and a most pleasant companion, with a fund of curious anecdote about everything and everybody. But woe betide those in great prosperity and renown; they had, like the Roman emperor, in Rogers the personification of the slave who bade them 'remember they were mortal.'

At an evening party many years since at Lady Jersey's, every one was praising [a duke] who had just come in, and who had lately attained his majority. There was a perfect chorus of admiration, to this effect: 'Everything is in his favour – he has good looks, considerable abilities, and a hundred thousand a year.' Rogers, who had been carefully examining the 'young ruler,' listened to these encomiums for some time in silence, and at last remarked, with an air of great exultation, and in his most venomous manner, 'Thank God, he has got bad teeth!'

His well-known epigram on Mr Ward, afterwards Lord Dudley –

'They say that Ward's no heart, but I deny it;
He has a heart, and gets his speeches by it' –

was provoked by a remark made at table by Mr Ward. On Rogers observing that his carriage had broken down, and that he had been obliged to come in a hackney-coach, Mr Ward grumbled out in a very audible whisper, 'In a hearse, I should think;' alluding to the poet's corpse-like appearance. This remark Rogers never forgave; and I have no doubt pored for days over his retaliatory impromptu, for he had no facility in composition: Sydney Smith[1] used to say that if Rogers was writing a dozen verses, the street was strewn with straw, the knocker tied up, and the answer to the tender inquiries of his anxious friends was, that Mr Rogers was as well as could be expected.

It used to be very amusing in London to see Rogers with his *fidus Achates*, Luttrell.[2,3] They were inseparable, though rival wits, and

---

[1] Sydney Smith (1771-1845), wit, journalist and from 1809 the kindly, good-natured parson of Foston-le-Clay, Yorkshire. He helped to found the *Edinburgh Review*, for which he wrote regularly.

[2] *Fidus Achates* – bosom friend. Achates was the faithful companion of Aeneas in Virgil's *Aeneid*.

[3] Henry Luttrell (*c.* 1765-1851). His mother was said to be a gardener's daughter. He was the 'most epigrammatic conversationalist' that Byron had ever met; while for Lady Blessington he was 'the one talker who always [made her] think'. He was often to be found at Holland House, where he once stared in silent astonishment at a man who had failed to laugh at one of Sydney Smith's jokes.

constantly saying bitter things of each other. Luttrell was the natural son of Lord Carhampton, Commander-in-Chief in Ireland. I consider him to have been the most agreeable man I ever met. He was far more brilliant in conversation than Rogers; and his animated, bustling manner formed an agreeable contrast with the spiteful calmness of his corpse-like companion. He was extremely irritable and even passionate; and in his moments of anger he would splutter and stutter like a maniac in his anxiety to give utterance to the flow of thoughts which crowded his mind, and I might almost say, his mouth.

On one occasion the late Lady Holland took him a drive in her carriage over a rough road, and as she was very nervous, she insisted on being driven at a foot's pace. This ordeal lasted some hours, and when he was at last released, poor Luttrell, perfectly exasperated, rushed into the nearest club-house, and exclaimed, clenching his teeth and hands, 'The very funerals passed us!'

The last time I saw him was at Paris, in June 1849, when [he was] above eighty years of age. We thought him quite delightful. He had lost none of the fire and eagerness of youth, but took the greatest interest in everything that was going on in Paris at that most exciting period, and I had for several days the great pleasure of acting as his cicerone.

Strange to say, on his return to England he married a second time, but died shortly afterwards. He was the author of *Advice to Julia*, and other poems; but nothing that he ever wrote gave an idea of the amusing variety of his conversation, and his brilliant wit and humour. He was the last of the 'Conversationists.'

BALZAC AND EUGÈNE SUE

It has been my good fortune, during the many years I have lived in Paris, to meet some remarkable characters, among whom I should wish particularly to name, the celebrated novelists Balzac,[1] Eugène Sue, and Dumas.

Balzac had nothing in his outward man that could in any way respond to the ideal his readers were likely to form of the enthusiastic admirer of beauty and elegance in all its forms and phases: the wonderful master-mind, which had so vividly drawn the pictures of his

---

[1] Honoré de Balzac (1799–1850) was born in Tours of peasant stock. He lived in an apartment in the rue Cassini, and later in a house in the suburb of Chaillot. His genius as a young writer was concealed behind a brash and noisy manner and clothes of extreme flashiness. He worked on occasions up to sixteen hours a day.

heroes and heroines, that one had ended by imagining one had lived in the charmed circle.

The great enchanter was one of the oiliest and commonest-looking mortals I ever beheld; being short and corpulent, with a broad florid face, a cascade of double chins, and straight greasy hair. The only striking feature in that Friar Tuck countenance was his eye; dark, flashing, wicked, full of sarcasm and unholy fire.

Balzac had that unwashed appearance which seems generally to belong to French *literati*, and dressed in the worst possible taste, wore sparkling jewels on a dirty shirt-front, and diamond rings on unwashed fingers. He talked little, but it was evident that nothing escaped him, and that bright eye seemed almost to read the secrets of the heart. No literary man, except perhaps Alexandre Dumas, ever ran through so much money as Balzac. The immense sums which he received for his writings were spent in the most absurd attempts at aristocratic luxury, which ended invariably in a steeple-chase between the great author and the bailiffs.

Eugène Sue was the very reverse of Balzac, both in appearance and manner.[1] Nothing could have been more correct and scrupulously neat than his dress, which was rather dandified, but in good taste, according to the notions of twenty or thirty years ago. He wore always a very broad-brimmed hat, of glossy newness, and remarkably tight, light-coloured trousers: which, by the bye, were not particularly becoming to a man built in a stout mould; but a Frenchman who cannot diminish the rotundity of his abdomen, generally revenges himself upon his legs, which he circumscribes in the smallest possible compass, giving himself very much the appearance of what we Englishmen are taught to believe to be his national characteristic and prototype – a frog.

Eugène Sue was rather above the middle height, strongly-built, with somewhat high shoulders. His hair and brows were very dark, his eyes blue, long, and rather closed, and his complexion of a livid paleness. In general society, he did not show off, and preferred rather being treated as a man of the world, than as a distinguished writer. But when he found himself among some kindred spirits, and felt he was appreciated, his conversation was particularly agreeable. He never had the sparkling wit and versatility of Dumas, or the extraordinary descriptive powers of

---

[1] Eugène Sue (1804–57). A naval surgeon before he became a writer of rather melodramatic novels, he inherited a fortune from his father and was well known for his extravagant way of life and smart attire. An opponent of Napoleon III, he went to live at Annecy in 1851.

Balzac; but he possessed the immense advantage over his great rivals in being veritably *un homme du monde*, living in the very best Parisian society. He could, therefore, make the men and women in his novels act and speak as people really do, and not like workmen in their Sunday coats, or actors in the old melodramas.

Sue's imagination was wonderful; but one can see that in his books he carried out his own principle, that the beginning of the novel was three parts of the battle. He always commenced his tales in a manner certain to fix the attention of the reader; but we generally find towards the close of the numberless volumes symptoms of weariness in the writer, which are apt to communicate themselves to the reader.

He was remarkable for the beauty of his horses; his cab was one of the best-appointed in Paris; his house in the Rue de la Pépinière (now an asylum) was a perfect *bonbonnière*,[1] and his dinners were renowned for their excellence. He was supposed (and to my knowledge with considerable reason) to lead a very Sardanapalian life.[2] Strange stories are told of his castle in Sologne, where he was waited on by a number of beautiful women, of all countries, and of all shades of colour.

In manners, Eugène Sue was particularly gentlemanlike and courteous, without servility. He held his own, but with good taste and good breeding. He had a wonderful passion for beautiful flowers, and was well skilled in botany. He had been in early life a navy surgeon, and in his distant voyages had become thoroughly versed in the names and properties of rare tropical plants. He had in his house a beautiful conservatory, full of valuable exotics. His handkerchiefs were always steeped in essence of bouquet; and he had generally a tuberose or a camellia in the button-hole of his coat. Though a man utterly devoid of moral principle, Sue was charitable and kind to the poor, and obliging to his friends. At the Revolution of 1848, he went all lengths with the Red Republican party; and, after being one of the members for Paris in the National Assembly, was obliged to leave France, and passed the few remaining years of his life in Savoy, in complete seclusion.

Eugène Sue had grown very unwieldy; and, as he lived in a village at the foot of a mountain called, I think, the Solève [Mont Salève], he had set himself, in order to grow thinner, on a course of training, which consisted in climbing to the top of this high hill. The weather, which was very sultry, and the over-exertion, brought on a fever, which carried him off in a few days. His death was attributed, among the ignorant

---

[1] Sweetmeat box, hence neat little house or apartment.
[2] Luxuriously effeminate – from Sardanapalus, last King of Nineveh.

peasantry, to poison given by the Jesuits, who had never forgiven the violent attacks he had made on their order in the ardent and eloquent pages of the *Juif Errant*.[1]

ALEXANDRE DUMAS

Of all the distinguished writers of the nineteenth century that have appeared in France, Alexandre Dumas is perhaps the most remarkable, from the versatility of his talent and the brilliancy of his imagination, which carries the reader along with unflagging interest through dozens of volumes.[2] Who among us has not in fancy shared the perils of the *Trois Mousquetaires?* or followed with unabated interest the avenging course of *Monte Christo?*

Alexandre Dumas is the son of General Alexandre Dumas, who served with some distinction in the republican armies of France, and was a native of one of the French West India Islands. In appearance, he is far above the middle height, and is almost a mulatto, with woolly curling hair, and copper complexion. This peculiarity of appearance has given rise to some amusing *traits d'esprit*, which, though well known in France, may be new to some of my English readers.

'A. Dumas fils' (the son of the writer), who has inherited all his father's wit, with a quiet and gentlemanlike demeanour, said the great novelist was so fond of 'show-off,' that he was always expecting him to get up behind his own carriage, in order to make people think that he had got a negro footman.

Dumas, who is the most generous and kind-hearted man in the world, had been away from his house in Paris on one of his many trips to foreign lands; and, with his usual munificence, had allowed his

---

[1] *Le Juif errant* (*The Wandering Jew*), was published in instalments in 1844–5.

[2] Alexandre Dumas (Alexandre Dumas Davy de la Pailleterie; 1802–70). His father, the natural son of the marquis de la Pailleterie and a black woman of San Domingo, was an ordinary soldier in the army of the *ancien regime* before becoming one of Napoleon's generals. Alexandre had come to Paris with the intention of becoming a lawyer before turning to writing plays and then historical novels. A most flamboyant personality, he characteristically travelled to Sicily when Garibaldi was dictator there, accompanied by two young Parisian friends (one acting as his secretary), a doctor, a Greek youth whom he had befriended and educated, a photographer, and the pregnant, nineteen-year-old daughter of a bucket-maker, stylishly dressed in a velvet sailor-suit and introduced by her lover sometimes as his son, sometimes as his nephew. Alexandre Dumas (Dumas *fils*) (1824–95), one of the illegitimate sons of Dumas *père*, was a far more respectable character than his father, as reflected in the content and message of his plays. Dumas *père* married the actress Ida Ferrier, after having lived with her for several years. She went to live in Italy not long after the marriage.

friends the run of his house and cellar during his absence. On his return home, he gave a great breakfast to celebrate the event. His numerous guests, towards the end of the repast, expressed a wish to drink his health in champagne, and the servant went downstairs, as if to look for some, but soon returned with the dismal intelligence that it had been all drunk. Dumas slipped a few napoleons into the valet's hand, and ordered him to buy some at the neighbouring *restaurateurs*; but having some suspicion, he followed the servant, when, to his great surprise, he beheld the fellow emerging from his own cellar, from whence he had brought up his own champagne. Dumas, though the soul of good-nature, was about to turn the rascal off on the spot, when the man fell at his kind master's feet, reminded him that he had a wife and family, and implored his mercy.

'Well, I will forgive you this time,' said the great writer; *'mais au moins une autre fois faites-moi crédit.'*

Dumas married an actress, from whom he separated, making her a liberal allowance, which was seldom or never paid. A friend of the lady went to expostulate on the distressed condition in which she found herself. 'I will double her annuity,' cried out the generous author. 'You would do better,' said the more matter-of-fact friend, 'to pay her the allowance you make her.'

The sums which the 'Père Prodigue' spent on his Monte-Christo villa near St Germain – so called from having been built at the time his novel of *Monte Christo* met with so much success, – were fabulous. He was horribly cheated by architects, builders, upholsterers, and in fact by everybody he employed; yet he did not succeed in making it a pretty house. Nothing could be more inconvenient, or in worse taste, than the way in which the rooms were laid out: the only thing that struck me as being pretty was the little dressing-room in white marble. This 'Folie Dumas' did not remain long in his possession, but was sold about twelve years ago.

Dumas is one of the most amusing men I ever met, and a most wonderful talker. His wit is prodigious, his fund of anecdote inexhaustible, the strength of his lungs overpowering. To give my English readers an idea of his Herculean powers of conversation, I may remark that I was present at a dinner some twelve or fifteen years ago, where Lord Brougham and Dumas were among the company, and the loquacious and eloquent ex-chancellor could not literally get in a single word, but had to sit, for the first and last time in his life, a perfect dummy.

CIVILITY REWARDED

We have all heard the story alluded to by Charles Lamb,[1] in the *Essays of Elia*, of the bank clerk who was in the habit, as he proceeded daily to his office, of giving a penny to a crossing-sweeper, and how in process of time the sweeper died and left £5000, which sum had been half a century in accumulating, to the charitable *employé*. The grandfather of the present Marquis of Hertford having been very civil to an old gentleman in a stage-coach during a journey to York, the said old gentleman very kindly died shortly after, and left his lordship a large fortune.

But I know of no incident more curious than the following; the moral of which would seem to be, that we ought all to go to church early and secure a good place. Like the novel of *Waverley*,[2] "'tis sixty years since,' when a young gentleman named Green, the son of a clergyman, wishing to hear a famous preacher, went one Sunday morning unusually early to church, and thereby secured a good place in a pew near the preacher. The church filled rapidly, and a venerable and rather infirm-looking old man, after walking up and down the various aisles, being unable to get a seat, was about to leave the church, when Green, who was a good-natured young fellow, took pity on him, as he looked very weak and ill, and offered him his seat; it was accepted with many thanks, whilst Green stood with his back against the wall during the service and sermon. On leaving the church the old gentleman again thanked him, and asked his name and address, which were given. A few days after, Mr Green received an invitation to dinner from the stranger, who was living in Grosvenor Square. It would appear that the acquaintance thus accidentally formed, became a fast friendship, for the old gentleman shortly afterwards died, and left the whole of his fortune, a very considerable one, to his young friend, with the condition that he should take the name of Wilkinson in addition to that of Green. I may add that the young gentleman made the most excellent use of the fortune which he owed to his good-nature and civility, and became the head of a very popular and prosperous family.

À propos of pews and pew-openers, I remember, when I was staying at Deal some years back, hearing of an incident in which a lady, who had

---

[1] Charles Lamb (1775–1834), the essayist, was the son of a lawyer's clerk. He himself had been a clerk at South Sea House and worked at the India House for over thirty years.

[2] Sir Walter Scott's novel *Waverley* was published in 1814, the first in his series of *Waverley* novels, which appeared until his death in 1832.

not the good-breeding of Mr Green, played a somewhat unenviable part.

The Duke of Wellington, then residing at Walmer Castle, had walked one Sunday evening into Deal, and entered Trinity Church. After wandering about for some time in search of the sexton (who, as a matter of course, was engaged elsewhere), the Duke ensconced himself in a roomy-looking pew, in front of the pulpit. After a short time a lady of portly and pompous appearance, the owner of the pew, entered. After muttering a prayer, she cast a scowl at the intruder, which was intended to drive him out of the place he had taken. She had not the least idea who he was, and would probably have given her eyes, had she known him, to have touched the hem of the great Duke's cloth cloak, or asked for his autograph. Seeing that the stranger bore the brunt of her indignant glance without moving, the lady bluntly told the Duke, as she did not know him, that she must request he would immediately leave her pew. His Grace obeyed, and chose another seat. When he was leaving the church, at the end of the service, and had at last found the sexton, who received him with many bows and salutations, he said –

'Tell that lady she has turned the Dule of Wellington out of her pew this evening.'

COUNTESS GUICCIOLI AND MADAME DODWELL

I knew Madame Guiccioli by sight in her youthful days,[1] when she was a celebrity, owing to her acquaintance with Lord Byron. I was rather disappointed with her personal appearance, as, though handsome, she give one more the idea of a healthy rosy, jolly-looking milkmaid, than a heroine of romance.

Madame Guiccioli was short in stature, and somewhat square-built; her hair was golden, her eyes were blue, her complexion and teeth beautiful in the extreme, and her face would have been much admired had she been taller. As it was, there was a great disproportion between

---

[1] Teresa Gamba-Ghiselli (1800–73) married the elderly Count Alessandro Guiccioli in 1818. The next year she fell in love with Byron, who was accepted as her lover by her husband. When the Countess returned to Ravenna, Byron followed her there. They later lived together in Venice. Byron refused to take her with him to Greece, where he died. 'She is pretty,' Bryon told his friend, John Cam Hobhouse, 'but has no tact; answers aloud when she should whisper – talks of old age to old ladies who want to pass for young; and this blessed night horrified a correct company . . . by calling out to me "mio Byron" in an audible key during a dead silence of pause in other prattlers, who stared and whispered to their respective serventi.'

her colossal head and her short figure. Her bust was also on a large scale, and very fine. She was, like most Italian women, unaffected, kind, and matter-of-fact, but had nothing in physical appearance or intellectual gifts to account for her having inspired a romantic passion. She was 'of the earth, earthy.'

At the same period I was introduced to a person who for many years passed for being the handsomest woman in Europe – a Roman lady, who had married a very ugly old antiquary named Dodwell.[1] The lovely Theresa had been offered the choice of a convent, or this ill-washed Briton. After much weeping and gnashing of her beautiful teeth, the lady, who was then only sixteen years of age, chose the latter.

Madame Dodwell was what English novelists describe as rather *petite* than otherwise, but her face was acknowledged by every painter, sculptor, and poet to be the most perfect in creation; she had crisp, black, waving hair, the large, hazel, almond-shaped eye, full of Italian fire or Eastern languor, the classical features, the full mouth, magnificent teeth, and clear, pale, brunette complexion, so rarely met with. Perfectly illiterate, but full of wit and fun, this beautiful woman amused herself by chaining many victims to her triumphal car; while, like a true Italian, her heart was faithful all the time to the one reigning attachment. She talked of her own beauty with as much simple composure as a man might have in dwelling on his horse or dog. With all this self-appreciation, she was perfectly unaffected, and had none of the grimaces of an acknowledged beauty, but remained calm and collected in the consciousness of her own undisputed superiority.

CHATEAUBRIAND

This great man passed many years of his life in absolute poverty and distress in London.[2] He was even obliged to wash his own linen. After the restoration of the Bourbons, Louis XVIII named Chateaubriand his ambassador in England, and during this period his great delight was to

---

[1] Edward Dodwell (1767–1832), the rich traveller, archaeologist and collector. His *Classical and Topographical Tour through Greece* was published in two volumes in 1819. According to Thomas Moore, he was 'a great favourite with the Pope [Pius VII] who always called him "Caro Doodle".' Moore added that his wife, thirty years younger than himself, was 'a beautiful creature'. She was the daughter of Count Giraud. After Dodwell's death she married the Count de Spaur, Bavarian Ambassador in Rome.

[2] François-René de Chateaubriand (1768–1848), the son of an impoverished nobleman, author of the *Mémoires d'outre-tombe*. From 1793 to 1800 he lived in London, where he supported himself by teaching and translating. He returned as Ambassador in 1822.

enumerate the many shifts he had employed to keep body and soul together; but what delighted him more than all was to revisit the banks of the Thames, near Chelsea, where he formerly washed his shirts and stockings.

THOMAS MOORE

During my residence in Paris, several distinguished men took up their abode for a time, and were universally well received. Thomas Moore stayed for a considerable length of time,[1] and was a favourite guest everywhere, but he was attracted only where a good *cuisine* would satisfy the taste of the *gourmet*. He realised (at least in Paris) Sir Edward Lytton Bulwer's admirable conception of Lord Guloseton, in his ever favourite novel, *Pelham*.[2] When Moore had received an invitation to dinner from an untried Amphitryon,[3] previous to returning an answer he cross-examined all who visited him. Had his friend an established kitchen, with a *chef* of his own? or did he depend upon a neighbouring *restaurateur*? Did the *chef* deserve the name of an *artiste*? Were the wines of a choice quality? Did they come direct from wine-growing countries? or were they likely to be the product of some Parisian wine-doctor? All these questions were asked with a serious earnestness that exhibited the great poet's exquisite taste in the pleasures of the table. It must, however, be added, that he was equally anxious that the invited should be intellectual or distinguished persons; and one stipulation in accepting the invitation was that English should be the language of the table: nothing seemed to annoy him more thoroughly than to find that, for the sake of a single individual, French should be the order of the day.

Whatever might be his peculiarities and his demands, however, they were amply repaid by the brilliancy of his conversation and the charm of his manners. He would now and then, when entirely at his ease with well-known friends, give an imitation of the great Irish orator Curran,[4] which those who had known the original pronounced to be perfect, while those who had never seen him were delighted with the wit and

---

[1] See note, p. 11. Moore lived in Paris in 1819-22.

[2] Lord Lytton's second novel, *Pelham, or The Adventures of a Gentleman*, was published in 1828. The character of Thornton in this book is based on John Thurtell, who was hanged at Hertford in 1824 for the murder of a London solicitor.

[3] Amphitryon, a host, a giver of dinners, from Molière's comedy *Amphitryon*, based on the *Amphitruo* of Plautus.

[4] John Philpot Curran (1750-1817). Like many great advocates, he was less successful in Parliament than in courts of law.

humour that were introduced; but it was when the dinner was ended, the drawing-room reached, and a few of his much loved countrywomen were present, that the charm of Moore's society was felt. Almost without an invitation he would unaffectedly sit down to the pianoforte and warble forth some of those enchanting melodies which he has given to a grateful nation, accompanying himself with exquisite taste; his voice was rich in tone, and the expression he threw into his own words, combined with his beaming face and genial manner, elicited the admiration of all. Those who have heard him sing 'Those Evening Bells,' and 'Oft in the Stilly Night,' will carry a recollection of one of the most agreeable moments of their lives. He fully deserved the cognomen of 'Anacreon,' by which he was much known in Parisian society.[1] The French are accustomed to Christian names of Greek origin; they have Achilles, Hector, and I have known several Nestors and one Epaminondas: indeed, it is their not unfrequent custom to drop the surname. Many men are distinguished entirely by the prenomen; and as 'Anacreon' Moore had been the sobriquet of the illustrious Irish lyric poet, from the time of his translation of the classic bard, he was soon christened 'Anacreon,' and as such generally known.

I remember once visiting M. Sommarivas's collection,[2] and on mounting the staircase, the domestic whispered into my ear that 'Monsieur Anacréon' was in one of the saloons; as that name had not then reached my ears, I asked him who was 'Monsieur Anacréon;' the man looked at me with something like astonishment at the question, and after a short pause said, 'It is your great English Béranger[3] that is looking at our collection.' On entering the saloon my mind was enlightened by recognising the bard of Erin,[4] who, with animated looks and lively gestures, was pointing out the beauties of an antique statue; he wore the earnest and intellectual expression which distinguished him when delighting his friends with a barcarolle, or one of his sweetest melodies. Moore always heard with infinite pleasure any compliment paid to his wife; indeed, one of his most remarkable characteristics was his intense fondness for her; he was in fact the most uxorious of mortals, and though he could smile on any pretty woman, all his affections were centred in his charming 'Bessy.'[5]

[1] Anacreon, the Greek lyric poet born in Ionia in about 570 BC.

[2] Giovanni Battista Sommariva (1760–1826), art collector.

[3] Pierre-Jean de Béranger (1780–1857), regarded in his day as the national poet of France.

[4] Erin, the ancient name for Ireland.

[5] Moore's wife, whom he married in 1811, was Bessie Dyke, a former actress.

FRANCIS HARE

Francis Hare, sarcastically nicknamed 'The Silent Hare,' from his extreme loquacity, was remarkable for his leanness, his appetite, and his conversational powers. He could not only speak every European language, but all the various *patois* of each tongue, with a rapid and effervescent utterance that reminded one of the rushing of some alpine torrent, or Pyreneean *Gave* battling with the impediments that obstruct its course. His memory was as surprising as his loquacity; he could repeat whole pages from almost any book that was mentioned in his presence, and 'come down' with effect on any unlucky wight who had made an incorrect quotation from some rare or obsolete volume, which might have been supposed to be unknown to all present.

One day, in a country house, his friends had made a bet that they would catch him napping, and start a subject on which he could have nothing to say. With this view they read up an article in an encyclopædia of that time, on Chinese music. At dinner one of the conspirators introduced the subject, a second took it up, and a third exhausted the knowledge they had gained by reading the learned essay. To their intense astonishment, Hare, in his excited, spluttering manner, took up the topic, contradicted all the statements that had been made, proved that they were all in the wrong, and concluded by saying, 'I see, my good fellows, where you have taken your impressions about the harmony of the Celestial Empire. You have found them in an article in such an encyclopædia, which I myself wrote ten years ago; but since then I have studied the subject and conversed with well-informed travellers, and I have arrived at conclusions diametrically opposed to those I held when I wrote the article.'

Hare was very fond of practical jokes and mystifications of all sorts. While passing a winter at Pisa, he amused himself (rather sacrilegiously, I must admit), one day that he was visiting the baptistry, by entering a confessional. In this quiet old town the priests have a good deal of rustic simplicity about them, and doubtless Hare would never have attempted the same joke either at Florence or Rome, where tales of deadly crimes are too common to astonish the confessor.

Hare, having selected a round-faced, innocent-looking priest as his victim, went up to the confessional, knelt down with a look of penitential sorrow, and poured forth in the purest Tuscan the most hideous tale of guilt that ever reached a good father's ear: robbery, blasphemy, sacrilege, rape, and murder were owned to in quick and horrifying succession; till at last the fat priest's placid countenance wore an expression of frantic terror, and opening the other door of the confessional, without cap or breviary, he rushed from the place, and tore down the street, never stopping till he had reached his own dwelling.

In mentioning the name of Hare, I am reminded of a circumstance which occurred to him during the Hundred Days. The English, including our embassy, were so frightened at the unexpected return of the Emperor, that they fled from France as if Old Nick had made his appearance. Hare, on the contrary, remained, and at the first levee held by Napoleon, he made his appearance at the Tuileries, where he was presented to his Majesty.

Napoleon addressed him in the following words: – 'Well, sir, what has kept you in Paris, when your countrymen have all left?' 'To see the greatest man in Europe, sir.' 'Ah, it is, then, your opinion, having seen and conversed with me, that I am not that wild beast I am represented to be by your ministers and the members of your Houses of Parliament.' 'Oh no, sir, it cannot be the opinion of the English ministers; but I blush when I call to mind the manner in which your name has been traduced by our garrulous members of both Houses.'

This little episode, and the remarks said to have been made by Hare, reached London in an incredibly short time, when our newspapers attacked him in no measured terms, stating that he was a traitor to his country, and ought to be prosecuted forthwith. But Hare could afford to laugh at their abuse and threats; and on his return to England after the fall of Napoleon, used often to relate with pleasure, and not without some emotion, the conversation he had held with the great French Emperor.

THEODORE HOOK

I remember being present at a dinner in London, when a very severe and saturnine Scotch Presbyterian was abusing Sunday newspapers, and concluded a violent tirade by saying, 'I am determined to set my face against them.' 'So am I,' said Theodore Hook, 'every Sunday morning.' He was well known at that time to be the editor of the *John Bull* weekly journal.[1]

---

[1] Theodore Edward Hook (1788–1841), writer and editor, celebrated at the time for his crude wit. Although he was almost innumerate, his influential friends, by whom he was considered a kind of court jester, obtained for him the post of Accountant-General in Mauritius, whence he was withdrawn when a deficit of 62,000 dollars was found in his accounts, or, as he put it himself, 'on account of a disorder in his chest'.

COSWAY THE PAINTER

The miniature painter Cosway enjoyed the reputation of drawing the long bow to a remarkable extent.[1] He was once relating, in my presence, to a large party of incredulous listeners, the story of a boy who had fallen from the top of a church steeple without sustaining any material injury. When he had come to a conclusion, there were a few murmurs, expressive of doubt as to the possibility of such a miraculous preservation, when Cosway, looking round on the company with a glance of solemn defiance, exclaimed, 'I was that boy!'

[1] Richard Cosway (1740–1821), the painter and miniaturist. His studio at 20 Stratford Place became a haunt of fashionable society. He was a favourite artist of the Prince Regent, who died with a miniature of Mrs Fitzherbert around his neck.

11

Actors and Musicians

THE ITALIAN OPERA: CATALANI

The greatest vocalist of whom I have a recollection is Madame Catalani.[1] In her youth, she was the finest singer in Europe, and she was much sought after by all the great people during her *séjour* in London. She was extremely handsome, and was considered a model as wife and mother. Catalani was very fond of money, and would never sing unless paid beforehand. She was invited, with her husband, to pass some time at Stowe, where a numerous but select party had been invited; and Madame Catalani, being asked to sing soon after dinner, willingly complied. When the day of her departure came, her husband placed in the hands of the Marquis of Buckingham the following little billet: - 'For seventeen songs, seventeen hundred pounds.' This large sum was paid at once, without hesitation; proving that Lord Buckingham was a refined gentleman, in every sense of the word.

Catalani's husband, M. de Valabrèque, once fought a duel with a German baron who had insulted the *prima donna*; the weapons used were sabres, and Valabrèque cut half of the baron's nose clean off. Madame Catalani lived for many years, highly respected, at a handsome villa near Florence. Her two sons are now distinguished members of the

---

[1] Angelica Catalani (1780-1849), the Italian soprano, was married to Paul Valabregue (not Valabrèque), who became her manager. She commanded an enormous salary, far higher than other singers of her time.

Imperial court in Paris; the eldest being Préfet du Palais, and the youngest colonel of a regiment of hussars.

I knew Madame Catalani when she lived in England. Her house was the rendezvous of many of the French *émigrés*; and as she was very rich and very generous, she frequently assisted those who were in the greatest distress. At the head of her profession, with the finest voice in the world, and the admired of all admirers, no whisper had ever been heard against her fair fame, and she lived in the utmost harmony with her husband, M. de Valabrèque. She was a most admirable woman in every relation of life, and as truly pious as she was kind and charitable. [A friend of mind] informed me that as he was seated in the stage-box at the opera one night, when Madame Catalani was about to appear in one of her greatest parts, he observed her in the *coulisse* [wings] before she had to come on, in an attitude of devotion, and evidently in earnest prayer, for the space of two or three minutes. When she had finished, she made the sign of the cross, and went on the stage, where, it is needless to say, she was received with unbounded applause. My friend, on calling upon the great singer next day, told her what he had observed; when she informed him, with a charming simplicity, that she never went upon the stage without first praying to God that He would grant her the favour to be enabled to sing well, and to meet with success; nor did she ever fail, on retiring to rest, to return thanks to Him for that and all the other mercies vouchsafed to her.

HER MAJESTY'S THEATRE

When George the Fourth was Regent, Her Majesty's Theatre, as the Italian Opera in the Haymarket is still called, was conducted on a very different system from that which now prevails.[1] Some years previous to the period to which I refer, no one could obtain a box or a ticket for the pit without a voucher from one of the lady patronesses. In their day, after the singing and the ballet were over, the company used to retire into the concert-room, where a ball took place, accompanied by refreshments and a supper. There all the rank and fashion of England were assembled on a sort of neutral ground.

At a later period, it became less difficult to obtain admittance; but

---

[1] The original theatre, known as the Queen's Theatre from 1705 to 1714 and as the King's Theatre from 1714 to 1837, was burned down in 1789. Rebuilt as an opera house in 1790-1, it was then the largest theatre in England, and one of the most exclusive. Even the audience in the pit was required to wear evening dress. This theatre was demolished in 1891. The present Her Majesty's Theatre was built on half the site in 1897.

the strictest etiquette was still kept up as regarded the dress of the gentlemen, who were only admitted with knee-buckles, ruffles, and *chapeau bras*. If there happened to be a drawing-room, the ladies would appear in their court-dresses, as well as the gentlemen; and on all occasions the audience of Her Majesty's Theatre was stamped with aristocratic elegance. The peculiar type of female beauty which these ladies so attractively exemplified, is such as can be met with only in the British Isles: the full, round, soul-inspired eye of Italy, and the dark hair of the sunny south, often combined with that exquisitely pearly complexion which seems to be concomitant with humidity and fog. You could scarcely gaze upon the peculiar beauty to which I refer without being as much charmed with its kindly expression as with its physical loveliness.

FANNY ELSSLER

In 1822 I saw this beautiful person for the first time.[1] She was originally one of the *figurantes* at the opera at Vienna, and was at this time about fourteen years of age, and of delicate and graceful proportions. Her hair was auburn, her eyes blue and large, and her face wore an expression of great tenderness. Some years after the Duke of Reichstadt, the son of the great Napoleon,[2] was captivated with her beauty; in a word, he became her acknowledged admirer, while her marvellous acting and dancing drew around her all the great men of the German court. The year following she went to Naples, where a brother of the king's fell desperately in love with her. Mademoiselle Elssler went soon afterwards to Paris, where her wit electrified all the fashionable world, and her dancing and acting in the 'Diable Boiteux' made the fortune of the *entrepreneur*.[3] In London her success was not so striking.

MARIA TREE

Miss Maria Tree was much admired as a vocalist, and her Viola, in *Twelfth Night*, was one of the most popular performances of the day. Mr

---

[1] Fanny Elssler (1810–84) made her début in Paris in 1834 and soon became the leading rival to Marie Taglioni, the celebrated Italian ballet dancer (1804–84), who was one of the first women to dance on the points of her toes.

[2] François-Charles-Joseph Bonaparte (1811–32). The son of Napoleon I and the Empress Marie-Louise, he was styled King of Rome at his birth and acknowledged by Bonapartists as Napoleon II after his father's defeat. He was created Duke of Reichstadt in 1818.

[3] Based on *Le Diable boiteux*, a novel by Alain-René le Sage, published in 1707.

Bradshaw became desperately enamoured of her during her engagement in London,[1] and having learnt that she was about to go by the
mail coach to Birmingham, where she was to perform her principal
characters, thought it a favourable opportunity of enjoying her society;
so he sent his servant to secure him a place by the mail, under the name
of Tomkins. At the appointed time for departure, Mr Bradshaw was at
the office, and jumping into the coach was soon whirled away; but great
was his disappointment at finding that the fair object of his admiration
was not a fellow-passenger: he was not consoled by discovering that
there were two mails, the one the Birmingham mail, the other, the
Birmingham and Manchester, and that whilst he was journeying by the
latter, Miss Tree was travelling in the other.

On arriving at Birmingham, early in the morning, he left the coach
and stepped into the hotel, determined to remain there and go to the
theatre on the following evening. He went to bed, and slept late the
following day; but on waking he remembered that his trunk with all his
money had gone on to Manchester, and that he was without the means
of paying his way. Seeing the Bank of Birmingham opposite the hotel,
he went over and explained his position to one of the partners, giving his
own banker's address in London, and showing letters addressed to him
as Mr Bradshaw. Upon this he was told that with such credentials he
might have a loan; and the banker said he would write the necessary
letter and cheque, and send the money over to him at the hotel. Mr
Bradshaw, pleased with this kind attention, sat himself down comfortably to breakfast in the coffee-room. According to promise, the cashier
made his appearance at the hotel, and asked the waiter for Mr
Bradshaw. 'No such gentleman here,' was the reply. 'Oh, yes, he came
by the London mail.' 'No, sir; no one came but Mr Tomkins, who was
booked as inside passenger to Manchester.' The cashier was dissatisfied;
but the waiter added, 'Sir, you can look through the window of the
coffee-room door, and see the gentleman yourself.' On doing so, he
beheld the supposed Mr Tomkins, *alias* Mr Bradshaw, and immediately
returned to the bank, telling what he himself had heard and seen. The
banker went over to the hotel, had a consultation with the landlord, and
it was determined that a watch should be placed upon the suspicious
person who had two names and no luggage, and who was booked to
Manchester but had stopped at Birmingham.

---

[1] Anna Maria Tree (1801–62) was the sister of Ellen Tree, who married Charles Kean.
After training at Drury Lane, she sang mostly at Covent Garden. Her husband, James
Bradshaw, was a rich property-owner.

The landlord then summoned 'boots,' – a little lame fellow, of most ludicrous appearance, – and pointing to the gentleman in the coffee-room, told him his duty for the day was to follow him wherever he went, and never to lose sight of him; but above all to take care that he did not get away. Boots nodded assent, and immediately mounted guard. Mr Bradshaw having taken his breakfast and read the papers, looked at his watch, and sallied forth to see something of the goodly town of Birmingham. He was much surprised at observing a little odd-looking man surveying him most attentively, and watching his every movement; stopping whenever he stopped, and evidently taking a deep interest in all he did. At last, observing that he was the object of this incessant *espionnage*, and finding that he had a shilling left in his pocket, he hailed one of the coaches that ran short distances in those days when omnibuses were not. This, however, did not suit little boots, who went up to him and insisted that he must not leave the town.

Mr Bradshaw's indignation was naturally excessive, and he immediately returned to the hotel, where he found a constable ready to take him before the mayor as an impostor and swindler. He was compelled to appear before his worship, and had the mortification of being told that unless he could give some explanation, he must be content with a night's lodging in a house of detention. Mr Bradshaw had no alternative but to send to the fair charmer of his heart to identify him; which she most readily did, as soon as rehearsal was over. Explanations were then entered into; but he was forced to give the reason of his being in Birmingham, which of course made a due impression on the lady's heart, and led to that happy result of their interviews – a marriage which resulted in the enjoyment of mutual happiness for many years.

MADEMOISELLE RACHEL

One cannot imagine a more striking contrast than that between Mlles Mars and Rachel,[1] each perfect and without a rival in her separate department. I confess that my own taste was far more gratified by witnessing the performance of *La Grande Tragédienne* in some of her parts, than it ever was by the more polished but colder talent of Mlle Mars; which charmed, but did not carry you away on the wings of enthusiasm.

---

[1] Rachel was the stage name of the diminutive Élisa Félix (1820–58). She made her début at the age of seventeen at the Comédie-Française in Corneille's *Horace* and was immediately successful. In later years she completely dominated the policy and players of the theatre. Her private life, as Gronow says, was notorious.

Rachel, in her moments of passionate declamation, bore all before her, as in a whirlwind. The spectators could not calmly criticise – they could only admire and weep.

I cannot conceive anything more splendid than Rachel's personification of [Racine's] 'Phèdre.' She looked the very woman consumed by her guilty passion, pursued by an avenging deity, the prey of conflicting powers struggling for mastery in that poor wasted bosom. The fire of unhallowed passion seemed to burn in her dark, hollow eyes, – the anguish and humiliation of rejected love to crush to the earth that frail form, – the gnawing of remorse to eat into her very heart. Those who have not seen Rachel in 'Phèdre' can have no conception of what she was as an actress: the dignity and grace of her bearing in the first scenes, contrasted with her passionate despair in the latter part, which at last found vent, each syllable forcing itself through her clenched teeth, as if the very words scorched her lips.

In those parts which brought into play her powers of fascination, such as 'Adrienne Lecouvreur,' [by Eugène Scribe] and others, nothing could be more coquettishly attractive, more irresistibly winning, than Rachel. Her deep rich voice had an inexpressible charm when softened into tenderness, and she possessed such a peculiar talent for enveloping her meagre figure in fleecy clouds of gauze and muslin, and decking it with rows of gold ornaments and pearls, that every man at the end of the performance thought his wife or mistress too much developed in figure, whilst every woman for the moment wished she were as devoid of all protuberances as the fair tragedienne.

I have had the pleasure of frequently meeting Rachel in society, and certainly it was impossible to have seen any one more high-bred in appearance, dress, and manner. There was nothing exaggerated in her style of dress, which was always of rich materials, but in perfect taste. She generally, in order to conceal the excessive spareness of her form, wore a high gown, fitting tight round the long, slight throat, and falling in heavy folds; the lace collar being fastened by some costly ornament. Her head, which was beautifully shaped, was generally adorned only by her thick waving hair. Her eyes were very deeply set, and too jet black to be soft or pleasing; her profile was regular in its outline, but her face was long and narrow, and bore evident traces of its Jewish origin. She had very small, well-formed hands, with long, thin, taper fingers, and pink nails remarkably *bien soignés*. Her manner in a drawing-room was particularly quiet, pleasing, and ladylike. She was neither forward nor servile; never forcing herself on any one's acquaintance, and yet never accepting a position of humiliation.

I could completely understand how thoroughly English society had been taken in during her first visit to London, and how the most strait-laced dowagers had invited her, almost on a footing of intimacy, to their houses and select parties. It is true that she had not then completely thrown all appearance of propriety to the winds, as in her later career. I think I may say, without subjecting myself to any accusation of scandal or exaggeration, that no woman ever went beyond Rachel in immorality.

I have heard men say that it was just that contrast between her 'company' manners, so distinguished, graceful, and dignified, and the coarse ribald tone which she assumed when at ease with her boon companions, that fascinated them. She must have studied vice as another might have studied virtue, and instead of feigning to appear better than she really was, it seemed to be her glory to show to her admirers the darkest shades of her character, and make them kneel down and worship the idol of mud they had set up.

Rachel had some redeeming points. She was extremely kind to her poor relations, and if a case of real distress was placed before her she would give generously and without ostentation.

JOHN KEMBLE

In the autumn of 1821, I met Mr and Mrs Kemble at Lausanne,[1] and a few weeks later I saw them again at Milan, where, as we lived at the same hotel, I had the pleasure of passing much time in their company. The first evening we went together to the 'Scala,' I remember the great tragedian exclaiming, as he surveyed the proportions of that magnificent theatre, 'How like old Drury!'

The opera pleased him well enough; but with the ballet he was quite delighted, and highly amused; for the dancers, by order of the police, were obliged to wear sky-blue pantaloons which reached down to their knees, but were so tight that the outline of the figure was more apparent, and the effect produced more indelicate, than if the usual gauze inexpressibles had been used. Kemble, after a hearty laugh, inveighed,

---

[1] John Philip Kemble (1757–1823), eldest son of Roger Kemble, the actor-manager, and brother of Sarah Siddons. Intended by his father for the Roman Catholic priesthood, he was educated at a seminary and at the English College at Douai. He played leading tragic roles for many years at Drury Lane, and later became manager of Covent Garden. He was considered the finest (and vainest) tragedian of his day, although his mispronunciation of certain words was notorious. Kemble retired to Lausanne, where, according to Samuel Rogers, he was jealous of the attention paid to Mont Blanc.

in no measured terms, against the imperial government, saying –

'What bullies and savages these Austrians are! They interfere with the unfortunate Italians in everything, even in their amusements, and make even the dancing-girls put on the breeches of their Hungarian infantry.'

I wish I could remember some of the numerous anecdotes of this remarkable man, who, without being actually witty, had a vein of rich dry humour; which, contrasting with his grave classical face, deep sepulchral voice, and serious manner, had a very ludicrous effect.

John Kemble had the honour of giving the Prince of Wales some lessons in elocution. According to the vitiated pronunciation of the day, the Prince, instead of saying 'oblige,' would say 'obleege,' upon which Kemble, with much disgust depicted upon his countenance, said –

'Sir, may I beseech your Royal Highness to open your royal jaws, and say "oblige"?'

Conway was a mediocre actor, but a very handsome man, and a great favourite with the fair sex.[1] On some one asking Kemble if Conway was a good actor, the only answer they could get from Kemble was, 'Mr Conway, sir, is a very tall young man.' 'But what do you think of him?' 'I think Mr Conway is a very tall young man.'

One day he was saying, before Lord Blessington, who was an amateur actor of no mean capacity, that the worst professional player was better than the best amateur performer. Lord Blessington, somewhat nettled by this observation, asked John Kemble if he meant to say that Conway acted better than he did?

'Conway,' replied Kemble, in his most sepulchral voice, 'is a very strong exception.'

MALIBRAN AND GRISI

Maria Malibran[2] was still in the zenith of her fame, when Giulia Grisi[3]

[1] William Augustus Conway (1789–1828). A leading player at Covent Garden, where he distinguished himself in various Shakespearean roles. He left for America in 1823, and threw himself overboard and was drowned on a passage to Charleston. Dr Johnson's by then ancient former friend, Mrs Piozzi, was an extravagant admirer of his acting and person. He entirely lacked John Kemble's self-possession and self-regard. His real name was Rugg.

[2] Maria Felicita Malibran (1808–36), the Spanish mezzo-soprano, was the daughter of the tenor and composer Manuel García. Her second husband was the versatile violinist, poet, painter and sculptor, Charles Auguste de Bériot, who designed her tomb, on which she appears as St Cecilia.

[3] Giulia Grisi (1811–69), the Italian soprano. Donizetti wrote Don Pasquale for her and her second husband, the tenor, Giovanni Mario.

made her appearance on the stage in Paris. She was not at that period of her life the consummate actress she afterwards became, but trusted a good deal to the power of her personal attractions, as well as to the singularly fine compass and sweet tones of her beautiful voice, to insure the applause of the public.

Malibran was, on the contrary, the soul of music. She was a grand being; that small, slight woman, with flushed cheeks and ardent expressive eyes, consumed by the love of her art, and that one passionate attachment which seemed woven into her soul, a part of her very being. I really believe that this blind idolatry for the man who afterwards became her husband, was the cause of the kind of frenzy with which she clung to her fame as an artist. She felt instinctively that she had been sought because she was celebrated, and that the applause which she elicited was the fuel which fed the flickering flame in De Bériot's heart. There can be no doubt that the dread that in losing the one, she might fail to keep the other, fastened on her heart and killed her.

Poor Malibran! Grisi's new-born fame was a canker-worm, eating into her very soul; and I truly believe not from a mean feeling of envy, but for the reason that I have assigned.

Malibran was not regularly handsome, but I always thought her in her young days remarkably attractive. As she grew older, her features became coarser, and a certain bold, hard look settled on her face. Her head was well formed; her mouth, though wide, was prettily shaped, and adorned with very good teeth, and her small figure was graceful. Her voice was splendid, full of passion and pathos. Who that ever heard her in Desdemona, could forget that cry of struggling agony, 'Se il padre m'abbandona' or the sorrowful wail of the blighted heart in the romance 'Assisa al pie d'un salice'? She identified herself so thoroughly with the part she acted that it required some courage to face her in the last scene. She died 'hard' and fought to the last; and Othello had to make a kind of steeplechase after her, and suffer many kicks and cuffs before he could, as an Irish friend of mine remarked, 'bring her to rason by taking her life.'

I was lucky enough to see the first representation of the Puritani with that grand galaxy of singers, Lablache, Rubini, Tamburini and Grisi.[1]

The bridal song, 'Son vergine vezzoza,' was one of Grisi's triumphs, and

---

[1] Luigi Lablache (1794-1858), Neapolitan bass; Giovanni Battista Rubini (1795-1854), tenor; Antonio Tamburini (1800-76), bass. Bellini wrote I puritani for them and Giulia Grisi.

it must be allowed that it was impossible to look on a fairer sight than
Giulia, with her long white veil flowing to her feet, carolling that sweet
happy lay. Grisi's head and face, bust, arms, and hands, were almost
faultless; her mouth and teeth were lovely beyond description; her hair
was black as jet, and luxuriant though not long, for which reason
probably she never let it fall completely down. But owing to her rather
thick waist, her large feet, and short legs, the spell was broken when she
attempted to run across the stage in pursuit of Edgardo or Arturo.

As Grisi's beauty waned, or her voice lost some of its rich, mellow
notes, her good sense taught her that she must study more, and act
better. She set herself conscientiously to work, and in the latter years of
her stage career gained the reputation of being an admirable actress.
She had not the pathos of Pasta,[1] nor the genius of Malibran, but she
had love for her art, and a desire to do the very best she possibly could.
She was neither huffy, capricious, nor tricky; she neither feigned illness
when she was well, nor allowed a passing whim or fancy to interfere with
her duty to the director or the public. A good warm heart beat in that
ample bosom, and no one, I believe, ever heard of Giulia Grisi doing a
mean or unkind action.

Madame Grassini[2]

One of the curious types of fifty years ago was the celebrated singer,
Madame Grassini. When I first met her in 1825, she still possessed some
remains of the remarkable beauty which had won for her the attention
and admiration of so many of the great men of the age. Napoleon and
Wellington, the Marshals of France, the Generals of the allied armies,
English, Russians, Prussians, Austrians, as well as the Dukes and
Marquises of the Restoration, had all bowed before Grassini's shrine,
and had all been received with the same Italian *bonhomie* and liberal
kindness. She would often say, 'Napoleon gave me this snuff-box; he
placed it in my hands one morning when I had been to see him at the
Tuileries, and added, "*Voilà pour toi; tu es une brave fille!*" He was indeed
a great man, but he would not follow my advice.'

All Madame Grassini's recollections came out quite naturally, with
true southern frankness, or rather cynicism; and she narrated her *liaisons*
in as unconcerned a manner before every one she met, as if she were
speaking of her drive in the Bois de Boulogne. Her face must have been

---

[1] Giuditta Pasta, *née* Negri (1797–1865), the Italian soprano.
[2] Josephina Grassini (1773–1850), the Italian contralto.

in her youth still handsomer than that of her niece, Giulia Grisi. The eyes were larger and more expressive, and she had more regular features and finer teeth. There was a tragic dignity in the contour and lineaments of her countenance, which formed a strange contrast with her unrefined language and gipsy style of dress; every colour of the rainbow was represented in her garments, which were tied on without the smallest regard to taste, and gave her very much the appearance of a strolling actress equipped at Rag fair.[1]

Grassini's once fine voice had, when I saw her, degenerated into a sharp, loud, unmelodious soprano, which grated harshly on the ear. She had no cleverness or wit, and the *bons mots* that are cited as hers are amusing only from the cynic *bonhomie* which inspired them, as well as the strong Italian accent with which they were spoken. One of her *mots* in the days of the Empire is often cited. Napoleon had given the order of the Iron Crown to the famous castrato singer, Veluti, who was at that time all the fashion.[2] This honour, at a period when decorations were given more sparingly than they are at present, created great discontent, especially amongst military men; several of whom were complaining in no measured terms that the Lombard order should have been bestowed upon a mere singer, when Grassini interposed, with great vehemence, and said, 'I am surprised that you soldiers should be so ungenerous, and not take into account *sa blessure.*'

ROSSINI

Rossini has been for some time a resident in Paris;[3] and whenever he receives, every one is anxious to be admitted to his *soirées*, where good music is sure to be heard, or to his dinner-table, where excellent macaroni is as certain to be served up. The master looks in perfect health, and has more of the Englishman than the Italian in his personal appearance. The photographs that are sold of him are perfect of their kind, and express the good-nature and sly humour for which he is remarkable. He lives a large portion of the year at Passy, where the Parisian municipality made him a present of the ground upon which he has built his villa in the Italian style.

---

[1] Rag fair - a market for the sale of old clothes, especially that held at Houndsditch since at least the sixteenth century.

[2] Giovanni Battista Velluti (1781-1861), one of the last of the *castrati*. He was performing in London as late as 1829.

[3] Rossini (see note, p. 106) went to live in Paris in 1823. After a time spent in Italy he returned to France in 1855 and died at his villa at Passy in 1868.

Rossini narrates, at his dinner parties, with great glee, some of the circumstances that occurred to him in London. He was made a great deal of by the Prince Regent; and on one occasion he could not help showing how little pleasure he derived from the attempts made by his Royal Highness to execute some passages, in which he totally failed owing to his inability to keep time: for the Regent, though a great lover of music, and not a bad player on the violin, constantly put out the *maestro*, to whom he at last offered an apology. Rossini accepted it with civility, and good-naturedly said, 'There are few in your Royal Highness's position who could play so well.'

Rossini was not aware of a law which then existed, by which a foreigner might be imprisoned for debt without any warning, and merely upon the affidavit of a creditor affirming that the stranger was about to leave England. He was once arrested in London by a bailiff, and carried to a sponging-house,[1] and though his incarceration was of short duration, it gave him a disgust for a city where he had otherwise been well received.

Rossini does not go as often to the opera as might be expected, preferring the agreeable society of a few friends. He has also a strong objection to go out to parties; even the Emperor's invitations have no weight with him, and he has frequently begged to be excused. Rossini is an enemy to modern innovations, and has never yet trusted himself to the railroad. No inducement could be found sufficiently strong for him to travel otherwise than in a coach drawn by horses, and that at so moderate a speed, that a week was occupied by him in his journey from Paris to Baden.

Madame Colbrand,[2] the *prima donna* at Naples when Rossini commenced his career as a composer, exercised considerable influence on the success of his earliest operas. They were written expressly for her, at a period when the heyday of her youth was gone by, she having long been an acknowledged favourite both with the manager and King Ferdinand. When 'Elisabetta' was produced in 1815 by the young *maestro*, Madame Colbrand retained all the beauty of her voice, which, added to her physical advantages and a commanding figure, fine features, and dignified bearing, called forth a shout of applause as she appeared on the stage of San Carlo, in the character of the English queen. The duet with Leicester secured the success of this the first opera that Rossini had produced at Naples, and others which followed in

[1] A place of preliminary confinement for debtors.
[2] Isabella Angela Colbran (1785–1845), Spanish soprano. She married Rossini in 1822.

quick succession were received with the enthusiastic admiration they so fully merited.

But it was reserved for that unrivalled *artiste*, Madame Pasta, to come up to the full exigencies of Rossini's musical genius. Her appearance at Her Majesty's Theatre electrified the house; and none who are old enough to remember her can forget the wonderful pathos and power of that richly toned thrilling voice.

MADAME ALBONI

About twelve years ago the inimitable Alboni, having finished her engagement at the Théâtre des Italiens, Paris, entered into one with the manager of the Opera at Nantes, to sing there and at the watering-places adjacent.[1] She left Paris dressed, as usual, in male attire, accompanied by a lady who passed as the wife. During the first week after their arrival at Nantes, they lived in furnished lodgings on the Place Royale, and thought of nothing but the piano and their scales; the incomparable singer attracting the other occupants of the house to the landing-place, ever and anon, by the power of her splendid voice. One day, something occurred which created a misunderstanding between Alboni and her friend: from high and violent words they came to blows, and a neat 'backhander' of Alboni's on the other's nose caused blood to flow. The injured lady ran downstairs, and implored the porter to go for a surgeon; but the man, alarmed for the respectability of the house, instead of obeying, went to the police and informed them what had occurred. On his returning with two policemen, Alboni and her friend were found in hysterics; nevertheless, they were hurried off, more dead than alive, to the police office.

When the Commissary began to interrogate the lady with the bloody nose as to the origin of their quarrel and other particulars, Alboni stepped forward, and addressing the man in authority, explained that they began to quarrel about a note in a song in 'La Gazza Ladra,' which opera was to be given that evening.[2] The Commissary, wondering what it all meant, asked their names, which were given by the ladies, and Alboni implored him to release them with as little delay as possible, as she had scarcely time left to dress for the theatre. The Commissary took the ladies by the hand, and conducted them to the door, saying that he

[1] Marietta Alboni (1826–94), Italian contralto.
[2] *The Thieving Magpie*, an opera by Rossini with libretto by Gherardini, was first performed in Milan in 1817.

was extremely sorry that his agents had acted in so precipitate a manner as to bring through the public streets two ladies of such standing, without first ascertaining that there were good reasons for their being arrested. Alboni bowed, and said she hoped to see the officer that night on the stage. The invitation was readily accepted; and when the vocalist perceived him at the conclusion of the opera, she flung her arms round his neck, to the astonishment of all present.

12

Soldiers and Sailors

SIR JAMES KEMPT

General Sir James Kempt,[1] who died at a very advanced age about ten or twelve years since, refused at different times the high posts of Commander-in-Chief in India, and Commander-in-Chief in England; and, I have heard, even that of Governor-General. His great abilities and bravery were only equalled by his modesty and simplicity of manners. It is said that he began life as a clerk at Greenwood's, the army agent's, and for his good conduct was recommended for a commission in the army.

The Duke of York took a great fancy to Kempt, and put him into one of our crack fighting regiments, where, if a man was not knocked on the head, he was sure to make his way. Kempt greatly distinguished himself, and rose rapidly to the highest honours of the profession.

AT NAPOLEON'S COURT

All anecdotes of Napoleon I are interesting, and I heard a few details respecting him in 1820, from an intimate friend of mine who was one of his household for many years, and which I do not remember to have seen published. The Emperor, though at times very magnificent, and

---

[1] Sir James Kempt (1764–1854). He commanded the 8th Brigade in Picton's Division at Waterloo and succeeded Picton in command of the Division. He was Governor-General of Canada from 1828 to 1830 and Master-General of the Ordnance from 1834 to 1838.

knowing (as his nephew does) how to reward services done to the country, was a man of much order in all his domestic arrangements, and would not allow certain sums, which he had laid down and allotted for special purposes, to be exceeded upon any account. He knew to a penny what was spent every day in his household. He gave one hundred francs for his own food, which was very simple, and allowed the Grand Maréchal of the palace, General Bertrand,[1] twenty francs a head for the persons who dined habitually at his table, and forty francs for those whom the Emperor invited to dinner. Napoleon generally dined alone, except on Sundays, when some of the most favoured members of his family were admitted to his table. A roast fowl was kept continually ready for his dinner, as the great man rarely dined at the same hour, and when he ordered dinner, expected it to be served immediately. His beverage was Chambertin and water.

With his abstemious habits, and a mind and body in constant activity, he did not merit the infliction of growing fat, which he suffered from during the last years of his life.

The Emperor allowed no one to approach him too familiarly, and ought, therefore, to have treated his inferiors with deference; but good-breeding was not the Emperor's *forte*, and he was accustomed to see his playful pinches received by his courtiers (and no prince ever had more servile ones) as the highest earthly favour. One day he so far forgot himself as to try the unpleasant caress of ear-pinching on Dr Hallé, one of the Iuminaries of medical science.[2] The doctor, more surprised than flattered at this pungent mark of imperial favour, observed, with dignity – '*Sire, vous me faites beaucoup de mal.*' This remark, made respectfully but firmly, prevented a repetition of this unpleasant liberty.

One of the great ladies of the Faubourg St Germain, whose son held a place in the imperial household, was obliged once or twice a year to put in an appearance, and make her courtesy to the Emperor and Empress. Napoleon, on one of these occasions, after fixing his eagle glance upon the lady, said, in an irritated voice – '*Je sais que vous ne m'aimez pas.*' The lady, with much presence of mind, replied, '*Sire, je ne suis encore qu'à l'admiration.*'

Napoleon I had not the courtesy and perfect breeding of the present

---

[1] Henri-Gratien, comte Bertrand (1773–1844), met Napoleon in Italy in 1797 and became his aide-de-camp in 1804. His companion in exile on the island of Elba, he was appointed Grand Marshal of the Palace in 1813. His account of Napoleon's life on St Helena was published in three volumes in 1949–59.

[2] Jean Noel Hallé (1754–1822), the physician.

Emperor. He took a spiteful pleasure in embarrassing women by disagreeable questions and remarks in public; and the kind and gentle Josephine had often much to do in healing the wounds her husband had made. However, it sometimes happened that the rude question or remark made in public was followed up by some private message of quite another nature. It has been supposed by many that the hatred with which Napoleon hunted down the beautiful Madame Récamier,[1] took its first origin in the admiration her beauty had inspired, and his displeasure at seeing his addresses rejected. Just as the famous Madame de Staël's[2] anger against him originated in the disdain with which he met her marked advances.

The Duke of Wellington and the Cavalry

About three weeks after the battle of Waterloo I arrived in Brussels, and dined, a few days afterwards, with General Sir George Cooke, who had commanded our division, and lost an arm.[3] He was still suffering from his wound, and was living at the hotel where supper had been ordered for the Emperor Napoleon, in anticipation of his certain triumph on the 18th.

Sir George observed to us that it was lucky for Lord Uxbridge that the field had been won by us; for had this not been the case, he would have got into an awkward scrape for having engaged the cavalry without orders from the Duke. From what Sir George seemed to think, it was evidently the Duke's intention to keep the cavalry in hand, and perfectly fresh, so that they might have charged the French squadrons when the latter had exhausted themselves in their attacks on our squares. To corroborate this opinion, he told us an anecdote of the war in Spain, which may be interesting, as showing how opposed the Duke was to the harum-scarum custom of our cavalry officers, who hurled their men at full gallop on the enemy, without supports, and without any actual plan or intimation beyond the ardour of a sportsman going at a five-barred gate.

---

[1] Jeanne-Françoise-Julie-Adélaïde, dame de Récamier (1777-1849). The daughter of a rich banker named Bernard, she married another rich banker much older than herself. Her wit and charm enabled her to become one of the leading hostesses of her day.

[2] Madame de Staël (1766-1817), the daughter of the financier Jacques Necker, married Baron de Staël Holstein, the Swedish Ambassador in Paris in 1786. Her salon became a meeting place for Paris's leading intellectuals. Her *Considerations sur les principaux événements de la Révolution française* was published in 1818.

[3] General Sir George Cooke (1768-1837).

He stated, when Sir Stapleton Cotton went out to take the command of the cavalry,[1] at his first interview with Lord Wellington, his chief addressed him as follows: – 'General Cotton, I am glad to see you in command of the cavalry; and I wish you to bear in mind that cavalry should be always held well in hand; that your men and horses should not be used up in wild and useless charges, but put forward when you are sure that their onset will have a decisive effect. Above all, remember that you had better not engage, as a general rule, unless you see an opportunity of attacking the French with a superior force. In Spain, the Germans,[2] the 14th Light Dragoons, and perhaps the 12th, under Fred Ponsonby, were the only regiments that knew their duty and did not get into scrapes of every description.'

THE DUKE'S RAZORS

My friend, George Smythe, the late Lord Strangford,[3] once told me that, staying at Walmer Castle[4] with the Duke of Wellington, the Duke informed him, one morning at breakfast, that he was obliged to go up to London immediately, as all his razors required setting, but he would be back to dinner. Lord Strangford very naturally offered to lend the Duke his razors, which, luckily for the Duke, he did not accept; for Lord S., who was somewhat careless about his personal appearance, shaved with razors something like miniature saws, which made one shudder to look at. Lord S. then offered to take the razors to Dover, but the Duke replied –

'The man who always sharpens my razors has sharpened them for

---

[1] Sir Stapleton Cotton (1773–1865) was created Baron Combermere on his return from the Peninsula and appointed commander-in-chief in India in 1825. He was promoted field marshal in 1855, at the age of eighty-two. Wellington had a high opinion of his talents as a cavalry commander and would have preferred him to Lord Uxbridge at Waterloo. On the day after the battle, the Duke declared, 'We must have Lord Combermere, if he will come.'

[2] Wellington is here referring to the cavalry regiments of the King's German Legion, a corps formed some years before. Its officers were mostly Germans who had come over to England after Napoleon had overrun Hanover in 1803 and had disbanded the Electoral army.

[3] George Augustus Frederick Percy Sydney Smythe, seventh Viscount Strangford and second Baron Penshurst (1818–57), a leading member of Disraeli's Young England Party and later Under Secretary of State for Foreign Affairs in Peel's second administration. Highly gifted both as politician and journalist, he was described by Lord Lyttelton as 'a splendid failure'. In 1852 he fought the last duel in England with Colonel Frederick Romilly, son of Sir Samuel Romilly, the law-reformer.

[4] Walmer Castle, near Deal in Kent, was the official residence of the Lord Warden of the Cinque Ports. Wellington died there in 1852.

many years: I would not trust them with any one else. He lives in Jermyn Street, and there they must go. So you see, Strangford, every man has a weak point, and my weak point is about the sharpening of my razors. Perhaps you are not aware that I shave myself, and brush my own clothes: I regret that I cannot clean my own boots; for men-servants bore me, and the presence of a crowd of idle fellows annoys me more than I can tell you.'

SIR JOHN ELLEY

I have alluded to the extraordinary personal bravery of General Sir John Elley on the field of Waterloo, and his series of hand-to-hand encounters with the French cavalry on that great day.[1] It is perhaps not generally known that this most distinguished officer commenced his career as a private in the Blues. He afterwards commanded that celebrated regiment, for which he always had a great liking; and on a lengthened tour he once made through Europe, after the war, although a major-general, he always wore the uniform of the Royal Horse Guards.

When he arrived at Vienna, he was invited to dine at a full-dress dinner at the British Ambassador's on the occasion of King George IV's birthday. He was covered with orders, bestowed by the different sovereigns of Europe in 1815; and amongst these gorgeous ribands and crosses the modest Waterloo medal appeared. Sir John happened to sit next to a French Secretary of the Embassy, who criticised the English decoration, and said, 'Surely, General, that is a very poor sort of order the Government have given you and the other brave officers of the English army. It cannot have cost them five francs.' 'True,' replied Sir John, making a low bow, 'it has not cost our country more than five francs; but it cost yours a Napoleon.'

GENERAL THORNTON AND THEODORE HOOK

On the return of the British army from Spain in 1814, the Prince Regent, desirous of rewarding the personal associates of the Duke of Wellington, decided on removing the Generals of the Guards, and giving their places to officers of the Duke's staff who ranked as Colonels. The Generals were mostly either useless and decrepit veterans, or officers whose ideas of service consisted in attending as little as possible

[1] See note, p. 67.

to their regiments, and giving the balance of their time to pleasure. One of them, General Thornton, was afflicted with the idea that of all persons in the world he was the only one who understood the art of waltzing.[1] In fact, it was quite a mania with him, and he might be seen at nearly every party of note, making himself exceedingly ridiculous by teaching young ladies to waltz: this dance having only shortly before come into fashion. Theodore Hook gave him the *sobriquet* of the 'waltzing General;'[2] this occasioned a violent altercation between them at a ball in Portman Square, where, it is said, the General received a more personal affront from Hook: which, however, the soldier did not resent according to the then received notions of honour, by calling him out. The inquiry into this affair by a committee of the other officers of the Guards, no doubt caused the sweeping change proposed by the Prince Regent; it was found that General Thornton had been guilty of cowardice in not demanding immediate satisfaction of Hook, and he was therefore desired to quit the regiment forthwith. His resignation, and the comments on it at the time, paved the way to the proposed changes in command.

ESCAPADE OF AN OFFICER OF THE 3D FOOT GUARDS

It is nearly fifty years since a young officer in the 3d Guards, smitten with the charms of Lady Betty Charteris, who was remarkable for her beauty and attainments, determined at all hazards to carry her off and marry her. Her father put a stop to any legitimate, straightforward wooing, by forbidding her to encourage the attentions of the young officer, who was too poor to maintain her in the position in which she had been brought up. When the London season was over, the family left for Scotland, and my friend, Andrew C——, decided on following his lady-love. Andrew was young, handsome, romantic, and sentimental; but a brave fellow, and had fought gallantly at Waterloo. After consulting several of his intimate friends, who recommended perseverance, he determined to further his scheme by disguising himself. So, with the aid of a black wig and a suit of seedy clothes, he engaged the services of an Italian organ-grinder, and took his place beside him on one of the Edinburgh coaches.

---

[1] Sir William Thornton (1779–1840). He became assistant military secretary to the Duke of York in 1812, and in 1813 commanded the 85th Foot in the Peninsula. He later served in America and was appointed deputy adjutant general in Ireland in 1819. He lost his reason in 1839 and shot himself the next year.

[2] See note, p. 195.

In the course of a few days the pair arrived at a village close to the mansion of the lady's father, and a correspondence was carried on between the lovers. They met, and after a great many urgent entreaties on the part of the enamoured swain, a day was arranged for the elopement. Andrew next gained over the head gardener, by stating that he had just arrived from Holland, and was up to the latest dodges in tulip-growing; then a mania in England. By this means he contrived to be constantly on the premises, and to obtain frequent interviews with the charming Lady Betty. The day fixed at length arrived, and the organ-grinder (then a rarity in Scotland) was introduced on the scene; his sprightly airs fascinated the servants, who thronged to listen to him, and meanwhile a post-chaise and four was driven up, out of sight of the house, according to a previous understanding between the lovers, who were ready for instant flight. Unluckily, there was an excessively vigilant governess in attendance on Lady Betty, and at the moment when affairs seemed most prosperous, this duenna was at her post at the young lady's side in the garden. Andrew, feeling that everything depended on some decisive action, suddenly appeared, and ejaculating, 'Now or never!' caught hold of his dulcinea's arm,[1] and attempted to hurry in the direction of the chaise. The dragon interposed, and clung to the young lady, screaming for assistance; her cries brought out the servants, the enraged father, and the inmates of the house to her assistance, and poor Andrew and the organ-man with his monkey were ejected from the premises. The young Guardsman, however, soon got over the sorrow caused by the failure of his scheme; but the nickname of 'Merry Andrew,' bestowed on him by his brother officers, stuck to him afterwards.

THE GOOD FORTUNE OF A PRETTY WOMAN

More than half a century ago a lady, conspicuous in the aristocratic world, on returning from a courtly *fête* and arriving at her mansion about four o'clock in the morning, was informed by her servants that a female child had been left at the door, wrapped up in a blanket. She desired that the infant might be taken care of; and, in the course of time, the child became a servant in the establishment. The girl grew to be a remarkable specimen of female beauty; her form was exquisitely modelled; her complexion was delicate and blooming; her features were

---

[1] Dulcinea del Toboso was Don Quixote's name for the peasant girl whom he so much admired – hence a sweetheart.

regular, and she was remarkable, for her large, blue, thoughtful eyes. But her greatest charm consisted in a most engaging and lovable smile. It was difficult to gaze upon that face without feeling an interest in Clotilde far beyond that which generally accompanies the contemplation of ordinary beauty. Although educated in the servants' hall, yet, by that singular instinct which some women possess, she had learned to make her conversation and manner acceptable and engaging to educated persons, whether male or female. The titled lady whom she knew as her protector made her her confidential maid, and Clotilde soon became the companion of her mistress.

She was not more than eighteen years of age when an Admiral of the British navy, who visited the house, fell desperately in love with her. It was during the period of the great wars of Napoleon the First, and the Admiral, being employed in cruising about the Mediterranean, was absent from London for long periods; but he never failed to correspond with Clotilde, and his letters were regularly placed before her mistress. The girl used to turn into ridicule the passionate language of the old sailor; but time passed on, and the Admiral returned, having distinguished himself, and become known as the intimate friend of the immortal Nelson; and, within six months afterwards, Clotilde became the wife of one of the most distinguished officers of the British navy.

As frequently occurs when a young and beautiful woman of humble extraction is allied to a man in advanced years, and finds herself surrounded by men occupying the highest position in society, Clotilde became susceptible to attentions which were paid with a view to undermine her virtue. Amongst her admirers was a royal Duke [the Duke of Clarence], who afterwards ascended the throne of Great Britain [as William IV]; and there is every reason to believe that many public acts of the navy and army originated in her influence. In short, the marriage was anything but a happy one, although the lady had daughters who were married to rich and noble foreigners. In the course of time the Admiral ignored her amours; and it was well known in London society that my lady had her friends, and the Admiral his.

As Clotilde advanced in life, she fascinated and formed an intimacy with one of the most wealthy of British peers. By pandering to the eccentricities of the noble Lord, her authority over him became absolute. It was through this nobleman that she bestowed magnificent dowries on her daughters, and became possessed of a colossal fortune. Although her conduct was notoriously immoral, she was countenanced and visited by persons who, as is too frequently the case, permit their morality to become exceedingly elastic in the presence of wealth.

COLONEL, OR 'BULL,' TOWNSHEND

When the Grenadier Guards returned to London from Cambrai, where they had been quartered some considerable time, the first thing that was proposed by the officers, was to invite their colonel, the Duke of York, to a banquet at the Thatched House, St James's Street. His Royal Highness, in a letter full of feeling and good taste, in which he alluded to the gallantry of the regiment he commanded, accepted the invitation, and, as was the custom upon such occasions, the army agents of the regiment were also invited. After dinner, Colonel Townshend, commonly called the Bull, addressed the Duke, stating that, as he was then in command of the old battalion, he hoped HRH would permit him to propose a toast. The Duke bowed assent, when the Bull bellowed out, 'I propose the health of Mr Greenwood, to whom we are all of us so much indebted.' This toast was ill chosen, for the Duke of York owed his army agents at that moment nearly fifty thousand pounds; but Townshend considered it a good joke, for he used frequently to boast of having astonished the Duke with his witty toast. Townshend was the brother of Lord Sidney. He was considered by the officers and men of the regiment to be intrepid and brave. He was unfortunately a slave to good cookery, which was the principal cause of his death. Townshend, despite his imperfections, was generous and full of compassion to the soldiers he commanded; he stooped to no flattery, disdained all disloyal arts, and, in a word, was replete with sterling and splendid qualities.

Many of my old comrades can remember the excellent dinners Townshend used to give his friends at Cambrai. I can call to mind that at one of those banquets, a young officer wilfully placed some ipecacuanha in one of Townshend's favourite *entrées*, of which he ate rather voraciously. The consequence was, the Colonel was obliged to quit the dinner-table sooner than the rest of the *convives*. In the hurry of the moment he sat down upon a brittle vase, which broke, and caused a wound so severe that he was confined to his room for many weeks, and the doctor of the regiment was apprehensive of mortification, for it baffled for a considerable time his skill in effecting a cure; but, fortunately, the gallant colonel recovered.

BEARDING THE LION IN HIS DEN

In 1820, a friend of mine, belonging to the same battalion of the Guards as myself, was sent from the Tower with a detachment to the Bank of

England.[1] On his arrival, he informed the porter that a lady would present herself at the door about dinner time, and that he was to escort her to the officers' room. The porter meanwhile communicated with the Governor, who sent strict orders that no female was to be admitted within the walls of the Bank. The lady in due time arrived, but was refused admission.

The officer having been informed by one of the sergeants that orders had been given by the Governor not to allow the lady to enter, ejected the porter from his lodge, with many oaths and threats, and gave it in charge to the sergeant. The porter ran to the Governor, stating that the officer would place the Governor and himself, if he caught him, in the black-hole; for he swore that he commanded at the Bank, and no one should interfere with him or his visitors.

The Governor kept out of the way, but sent a clerk to the commanding officer of the regiment, stating what had occurred, who in his turn sent a report to the Horse Guards of the whole affair. The Duke of York desired my friend to appear before him next day, when he was asked by his Royal Highness for an explanation. The officer admitted all that had been reported of him, but declared that, as he had been entrusted with the custody and safe keeping of the Bank of England, he regretted not having put the Governor into the black-hole for his interference.

The Duke of York was so amused and tickled by the coolness and *sang froid*, and I may say impudence, of my friend, that he could not help laughing; and after a slight reprimand, asked him to dinner. The Duke used frequently to mention this anecdote to his particular friends as a very good joke; but he was the kindest of men, and I am not sure whether the young officer would not have found his escapade taken up in a very different manner by most commanding officers.

COLONEL THE HONOURABLE H. STANHOPE

Next to the death of the Duke of York, there was no event which pained the Grenadier Guards so much as the untimely death of the Honourable Colonel Stanhope.[2] He had seen much service; served as aide-de-camp

---

[1] A military guard had been placed on the Bank of England ever since the Bank had been attacked by the mob in the Gordon Riots of 1780. The Bank continued to be guarded until 1973.

[2] Hon. James Hamilton Stanhope (1788–1825). He married Lady Frederica Louisa Murray, eldest daughter of the third Earl of Mansfield in 1820. Lady Hester Stanhope was the eldest daughter of his father by his first wife.

to Sir John Moore and to Lord Lynedoch, and distinguished himself greatly at Waterloo. He was the only one of the staff accompanying the Duke of Wellington when the Duke took refuge in our square from the enemy's cavalry, as related in the previous volume.

The sensation the death of Colonel Stanhope created in the public mind was partly due to the melancholy circumstance of his suicide. He had never recovered from the effects of a gun-shot wound he had received at the siege of St Sebastian, and under the combined influences of pain and nervous depression, he hanged himself in Caen Wood, the property of his father-in-law, the Earl of Mansfield. Besides his merits as a soldier, Colonel Stanhope was a most accomplished scholar and gentleman. In his youth he lived with his uncle, Mr Pitt, the great minister, and he entered the army at the age of sixteen.

The Duke of Wellington and Lord Strangford

Not long before the death of the Duke of Wellington, the late Lord Strangford,[1] on his return from Paris, was invited by the Duke to pass a few days at Walmer Castle. His Grace inquired whether, during his sojourn in the French capital, he had seen Lord Hertford; upon which Lord Strangford replied he belonged to the same club, where they frequently met. 'Ah!' added the Duke, 'Lord Hertford is a man of extraordinary talents. He deserves to be classed among those men who possess transcendent abilities. What a pity it is that he does not live more in England, and occupy his place in the House of Lords. It was only the other day,' added the Duke, 'that Sir Robert Peel observed, when speaking of Hertford, that he was a man of great comprehension; not only versed in the sciences, but able to animate his mass of knowledge by a bright and active imagination. In a word, if he had lived in London, instead of frittering away his time in Paris, he would have no doubt become Prime Minister of England.'

'Taking the Bull by the Horns'

The late Lord John Churchill, prior to his appointment as equerry to the lamented Duke of Sussex, commanded a frigate of HM Navy in the Mediterranean. The doctor of the ship, a man of great medical experience and decision, was one day expatiating to his Lordship on the

---

[1] Percy Clinton Sydney Smythe, sixth Viscount Strangford and first Baron Penshurst (1780–1855), successively Ambassador in Stockholm, Constantinople and St Petersburg.

efficacy of blisters, which, he stated, had cured all the sailors who had been attacked with fevers. Lord John replied, 'All this may be quite true; but if ever you apply a blister to any part of my body, by God, doctor, I will order my ship's company to throw you overboard.' 'Be it so, my Lord; but you know I invariably take the bull by the horns,' replied the medico: and the matter then dropped.

A short time afterwards, the noble captain was seized with violent headache and fever, and his pulse was very high; the doctor therefore determined, '*coûte que coûte*,' to apply his favourite remedy. Having prepared the blister, he contrived, while Lord J. slept, to place it on his chest without awakening him; he then retired to rest, but gave orders to be called if his presence was necessary. At an early hour the following morning, he was awoke by the captain's servant, who, looking more dead than alive, said that his Lordship was very violent, foaming with rage, and calling out with all his might, 'Where's that damned doctor?' The terrified medico found his patient in a state of exasperation and excitement; but, upon feeling his pulse, ascertained that the fever had greatly abated. Lord J., though furious at the pain he was enduring, asked what the doctor had done to him, and quoting the *Corsair*,[1] added, –

Prepare thee to reply
Clearly and full; I love not mystery.

'In a word, sir, what does it all mean? I am suffering from blisters all over my body.' The doctor, unconscious of what had occurred during the night, opened the captain's shirt collar to look at the effects of the blister; but the sufferer pushed him aside, saying, 'No, doctor, it is not there; you will find it lower down.' Lower down it certainly was, for it was discovered, like the one mentioned in *Tom Cringle's Log*,[2] in a very awkward place. It had, no doubt, during the night, got rubbed off the chest and had slipped down to a very opposite part of the body, which was blistered severely. The doctor, to appease the captain's anger, explained: 'I found your Lordship last night in a violent fever, and had no alternative left but to take the bull by the horns: the blister was placed contrary to my orders, I confess; but "all's well that ends well," and I am happy to see your Lordship so much better.'

---

[1] A poem by Lord Byron, published in 1814.
[2] 'Tom Cringle's Log' by Michael Scott (1789–1835) appeared in *Blackwood's Magazine* in 1829–33. It describes life in the West Indies in the early nineteenth century.

13

Politics and Politicians

THE CORN-LAW RIOTS AND LORD CASTLEREAGH

When I call to mind the dangerous state of the country at that time, the very bad feeling of the people towards the upper classes, the want of employment in the manufacturing districts, and the great misery all over England from the high price of bread, – when I recollect, at the same time, the total absence of any sort of police, and the small military force we possessed, I am astonished that some fatal catastophe did not occur in the years immediately following the war.[1]

Those who remember the Luddite riots, the Corn-Law riots, the Spitalfields meetings, and other public demonstrations of a people driven to madness by every sort of oppression, will agree with me in thinking that those were days of great peril. I recollect, during the Corn-Law riots in London, having walked from St James's Palace (where I was on guard) to St James's Square. I there beheld, collected together, thousands of the lowest of the London rabble. These ruffians, with loud shouts, and threats of summary vengeance on the Ministers, were at the time I arrived breaking the windows of most of the houses in the square. The Life Guards were patrolling in the neighbouring streets, and, whenever they appeared, were received with volleys of stones mingled

---

[1] The Corn Laws were passed in an attempt to protect British farming by charging duties on imported corn. They were denounced as being designed to protect landowners at the expense of the public at large. They were repealed in 1846.

with mud, and cries of 'Down with the Piccadilly butchers!' The mob
was evidently bent on more mischief.

I was afterwards returning towards King Street, when I was accosted
by Lord Castlereagh. He thanked me for the energy I had displayed,
but recommended a little more discretion in future; 'for the mob,' said
he, 'is not so dangerous as you think.' This remarkable man was quietly
looking on while his windows were being broken by these ruffians. I see
him before me now, dressed in a blue coat buttoned up to the chin, a
blue spenser, kerseymere breeches, long gaiters, shoes covered by
galoshes, and a white neckcloth. He was a particularly handsome man,
possessed great pluck and energy, and on this occasion appeared
perfectly calm and unconcerned, and not in the slightest degree ruffled
by the popular excesses and the abuse which was liberally heaped upon
himself and his colleagues in the government.

SHERIDAN AT STAFFORD

I heard from some very old men amongst my constituents the singular
history of the canvass of Sheridan for this immaculate borough.[1] His
reputation had already reached the town, but the defects which
unfortunately also rendered him conspicuous were then unknown. He
was reported to possess, besides, unbounded influence with the
Government, and to have the entire management of Drury Lane
Theatre. His voters, being fully convinced that they ought to receive a
quid pro quo for their 'most sweet voices,' every one had a favour to ask.
One had a son who had great dramatic talent, another was an
admirable scene-painter, others had cousins and nephews who would
make excellent door-keepers, lamp-lighters, check-takers, or box-
openers; there were tailors, coiffeurs, and decorators, who could dress
with inimitable effect the dramatis personæ. Sheridan listened with his
usual bland smile to every request, and complied with them all; each
individual being furnished with a letter to the stage-manager of Drury
Lane, they all started off for the metropolis, full of eager expectation. On
their arrival they were favourably received, and each person obtained
the situation that he had desired. When letters from London
announcing the fulfilment of Sheridan's promises reached the hungry
constituents of Stafford, a fresh batch of aspirants for office posted off,
and all were equally successful; the consequence was that, on the day of

[1] Sheridan (see note, p. 103) was returned as Member of Parliament for Stafford in 1780.

election, the favourite was returned with every demonstration of admiration and confidence.

Scarcely, however, had the member of Parliament left the town than innumerable reproaches were heaped upon his head; it was found that upon application for the payment of the salaries due to the different persons employed there was no money in the treasury. On Saturday night the receipts were carefully handed over to Sheridan, who carelessly spent the money; so that the whole of the humbler *employés* received nothing, whilst the higher order of actors contrived to dun and worry the thoughtless and extravagant *entrepreneur* out of a portion of their salaries.

Great was the indignation excited amongst Sheridan's constituents on finding that they had placed their political interests in the hands of such a man, and a deputation of three persons was despatched to London to remonstrate with him. They went at a fixed hour to the residence of the great man where they found a large crowd of his creditors assembled, many of them apparently bent on saying some very disagreeable truths. After waiting for some time, the folding-doors were thrown open, and out stepped the delinquent, in the first style of fashion. Looking around him with a fascinating smile, he addressed a few words to each of his would-be tormentors in succession; each one in his turn was delighted, and quite incapable of making unpleasant observations. They saw before them the man whose speech they had just read in the *Times* and *Courier*, which had proclaimed him in their leading articles the first orator of the age; and they had seen in the *Morning Post* a paragraph describing the irresistible wit which had convulsed Brookes's with laughter, and which concluded by pronouncing the honourable member an ornament to British society.

On this occasion, Sheridan soon observed that the deputation from Stafford was an angry one; so he walked quietly up to each individual, and put some questions to him relating to his domestic concerns. He had not forgotten anybody or any circumstance. He asked one of his constituents if Mrs Grundy's preserves and jams, which she was making when last he saw her, had proved of first-rate quality; whether Miss Grundy the elder continued to charm the world with playing Steibelt's 'Storm' on the piano; if Miss Grundy the younger still took lessons from Mr Town in velvet-painting; and whether Dr Squill had successfully vaccinated Master Tommy. To each the great man had something to say which seemed calculated to soothe the irritation of the hearer, and to prevent him from uttering a word of blame. Each man saw before him the most fascinating individual in the kingdom fixing upon him his dark flashing eye, and addressing him in persuasive accents, with the blandest smile. Sheridan moved through the admiring circle with graceful step, no one venturing to stop him; and as he reached the door he turned round, made an enchanting bow, and having entered his carriage, kissed his hand gracefully to his surrounding friends, and loudly told the coachman to drive to Carlton House. Away he went in a carriage for which the coachmaker had received no money, driven by a coachman and footman whose wages had not been paid for months, but who were still so pleased with their master that they were willing to wait, and in fact rather starve in his service, than live in the family of the richest nobleman upon the fat of the land.

Upon the dissolution of Parliament, Sheridan went down to Stafford; but he found circumstances completely changed; he could not obtain the promise of a single vote from his old friends. In consequence of his continued excesses, he had lost much of the charm of outward appearance that had won him friends at an earlier period, and nothing remained of his once expressive face but the remarkable brilliancy of his eyes; his cheeks were bloated, his nose was of a fiery red, and his general aspect bespoke the self-indulgence of the reckless man. His appearance on the hustings was the signal for a volley of opprobrious terms. One man in the crowd bawled out, 'We won't send you to parliament, for your nose will set the House of Commons on fire;' another had some doggerel rhymes to recite about

> The Whigs' banners are blue;
> Your nose and your cheeks are red,
> From port-wine and brandy too,
> And there's *sherry* in your head.

In vain did the once-admired orator attempt to gain a hearing; he was driven away amid the derision of the crowd, and never again was enabled to show his face in Stafford.

It has been said that his first election cost him £2500; but this has been strenuously denied. An anecdote, however, was in circulation, and had reached his biographer, Thomas Moore, to the effect that a deputation from Stafford had waited upon Sheridan, requiring that he should give a vote contrary to his own views, and that his answer was a decided negative, expressed in these words, 'Gentlemen, I bought you, and I assure you that I shall sell you whenever it suits my convenience.'

Many of the follies and extravagances that marked the life of this gifted but reckless personage must be attributed to the times in which he existed. Drinking was the fashion of the day. The Prince, Mr Pitt,

Dundas, the Lord Chancellor Eldon,[1] and many others, who gave the tone to society, would, if they now appeared at an evening party, 'as was their custom of an afternoon,' be pronounced fit for nothing but bed. A three-bottle man was not an unusual guest at a fashionable table; and the night was invariably spent in drinking bad port-wine to an enormous extent.

SHERIDAN AT DRURY-LANE THEATRE

However, many of the tricks played by Sheridan were quite unjustifiable. A very old man, and who had suffered severely by his confidence in the great orator, was pointed out to me. On a Friday evening, after the second price had been received,[2] the treasurer of Drury-Lane Theatre came to Sheridan with a wofully long face, and told him that there was not money enough to pay even the subordinates on the following day; and that unless a certain sum could be found he was persuaded that the house could not open on Monday. Sheridan suggested several plans for raising the wind, but all were declared by Mr Dunn to be useless. Sheridan gazed round at the thinly-peopled boxes, and at length called to one of the porters in waiting, 'Do you see that stout, good-tempered-looking man seated next a comely lady in the third box from the stage, in a front row? Immediately the play is over, go to him; have a couple of wax candles carried by a boy who can make graceful bows; open the box door, and in a voice loud enough to be heard by every one, say, 'Sir, Mr Sheridan requests the honour of a private interview with you in his own room.' Let every one on the way treat him with the greatest civility; and, Mr Dunn, will you have the kindness to see that a bottle of the best port and a couple of wine glasses are placed on the table in my study.'

The orders were duly obeyed. The gentleman was ushered into the presence of Sheridan with honours almost approaching those shown to royalty, and was received by him with the most cordial marks of

---

[1] Henry Dundas, first Viscount Melville (1742–1811), was First Lord of the Admiralty in Pitt's second administration; John Scott, first Earl of Eldon (1751–1838), the son of a coal merchant and hence known in the Royal Family as 'Old Bags', was Lord Chancellor. According to Gilbert Eliot, 'men of all ages [drank] abominably'. Fox a 'great deal', Sheridan 'excessively', Pitt 'as much as either' and Grey 'more than any of them', but none was a match for Dr John Campbell, who – while Pitt and Sheridan were content to drink six bottles a day – was said to get through thirteen and they were of port.

[2] When double bills were presented at theatres, prices were reduced for those who came only for the second half of the performance.

friendship and regard. 'I am always so happy to see any one from Stafford. I was glad you called at my house for an order to this theatre, where I hope you will come when you please; you will find your name on the free list. I think I remember you told me you always came twice a year to London.' 'Yes,' was the reply; 'January and July, to receive my dividends.' 'You have come for that purpose now,' continued Sheridan. 'Oh, yes; and I went to the Bank of England and got my six hundred pounds.' 'Ah,' said the manager, 'you are in Consols,[1] whilst I, alas, am Reduced, and can get nothing till April, when, you know, the interest is paid; and till then I shall be in great distress.' 'Oh,' said his constituent, 'let that not make you uneasy; if you give me the power of attorney to receive the money for you when it is due, I can let you have three hundred pounds, which I shall not want till then.' 'Only a real friend,' said Sheridan, shaking his dupe by the hand with warmth, 'could have made such a proposition. I accept it thankfully.' And the three hundred pounds were immediately transferred from the pocket-book of the unwary man of Stafford into that of the penniless manager of the theatre.

April arrived, a power of attorney was one morning handed over for signature to Sheridan, [who refused to sign it]. The Stafford man, burning with indignation, rushed up to London, and found his cajoler calmly seated in his room at Drury Lane. Sheridan, apparently not at all disconcerted, with outstretched hand and benignant smile welcomed his victim, whose rage was at first uncontrollable; but his attack was met by the manager with an acknowledgment that, in a moment of urgent necessity, he had been compelled to throw himself on the generosity of a man whom he had heard from every one was a model of worth, and whose acquaintance would be acceptable in the highest quarters. 'But excuse me, my dear sir,' he added; 'I am now commanded to go to the Prince of Wales, to whom I shall narrate your noble conduct. My carriage is waiting, and I can take you to Carlton House.' The eye of the provincial sparkled with delight. Was it possible that he meant to take him to the Prince of Wales? It sounded something like it. He shook Sheridan by the hand, saying, 'I forgive you, my dear friend; never mention the debt again.' 'I will take care never to do so,' said the manager. The carriage came round to the door, the two friends entered it, and when they arrived at Carlton House, Sheridan got out, and closing the door, told the coachman to drive the gentleman to his hotel.

---

[1] Consolidated Annuities, British government securities which were consolidated in 1751 into a single stock bearing interest at 3 per cent.

The Stafford man, with a last hope, naïvely said, 'I thought I also was going into Carlton House.' 'Another mistake of yours,' replied Sheridan. The worthy constituent returned that night to Stafford; and in future his vote was given against Sheridan.

LORD NORMANBY

The first time I ever saw Lord Normanby was in 1816,[1] during a morning visit at the Right Hon. George Tierney's, in Stratton Street.[2] He was then a remarkably pleasing and good-looking young man; and I remember a circumstance which may account for his entering political life as a Liberal.

His father, Lord Mulgrave, was a high Tory, had long been a member of the administration of Pitt and his successors, and at the time of which I speak was Master-General of the Ordnance. On the occasion to which I refer, Lord Normanby, in the course of conversation, informed those present that his father had in a most unceremonious manner been dismissed from his high post to make way for the Duke of Wellington. He denounced, in the bitterest terms, the conduct of the Government towards so old a public servant as his father, and swore he never would forgive them.

He shortly afterwards entered Parliament as an advanced Liberal, always voted with the Whigs; and when they came into office in 1830, he was appointed Governor of Jamaica. On his return thence to England, he filled the post of Lord-Lieutenant of Ireland, under very difficult circumstances, and at a period of great importance, with general applause. His pleasing and conciliating manners made him a general favourite; and the Vice-Regal Court during his stay was a very brilliant one. He afterwards became Secretary of State; and in 1847, ambassador at Paris. He conducted himself with considerable tact, and showed a certain amount of ability during the latter part of the reign of Louis Philippe. On the establishment of the Republic, he had the good sense to keep quiet, and to remain on good terms with the poets, wood-merchants, and journalists who successively held office. But I do not think he conducted his relations with the present Emperor in a very adroit manner. He misjudged the Prince's capacity and character, and

---

[1] Constantine Henry Phipps, first Marquess of Normanby (1797–1863), was Ambassador in Paris from 1846 to 1852. He was the eldest son of Henry, first Earl of Mulgrave. Guizot said of him, 'Il est bon enfant, mais il ne comprend pas notre langue.'

[2] George Tierney (1761–1830), a rich politician of Irish extraction renowned for his biting sarcasm. A prominent Whig, he fought a duel with Pitt in 1798.

assumed rather a protecting tone with him; and when the *coup d'état* took place, he did not believe that Lord Palmerston would, with his usual decision and foresight, recognise Louis Napoleon as Emperor, immediately the choice of the French nation became known. Lord Normanby afterwards engaged in intrigues against his chief at the Foreign Office, and the latter period of his embassy was not a very satisfactory one, either to himself or to his admirers.

On his resignation, and after an attack of paralysis, he was appointed minister to Florence. This post was given him in lieu of a retiring pension, and because the climate suited him; and Lord Normanby, with his palazzo in town and the Villa Normanby near Fiesole, recalled to his old friends the pleasant days they had spent with him thirty years before, when he resided there as a private gentleman before his accession to office, and when his theatricals were the delight of all who visited Italy.

On the accession of the Tories to power, Lord Normanby and Lord Howden, our envoy to Madrid,[1] were, with an unparalleled want of courtesy, immediately informed by a telegraphic despatch that her Majesty had no longer any occasion for their services. The insulting nature of this dismissal at the hands of Lord Malmesbury had no effect upon the fixed determination of Lord Normanby to leave his old friends the Whigs.[2] It is supposed that the immense success of the paternal governments of Naples, Florence, Parma, Lucca, and Modena, in making their people happy and contented, must have produced this change in Lord Normanby's opinions; for, immediately on his return to England, he became a most violent Tory; and in his frequent speeches in the House of Lords arraigned and attacked on all occasions the foreign policy of the Whigs, and that with a blind and almost rabid violence, and a degree of bitterness and ill-nature, which astonished and disgusted his old friends.

Let us hope that this extraordinary change both in the opinions and feelings of so generally popular and amiable a man was the effect of disease, and attributable to the severe attack of illness from which he had suffered for several years before his death. He was *the* man of all others who should *not* have left the Liberal party. He was the spoiled child of the Whigs, and had received from them every great appoint-

---

[1] John Hobart Caradoc, second Baron Howden (1799–1873), became Ambassador in Madrid in 1850.
[2] James Howard Harris, third Earl of Malmesbury (1807–89), was Foreign Secretary in the Earl of Derby's Cabinet.

ment and every distinction it was in their power to give. Besides the high offices I have before enumerated, he was made a Marquis, a Grand Cross of the Bath, and a Knight of the Garter.

I remember, *à propos* of this, that when Lord Melbourne was minister, Edward Ellice[1] and the Premier were looking one morning from the windows of the First Lord's residence in Downing Street into St James's Park, and saw Lord Normanby approaching. On Mr Ellice inquiring what he could be coming for, Lord Melbourne said, in his off-hand manner, 'I don't know what the devil the fellow can want, unless he comes to ask for a second garter for his other leg.' In fact the commonest gratitude should have made Lord Normanby pause before he took the fatal step which sullied the close of his political career.

Let me turn from this last lamentable error, and remember only his many good and amiable qualities. He was certainly one of the most courteous and agreeable of our ministers and diplomatists. There was no hauteur or reserve in his manner, and yet a natural dignity which prevented all undue familiarity. He was a fluent and ready speaker, and wrote with ease and elegance. When in Dublin he was much beloved by all around him, for he was a thoroughly good-natured man; and because this expression has been often misunderstood and supposed to mean weak or silly, let us not despise this rare and precious gift, much oftener bestowed on men of intellect than on fools. Till his illness, Lord Normanby was never heard to say an unkind thing of any one; and though in the latter years of his life he carried this amiable quality too far, yet this kindness in the days of his prosperity had a winning charm, because it was genuine, and sprang from a really good heart.

Had Lord Normanby not taken to politics and become a Viceroy and Secretary of State, he would have achieved great success as a literary man.[2] His two novels, *Matilda*, and *Yes and No*, were worthy to be placed on a par with the best of their day; and had he been obliged to earn his bread, he might have been a Bulwer or a Kemble. For, besides his literary acquirements, he had a remarkable talent for acting; and his theatre at Florence, some forty years ago, might have vied with many of the best establishments in London or Paris. Lord Normanby had a thousand good and amiable qualities; and those who knew him will long remember with regret his pleasant conversation, his genial smile, and kind, open-hearted manner.

---

[1] Edward Ellice (1781–1863) was Secretary at War in Melbourne's first Cabinet.
[2] Most of his books were romantic novels published anonymously. The two that Gronow mentions were scarcely worthy of the praise which he bestows upon them.

LORD CASTLEREAGH AND SIR E. PAKENHAM

The following incident occurred in London in 1814. When the war had terminated in the Peninsula, Sir Edward Pakenham, with his physician, Dr John Howell, arrived in England, *en route* to North America, where Sir Edward had been named by the Duke of York Commander-in-Chief of the British forces.[1] Before the departure of the gallant General, he had promised Lord Castlereagh to breakfast with him, and at the same time to introduce his physician to the minister. After breakfast, Lord C. inquired of the Doctor the precise place where the jugular vein was situated. Dr Howell explained it to the satisfaction of his Lordship, stating that it would be a dangerous experiment for any man to take the slightest liberty with that artery, for death would inevitably follow if it were pierced. When the General and his friend were returning to their hotel, the former said, 'I am afraid, Doctor, you were too explicit about the jugular artery, for I observed Castlereagh to be in a strange mood when you finished your anatomical lecture.' It is needless to state that many years did not elapse before Lord C. committed suicide by cutting his throat with a penknife.

Dr Howell related this incident to me at Brighton in 1849.

LORD ALTHORPE

Mr Morier,[2] formerly our minister in Switzerland, who had been Lord Althorpe's fag at Westminster,[3] and always remained on terms of great intimacy with him, was calling one morning in Downing Street, at the time the noble lord was Chancellor of the Exchequer, and found him at breakfast. Mr Morier, appearing to be struck by something he saw on the table, Lord Althorpe asked him what he was thinking of, when Mr Morier said, 'I am looking at your teapots, Althorpe, for they appear to me to be wonderfully like those I used to clean for you when I was your fag.'

'They are the very same teapots,' replied the Chancellor of the

[1] See note, p. 50.
[2] David Richard Morier (1784–1877), born at Smyrna, the son of a diplomat. He had played a leading role in the post-Napoleonic settlement of Europe. He was appointed Minister in Switzerland in 1830. His son, Sir Robert Morier, became Ambassador at St Petersburg.
[3] John Charles Spencer, Viscount Althorp and first Earl Spencer (1782–1845). Gronow is mistaken in saying he was at Westminster. He and Morier were at Harrow. He became Chancellor of the Exchequer in 1830. He never seemed at home in the House of Commons; and it was said of him that he was heard only once to speak with any enthusiasm and that was on the subject of prize-fighting.

Exchequer. 'They remind me of my happy school-days, and I like to stick to my old acquaintances.'

Lord Althorpe was rather singular in his dress. Even in the dog-days, he was always buttoned up to the chin; and I once heard O'Connell say, that no one had ever been able to discover whether his lordship wore a shirt or not, for there were no visible signs of one, either on the neck or wrists; but that it was evident he had made 'a shift' to do without one.

Lord Althorpe was a bad and tedious speaker; his financial statements, given out as they were with endless humming and hawing, and constant hesitation, made his hearers feel quite nervous and uncomfortable; but he was possessed of great good sense, and was so upright and honourable a man, and such a thorough gentleman, that the Reformed House of Commons – a difficult one to manage – had more confidence in him than they would have had in any one else, however eloquent and fluent he might have been.

O'CONNELL

During the time I was in the House of Commons, I saw a good deal of O'Connell, and frequently dined at his house in Great George Street.[1] He was nowhere seen to more advantage than presiding at his own table, in all the pride of hospitality, surrounded by a numerous body of friends and relations. His dinners were plain but good; there were always large joints and plenty of wine. His conversation was most interesting: he had a fund of anecdote, and used to relate most curious stories about the Union and the state of society in Ireland when he was a young man. Though a good hater, he could do justice to political opponents; and I once heard him say, in speaking of Lord Castlereagh, the minister, 'Castlereagh, with all his faults, was a fine fellow, and as brave as Achilles.'

In the House I very often sat next to him; he was always gay and cheerful, and sometimes very amusing: like most Irishmen, he was at all times ready for a joke.

THE SPAFIELDS RIOTS

The years 1816 and 1817 were a most dangerous period. The spirit of the people of England, exasperated by heavy taxation, the high price of bread, and many iniquitous laws and restrictions now happily done

[1] Daniel O'Connell (1775-1847), the Irish political leader.

away with by successive liberal administrations, was of the worst possible nature. In the riots and meetings of those troublous times, the mob really meant mischief; and had they been accustomed to the use of arms, and well drilled, they might have committed as great excesses as the ruffians of 1793 in France.

On the 15th November 1816, a monster meeting was held in Spafields, to petition the Prince Regent.[1] Early in the morning of that day, I was sent with a company of the Guards to occupy the prison of Spafields, and to act, if necessary, in aid and support of the civil power. On our arrival, we found that a troop of horse artillery, with their guns, had already taken up their position within the yard. We lost no time in making loopholes in the walls, in the event of an attack from without, and made ready for action. The mob, which was not very numerous on our arrival, had by this time increased to an enormous multitude. Sixty or seventy thousand persons must have been present. Their principal leaders appeared to be Major Cartwright,[2] Gale Jones,[3] and the notorious Henry Hunt, the blacking-maker.[4] The major was an old, grey-headed, vulgar-looking man. Hunt was a large, powerfully made fellow, who might have been taken for a butcher: he always wore a white hat, which was, I never knew why, in those days supposed to be an emblem of very advanced liberal, or even republican opinions.[5] These two demagogues, and two or three more of the leaders of the mob, got into a cart, that had been brought up as a sort of tribune or rostrum, from which they harangued the people. More violent and treasonable discourses it was impossible to make; and the huge multitude rent the air with their shouts of applause.

After a time, a magistrate and some constables appeared, and

[1] The Spafield Riots actually took place on 2 December 1816. They were provoked by demands for parliamentary reform.

[2] Major John Cartwright (1740–1824), a major in the Nottinghamshire militia, had formerly been a naval officer but his refusal to serve against the American rebels in the War of Independence had put a stop to his life at sea. The author of numerous tracts on parliamentary reform, he became known as the Father of Reform. Although respected for his good nature and bravery, and as a gentleman from an old Nottinghamshire family, his extreme views prevented him obtaining a seat in Parliament and blocked his promotion in the militia.

[3] John Gale Jones (1769–1838), a surgeon and apothecary, well known for his inflammatory addresses at public meetings. He was committed to Newgate Prison in 1810.

[4] Henry Hunt (1773–1835), a farmer from Wiltshire who later became a blacking manufacturer. Known as 'Orator' Hunt and described by Sir Samuel Romilly as 'a most unprincipled demagogue', he was sentenced to imprisonment after the Peterloo Massacre of 1819. He later, for a short time, was Member of Parliament for Preston.

[5] Henry Hunt's habitual wearing of a white hat led to other radicals adopting it.

summoned the people to disperse; and, at the same moment, a messenger arrived from the prison, who whispered in Hunt's ear that if the mob committed any outrage, or made any disturbance, and did not quietly disperse, they would be dealt with by the soldiers, who had orders above all to pick off the ringleaders, should any attack be made upon the prison. This intelligence, conveyed to the gentlemen in the cart by one of their friends, produced a very marked effect. In a very short time they got down, as they seemed to consider themselves in rather an exposed position, declared the meeting at an end, and hurried off, leaving the crowd to follow them; which they shortly afterwards did.

Several years after this event, at the time of the Reform Bill, Hunt was elected member of Parliament for Preston, and I was elected for the immaculate borough of Stafford. I well recollect, but cannot describe, the amazement of the blacking-man when I told him one evening, in the smoking-room of the House of Commons, that if any attack had been made upon the prison at Spafields, I had given my men orders to pick off Major Cartwright, himself, and one or two more who were in the cart. Hunt was perfectly astonished. He became very red, and his eyes seemed to flash fire.

'What sir! do you mean to say you would have been capable of such an act of barbarity?'

'Yes,' said I; 'and I almost regret you did not give us the opportunity, for your aim that day was to create a revolution, and you would have richly deserved the fate which you so narrowly escaped by the cowardice or lukewarmness of your followers.'

14

Lord Alvanley and Company

LORD ALVANLEY

From the time of good Queen Bess, when the English language first began to assume somewhat of its present form, idiom, and mode of expression, to the days of our most gracious sovereign Queen Victoria, every age has had its punsters, humourists, and eloquent conversationists; but I much doubt whether the year 1789 did not produce the greatest wit of modern times, in the person of William Lord Alvanley.[1]

After receiving a very excellent and careful education, Alvanley entered the Coldstream Guards at an early age, and served with distinction at Copenhagen and in the Peninsula; but being in possession of a large fortune, he left the army, gave himself up entirely to the pursuit of pleasure, and became one of the principal dandies of the day. With the brilliant talents which he possessed, he might have attained to the highest eminence in any line of life he had embraced.

Not only was Alvanley considered the wittiest man of his day in England, but, during his residence in France, and tours through Russia and other countries, he was universally admitted to possess, not only great wit and humour, but *l'esprit français* in its highest perfection; and no greater compliment could be paid him by foreigners than this. He was one of the rare examples (particularly rare in the days of the dandies, who

---

[1] William Arden, second Baron Alvanley (1789–1849). His father was Lord Chief Justice. He himself joined the army, retiring as lieutenant-colonel. With the death of his brother, the peerage became extinct.

were generally sour and spiteful) of a man combining brilliant wit and repartee with the most perfect good-nature. His manner, above all, was irresistible; and the slight lisp, which might have been considered as a blemish, only added piquancy and zest to his sayings.

In appearance, he was about the middle height, and well and strongly built, though he latterly became somewhat corpulent. He excelled in all manly exercises, was a hard rider to hounds, and was what those who do not belong to the upper ten thousand call 'a good-plucked one.' His face had somewhat of the rotund form and smiling expression which characterise the jolly friars one meets with in Italy. His hair and eyes were dark, and he had a very small nose, to which, after deep potations, his copious pinches of snuff had some difficulty in finding their way, and were in consequence rather lavishly bestowed upon his florid cheek. He resided in Park Street, St James's, and his dinners there and at Melton were considered to be the best in England. He never invited more than eight people, and insisted upon having the somewhat expensive luxury of an apricot tart on the sideboard the whole year round, and his *maître d'hôtel* remonstrating with him upon the expense, Alvanley replied, 'Go to Gunter's, the confectioner, and purchase all the preserved apricots, and don't plague me any more about the expense.'

Alvanley was a good speaker; and having made some allusion to O'Connell in rather strong terms in the House of Lords, the latter very coarsely and unjustly denounced him, in a speech he made in the House of Commons, as a bloated buffoon. Alvanley thereupon called out the Liberator, who would not meet him, but excused himself by saying, 'There is blood already on this hand,' – alluding to his fatal duel with D'Esterre.[1]

Alvanley then threatened O'Connell with personal chastisement. Upon this, Morgan O'Connell, a very agreeable, gentlemanlike man, who had been in the Austrian service, and whom I knew well, said he would take his father's place.[2] A meeting was accordingly agreed upon

---

[1] After referring to the corporation of Dublin as 'beggarly', O'Connell had been challenged to a duel by one of the city's guild merchants, d'Esterre, whom he wounded fatally. Thereafter he swore never to fight a duel again.

[2] Morgan O'Connell (1804-85), second son of Daniel, served with the Irish South American Legion before joining the Austrian army. He entered Parliament as one of the Members for Meath in 1832. After his duel with Alvanley he received a challenge from Benjamin Disraeli, who had been castigated by Daniel O'Connell as a 'reptile', a 'vile creature' and a 'living lie'. 'His name shows that he is of Jewish origin,' O'Connell added. 'I do not use it as a term of reproach; there are many most respectable Jews. But there are, as in every other people, some of the lowest and most disgusting grade of moral turpitude; and of those I look upon Mr Disraeli as the worst.' Morgan O'Connell, in replying to Disraeli's challenge, said that he was not responsible for his father's opinions.

at Wimbledon Common. Alvanley's second was Colonel George Dawson Damer, and our late consul at Hamburgh. Colonel Hodges, acted for Morgan O'Connell. Several shots were fired without effect, and the seconds then interfered, and put a stop to any further hostilities.

On their way home in a hackney-coach, Alvanley said – 'What a clumsy fellow O'Connell must be, to miss such a fat fellow as I am! He ought to practise at a haystack to get his hand in.' When the carriage drove up to Alvanley's door, he gave the coachman a sovereign. Jarvey was profuse in his thanks, and said, 'It's a great deal for only having taken your lordship to Wimbledon.'[1]

'No, my good man,' said Alvanley, 'I give it you, not for taking me, but for bringing me back.'

Everybody knows the story of Gunter the pastry-cook.[2] He was mounted on a runaway horse with the King's hounds, and excused himself for riding against Alvanley, by saying, 'O my lord, I can't hold him, he's so hot!' 'Ice him, Gunter – ice him!' was the consoling rejoinder.

Alvanley had a delightful recklessness and *laisser aller* in everything. His manner of putting out his light at night was not a very pleasant one for his host for the time being. He always read in bed, and when he wanted to go to sleep, he either extinguished his candle by throwing it on the floor in the middle of the room, and taking a shot at it with the pillow, or else quietly placed it, when still lighted, under the bolster. At Badminton, and other country houses, his habits in this respect were so well known, that a servant was ordered to sit up in the passage to keep watch over him.

Alvanley's recklessness in money matters was almost incredible. His creditors having become at last very clamorous, that able and astute man of the world, Mr Charles Greville,[3] with the energetic and bustling

---

[1] Hackney-coach drivers were known as 'jarveys', possibly an allusion to St Gervaise, whose symbol in art is a whip.

[2] Gunter's Tea Shop was in Berkeley Square. It was founded in 1757 by an Italian pastry-cook, Domenico Negri, who took Gunter into partnership in 1777. The shop moved to Curzon Street in the 1930s and was closed in 1956.

[3] Charles Greville (1794–1865), the diarist, was Clerk of the Privy Council from 1821 to 1859. He also managed the racing establishment of the Duke of York. Through the influence of his grandfather, the third Duke of Portland, he acquired the sinecure secretaryship of Jamaica whose duties were performed for him on the island which he never himself visited. He was 'a friend of many', said Sir Henry Taylor, 'and always most a friend when friendship was most wanted.' 'No power on earth would induce him to get out of an arm chair he had selected,' it was also said of him. Yet 'he would go from London to Berwick to serve a friend.'

kindness in mixing himself up in all his friends' affairs which still distinguishes him, had undertaken to settle those of Alvanley. After going through every item of the debts, matters looked more promising than Mr Greville expected, and he took his leave. In the morning he received a note from Alvanley, to say that he had quite forgotten to take into account a debt of fifty-five thousand pounds.

In his latter years Lord Alvanley was a martyr to the gout, but preserved his wit and good-humour to the last.

*

When Alvanley was at college, he was smitten with a sudden thirst for military glory, and a pair of colours in the Coldstream Guards, then commanded by the late Duke of York, was given him. He became the Duke of York's bosom friend, and this unfortunately led him to become reckless in money matters. Upon one occasion George Anson, afterwards General Anson,[1] asked Alvanley at White's if he felt disposed to join a water party on the Thames, at which several pretty women of fashion, would assemble. He assented, inquiring where they were to dine. Anson replied, he never thought of dining. 'Well, never mind, Anson; I will give instructions on that head.' Accordingly, he told Gunter to supply the party with a good dinner, to hire the largest boat on the Thames, to have it carpeted and covered with an awning, and make it as comfortable as possible, and to hire twelve boatmen: in short, nothing was to be wanting. The *fête* succeeded to the satisfaction of all parties; but Alvanley paid Gunter two hundred guineas for his folly.

Apart from his extravagance, Alvanley, the magnificent, the witty, the famous, and chivalrous, was the idol of the clubs, and of society, from the King to the ensign of the Guards. All sorts of stories used to be told of his recklessness about money. When Lord Alvanley succeeded to his father's fortune, he inherited an income of eight thousand pounds a year; when he died, he did not leave to his brother, who succeeded to the title, above two thousand.

The great charm of Alvanley's manner was its naturalness, or *naïveté*. He was an excellent classical scholar, a good speaker, and whatever he undertook he succeeded in. He had lived in nearly every court of Europe, had a vast acquaintance with the world, and his knowledge of languages was great.

[1] See note, p. 134.

PARSON AMBROSE

During the winter of 1816, I had the honour to receive a general invitation to the Sunday *soirées* of the Duchess of Orleans, the mother of Louis Philippe. Upon one occasion I remember seeing two celebrated ladies there, Madame de Staël and Madame Recamier. There were many English present also. Among the most remarkable was a gentleman known by the appellation of 'Parson Ambrose,' a natural son of Lord de Blaquiere's.[1] He was good-looking, and dressed like a gentleman of the old *régime*. He wore black silk breeches, with buckles both to his knees and shoes, and the frills to his shirt were of the finest Malines lace. Sir Charles Stewart, upon entering the saloon, beckoned to the parson, who said, 'Well, Sir Charles, I am in a bad state.' 'What is the matter with you?' 'I have a complaint in the chest, your Excellency.' 'What doctor have you consulted?' 'Lafitte,' replied the parson. 'I never heard of him except as a banker. Well, what has he done for you?' 'Nothing.' Sir Charles, now discovering the meaning of the '*chest* complaint,' said, in his good-natured way, 'Come to the Embassy to-morrow morning, and I will see what can be done to cure your complaint.' The parson accordingly went, and found the ambassador at breakfast with the Duke of Wellington. After talking over olden times, when the Duke was merely Captain Wellesley, and lived on intimate terms with the parson in Dublin, his grace kindly presented Ambrose with a hundred guineas, to take him back to England for change of air; which, he trusted, would contribute to the restoration of his health.

'KING' ALLEN

The late Viscount Allen, commonly called 'King' Allen, was a well-known character in London for many years. He was a tall, stout, and pompous-looking personage, remarkably well got up, with an invariably new-looking hat and well-polished boots. His only exercise and usual walk was from White's to Crockford's, and from Crockford's to White's.

Who in this ponderous old man would have recognised the gallant youth who, as Ensign in the Guards, led on the men with incredible

---

[1] John Blaquiere (1732–1812), the son of a French merchant who had emigrated to London, became a distinguished politician and was created Baron de Blaquiere in 1800. He had a very large number of legitimate children as well as 'Parson Ambrose'.

energy and activity across the ravine at Talavera; where, if the great Duke had not sent the 48th Regiment to their assistance, very little more would have been heard of 'King' Allen and his merry men? But one of the most famous dandies of the day was not fated thus to perish; and he was preserved for thirty years after the great battle, to swagger down Bond Street or lounge on the sunny side of Pall Mall, to become an *arbiter elegantiarum* amongst the tailors, and a Mæcenas at the opera and play.

To render the 'King' perfectly happy, one little item was wanting – money. His estates, if he ever had any, had long passed from him, and he had much difficulty in making the two ends meet. When, for economy's sake, he was obliged to retire for a short time to Dublin, he had a very large door in Merrion Square, with an almost equally large brass plate, on which his name was engraved in letters of vast size; but it was very much doubted whether there was any house behind it. He was a great diner out; and one spiteful old lady, whom he had irritated by some uncivil remarks, told him that his title was as good as board wages to him.

Strange to say, this *mauvais sujet* was a great friend of the late Sir Robert Peel, when Chief Secretary for Ireland; and on one occasion, when they were proceeding in an open carriage to dine with a friend a few miles from Dublin, in passing through a village, they had the misfortune to drive over the oldest inhabitant, an ancient beldam, who was generally stationed on the bridge. A large mob gathered round the carriage; and as Peel and the Tory Government were very unpopular at the period to which I refer, the mob began to grow abusive, and cast very threatening and ominous looks at the occupants of the barouche; when the 'King,' with a coolness and self-possession worthy of Brummell, rose up, displaying an acre of white waistcoat, and called out, 'Now, postboy, go on, and don't drive over any more old women.' The mob, awe-struck by 'King' Allen's majestic deportment, retired, and 'the industrious and idle apprentices' went on their way rejoicing.

The 'King' was not a very good-natured person; and as he had a strong inclination to, and some talent for, sarcasm, he made himself many enemies. To give an idea of his 'style.' When the statue of George III[1] was erected in front of Ransom's banking-house,[2] Mr Williams, one

---

[1] The statue of George III in Cockspur Street is by Matthew Cotes Wyatt. It was unveiled by the King's fifth son, the Duke of Cumberland, in 1836 after two months of 'tedious and expensive' litigation by Mr Williams.

[2] Ransom, Bouverie and Company was founded in 1786. With several other banks it was merged with Barclays in 1896.

of the partners, commonly known by the name of 'Swell Bill,' petitioned the 'Woods and Forests' to remove that work of art, as it collected a crowd of little boys, who were peculiarly facetious on the subject of the pigtail of that obstinate but domestic monarch, and otherwise obstructed business. Lord Allen, meeting Williams at White's, said, 'I should have thought the erection of the statue rather an advantage to you, because, while you are standing idle at your own shop door, it would prevent you seeing the crowds hurrying to the respectable establishment of Messrs Coutts & Co., close by in the Strand.'[1]

Lord Allen greatly resembled in later life an ancient grey parrot, both in the aquiline outline of his features, and his peculiar mode of walking, with one foot crossed over the other in a slow and wary manner. He was a regular Cockney, and very seldom left London; but on one occasion, when he had gone down with Alvanley to Dover for the sake of his health, and complained to his facetious friend that he could get no sleep, Alvanley ordered a coach to drive up and down in front of the inn windows all night, and made the boots call out, in imitation of the London watchmen of that day, 'Half-past two, and a stormy night.' The well-known rumble of the wheels, and the dulcet tones of the boots, had the desired effect; the 'King' passed excellent nights, and was soon able to return to his little house in South Street with renewed health and spirits.

Lord Allen was at last obliged to leave London, after coming to an understanding with his creditors; and after passing some time at Cadiz, died at Gibraltar in 1843, when his title became extinct.

MARTIN HAWKE

The Hon. Martin Hawke was a remarkable character, of a somewhat original and eccentric turn of mind.[2] He lived many years abroad, and was the principal person who introduced, and rendered popular on the Continent, horse-racing, cricket, and other manly sports. He was well known in Paris, Tours, and Boulogne. He was an excellent horseman, a first-rate pugilist, a capital shot, was passionately fond of field sports, and had a great aversion to anything in the shape of poaching. He had several very serious encounters in France with some very rough

---

[1] Coutts & Co., founded in 1692, was then at 59 Strand, where it remained for 165 years. In 1904 it moved to its present site at 440 Strand.

[2] The Hon. Martin Bladen Edward Hawke (1777–1839), second son of the second Baron Hawke.

customers, whom he found shooting on the manors he had hired; and nothing but his great strength and courage prevented him from falling a sacrifice to their vengeance.

When in Paris some forty years back, Hawke received, through Sir C. Stewart, our ambassador, an invitation to accompany the Duc de Berri on a shooting excursion in the forest of St Germain. Prior to the chase, Alexandre de Girardin,[1] the *grand veneur*, or huntsman, informed the gentlemen who were invited that it was not etiquette for them to fire before his Royal Highness had discharged his gun. As bad luck would have it, Hawke, in the ardour of the moment, had completely forgotten the hint given him; for on the first cock-pheasant getting up, Hawke, who was rather quicker than the royal sportsman, knocked it over close to the feet of the Duke, who in a great rage cried out, in English, 'Who the devil are you, sir, who have disobeyed my orders?' Martin, rather ashamed, mentioned his name. The Duke replied, 'A droll name yours is, Mr "Hock;"' upon which Martin, nothing abashed, said, 'Oh, sir, your Royal Highness must be acquainted with it already, for my grandfather Admiral Hawke's name was well known in the French navy.'[2] The Duc de Berri took this retort very good-humouredly, and said, 'Well, well, Mr Hawke, you are a plain-spoken sort of fellow; I like your frankness and spirit, and therefore hope, the next time I have a shooting party at St Germain, you will accompany me again.' Alas! the following night the good-natured Prince, on entering the opera, was assassinated.

A Mother in Israel

Old Madame Rothschild, mother of the mighty capitalists, attained the age of ninety-eight;[3] her wit, which was remarkable, and her intellectual faculties, which were of no common order, were preserved to the end. In her last illness, when surrounded by her family, her physician being present, she said in a suppliant tone to the latter, 'Dear doctor, try

[1] See note, p. 175.
[2] Edward, first Baron Hawke (1705–81), Admiral of the Fleet. He defeated the French fleet at Quiberon Bay in 1759.
[3] Gudule Rothschild (1753–1849) married Meyer Amschel Rothschild in 1770. She was the daughter of Baruch Schnappe, a merchant of Frankfurt. She had ten children, five of them sons. The eldest son assisted in his father's business in Germany, the others leaving to open branches in other countries. The third son, Nathan Meyer Rothschild, established the London branch at New Court, St Swithun's Lane, where N. M. Rothschild and Sons Ltd are still in business as merchant bankers.

to do something for me.' 'Madame, what can I do? I can't make you young again.' 'No, doctor, I don't want to be young again, but I want to continue to grow old.'

THE MARQUESS OF WORCESTER

The Marquis of Worcester,[1] a spirited, dashing, handsome young man, was much admired by the fair sex, and led a life of great gaiety. His father, the Duke of Beaufort, receiving some hints that this promising youth was in danger of becoming the victim of a siren who had almost extorted from him a promise of marriage, the Marquis was sent to join the Duke of Wellington, became his aide-de-camp, and upon every occasion showed that he was worthy the race of John of Gaunt, from which he sprang.

The lady in question (Harriet Wilson) was one of the most notorious *traviatas*[2] of the day, had written her memoirs, and become the scandal of the metropolis; one of her sisters had married a peer of the realm,[3] and another a famous harpist of very doubtful character, who had been one of the most licentious men of the day, and afterwards carried off the wife of a distinguished English composer.[4]

Upon the return of the Marquis from the army, he devoted his time to the sports of the field, his father's hunting establishments, both in Gloucestershire and Oxfordshire, being the admiration of every lover of the chase.

---

[1] William Somerset, Marquess of Worcester (1792-1853), succeeded his father as seventh Duke of Beaufort in 1835.

[2] Harriette Wilson (1789-1846), courtesan and author of the celebrated and libellous *Memoirs*, which appeared in instalments from 1825 accompanied by threats of further revelations issued with the intention of extracting blackmail from her former lovers, including the Duke of Wellington, who responded to her blackmail with the famous riposte, 'Publish and be damned!' The Duke of Beaufort promised her an annuity of £500, which he reduced to a single payment of £1,200, much to her annoyance. She was born in Mayfair, the daughter of a watchmaker of Swiss descent, John Dubochet. She was one of fifteen children, few of whom were virtuous.

Traviata, a feminine noun meaning literally the led-astray; in Gronow's sense, the leader-astray.

[3] This was Sophia, who in 1812 married Thomas Noel Hill, second Baron Berwick (1770-1832). She died in 1875.

[4] Robert Nicolas Charles Bochsa (1789-1856), harpist to both Napoleon and Louis XVIII. He left France to escape imprisonment for forgery and settled in London, where he bigamously married Amy Dubochet whom he abandoned to run away with Lady Bishop, second wife of the opera conductor and composer Sir Henry Rowley Bishop, whose music for John Howard Payne's lyric 'Home Sweet Home' was performed in Bishop's opera *Clari, the Maid of Milan*.

TOM PIPES

In the days of which I speak there were amateur coachmen, who drove with unflinching regularity, and in all weathers, the public stage-coaches, and delighted in the opportunity of assimilating themselves with professional Jehus.[1] Some young men, heirs of large landed proprietors, mounted the box, handled the ribbons, and bowled along the highroad; they touched their hats to their passengers, and some among them did not disdain even the tip of a shilling or half-crown, with which it was the custom to remunerate the coachmen. One of the members of the Four-in-hand Club, Mr Akers, was so determined to be looked upon as a regular coachman, that he had his front teeth so filed that a division between them might enable him to expel his spittle in the true fashion of some of the most knowing stage-coach drivers.

Lord Onslow[2] devoted his time to his stud, and being the master of four of the finest black horses in England, was always conspicuous in the parks; but he was too eccentric to obtain the suffrages of any of the Four-in-hand Club, for his carriage was painted black, and the whole turn-out had more the appearance of belonging to an undertaker. Mrs Humphrey, at whose shop in St James's Street were exhibited all the best caricatures of the day,[3] had a capital one in her window, in which the noble Lord was depicted driving his mournful equipage, and the following lines at the bottom were read with great glee by those who had seen the original: –

> What can Tommy Onslow do?
> He can drive a curricle and two.
> Can Tommy Onslow do nothing more?
> Yes, he can drive a phaeton and four.

There was an individual once familiar in the dandy circle, whose turn-out made always a sensation from its excessive elegance; his name was Richards, but he acquired the cognomen of 'Tom Pipes' from the following circumstance. Having run through an enormous fortune, he

---

[1] Jehu, King of Israel (c. 842–815 BC), celebrated for his chariot-driving.
[2] Thomas Onslow, second Earl of Onslow (1754–1827).
[3] Hannah Humphrey's shop was at 27 St James's Street. She moved there in 1797 from 37 New Bond Street. The caricaturist James Gillray lived in lodgings over the shop, where he died insane in 1815. He depicted Miss Humphrey as the elderly bespectacled whist-player in 'Two-Penny Whist' (11 January 1796: BM 8885). Gillray's biographer describes her as 'a shrewd, direct person of limited education and simple tastes' (Draper Hill, *Mr Gillray, the Caricaturist*, Phaidon Press, 1965, p. 38). Her shop is shown in Gillray's 'Very Slippy Weather' (10 February 1808: BM 11100).

was compelled to borrow money at an exorbitant interest, and a well-known tobacconist in Oxford Street lent him large sums on the condition that Richards should take one-half of the amount in tobacco pipes, and other such commodities, and the needy man was always inviting his friends to take off his hands a portion of this stock in trade. He, of course, like all other borrowers upon post-obit bonds, became completely ruined, and one kind friend obtained for him what in those days was a refuge of the destitute – a consulship. It was to Nantes he went; but his pecuniary difficulties hung about him, and he got into scrapes, and lost his appointment.

Richards had one redeeming point; he was a learned naturalist, and spent his little all in the purchase of animals. He got into trouble about a rare snake which he petted. Travelling in the Bath mail, he had placed the reptile in a basket under his feet; it crawled out and glided up the petticoat of a lady, who, suddenly waked up with an unusual sensation, pressed her hand upon the visitor, and irritated the snake, which gave her a severe bite.

ONE WAY OUT OF A DILEMMA

I recollect when a boy seeing a strange couple, a Mr and Mrs Turbeville, who were famed for their eccentricities. Mr Turbeville was related to Sir Thomas Picton, but did not possess the talent or discretion of the gallant General. Upon one occasion, at a dinner at Dunraven Castle, after the ladies had retired, Mr Turbeville observed to a gentleman present, that the woman who had sat at his right was the ugliest he had ever seen; upon which the gentleman said, 'I am sorry to hear that you think my wife so ill-looking.' 'Oh, no, sir, I have made a mistake; I meant the lady who sat on my left.' 'Well, sir, she is my sister.' 'It can't be helped, sir, then; for if what you have said is true, I must confess I never saw such an ugly family during the course of my life.'

ANECDOTE OF A LORD-LIEUTENANT OF IRELAND

In times gone by when Lords-Lieutenant thought more of love and beauty than the land they were sent to govern, and considered they had a right to monopolise every pretty girl who appeared at the Castle balls, two sisters, the beautiful Misses Gunn, were the objects of the Viceroy's assiduous attention.[1] Of course, they were much envied both by

---

[1] The Viceroy in question is Charles Lennox, fourth Duke of Richmond (see note, p. 126). He was Lord-Lieutenant of Ireland from 1807 to 1813.

mothers and daughters for the attention shown them by the Viceroy and his family. All went on swimmingly until one day a young lady, only about sixteen years of age, and of surpassing beauty, a Miss Woodcock, made her appearance at one of the drawing-rooms. She came as if from the waves of the Channel, for nobody knew her name or family, and she was known by the cognomen of the beautiful Venus. The Lord-Lieutenant at once discarded the Misses Gunn, and lavished jewellery and presents upon the youthful Venus in so barefaced a manner, that society began to be alarmed, and gave the new beauty the cold shoulder. Bunbury, the celebrated caricaturist, happening to be at Dublin, turned the scandal to good account, by drawing a capital likeness of the Viceroy, dressed as Robinson Crusoe, carrying a *Gun* upon each shoulder, and a *Woodcock* at his left side; denoting that his affections lay in that quarter.[1]

MR LAWRENCE, THE CELEBRATED SURGEON

It was my good fortune to have known Mr Lawrence, who was allowed to have been the most scientific, as well as one of the most skilful surgeons England or Europe could boast of at that time.[2] The opinion entertained of him by the faculty was evinced by the many high encomiums passed upon his talents by his contemporaries. He was the most accomplished and gentlest of mankind, and ever ready to render the slightest service to a friend in distress. Upon one occasion I called upon him at his house in Whitehall, opposite the Admiralty, and told him that half-an-hour before I had seen a pretty girl, an opera-dancer, unable to move from her sofa owing to 'soft corns,' which precluded her from appearing on the stage. 'Bring her here, my friend Gronow, and I will endeavour to cure her; but do not mention to any one that I have turned chiropodist.' I lost no time in calling upon the *danseuse*, and prevailed upon her to place herself under the care of my skilful friend. Some few days elapsed, when I met Lawrence in his carriage and was invited by him to take a drive, during which he asked me if I had seen the young lady, whom he had operated upon and completely cured. Upon my replying in the negative, he said, 'It is always so when you render a service to persons possessing neither principle nor feeling; you

[1] Henry William Bunbury (1750-1811), the son of the Rev. Sir William Bunbury, Bart. After coming down from Cambridge, he studied drawing in Rome. Horace Walpole compared him to Hogarth.
[2] Sir William Lawrence (1783-1867) was employed as a surgeon at St Bartholomew's Hospital for almost sixty-five years.

are sure to be treated with ingratitude.' This lady became immensely rich, and I regret to add that the surgeon's fee was never paid, which I had good reason to know amounted to twenty guineas.

LORD DEERHURST (AFTERWARDS LORD COVENTRY)

Persons are still living who remember this nobleman hastening down Piccadilly after some pretty girl or other.[1] Lord Deerhurst was distinguished for his good looks and manly bearing; but he always seemed in a hurry: his habits and appearance were in other respects singular, though they did not lessen the respect his rank and abilities deservedly commanded. His wit was proverbial: in short, such were his talents in society, that he was considered a match for Alvanley. Another good trait in his character was the attention he paid to Lord Coventry, who was blind.

His marriage proved a very unhappy one. After living some time with his wife on very bad terms, a separation ensued, which caused him great misery. I recollect, after this occurrence, seeing a letter dated from his father's place in Worcestershire, in which he said, 'Here I am at leisure, free to indulge in my grief, and to correct those errors that have brought upon me so much mental suffering.' He never completely recovered, and contrived to kill time by travelling from London to his seat in Worcestershire and back, once a week. Before his death poor Deerhurst became excessively irritable, and subsequently insane. He recovered his reason slightly, but died shortly after, attended only by a few trusty servants.

I recollect dining at Madame Vestris's pretty house in St John's Wood.[2] Deerhurst was the life and soul of the party; and although there was, of course, a little sparring between him and Alvanley, he was 'cock of the walk.' He was then in good health and spirits, and conversed easily, and without appearing conscious that he was delighting us all with his witty sayings. Of all the dinners I have been present at, I recollect this as being the most pleasant; it might be called a dinner of dandies, as most of those present belonged to White's, and led the *beau monde* at that period. Of Madame Vestris I can only say, that I never knew any lady more perfectly natural and agreeable in manner and conversation, and she did the honours of her house in admirable style.

[1] George William Coventry, sixth Earl of Coventry (1722–1809).
[2] See note, p. 73.

MR NEELD

Lord Alvanley having been invited to dine in Grosvenor Square, at the house of Mr Neeld, the heir to Mr Rundell the wealthy goldsmith,[1] was, previous to sitting down to table, shown some fine pictures which hung on the walls of the drawing-room, together with many articles of *virtù* that crowded the apartment; the host praising and describing each, and stating the cost, in by no means a well-bred manner. One would have thought that the infliction would have been discontinued on entering the dining-room; but, on the guests being seated, Mr Neeld began excusing himself for not having a haunch of venison for dinner, and assured his guests that a very fine haunch of Welsh mutton had been prepared for them. He then returned to his favourite topic, and began praising the room in which they were dining, and the furniture; he had got to the gilding, which he assured his guests had been done by French artists at an enormous expense, when the mutton made its appearance. Lord Alvanley, who had been intensely bored, exclaimed, 'I care not what your gilding cost; but, what is more to the purpose, I am most anxious to make a trial of your carving, Mr Neeld, for I am excessively hungry, and should like to attack the representative of the haunch of venison.'

The *nouveau riche*, though rather astonished by this remark, was obliged to let it pass without notice; his anxiety to form a circle of aristocratic acquaintances preventing his taking offence at anything said by such a person as his Lordship.

MRS BEAUMONT

There are probably many persons who remember this lady. She was reported to have been of low origin, but inheriting vast estates in the north, and having married a colonel of militia, who became member for the county where her large estates lay, she became one of the leaders of the fashionable world in 1812. From that time to 1820, it was impossible, during the London season, to walk from St James's Street to Hyde Park at a certain hour in the afternoon, without seeing her and her daughters in her large yellow landau. Her style of living was most luxurious and full of ostentation. Her preference of a nobleman before a gentleman of no title was shown in a manner that was perfectly ridiculous, and

---

[1] Philip Rundell, whose firm of jewellers bought the lease of No. 76 Dean Street in 1810.

evinced a great want of good sense and tact. Her *fêtes* were thronged with the *grand monde*, and her system of excluding all but persons of rank amused the fashionable world: even men of talent and good family rarely got the *entrée* of her saloons.

This recalls to my mind a rather ludicrous incident. Through the kindness of the Duchess of Marlborough, I was present at one of Mrs Beaumont's balls, and this led to my being invited to the rest of them during the season. In fine, I became a constant visitor at her house in Portman Square, till one day I ventured to ask for an invitation for a friend of mine, a distinguished officer in the Guards, good-looking, and in every respect fit company for the best saloons. I was of course asked what was his rank; and on my replying that he was a captain in the regiment in which I had the honour to serve, Mrs Beaumont exclaimed, 'I want no more captains at my balls: you should consider yourself lucky in getting an invitation.' I bowed and took my leave; and, reflecting on the injustice I had done Mrs Beaumont in presuming to appear at her assemblies, I never again perpetrated the offence.

Mrs Beaumont had three sons, two of whom died insane; the other sorely wounded her pride by marrying Miss Atkinson, the daughter of a hatter. When his mother died he succeeded to her large property, and this somewhat turned his head. Like all *parvenus*, he was ambitious of being raised to the peerage; but he threw away the only chance he had, by quarrelling with the only great man likely to forward his views – the celebrated Lord Grey. Mr Wentworth Beaumont fought a duel with the late Lord Durham,[1] and had to pay his second an annuity for life, – why or wherefore no one could tell. The issue of his marriage was a son, of whom he was very proud. Soon after the birth of his heir, poor Beaumont became in a measure insane; but there was method (or satire) in his madness, for in his last moments he ejaculated, 'I cannot say that I have lived for nothing, for my son, besides inheriting my vast fortune, will become the "Duc de Feltre."'

In spite of all the anxiety and trouble Mrs Beaumont had taken in bringing up her daughters, in the hope of their marrying men of exalted rank, she had the mortification of knowing that they had married men of low origin in Italy.

---

[1] John George Lambton, first Earl of Durham (1792–1840). The duel was fought in 1820 following a speech, made during the Northumberland election, in which Wentworth Beaumont insulted him personally.

Sir Charles Shakerley[1]

This gentleman had a great horror of a dead body. On one occasion Henry Williams and some others were stopping at his house, when, some slight difference having arisen between him and Sir Charles, the latter spoke in rather an abrupt manner. The visitors, knowing their host's antipathy, determined to pay him off by a practical joke, and accordingly came down the next morning looking very grave, and informed him that Williams was seriously ill. Shakerley hastened upstairs, and found Williams lying in bed, foaming at the mouth and rolling his eyes wildly. Sir Charles, struck with the thought that his guest might die, became alarmed, and was about to send for a conveyance to remove him; but the 'dying man' found it convenient to get better. When Sir Charles left the room, Williams took from his mouth a piece of soap, with which he had imitated the froth on the mouth of a man in a fit. Sir Charles was, however, so frightened, that he never said an unkind thing to the practical joker during the remainder of his visit.

[1] Sir Charles Peter Shakerley (1792–1857).

15

Parisiens and Parisiennes

The Duc de Grammont

The Duc de Grammont, better known as the Duc de Guiche, was the type and model of the real French gentleman and *grand seigneur* of the olden time.[1] He was the handsomest man at the court of the elder branch of the Bourbons; and during the Empire, when in exile, had served in the English army. I knew him well in Spain, in 1813, when a captain in the 10th Hussars, and subsequently at Bordeaux, in 1814, when he accompanied the Duc d'Angoulême, and having then left our service, was arrayed in a French uniform as aide-de-camp to the Dauphin. He spoke English perfectly, was quiet in manner, and a most chivalrous, high-minded, and honourable man. His complexion was very dark, with crisp black hair curling close to his small, well-shaped head. His features were regular and somewhat aquiline, his eyes large, dark, and beautiful; and his manner, voice, and smile were considered by the fair sex to be perfectly irresistible.

He served with distinction as a general officer in the Spanish campaign of 1823, and was specially attached to the person of the Dauphin, whom he was obliged to keep in great order. As is often the case with princes, the Dauphin, or Duc d'Angoulême, as he was

---

[1] Antoine Héraclius Geneviève Agénor, duc de Gramont and de Guiche (1789–1855), the son of Antoine Louis Marie, duc de Gramont, who had emigrated from France during the Revolution. Having served in the British army during the Peninsular War, he became a lieutenant-general in the French army in 1823.

sometimes called, would frequently emancipate himself, and take liberties with those around him, if permitted to do so. Once, when driving with the Duc de Guiche, the Prince, in his somewhat ape-like manner, pinched his companion. A few moments afterwards, the Duke returned the caress with interest, to the great surprise of the Dauphin, who started and turned angrily round, to meet the winning, placid smile of his friend and mentor.

The Duke was universally beloved and regretted; and I should instance him as being, perhaps, the most perfect gentleman I ever met with in any country.

OUVRARD, THE FINANCIER

Before the French Revolution, the largest fortunes in France were possessed by the farmers of the revenue, or *fermiers-généraux*. Their profits were enormous, and their probity was very doubtful. It is related that one evening at Ferney, when the company were telling stories of robbers, they asked their host, Voltaire, for one on the same subject.[1] The great man, taking up his flat candlestick, when about to retire, began, 'There was once upon a time a *fermier-général* – I have forgotten the rest.'

No man was more reckless in his expenditure, or more magnificent in his manner of living, than Ouvrard.[2] At the time of the Directory, the *fêtes* given by him at Le Raincy were the theme of the whole of Parisian society of that time. At his splendid villa near Rueil, during the Empire, he was in the habit of giving suppers to all the *corps de ballet* of the opera twice a week; and he used to send several carriages, splendidly equipped, to bear away the principal female performers when the performance was over. There an enormous white marble bath, as large as an ordinary-sized saloon, was prepared for such of the ladies as, in the summer, chose to bathe on their arrival. Then a splendid supper was laid out, of which the fair bathers, and many of the pleasure-seekers of the day, partook; and, besides every luxury of the culinary art, prepared by the best cooks in Paris, each lady received a donation of fifty louis, and the one fortunate enough to attract the especial notice of the wealthy host, a large sum of money.

Mademoiselle Georges, the celebrated tragedian of that day,[3] cost

---

[1] François-Marie Arouet, known as Voltaire (1694–1778).
[2] Gabriel Julien Ouvrard (1770–1846).
[3] Marguerite Georges, the French actress, was born in 1786.

him (as he was fond of relating) two millions one hundred thousand francs for a single visit. He had invited her to sup with him at his villa, but the very day she was to come, a note informed him that she was compelled to give up the pleasure of supping with him, as the Emperor Napoleon had given her a rendezvous for the same hour, which she dared not refuse. Ouvrard was furious at this *contretemps*, and (as he said when I heard him tell the story) he could not bear to yield the *pas* to '*le petit Bonaparte*,' whom he had known as a young captain of artillery, too happy to be invited to his house in the days of the Directory. This feeling, and his pride of wealth, got the better of his prudence, and he sent to Mademoiselle Georges to insist upon her coming to Rueil, adding, as a postscript, that she would find a hundred thousand francs *sous les plis de sa serviette* at supper. This last argument was irresistible, the lady sent an excuse to the Emperor, pleading a sudden indisposition, and was borne rapidly in one of Ouvrard's carriages to his country residence.

The following day the great financier received a summons forthwith to appear at the Tuileries, and was ushered into the Emperor's presence. After walking once or twice up and down the room, the great man turned sharply round on his unwilling guest, and, with his eagle glance riveted on Ouvrard's face, sternly demanded, 'Monsieur, how much did you make by your contract for the army at the beginning of the year?' The capitalist knew it was in vain to equivocate, and replied, 'Four millions of francs, sire,' 'Then, sir, you made too much; so pay immediately two millions into the Treasury.'

Ouvrard passed several years in prison for a considerable debt owed by him to Séguin, another army contractor; but he lived magnificently even when in prison, and his creditor, strange to say, used frequently to go and dine with him there. I saw Ouvrard shortly before his death, which took place in 1846.

MADAME DE STAËL

I frequently met the famous Madame de Staël in Paris during the years 1815 and 1816. She was very kind and affable to all the English, and delighted to find herself once more in sight and smell of the *ruisseau* de la Rue du Bac, which she once said she preferred to all the romantic scenery of Switzerland and Italy. She was a large, masculine-looking woman, rather coarse, and with a thoracic development worthy of a wet nurse. She had very fine arms, which she took every opportunity of displaying, and dark, flashing eyes, beaming with wit and genius.

Her career was a chequered one, and her history is a romance. The only child of the Minister Necker, in troublous times she married the Swedish ambassador at Paris, the Baron de Staël, in 1786. Full of great and noble sentiments, she took up the cause of the unfortunate Louis XVI and his Queen with generous ardour. She arranged a plan of escape for the King in 1792, and did not fear to present to the revolutionary tribunal, in 1793, a petition in favour of Marie-Antoinette. She remained in Paris during the Directory; and it was under her influence and protection that Talleyrand obtained office in 1796.[1] She was always opposed to Napoleon, and was exiled by him from Paris in 1802. She returned, however, and her presence was tolerated till the appearance of her book *De l'Allemagne*, the sentiments and allusions of which were decidedly hostile to the imperial despotism which then oppressed nearly the whole of Europe. The book was seized by the Emperor's police, and Madame de Staël was again exiled, and did not return till 1815 to Paris, where she died in 1817, aged fifty-one.

Admirable as her writings were, her conversation surpassed them. She was 'well up' on every subject – '*nihil quod tetigit non ornavit.*'[2] Her *salons* were filled with all the most celebrated persons of her time. The statesmen, men of science, poets, lawyers, soldiers, and divines, who crowded to hear her, were astounded at her eloquence and erudition. Disdain and contempt for her personal charms or mental powers was one of the causes of the hatred she had vowed to the first Napoleon; and, unequal as a contest between the greatest sovereign of the age and a woman would at first sight appear, there is no doubt that, by her writings and her sarcastic sayings, which were echoed from one end of Europe to the other, she did him much injury.

Talleyrand, when he married Madame Grant, a beautiful but illiterate idiot, said he did so to repose himself after the eternally learned and eloquent discourses of Madame de Staël, with whom he had been very intimate. On one occasion, alluding to her masculine intellect and appearance, while she was holding forth at great length, he said, '*Elle est homme à parler jusqu'à demain matin.*' At another time, when he was with

---

[1] Charles Maurice de Talleyrand-Périgord, Prince of Benevento (1754–1838), the statesman and diplomat, renowned for his political survival. In 1803 Talleyrand married Madame Grand (not Grant), a divorcée who had been his mistress for some time. He separated from her in 1815.

[2] Samuel Johnson's epitaph on Oliver Goldsmith has it thus: *Nullum quod tetigit non ornavit* (He touched nothing that he did not adorn).

her in a boat, and she was talking of courage and devotion, qualities in which the *ci-devant* bishop was notoriously deficient, she put the question, 'What would you do if I were to fall into the water?' Looking at her from head to foot, he answered, 'Ah, madam, you must be such a good swimmer' (*'vous savez si bien nager'*).

The person in England who was the great object of Madame de Staël's admiration, and in the praise of whom she was never weary, was Sir James Mackintosh, one of the greatest men of the age, and certainly the best read man of the day.[1] She also lived on most intimate terms with the celebrated orator and publicist, Benjamin Constant;[2] but her *liaison* was supposed to be a Platonic one: indeed, she was secretly married, in 1810, to M. de Rocca, a young officer of hussars, who was wounded in Spain, and who wrote a very interesting account of the Peninsular war.[3]

Madame de Staël was perhaps at times a little overpowering, and totally deficient in those 'brilliant flashes of silence' which Sydney Smith once jokingly recommended to Macaulay.[4] In fact, as a Scotchman once said of Johnson, she was 'a robust genius, born to grapple with whole libraries, and a tremendous conversationist.'

A story is told of the Duke of Marlborough, great-grandfather of the present Duke, which always amused me.[5] The Duke had been for some time a confirmed hypochondriac, and dreaded anything that could in any way ruffle the tranquil monotony of his existence. It is said that he remained for three years without pronouncing a single word, and was entering the fourth year of his silence, when he was told one morning that Madame la Baronne de Staël, the authoress of *Corinne*, was on the point of arriving to pay him a visit. The Duke immediately recovered his speech, and roared out, 'Take me away – take me away!' to the utter astonishment of the circle around him, who all declared that nothing but the terror of this literary visitation could have put an end to this long and obstinate monomania.

---

[1] Sir James Mackintosh (1765–1832), the writer and philosopher. He had an 'uncommon facility' in speaking French. His *Vindicae Gallicae* was published in 1791 as a reply to Burke's *Reflections on the French Revolution*.
[2] Henri Benjamin Constant de Rebecque (1767–1830), the author and politician, met Madame de Staël at Lausanne in 1794; and, having left his wife, he returned to Paris with her in 1795. Their intimate friendship, interrupted by passionate quarrels, continued until 1806.
[3] Madame de Staël married Rocca, a young Swiss officer in 1811, not 1810.
[4] Macaulay, said Smith, had 'occasional flashes of silence that [make] his conversation perfectly delightful'.
[5] George Spencer, fourth Duke of Marlborough (1739–1817).

MADEMOISELLE LE NORMAND

One of the most extraordinary persons of my younger days was the celebrated fortune-teller, Mademoiselle le Normand. Her original residence was in the Rue de Tournon, but at the time of which I write she lived in the Rue des St Pères. During the Restoration, the practice of the 'black art' was strictly forbidden by the police, and it was almost like entering a besieged citadel to make one's way into her *sanctum sanctorum*.

I was first admitted into a good-sized drawing-room, plainly but comfortably furnished, with books and newspapers lying about, as one sees them at a dentist's. Two or three ladies were already there, who, from their quiet dress and the haste with which they drew down their veils or got up and looked out of the window, evidently belonged to the upper ten thousand. Each person was summoned by an attendant to the sibyl's boudoir, and remained a considerable time, disappearing by some other exit without returning to the waiting-room. At last I was summoned by the elderly servant to the mysterious chamber, which opened by secret panels in the walls, to prevent any unpleasant surprises by the police. I confess that it was not without a slight feeling of trepidation that I entered the small square room, lighted from above, where sat Mademoiselle le Normand in all her glory.

It was impossible for imagination to conceive a more hideous being. She looked like a monstrous toad, bloated and venomous. She had one wall-eye, but the other was a piercer. She wore a fur cap upon her head, from beneath which she glared out upon her horrified visitors. The walls of the room were covered with huge bats, nailed by their wings to the ceiling, stuffed owls, cabalistic signs, skeletons – in short, everything that was likely to impress a weak or superstitious mind. This malignant-looking Hecate[1] had spread out before her several packs of cards, with all kinds of strange figures and ciphers depicted on them. Her first question, uttered in a deep voice, was whether you would have the *grand* or *petit jeu*, which was merely a matter of form. She then inquired your age, and what was the colour and the animal you preferred. Then came, in an authoritative voice, the word '*Coupez*,' repeated at intervals, till the requisite number of cards from the various packs were selected and placed in rows side by side. No further questions were asked, and no attempt was made to discover who or what you were, or to watch upon your countenance the effect of the revelations. She neither prophesied

---

[1] Hecate, the Greek goddess, was associated with the world of the dead. She was a goddess of magic and depicted by artists with three bodies set back to back so that she could look in all directions at crossroads.

smooth things to you nor tried to excite your fears, but seemed really to believe in her own power. She informed me that I was *un militaire*, that I should be twice married and have several children, and foretold many other events which have also come to pass, though I did not at the time believe one word of the sibyl's prediction.

Mademoiselle le Normand was born in 1768, and was already celebrated as a fortune-teller so early as 1790. She is said to have predicted to the unfortunate Princesse de Lamballe her miserable death at the hands of the infuriated populace.[1] She is also reported to have been frequently visited and consulted by Robespierre and St Just;[2] to have reported his downfall to Danton,[3] at that time the idol of the people; to have warned the famous General Hoche of his approaching death by poison;[4] to have foretold to Bernadotte a northern throne,[5] and to Moreau exile and an untimely grave.[6]

The Empress Josephine, who, like most creoles, was very superstitious, used frequently to send for Mademoiselle le Normand to the Tuileries, and put great faith in her predictions; which she always asserted in after years had constantly been verified. But, unfortunately for the sibyl, she did not content herself with telling Josephine's fortune, but actually ventured to predict a future replete with malignant influences to the Emperor himself. This rash conduct entailed upon her great misfortunes and a long imprisonment; but she survived all her troubles, and died as late as 1843, having long before given up fortune-telling, by which she had amassed a large sum of money.

[1] Marie Thérèse de Savoie-Carignan, princesse de Lamballe (1749–92), the excessively sensitive Superintendent of Marie Antoinette's household, lost consciousness so readily that she once swooned away at the sight of a lobster in a painting. She was murdered by the mob in the September Massacres. Having been stripped and raped, her breasts were cut off and the rest of her body mutilated. A man was later accused of having cut off her genitals which he impaled upon a pike and of having ripped out her heart which he ate 'after having roasted it on a cooking stove in a wine shop'.

[2] Maximilien-François-Marie-Isidore de Robespierre (1758–94); Louis-Antoine-Léon de Saint-Just (1767–94).

[3] Georges-Jacques Danton (1759–94).

[4] Louis-Lazare Hoche (1768–97), the son of a stableman, enlisted in the French army in 1784, became a captain in 1792 and a highly successful general in the revolutionary wars. A rival to Napoleon, he was rumoured to have been poisoned but more probably died of pneumonia. The Empress Josephine also fancied herself as a clairvoyant and once at a party persuaded Napoleon to tell fortunes. Having inspected Hoche's palm, Napoleon predicted that he would die in his bed, a prophecy that the gallant soldier took as an insult.

[5] See note, p. 26.

[6] Jean-Victor-Marie Moreau (1763–1813), the Revolutionary general and critic of Napoleon's regime, was banished from France and emigrated to the United States. Returning to France in 1813 to fight Napoleon, he was mortally wounded in both legs.

LOUIS PHILIPPE AND MARSHAL SOULT

Louis Philippe's cunning was proverbial, and he showed great talent and ingenuity in managing his ministers; but he had great difficulties to encounter. The most *exigeant* of all his officials was the celebrated Marshal Soult, who was perpetually asking the King for some place or appointment for one or other of his friends or relations, to the disgust of Louis Philippe. Upon one occasion, when all the ministers had assembled in the royal closet, the King, observing that the Marshal appeared displeased, inquired, 'What is the matter, Marshal?' 'Oh, nothing, sire; except that I intend giving into your Majesty's hands my resignation.'[1] This untoward and unexpected announcement alarmed the rest of the ministers, who, one and all, intimated that in such case they also must tender their resignations. The King, not alarmed in the slightest degree, requested the Marshal would follow him into his private room, and begged the rest of the ministers to remain until his return. The interview lasted a considerable time, and the King, fearing that he had kept the ministers too long waiting, and that their patience was exhausted, popped his head into the council-room, crying out, 'A little more patience gentlemen. All will be well; for the Marshal and myself have already shed tears.' The truth became known the following day; at all events it was generally whispered that Soult had frightened out of the King a promise that all places of emolument and advancement in the army should centre in him, which promise was religiously adhered to until Soult left the Ministry of War.

M. GUIZOT

M. Guizot, when he commenced his lectures on public history at the Sorbonne, appeared like a luminous meteor on the political horizon.[2] The expression of his views of ancient literature, the energy and the dignity with which he explained to his admiring audience the philosophy and the religion of Rome and Greece, his ironical comparison of the present claimants to renown, were listened to with an enthusiasm which proved how thoroughly they were understood, how fully they were appreciated. It was a sight which can never be effaced from memory, when the crowded hall was filled with impatient students

---

[1] Marshal Soult (see note, p. 46) had been appointed Minister of War in 1830.
[2] François-Pierre-Guillaume Guizot (1787–1874), the historian and politician, was Foreign Minister from 1840–8. He married Pauline de Meulan in 1812.

awaiting the presence of their much loved professor, who with difficulty threaded his way, amid immense applause, with a slow and solemn step, to the professorial chair. He poured forth, at first slowly, in a continued flow of elegant language, eulogiums upon the great writers in his own language, and then, with an impetuosity that seemed to convey an electric impetus around, his face, at first sombre and inexpressive, lighted up with supernatural animation; and as he gazed around, he inspired each of his auditors with the conviction that he was listening to a being of a superior order.

In the Assembly, M. Guizot spoke in a different style from what he did at the Sorbonne; and it was somewhat difficult to define the emotion that predominated in him: no sense either of triumph or of defeat was apparent. Cold, sombre, and meditative, he spoke with authority; and it was only at rare intervals that any great animation was visible in his countenance. It is no discredit to those statesmen that they earned their livelihood by writing for the newspapers; indeed, M. Guizot, aided by Madame Guizot, derived his subsistence for a long time from his literary labour. But they were the innocent cause of much mischief; for many a scribe who contributed a few lines to some journal anticipated the time when he might become Prime Minister of France.

LAMARTINE

There was a period when much was expected from Lamartine.[1] Certainly no one did more for the safety of Paris than he did during the first days of the revolution of 1848; but there was too much poetry in his head for a statesman. He was too much absorbed in himself to think of his friends; the consequence was, that he never made up a party to support him; indeed, he always stood aloof from any associations. His soirées on Saturday evenings in the Rue de l'Université were most agreeable, but were only social: every one sought access to them. They were presided over by Madame Lamartine, a highly-accomplished Englishwoman, daughter of Colonel Birch of Norfolk. She was an amateur artist, and took great delight in sculpture; a bust of her husband from her chisel is one of the best likenesses we have of Lamartine. At his reunions were to be seen the principal literary and political persons of the day, and all the distinguished artists; but

---

[1] Alphonse Marie Louis de Lamartine (1790–1869), the poet, was recognised as leader of the provisional government when the Second Republic was proclaimed in 1849. He married his English wife, Maria Ann Birch, in 1820.

amongst them were no attached friends. Many persons expected that he would be elected the first President of the [Second] Republic; and this most probably would have been the case, had not Louis Napoléon presented himself, for Lamartine was preferred to Cavaignac.[1] The poet foresaw that the name of Bonaparte would carry everything before it, and was one of those who opposed the admission into France of all who belonged to that family.

PRINCE LOUIS NAPOLÉON

Great was the eagerness of every one to know the opinion that had been formed in England of the Prince Louis Napoléon.[2] It was only known that he was looked on there as a perfect gentleman; but nobody could understand why he should have had himself sworn in as a special constable on the occasion of the Chartist demonstration of the 10th of April, and various were the reasons assigned.[3]

His first speech in the Legislative Assembly was expected to be an explanation of his policy; it was, however, brief and modest. The election of the Prince as President of the Republic may be considered as a national triumph, as it certainly proved a national benefit; for he immediately took steps to organise a competent Ministry, and commenced carrying into effect the improvements that his mind had long been engaged in studying. His speeches, his addresses, gave evidence of a vigorous intelligence, and he now and then astonished his Ministers by the boldness of his language. This was the case at the inauguration of the railroad at Dijon, on which occasion he delivered an address, which M. Leon Faucher,[4] his then Prime Minister, took care to alter before he gave it publicity. The Prince had occasion sometimes to change his Ministry, according as circumstances permitted, but his selections uniformly gave satisfaction to the country. The station of Minister of

[1] Louis-Eugène Cavaignac (1802–57) was appointed Minister of War in the provisional government of 1848. After suppressing the workers' revolts in Paris, he and Lamartine had hopes of being elected President of the Second Republic but they were defeated in the election by Louis-Napoleon Bonaparte, later Napoleon III.

[2] See note, p. 158.

[3] The Chartists took their name from *The People's Charter* of 1838 which demanded universal male suffrage, annual parliaments, equal electoral districts, voting by ballot, an end to property qualification for Members of Parliament and salaries for Members. A mass procession to Parliament was planned for April 1848; but, when the government showed itself determined to resist the demonstration by calling in troops and enrolling special constables, it was called off.

[4] Léon Joseph Faucher (1799–1854).

Finance was filled for the most part by M. Achille Fould,[1] who, amid all the varied changes in the political world, has maintained a well-deserved popularity, whilst his attachment to the Emperor has been both political and personal.

LOUIS PHILIPPE AT TWICKENHAM

Early in this century Louis Philippe lived with his brothers in a small cottage at Twickenham, where, though fond of conviviality, he practised the most rigid economy.[2] They had only one man-servant and a maid-of-all-work. Towards the end of his chequered life he was heard to say in passing the cottage, 'There I passed some of the happiest days of my life; but during that period I had to struggle against poverty, without receiving aid from any one.' The three royal brothers had a tilbury, which they drove by turns; but they gave both man and horse a holiday on Sundays.

I received this little anecdote from a friend who when young resided at Richmond and was intimately acquainted with the fallen monarch. Louis Philippe resided in England till 1808, when he embarked for Malta, carrying thither, for change of climate, his surviving brother, the Count Beaujolais, then in a rapid consumption. The Count's health was such that it was found necessary to stop at Gibraltar, where HRH died. Louis Philippe afterwards proceeded to Sicily to return thanks for various favours he had received from the King of Naples, and there he met his future wife in the king's second daughter, the Princess Amélie.[3] There can be little question but that it was a love match, as at that period there did not appear to be the remotest chance of Louis Philippe succeeding to his patrimonial estates, much less to the crown of France; and it was by many considered a foolish marriage. There were many difficulties in the way of their being married; but these were, however, surmounted, and the royal pair were united on the 25th November 1809, at Naples.

---

[1] Achille Fould (1800–67) served as Minister of Finance during the Second Republic and the Second Empire.

[2] This was a villa built in 1710 for James Johnson, Joint Secretary of State for Scotland under William III. It then belonged to a Mr Pococke, who leased it to Louis-Philippe, then Duke of Orleans, who lived there with his two brothers, the duc de Montpensier and the comte de Beaujolais, until Montpensier's death in 1807. It later became known as Orleans House. Most of the building was demolished in the 1920s, apart from the Octagon added to the original house in 1730 by James Gibbs.

[3] See note, p. 112.

After the downfall of Napoleon the First, Louis Philippe returned to Paris, contrary to the wishes of Louis XVIII, whose jealousy was sharpened by the wily Talleyrand. There he occupied himself with the culture of his vast estates, the education of his children, and the formation of a political party, which a few years later placed him on the throne of France.

*

I remember an amusing adventure happening to my friend the Count de M——, then an *homme à bonnes fortunes* with beautiful fair hair and a light active figure, but now an elderly gentleman, somewhat bald, and very stout. He was, I am sorry to say, paying an evening visit to a fair lady during her husband's absence, when that gentleman unexpectedly returned, and the room having only one door, which was to give ingress to the jealous husband, the gallant gay Lothario, after looking wildly round the room for a hiding-place, took refuge in a large old-fashioned clock-case which stood in a corner of the room. There he ensconced himself; and, as his entry stopped the pendulum, he tried with his tongue against his palate to imitate the ticking noise of the clock; hoping that the husband would make a short stay, and that he would be soon released from his uncomfortable situation.

But that gentleman, who had been privately warned by an anonymous letter that all was not right at home, showed no symptoms of moving from the large arm-chair, just in front of the clock, where he had taken up his position. My unfortunate friend could no longer keep on the clicking noise, – his tongue clove to the roof of his mouth, – and he had to keep silence. The husband arose, crying out to his wife, '*Chère amie*, the clock is stopped: I must wind it up.' Before the lady could arrest his progress, he had opened the door and found the young Lovelace tightly wedged in.[1] 'What are you doing there, you villain?' shouted the enraged husband. '*Je me promène*,' replied the young man.

PARTING OF NAPOLEON AND MADAME MÈRE

Talma[2] was present at the last parting at the Malmaison between the Emperor and his mother,[3] and he said that it was one of the most tragic

---

[1] A libertine. The name comes from the character Robert Lovelace, the selfish seducer in Samuel Richardson's novel *Clarissa Harlowe* (1747-8).

[2] See note, p. 145.

[3] Napoleon's mother, Madame Mère, was Letizia Ramolino (1750-1836), the wife of Carlo Buonaparte (1746-85). She was only fourteen years old at the time of her marriage.

scenes he had ever witnessed. When the last moment arrived, the Empress-mother, prostrated with grief, and with tears streaming from her eyes, could only utter, in a tremulous voice. '*Adieu, mon fils! adieu!*' And Napoleon was so affected, that he caught hold of both her hands, cried, '*Adieu, ma mère!*' and burst into tears as he left her.

THE PRESENT EMPEROR OF THE FRENCH WHEN A BOY

Prince Louis Napoléon, when at the age of six, lived with his mother, Queen Hortense,[1] at the Malmaison,[2] with whom resided the Empress Joséphine; who, it will be remembered, received the allied sovereigns there in 1814, after Napoleon I was exiled to Elba. The Emperor of Russia when in Paris scarcely passed a day without visiting those exalted ladies, and on each occasion he breakfasted or dined with them. The Queen told her children, that when the Emperor Alexander called, every mark of attention and respect was to be paid to his Imperial Majesty; for to him, and him alone, they owed everything they possessed in the world. Prince Louis listened to his mother's precepts with great attention, but said nothing. The next time the Czar came, however, the little fellow sidled up to him and quietly placed on one of the Czar's fingers a ring, which his uncle Prince Eugène,[3] the Viceroy of Italy, had given him. The boy, on being asked by his mother what he meant, said, 'I have only this ring, which my uncle gave me; but I have given it to the Emperor Alexander, because he has been so kind to you, dear mamma.' The autocrat smiled, and placing the gift on his watch-chain, said he would never part with it, but would keep it in remembrance of the noble trait of generosity shown by one so young. The Queen replied, 'Sire, my son Louis keeps nothing for himself.'

JÉRÔME BONAPARTE AND CARDINAL FESCH

Jérôme, the youngest brother of the great Emperor, was when young extremely wild and extravagant.[4] He was always in debt, and would

[1] Queen Hortense (Eugénie-Hortense de Beauharnais; 1783-1837) was Napoleon I's stepdaughter. She was married to his brother, Louis Napoleon, who became King of Holland in 1806. Napoleon III was their son.
[2] Malmaison, in the western suburbs of Paris, was built by Christophe Perrot in 1622. In 1799 it was bought for Napoleon's first wife, Josephine, who much enlarged it. It is now a museum.
[3] Eugène de Beauharnais (1781-1824), later Duke of Leuchtenberg, Napoleon I's stepson and Queen Hortense's brother, became Viceroy of Italy in 1805.
[4] See note, p. 135.

borrow money of any one who would trust him. Upon one occasion he called upon his uncle, the Cardinal Fesch, who invited him to dinner.[1] The Cardinal was a great amateur of paintings, and his gallery contained some of the finest specimens of the old masters. After dinner, the Cardinal was on the point of quitting the dining-room, when Jérôme followed him, and asked for the loan of 500 francs. The old Cardinal refused to lend him the money, whereupon Jérôme became furious, drew his sword, swore vengeance against his uncle, and began cutting at everything about him. Unfortunately his sword fell upon a *chef-d'œuvre* by Vandyke, which the Cardinal, upon his return to the dining-room, observing, called out in a loud voice, 'Stop, young man! sheathe your sword, and here are your 500 francs!'

BREGUET, THE FRENCH WATCHMAKER

This celebrated man was greatly encouraged by the Allies in 1815. The Emperor Alexander purchased several of his unequalled watches, and the Duke of Wellington also had one which, on touching a spring at any time, struck the hour and minute. The Duke carried it for many years, and it proved of great service to him on many occasions: it cost, I was told, three hundred guineas.

I frequently visited [Breguet's] shop, and had many conversations with him; and, although at that time getting old, he was full of energy and vivacity. He was not an advocate for flat watches, as he said they impeded the proper action of the wheels and could not be depended upon as time-keepers: he defied any one to make a watch so good as those made on his own principle. The prices he paid to his best workmen were enormous; there being few to whom he could confide his watches, as so many were drunkards, and could only work a day or two in the week. He told me that he paid some of them thirty francs a day, and none less than a napoleon; and that throughout Paris there were only fifteen or twenty able to execute the delicate work necessary for such watches as he made.

Breguet was a great encourager of merit: he used to say to his young workmen, 'Don't be discouraged, or allow a failure to dishearten you; accidents will happen, miscalculations cannot altogether be avoided: be persevering, industrious, sober, and honest.' Such was the advice he

---

[1] Joseph Fesch (1763–1839), Napoleon I's uncle, became a cardinal in 1803 when he also took up the appointment of French Ambassador in Rome. He had left the Church for a time and had made a fortune in various business ventures.

gave, and he frequently enabled those in his employ who were skilful, steady, and industrious, to arrive at opulence. Breguet, besides his scientific knowledge and mechanical skill, possessed great general information. Napoleon himself, knowing his abilities, frequently went incognito to the workshop and conversed upon the improvements which he was anxious to effect in cannons and fire-arms. The Russian campaign and its disasters put an end to all projects on that score.

POTAGE À LA POMPADOUR

We are apt to talk a good deal of the wisdom of our ancestors; but in the midst of a certain amount of civilisation, much rude magnificence, and great display, those good people were completely ignorant of, and unacquainted with many of the refinements and even necessaries of life, as the following anecdote will prove.

About a hundred years ago, in the reign of Louis the Fifteenth, when his mistress, the Marquise de Pompadour, governed France with absolute power, the Duke of Norfolk was much in favour with that lady.[1] One morning, at her toilette, – to the close of which, consisting of powdering and hair-dressing, her friends were admitted, according to the custom of that time – when the usual compliments had passed, his Grace's attention was riveted to a certain article of furniture in a distant part of the room, of a somewhat octagonal shape, which was entirely new to him. As a considerable crowd of courtiers surrounded the royal favourite, he was able to approach something closer, and to discover that the object of his curiosity was of solid gold, with the Marquise's arms richly engraved, and that it was placed upon a wooden stand.

The Duke of Norfolk took an opportunity of inquiring from one of the *femmes de chambre* for what purpose this magnificent piece of plate was used; and the reply, given without any signs of bashfulness, struck him with utter amazement and some confusion. In the course of the day, the *soubrette* communicated this incident to her mistress, as rather a good joke; and Madame de Pompadour, who was anxious that the Duke should have some souvenir of his stay in France, and of her friendship for him, gave instructions to her silversmith to make another piece of plate exactly similar to that which had so much attracted his Grace's attention. It was very richly ornamented, and had the Duke's arms

[1] Jeanne-Antoinette Poisson, Marquise de Pompadour (1721–64), became Louis XV's mistress in 1745.

engraved on one side, and those of Madame de Pompadour on the other. It was carefully packed up, and forwarded to the Duchess of Norfolk, by a messenger belonging to the French court.

Upon receiving the present from the Marquise de Pompadour, the Duchess was delighted, and said –

'How very kind of the Marquise! I never saw so beautiful a soup tureen; I suppose its shape is *la grande mode* of the day!'

A few days after the present had been received, the Duke of Norfolk arrived from Paris, and a great dinner was given at Norfolk House to celebrate his safe return. In those days *les diners à la Russe* were not invented,[1] and the dishes, of magnificent silver gilt, were placed upon the table, and served by those who sat opposite to them.

When dinner was announced, and the guests had sat down, the Duke was perfectly aghast with horror and amazement; for there in front of him he beheld the mysterious piece of plate filled with excellent mutton broth. The present of the fair Marquise is said to be still in existence in one of the country residences of the chief of the noble family of Howard, but restored from its culinary duties to the original legitimate purpose for which it was intended. But it is only on rare occasions, such as the visits of royalty, that this heirloom is displayed; when the taste of the fair Marquise is highly admired.

Louis Philippe's Sons at a Masked Ball

I witnessed a strange sight at one of the masked balls at the opera in Paris. A young man of herculean strength had intruded himself among a party of dancers in a quadrille, and laid violent hands on a young lady already engaged. The gentlemen of the party flew to the rescue, and for a few minutes all was confusion; but four or five of the secret police presently appeared on the scene, and arrested the cause of the disturbance. I was surprised to observe that none of the other persons engaged in the disturbance were molested, but allowed to dance as if nothing had occurred, and on quitting the ball I determined to unravel the secret. After some trouble, I found that the party was composed of the sons of Louis Philippe and some of their friends, who

---

[1] The eighteenth-century practice had been to place several dishes on the table at once, the guests helping themselves when the covers had been removed, offering to help their neighbours, and sending a servant to fetch anything they could not reach. In the nineteenth century, when *diners à la russe* became fashionable, each course was served separately and handed round by servants from guest to guest.

were completely metamorphosed by the aid of false wigs, &c.[1]

On my mentioning the circumstance to a friend of mine, he said that they often disguised themselves, and appeared thus in public; and that one day during the preceding summer, after dining with them at Chantilly, the Duke de Nemours proposed a stroll, and taking out of his pocket his false wig and whiskers, said, 'You, sir, have no occasion to disguise yourself; but as it fell to my lot to be the son of a king, I am obliged to have recourse to disguise and strategy from morning till night.'

COUNT TALLEYRAND PÉRIGORD'S PRIVATE THEATRICALS

Among the many ludicrous incidents that occurred during the reign of Louis XVIII, I recollect the following: – The Count Talleyrand Périgord having been appointed Ambassador – or, more properly speaking, minister – at Berne, determined to amuse his friends with theatrical representations; accordingly his dining-room was arranged with side-scenes, drop-scenes, and all the stage requisites, and he invited the dignitaries of Berne to witness the opening of his little theatre. The Count intended to have represented the part of a miller, and therefore ordered his *valet de chambre* to take off his coat, and to bring him some flour from the kitchen, with which to cover himself in a manner that would make the disguise appear natural. The valet obeyed his master's instructions to the letter, and, begging the Count to shut his eyes and remain motionless during the operation, the servant emptied the contents of a box of flour over his master's head. At that moment a courier arrived with the news that the Emperor Napoleon had disembarked at Fréjus. This intelligence excited the diplomate to that degree that he flew out of the house, with the intention of calling upon the English minister to know whether he had received any tidings of the kind. The strange appearance in the streets of the Count covered with flour, occasioned a commotion in the quiet town of Berne. Men, women, and children followed the French minister, crying out, 'Take care of him, for he is mad.' In a word, it was with difficulty he got back to his hotel, where he found the company assembled and waiting for the

[1] King Louis-Philippe had five sons. The eldest, Ferdinand-Philippe, duc d'Orléans (1810-42), died after being thrown from his carriage in a street accident. The others were Louis Charles, duc de Nemours; François-Ferdinand, prince de Joinville (see note, p. 275); Henri Eugène, duc d'Aumale; and Antoine Philippe, duc de Montpensier, who married the Infanta, younger sister of Queen Isabella of Spain. The duc d'Aumale (1822-97) became a general. His *Histoire des princes de Condé* was never completed.

performance which had been promised; but, alas! the nerves of the Count were so terribly disturbed that he relinquished the idea of enacting the part of the miller.

It is much to be regretted that we English are even now in the habit of regarding all foreigners in an unfavourable light. The vulgar brag that any John Bull is a match for three Frenchmen, and other extravagances of a similar description, are becoming obsolete; but English tourists are still apt to disparage foreigners, and entertain the notion that when we set foot on the Continent, a system of cheating and extortion commences. These and similar prejudices, arising from ignorance of the language and usages of foreign nations, naturally create a bad feeling towards England and Englishmen. Foreigners say, and not without justice, that we are pre-eminently self-conceited, boastful, and proud.

SIR ASTLEY COOPER

I recollect meeting this celebrated surgeon in South Wales about thirty years back, when on a visit to some of his friends. I had only returned the day before from Paris, and Sir Astley was very inquisitive about everything I had seen there.[1] He eulogised the French surgeons, but objected to the means employed after amputation; for instead of giving beefsteaks, port wine, and other stimulants, the French surgeons recommended lemonade and *tisanes*, whereby eight patients out of ten died, whereas by the English system only two succumbed out of ten. Nevertheless, he spoke of Dupuytren in the most enthusiastic terms, and acknowledged him to be the most skilful surgeon in Europe. I asked him his opinion of French cookery; he replied, 'It suits the French; but it would never do in England; for our men require animal food twice a day, and porter; but the French, from their birth, live upon fruit and vegetables, and their meat is boiled down to rags; this is, however, congenial to their stomachs, and proves that digestion begins in the kitchen.'

Our great surgeon, perceiving that I was fond of smoking, cautioned me against that habit, telling me it would sooner or later be the cause of my death. If Sir Astley were now alive he would find everybody with a cigar in his mouth: men smoke now-a-days whilst they are occupied

---

[1] Sir Astley Paston Cooper (1768–1841) was appointed President of the College of Surgeons in 1827 and in the following year surgeon to the King, who bestowed a baronetcy upon him after he had successfully removed a wen from the royal head.

in working or hunting, riding in carriages, or otherwise employed. During the experience of a long life, however, I never knew but one person of whom it was said that smoking was the cause of his death: he was the son of an Irish earl, and an *attaché* at our Embassy in Paris. But, alas, I have known thousands who have been carried off owing to their love of the bottle; ay, some of the noblest and famous men in our land, splendid in youth, strength, and agility. I regret to add, I have met with refined ladies, too, who never went to bed without a little brandy 'to drive away the colic.'

16

Revolutions and Coups d'État

REVOLUTION OF 1848

The character of the two great outbreaks of popular feeling in 1830 and 1848 was widely different. The first had a far grander aspect, from the simple fact that, under the elder branch of the Bourbons, there were real grievances to redress. It was absolutely necessary to arrest the wide-spreading encroachments of the priesthood, and to crush the infatuated pride of aristocracy, which would have ignored the reforming work of 1789. The Revolution of 1830 was the expression of a strong genuine feeling, the death-struggle between blind superstition and that latent love for truth and liberty which cannot be trampled out of the human breast. But that of 1848 was of a very different kind.

On the eve of the day [23 February 1848] which was to see Louis Philippe hurled from his throne, I remember walking down the Boulevards, which were crowded with people. It has been generally remarked, that revolutionary movements in France never take place during very cold weather, and the last week of February 1848 was singularly mild and warm. It seemed to me, during my promenade, that there was about the assembled masses that peculiar aspect of sullen defiance which characterises the Paris mobs before an outbreak.

I had had some experience in these matters, owing to my long residence in France, and I felt quite certain that the persons assembled at various points, and in divers groups, were combining their plans, and that we might look out for squalls. The only soldiers one saw on that day were the municipal guards; for the troops of the line were confined to their barracks. Unfortunately, the municipal guards did not show much forbearance in their treatment of the people, invariably answering their vociferations by a charge. It would have been far wiser, in my opinion, not to have irritated the mob by these half-measures, which could be productive of no beneficial result. When the troops were called out, instead of being made to act immediately, they were allowed to stand all day and all night in the streets, weary, unoccupied, and without provisions, to endure the jeering of the *gamins* and the cajoling of the workmen, or rather *émeutiers* [ringleaders] disguised as workmen and carrying arms under their blouses. This long inaction, coupled with physical exhaustion, brought about their fraternising with the mob, which lost the Orleans dynasty one of the finest thrones in the world.

I lived at this period in the Place de la Madeleine, and could observe from my windows the increasing numbers of the populace, and the insolence of their bearing. As I went to my club at the Café de Paris, I saw a battalion of the 14th Regiment of the line, stationed in the garden of the Foreign Office, which was then on the Boulevards.

The king, at the time I mention, had at last consented to dismiss his ministers, and to replace them by members of the Liberal party. There was great joy at this news, and even a commencement of illuminations in consequence. At the club where I was dining, the friends of the monarchy were rejoicing at the prospect of matters being satisfactorily arranged; when, just as we were all congratulating ourselves on the peaceful termination of the *émeute*, a terrific yell burst upon our ears. Its cause was soon explained. On rushing to the windows, we beheld a large cart full of dead and dying persons, followed by an immense concourse of men and women in the highest state of excitement, flinging their arms up towards heaven, and shouting out, '*Aux armes!*' '*Vengeons nos frères!*' We soon learnt what had occurred.

A large and peaceable crowd had collected before the Foreign Office, the garden of which looked upon the Boulevard des Capucines, and were gazing with Parisian delight at the illumination, when it is supposed that the republican party, enraged at seeing peace restored by the announcement of a change of ministry, determined to strike a murderous blow at the tottering monarchy, and – with that utter disregard of human life, which characterises Frenchmen when they have a political end in view – put forward an agent, who fired a pistol-shot at the officer commanding the battalion. The soldiers immediately responded by a volley of musketry upon the unsuspecting people, and strewed the Boulevard with dead and wounded. Many of the corpses were placed by the revolutionary party upon a cart to excite the passions of the people, and followed by vast crowds shouting vengeance.

From my club window that evening, I witnessed another extraordinary sight. An infuriated mob broke into the shop of a gunmaker opposite, and robbed him of every weapon he possessed: guns, pistols, swords, sabres, carbines, were slung round the shoulders, or fastened round the waists of men and boys, who were all singing the forbidden 'Marseillaise,'[1] and the 'Chant de Départ,'[2] and shouting seditious cries. In a few hours, barricades were raised, as if by magic, on every point of Paris, ready for the conflict that commenced at break of day.

I went out early on the following morning, and visited the Place de la Concorde, where several regiments of cavalry had bivouacked; and owing to the blundering and mismanagement of the military authorities, - who all seemed to have taken leave of their senses, - the troops had remained all night, the men without any food, and the horses with neither corn nor hay. From the Place de la Concorde, I directed my steps to the Boulevard Montmartre, by the Palais Royal, and the Rue Vivienne.

I spoke to several persons, all of whom appeared disgusted at the unaccountable apathy shown by the Government. As I passed along the Boulevard Bonne Nouvelle, I witnessed a strange scene: a regiment of the line, who, if they had been well led, would have put to flight all the mob of Paris, were actually in the hands of the émeutiers, who had persuaded the soldiers to give up their muskets. A General rode up and addressed the crowd, saying that the soldiers would never more fire on their brethren. Upon which there was a tremendous shout of applause.

I then endeavoured to make my way to the Chamber of Deputies, but could not reach it owing to the denseness of the crowd. I met a member of my club, Emmanuel Arago, son of the great astronomer.[3] Having always been a republican, and opposed to Louis Philippe's government, he was radiant with joy; and after leaving me, he placed himself at the

---

[1] Written by Rouget de Lisle in 1792 at the request of the Mayor of Strasbourg, who lamented the lack of a French national anthem when France declared war on Austria. It was first known as the 'Chant de guerre pour l'armée du Rhin'. It was sung in Paris by the citizen soldiers who came to the capital from Marseilles for the Festival of the Federation on 14 July 1792 and adopted by the Parisians who renamed it La Marseillaise.

[2] Also known as 'The Second Marseillaise', a revolutionary song with words by Chenier and music by Mehul. It was sung in 1794 when the body of the murdered Marat was taken to the Pantheon.

[3] Dominique-François-Jean Arago (1786–1853), director of the Paris Observatory. He had played a leading part in the July revolution of 1830, and became a member of the provisional government in 1848.

head of sixty or seventy of the armed mob, and forced his way into the Chamber.

In this extraordinary manner, and almost I may say by chance, the Orleans dynasty ceased to reign over the French people; and Louis Philippe – long reputed the Nestor of monarchs,[1] the wisest sovereign in Europe – was driven from the throne, as he constantly exclaimed during his flight – '*Absolument comme Charles X! – Absolument comme Charles X!*'

THE COUP D'ÉTAT

The simple narrative of an unprejudiced individual who has witnessed some of the scenes of that extraordinary event, the *coup d'état* of 2d December 1851, and who has had opportunities of forming a judgment for himself of many of the circumstances attendant upon it, will, I am persuaded, be received with indulgence as a contribution of facts, for the accuracy of which I am able to vouch from my personal knowledge.

Every thinking person in Paris, towards the close of the year 1851, anticipated, with considerable apprehension, that early in the ensuing spring a great change must take place in the government of the country. The constitution, which had been proclaimed with apparent enthusiasm in the year 1848, appeared likely to produce anarchy and confusion; for a new President and an Assembly had to be elected, and whatever claims the individual who had once acted as head of the state might have upon the country, he was, according to the constitution, ineligible again to fill that high position. There was every reason to fear that the Red Republicans would make a desperate effort to gain power, even should the streets of Paris again be deluged with blood; indeed, the language of some of their adherents boldly proclaimed that liberty could only be secured by means of the guillotine. In effect, a struggle for power had commenced between the Prince-President and the representatives of the people. The Assembly had refused to grant to the chief of the state the funds necessary to defray the expenses attendant upon his position; it manifested distrust of his Ministers, and jealousy of his popularity with the army, of which Changarnier had the command;[2] and so mean were the devices resorted to to annoy Louis Napoléon, that he was compelled to wear at reviews the uniform of a general of the National Guard. A decided opposition was being organised against his

[1] Nestor was King of Pylos, the most venerable of the chiefs who went to the siege of Troy.

[2] General Nicolas Anne Théodule Changarnier (1793-1877).

re-election; and there is no doubt that his personal liberty was menaced by his opponents, and that, had not the *coup d'état* taken place, his career would have terminated in the fortress of Vincennes.[1] The candidature of the Prince de Joinville for the Presidency of 1852,[2] which was very popular in France, even among the Liberal party, and seemed likely to be successful, disquieted the Bonapartists; and the violent and insolent language of General Changarnier aroused Louis Napoléon to the conviction that the time for action had arrived. It was the general opinion that a crisis was rapidly approaching, and only the President had the skill and courage to place himself at the head of the movement, and act decisively.

The Prince-President naturally looked to that great source of power in all governments, the army, as his strongest support; as military discipline secures prompt and efficient action at the bidding of one directing mind. The army, having already been disgusted by the interference of the Legislative body, felt humiliated by the Republicans, and hailed with delight the expected advent of a bold leader. At the end of November the principal military authorities met at the house of General Magnan,[3] and unanimously resolved to co-operate in any measures necessary to secure the tranquillity of Paris, and establish a firm and resolute government. The whole army being stationed in the vicinity of the metropolis, was prepared for some decisive movement; and although its precise nature was not understood, yet there was a determination to obey any orders emanating from the military authorities, whatever might be the consequence.

Relying on the support that he was thus to receive, the Prince-President announced to some of his faithful followers that the time had at length arrived when it was necessary for the welfare of the country, as well as for his own preservation, that measures should be adopted to dismiss the Assembly, and to give into his own hands the reins of government. Upon every occasion Louis Napoléon has secured to himself many attached adherents and friends, who have devotedly followed his fortunes on desperate occasions, and have not failed him in adversity. Such fidelity and devotion, while it reflects honour on them, also indicates rare qualities in the Prince, who exercises so powerful an

---

[1] The castle at Vincennes was begun in the fourteenth century; it became a state prison in the seventeenth.

[2] François-Ferdinand-Philippe-Louis-Marie d'Orleáns, prince de Joinville (1818–1900), was a son of King Louis-Philippe.

[3] Bernard Pierre Magnan, Marshal of France (1791–1865).

influence over his adherents. His winning, unaffected manners, his calm self-possession, the deliberation and coolness of his judgment, and his firm conviction of his ultimate success, which have borne Louis Napoléon through difficulties apparently insurmountable, have never failed to impress all who have been admitted to his intimacy. He has also obtained the well-merited reputation of never having alienated or forgotten a friend.

M. DE MORNY

The friend who stood forward on this occasion, and in whom the President felt that he could place the utmost reliance, was M. de Morny,[1] a man of firm determination and keen intellect, who was well acquainted with the state of political feeling in France, and was friendly with some of the most distinguished men of the day. He entered into the plan proposed with a full conviction that he was acting the part of a good citizen and an attached friend, and zealously devoted himself to the cause of the Prince; indeed, much of its success must be attributed to his admirable arrangements. Throughout he exhibited that calm but energetic and indomitable spirit essential on great occasions. He was at the Opera Comique on the very night when the storm was to burst forth; but nothing in his manner or appearance betrayed that his mind was absent from the dramatic scene.

The following anecdote is related of him, of the truth of which there can be no doubt. Being seated beside a lady of high rank, she asked him if the rumour in circulation was true, that it was intended to sweep out the Legislative Assembly; the prompt reply of the future Minister of the Interior was, 'I trust that I shall be near the handle of the broom that is to produce this effect.' His tact, his temper, and his moderation may be judged of by the telegraphic despatches which passed, during the tumult of the day, between himself and the Minister of Police. The celebrated Dr Veron occupied himself for some time in copying these messages as they were transmitted;[2] and the experienced editor of the *Constitutionnel* has enabled the public to judge how rapidly M. de Morny entered into the ideas of the Minister of Police, and how cautiously yet vigorously he answered the somewhat hurried and imprudent communications that he received.

[1] Charles-Auguste-Louis-Joseph, duc de Morny (1811–65), Louis-Napoleon's half-brother, became Minister of the Interior in 1852.

[2] Louis-Désiré Veron (1798–1867), formerly a medical practitioner, founded the *Revue de Paris* in 1829 and *Le Constitutionnel* in 1844.

The Night of December 1

On the evening of the 1st of December, a gay and fashionable assembly congregated at the palace of the Elysée; all was gaiety and animation as usual; it was a *fête* of social life, into which care never seemed to enter: to-morrow seemed never dreamt of. The Prince joined the lively throng; no trace of care was upon his brow: he was apparently bent only on making happy the friends by whom he was surrounded; and, with his usual affability and kindness, he spoke to several of those who were for the first time present, giving to all a hearty welcome. At eleven o'clock the party broke up, and the visitors departed.

Then the Prince entered the private cabinet of the President, to arrange definitively the course of proceeding on the morrow. It was at this meeting that the final orders were issued to the various functionaries by whom the plan of operations was to be carried into effect. Everything had been well and maturely considered; even the minor details had been decided upon. To obtain possession of the Government press – to arrest some of those whose violent opposition was most to be dreaded – to prevent the meeting of the Legislative body – to distribute the different regiments in commanding position – to name a new ministry, – these were objects of vital importance, the failure of any one of which might endanger the success of the whole movement; and each of the members of this cabinet council had important duties to perform, which if neglected would produce irremediable confusion. Not one of these determined men failed in his purpose, and all acted in concert; each one felt that upon his own efficiency rested the lives and fortunes of his associates, and the complete success of the *coup*.

The first step taken by Louis Napoléon was to sign the dismissal of the existing ministry, the appointment of the new ministers to their respective offices, and to prepare those energetic proclamations which on the following morning were read with eager eyes by the astonished Parisians. An active and intelligent officer had been selected to carry to the printing-office the decrees that were to be disseminated; these consisted of appeals to the people, orders to the army, and the proclamation of the Préfet of Police. He took them to the national printing-office, where he found that a hundred of the Garde Municipale had, with prudent foresight, been installed, with orders to obey his commands. The director, of course, complied with the injunctions of the Préfet of Police, and the printers were kept at work during the night under strict surveillance; and in the morning Paris was placarded with the President's decrees.

The account given by Mr Kinglake[1] of what occurred on the eve of the *coup d'état* is so far from being correct, that instead of manifesting the perturbation, nervousness, and apparent anxiety of mind so graphically described, the Prince quietly retired to rest, and simply gave orders that he should be awakened at five in the morning. He betrayed not the slightest emotion, and nothing transpired that could give the household the most remote intimation of what was about to occur: indeed, it is a well-known fact, that the domestics were as much surprised the following morning at learning that a revolution had taken place in Paris, as any other inhabitants of the city, for some of them actually sallied out to inquire of the servants of the English Embassy whether there was any truth in the reports that had reached them from without.

The Arrests

The Minister of Police instantly summoned all the commissioners of the different arrondissements into his cabinet, and signed orders for the arrest of the leading members of the Legislative Assembly, which were to be carried into effect before the break of day. Strange to say, there was not a word of inquiry, not a sign of hesitation. These functionaries recognised at once the authority under which they were called upon to act, and performed their duties with marvellous promptitude and with unfailing efficiency. The prisons of Paris received the men who the day before were the legislators and governors of France. Nor did the jailers hesitate (as was the case when Robespierre was overthrown) to open their gates for the reception of their late masters.

An anecdote is related, that General Changarnier was very nearly being made acquainted with the impending events. A young officer whose regiment was stationed at Courbevoie, had come up to Paris to pass the night; he was awoke by his servant, who told him that his presence was required immediately, as his regiment had been suddenly called out. The officer, surprised at this intelligence, and thinking that he ought to acquaint General Changarnier with this unusual order, went to the General's hotel; but finding that the porter was slow in opening the doors, he abandoned his intention and went to his quarters; whence he was obliged to accompany his regiment on the following day to overthrow the authority of General Changarnier and his friends. No

---

[1] Alexander William Kinglake (1809-91), historian of the Crimean War and author of *Eōthen*, renowned for his animosity towards Napoleon III. His partisan account of the *coup d'état* of 1851, to which Gronow, no less partisan, takes such exception, is given in Chapter XIV of the first volume of his *Invasion of the Crimea*.

delicacy was shown in the manner of arresting the most distinguished men of the day; and the volume of M. Granier de Cassagnac,[1] narrating what occurred in each case, has not met with general approbation: a little more consideration for men woke up in the dead of the night to be thrown into prison, would have better become that injudicious writer.

M. de Morny, after playing at whist at the Jockey Club, went to the hotel of the Minister of the Interior at five in the morning, and found the actual possessor of the office enjoying a peaceful slumber, from which he was speedily awakened to find himself superseded. The Chamber of Deputies was dissolved; some of the members in vain attempted to assemble and form a house, but they were removed and imprisoned for the day in the barracks on the Quai d'Orsay, whilst others were distributed amongst the neighbouring forts. Everything worked well, and the Government was soon in the hands of those who had so adroitly planned and so boldly carried out the *coup d'état*.

It now remained to keep the people tranquil, and to preserve the public peace from those daring Republicans, who would be certain to take advantage of any movement that might afford them an opportunity of seizing power, and to whom any amount of bloodshed would be considered of little consequence, so that their ends could be obtained.

PARIS ON DECEMBER 2

Upon the 2d of December, totally unsuspicious of what was going forward, I left my house, and was somewhat surprised to witness great agitation amongst the people in the streets, who, for the most part, seemed anxious to return to their homes. I saw various groups reading placards of a large size upon the walls of every street, that had evidently been posted up by order of Government, as they were printed on white paper; for since the revolution of 1848, all private announcements have, by order of the police, been printed upon coloured paper. Knowing that at the mayoralty of my arrondissement every authentic document would appear on the *façade*, I hastened thither; besides, I was anxious to know what was said by the street politicians, who are in the habit of daily visiting the public office, outside which the *Moniteur* is daily affixed.[2]

---

[1] Bernard Adolphe Granier de Cassagnac (1803–80). His *Souvenirs du Second Empire* were published in three volumes in Paris in 1881–4. A more reliable account of these days is to be found in F. A. Simpson's *The Rise of Louis Napoleon* (3rd edn, 1950).

[2] *La Gazette nationale ou le Moniteur universel* was founded in 1789. It was replaced by the *Journal officiel* in 1868.

I found two proclamations attracting the eager attention of the readers: one was a *plébiscite*, countersigned De Morny, decreeing that votes should be taken at the different mayoralties for or against the maintenance of the power of Louis Napoléon; the other emanated from the Préfet de Police, demanding the maintenance of order, and recommending people to remain at home. Little was said by the readers; but in the group I espied a well-known Figaro of the neighbourhood, who whilst shaving his customers usually launched out into politics. He was a stanch Bonapartist, for his father, a soldier, had been raised to the rank of sergeant in consequence of a brave but ineffectual attempt to rescue Prince Poniatowski from a watery grave at the battle of Leipsic.[1] I determined to submit my chin to the operation of this worthy during the afternoon, feeling sure that I should hear information from him as to what was the general opinion of his customers. In the meantime I strolled into the Faubourg St Honoré, where a squadron of the 12th Regiment of Dragoons was stationed before the British Embassy, another being drawn up in front of the palace of the Elysée, whilst there was a third doing duty at the garden gate. A few individuals stood gazing on the unusual military display; but not a word was uttered, and they soon passed on. Now and then a carriage drove up to the gate, and after a scrutiny from the porter, was admitted or rolled away. So far as I could learn, no demonstration of any kind was made that day at the fashionable end of the town; but it was said that the Republicans were to have, at ten o'clock at night, meetings to take into consideration the incidents of the day; and that in the Faubourg St Antoine, the Barrière du Trône, and the Faubourg du Temple, cries had been heard of '*Vive la République sociale!*' and '*À bas le Prétendant!*'

After reconnoitring the principal streets, and seeing nothing remarkable, beyond the anxiety and curiosity written upon the faces of most persons, and witnessing, what is not unusual in the streets of Paris, the marching by of several regiments evidently in high glee, I adjourned to the barber's, and seated myself in his chair. He was in a state of great excitement, and expatiating on the many virtues of Prince Louis Napoléon, with which he had become acquainted from having on two occasions dressed the hair of the chambermaid whose duty it was to lay the fire over-night in the cabinet of the President, which he himself generally lighted at an early hour in the morning. The excellent *soubrette*

---

[1] Prince Józéf Antoni Poniatowski (1763–1813), Marshal of France, was drowned while trying to cross the Elster on the last day of the battle of Leipzig.

could never speak in sufficiently high terms of the gentleness and amiable temper of her master, and the worthy barber had caught the infection. Deriving his information from her as to the Prince's domestic virtues, and inheriting his father's admiration of the great Napoléon, he launched out in no measured terms against all those who opposed the re-election of the President, though his animosity to the Republicans was somewhat restrained by the presence of two doubtful-looking statesmen in blouses, who now and then interrupted him, by expressing their faith in General Changarnier. My eloquent friend, however, soon resumed his discourse. He had heard some cries in the street of '*Vive l'Empereur!*' from the military, and they had delighted him. Some of the surrounding persons, waiting to have their beards trimmed, differed from the knight of the brush; doubts were expressed of the talent of the Prince-President, and there was evidently a Republican tendency springing up; but the announcement that the Prince, attended by a numerous staff, was passing by, put a stop to the conversation; away every one rushed out to see the passing show, and upon their return there was a universal opinion expressed, that the Prince-President looked like a noble soldier, and 'every inch a king:' his gallant bearing had evidently produced a strong impression upon the spectators, the majority of whom from that moment were evidently in favour of the changes that had taken place.

LOUIS NAPOLÉON AT THE ELYSÉE

It has been asserted that the Prince-President remained in his cabinet, during these eventful days, solitary and gloomy, and solely occupied in issuing his edicts for the destruction of his opponents. This story originally emanated from an author more distinguished for the brilliancy of his imagination than for the soberness of his judgment, or the accuracy of his knowledge; and who was conspicuous for his political malevolence, and the virulence of his speeches in the Legislative Assembly. He has been followed by some who, whilst they claim to write history, have no hesitation in copying the errors and exaggerations of others; but it can safely be asserted that, so far from Prince Louis Napoléon being left to himself, the Princesse Mathilde remained with him the greater part of the day;[1] King Jérôme and most of the new

---

[1] Princess Mathilde (1820–1904), only daughter of Napoleon I's youngest brother, Jérôme Bonaparte. A patroness of arts and letters in Paris, she was married to an extremely rich Russian, Anatole Dimidoff, Principe di San Donato.

ministers were admitted,[1] and the Elysée was not closed to any visitors
who had a right to present themselves to the President. Those who were
received, found him calm, collected, and urbane as usual; and as notes
and messages were placed in his hands, he received them with coolness,
and quietly read their contents; but never, by his countenance, his
gestures, or his words, could the effect or import of these communications be inferred. He addressed all with his customary affability and
kindness, and conversed freely upon various topics. The Emperor, it
is true, does not possess that volubility for which Frenchmen are
remarkable; he thinks and weighs his words before he speaks, and what
he says is concise and to the point: his manner is quiet and reticent, like
that of a grave and thoughtful man; but this quietude is amply made up
for by the flattering attention which he gives to the words of all with
whom he speaks: nothing escapes him; he listens intelligently to all that
is said, and his replies and observations evince a wish not to express his
own opinion, but to learn that of others; and he never fails to appreciate
at their due the value of the views and opinions brought before him.
Upon these eventful days the Prince maintained his usual equanimity,
and was not more grave and silent than usual; he never for an instant
flinched from possible danger; he was always prepared to meet it and his
followers had seen enough of his conduct in such emergencies, to be
satisfied of his presence of mind and personal courage.

M. de Persigny,[2] whose attachment to the Emperor is such that he
would at any moment lay down his life for him and for his dynasty,
was constantly at the Elysée; for to him had been intrusted the task
of effecting an honourable retreat, in case of an adverse turn of
circumstances. His duty it would have been, had the day gone against
the President, to have collected the household, and to have conducted
the Prince, with all the troops that were faithful, to the palace of the
Tuileries, where the active leaders were determined to make a last
stand, and succeed, or perish with arms in their hands. This was the only
alternative proposed; no preparations had been made for flight; no
horses and carriages kept ready, no money had been sent to foreign
countries, and nothing had been packed up to be carried off at a
moment's notice. There was a firm resolve that death or victory was to
be the result of this great enterprise.

In the course of the first day, I paid a visit to an old comrade, that

---

[1] Jérôme Bonaparte (see note, p. 135).
[2] Jean Gilbert Victor Fialin, duc de Persigny (1808–72), was Napoleon III's Minister of
the Interior and Ambassador in London from 1855 to 1860.

distinguished officer Sir de Lacy Evans,[1] who had just come to Paris, and was residing in the Place de la Madeleine; the conversation naturally turned on the events passing before our eyes, and the General expressed much satisfaction at the apparent promptitude with which the affair had been carried out; for we believed that public tranquillity had not been disturbed. He observed that the enemies of the Prince-President had brought the whole thing upon themselves, by their shameful treatment of the chief of the state; adding, that he felt persuaded that if Louis Napoléon would give the people a liberal constitution, which should include the freedom of the press, he would prove himself a greater man than his uncle.

I had been told that a column of the National Guard had marched with the infantry, but I found that this was not the case; in fact the utmost care had been taken not to call out the National Guard, for it was well known that in some of the regiments there were Republicans, who might be induced to leave their brethren and join the insurgents, if they were disposed to raise barricades. The consequence was that everything depended upon the regular troops.

RECEPTION OF THE PRINCE-PRESIDENT

When the Prince, attended by a numerous staff, accompanied by the ex-King Jérôme and by Count Flahault,[2] rode through the streets, he exhibited that bravery which has never deserted him in the hour of danger; notwithstanding the calumnies of his traducers, who choose to assert that he is deficient in personal courage and nerve. He was remarkably well received by the army, and shouts of '*Vive le Prince!*' were heard from every regiment, as he cantered along the Champs Elysées. The people of Paris are never demonstrative in their reception of their monarchs; even the ordinary token of respect to royalty, the lifting of the hat, is rare, and on this occasion there was no observable departure from the usual habit. The Prince-President returned at an early hour to the Elysée, where M. de Persigny received him with the

[1] General Sir George de Lacy Evans (1787–1870) distinguished himself as commander of the 2nd Division in the Crimean War. A radical in politics, he was for a time Member of Parliament for Westminster.

[2] August-Charles Joseph, comte de Flahaut de la Billarderi (1785–1870), supposed to be the natural son of Talleyrand. He was the lover of Napoleon's sister Caroline, wife of Joachim Murat, and of Hortense de Beauharnais, whose son by him became duc de Morny. Flahaut was Ambassador in Vienna from 1842 to 1848 and in London from 1860 to 1862.

intelligence that all the steps hitherto taken were successful, and that the military were fully prepared to fulfil the orders of their superiors; indeed, so obedient were the sentries to the commands which had been given, that when the President, preparing to leave the garden of the palace, presented himself at the gate, the advanced guard of the 12th Regiment, then on duty, would not allow him to pass without giving the countersign.

That the 4th of December was a melancholy day for France, and will long remain remembered by Europe, is not to be denied; but it is neither just nor honest to attribute the lamentable events which then occurred to cold-heartedness on the part of Louis Napoléon. No man ever more deeply deplored them; and where the opportunity offered, he gave what indemnity he could to the families of those who had suffered. There are young persons who lost their parents on that day who have been educated at his expense, the cost being defrayed out of his private purse; and I know myself one instance in which the children have had a regular quarterly stipend paid to them, from their infancy, and which is continued, without interruption or diminution, to this day.

The first impression made upon the minds of people in England as to what occurred on the 4th of December, was the result of a letter which appeared in the *Times*, from an officer of the British army, who, from a window on the Boulevard Montmartre, was a personal witness of the scene that took place in the street beneath him, where many persons fell victims to the fire of the soldiery. The infantry, quartered in sub-divisions, suddenly fired, not only upon the men, women, and children in the footpath, but at the windows above them, and with sad results: volley succeeded to volley, and it was evident that a panic had taken possession of the soldiery. Their officers had given no commands; for they were quietly smoking their cigars when the firing began.

What the Author Saw

I happened on that day to pay a visit, in company with [a friend from] the British Embassy, to my banker in the Rue Basse du Rempart: M. Charles Lafitte then gave us to understand that orders had been given to the military to act with great moderation; but if there existed the slightest disposition to riot, they were to 'take the bull by the horns,' and to destroy all barricades with cannon. During our short interview the bugles were heard close at hand, the windows were opened, and we took up a position on the balcony, whence we saw marching, in good military order and at double-quick time, the Chasseurs of Vincennes.

M. Lafitte, without anticipating what was about to occur, good-naturedly said, 'If you wish to see the fun, you had better follow the troops; for I am confident, from the information I have this moment received, that they are bent on mischief.'

[My friend] and I then bent our steps towards the Rue Richelieu, where the rattling of musketry was distinctly heard. My friend left for the British Embassy, saying that, as a diplomatist, his place was in the Faubourg St Honoré and not upon the Boulevards. Immediately afterwards a brigade of Lancers arrived opposite the spot where I had placed myself, at the angle of the Rue Grange Batelière and the Boulevards. A considerable crowd had there collected; and such was their hostile attitude, and so loud their vociferations, that I was convinced the Lancers would not long remain inactive, especially if the slightest insult was offered them. From amongst these persons thus collected came a pistol ball with a loud detonation, and a soldier was wounded. The Colonel immediately charged at the head of his regiment; the consequence was that several of the crowd were severely wounded, and a bad feeling sprang up amongst the soldiery. I thought it prudent to quit this scene and return to my home, which I reached with considerable difficulty.

Certainly, all that occurred was of a nature to excite uneasiness and alarm; but 'that it was seen with frenzied horror by thousands of French men and women' is an absurd exaggeration. The upper classes of Paris were no doubt exceedingly angry and irritated, because during every *émeute* in the metropolis, the Boulevards on the Madeleine side of the Rue Richelieu always continued to be the resort of the *flâneur* [idler], and had escaped the slaughter consequent on the erection of barricades; and they went there attracted by 'the pomp and circumstance of war,' and thought themselves safe; for they looked upon the soldiers as their national defenders against insurgents, and they were maddened at the idea of the slaughter of unarmed saunterers, who had gone out as it were under the shield of the military, to see what was going forward.

GROUNDLESS FABRICATIONS

The occurrences of that day undoubtedly struck terror into the hearts of the people of Paris which will never be obliterated, and they certainly have tended to affect the popularity of the Emperor Napoléon in the capital; more especially as his political adversaries have never failed to throw upon him the responsibility of events over which he had no control. So dishonest have been some of the writers who have furnished the public with their tales, that it has been stated that in the gardens of the Tuileries, and the Luxembourg, military executions of prisoners took place in the dead of night! The overthrow of a pile of the chairs, which in winter are generally to be seen in the garden of the Tuileries, and the consequent alarm given by the sentry, was even magnified into an attack upon the palace and the consequent carnage of the assailants. As for the statement that platoons of soldiers performed the office of executioners in the night, it is a pure invention; and the rumour alleged to have been credited in Paris, that during the night of the 4th and 5th of December prisoners were shot in batches and thrown into pits, is an equally groundless fabrication. I never heard that such a falsehood was propagated, until I read this shameful insinuation in a volume which claims to be a contribution to history. As for the 'nine kinds of slaughter' which the eccentric writer discovers that military men may unhesitatingly indulge in, I do not think that any of these have relation to the melancholy events of the 4th of December.

Those events are deeply to be deplored; but they arose out of accidental circumstances. No one has ever attempted to defend them; and they ought not to be exaggerated, either for the purpose of exciting the sympathy of nations, or for the sake of blackening political enemies. There was no wanton massacre of the people, as has been asserted; there were sad mistakes, and people ran into danger notwithstanding the warnings that were distributed everywhere – for placards were upon the walls in every direction, entreating every one to stay at home. There were insurgents, there were barricades, there was firing upon the soldiers; there was therefore a necessity for martial law to be enforced; but the Emperor is not chargeable either with the wild excesses of the soldiery, or the credulity of the Minister of Police.

The Parisians, even at the height of their excitement, did not hold the Prince-President responsible for these deplorable consequences; neither had he the least apprehension of being the object of vindictive feelings. So far from entertaining any personal fear, his calm self-possession was never more conspicuous than during these eventful days. I will only mention one corroborative circumstance in proof of this.

On the fourth night after the *coup d'état*, my daughter and myself were present at a ball, given by the Duchess of Hamilton in honour of the Prince-President, at the Hôtel Bristol, Place Vendôme.[1] At ten o'clock

---

[1] The Duchess of Hamilton was the Princess Marie-Amélie Baden, youngest daughter of Charles Louis Frederick, Grand Duke of Baden, a cousin of Napoleon III. She married the Duke in 1843 and died in 1888. She and her husband spent most of their lives in Paris and Baden. Although Gronow refers to her as the Duchess of Hamilton, her husband, the eleventh Duke, did not, in fact, succeed to the title until 1852.

precisely, the President entered the ball-room when a quadrille was formed; the Prince dancing with the Duchess of Hamilton, Lady Poltimore[1] and the Duke of Hamilton being the *vis-à-vis*. The second quadrille soon followed; when the Prince chose the Princess Mathilde as his partner, Lord Poltimore and Lady Cowley making the *vis-à-vis*.

The Prince appeared perfectly cool and collected; he conversed with a great many persons, but more particularly with Lord Cowley, who had only arrived in Paris that morning, to fill his post of British Ambassador.[2] The instant the clock struck twelve, the Duke of Hamilton, taking two wax-candles, conducted his imperial guest downstairs, and handed him into his plain brougham. On the return of the Duke to the ball-room, he observed to several friends who had collected round him, 'How extraordinary! There were neither military nor police in the courtyard of the hotel, to protect the President in case of danger.' In fact, the Prince returned at midnight, without an escort, to the Elysée, in a one-horse brougham.

And this is the man whom Mr Kinglake, in his account of the *coup d'état*, has insinuated to be constantly occupied in guarding himself against attacks from assassination, and living in fear and trembling.

Let those who have been influenced by these calumnies, consider what have been the results of the *coup d'état* upon the position and prospects of France. The nation enjoys greater prosperity and happiness, and its power and influence are stronger and more undisputed than ever in Europe; while the Emperor of the French holds a firm and lofty place amongst the monarchs of the world, in right of the wisdom with which he governs the people and develops the resources of the country.

---

[1] Lady Poltimore, second wife of George Warwick, first Baron Poltimore (1786–1858), was Caroline, eldest daughter of Lieutenant-General Frederick Buller.

[2] Henry Richard Charles Wellesley, first Earl Cowley, was appointed Ambassador in Paris in 1852. His father had been Ambassador there before him. His wife was Olivia Cecilia, a daughter of Lord Henry Fitzgerald, whose self-confidence in society compensated for her husband's diffidence.

17

Random Observations

IMPROVEMENTS IN PARIS

Paris has within four or five years undergone marvellous changes, which reflect the highest honour on those who have contributed to its splendour at the present time.[1] The melancholy, gloomy, miserable portion of the city might be very charming to the artist and archæologist, who admired mediæval pointed roofs, fantastic domes, labyrinths of galleries, and windows that seemed as if not intended to admit the air or the sunlight; whilst liquid mud and filthy streams sluggishly meandered through the dark and narrow streets and passages, from which the frightened foreigner could scarcely extricate himself. A beautiful, fairy-like city has replaced the crowded heaps of dingy, dark dwellings; the blind alleys and the fetid courts have been exchanged for lofty and elegant mansions, wide and well-paved thoroughfares, and spacious open places. A writer of antiquity denominated Paris *Leukotokia*, the white city. Well now does it merit that name. All that was may have been picturesque; but all that is must be pronounced delightful.

Upon sites once covered with cemeteries, with sewers, with pits, and with abominations indescribable, have arisen verdant lawns, squares, and gardens, where, at the vernal season, flowers charm the eye and

---

[1] Georges-Eugène, Baron Haussmann (1809–91), Subprefect of Paris from 1832 to 1848 and Prefect from 1853 to 1870, was largely responsible for the transformation of Paris which Gronow describes.

gratify the sense, while sparkling fountains pour forth their cool streams; spaces where the sun and air give life and animation to all around; mansions where domestic or polished society can enjoy all the luxuries and comforts which art and taste have introduced.

This transformation has been effected at an enormous expense, by skilful architects and sculptors, under the control of one great sovereign; it has been the result of unremitting energy on the part of those who planned the improvements, and the indomitable toil of those who carried them out. It was indeed a sight worthy this engineering age, to see the thousand workmen congregated upon various spots, the tramroads, and trains of horses and waggons bearing enormous weights of stone from the neighbouring quarries, the crumbling houses marked for destruction, and the deep foundations dug for new Boulevards on both banks of the Seine, the delight of Paris.

One of the most glorious achievements of the present reign has been the completion of that magnificent edifice, the Louvre. Its saloons, lined with treasures of fine art, were the glory of France; but a large portion of this vast structure, only a very short time ago, wore a most ignoble aspect: columns, with rich capitals, were at their base disfigured by all that was filthy and disgusting. The square that had displayed the talents of Jean Goujon,[1] and of Perrault[2] adjoined stalls where squalid people offered for sale dogs, birds, the sweepings of *bric-à-brac* shops; spots infested by the lazzaroni of Paris, thieves, and courtesans. A more painful contrast of luxury and misery never disfigured the most attractive part of a luxurious city. Napoleon I, in the plenitude of his power, and Louis Philippe, with all the *bourgeoisie* of Paris to back him, could not drive away the human vermin that infested the place; nor did they add a single stone to improve this *chef d'œuvre* of architecture. At length, to the immortal honour of the Emperor Napoleon III, the work has been accomplished, and the Louvre is now a palace worthy of the *chefs d'œuvre* of art which enrich its interior. Indeed, the inauguration of the Louvre is an era in the annals of Paris.

The cleansing, draining, and lighting of the streets have also been admirably carried out; and the famous city of Paris now appears with renovated grace and beauty, and decorated with a thousand ornaments, which attract the eyes of the whole world.

[1] Jean Goujon (*c.* 1510-*c.* 1568), whose sculpture decorated the façade of the Cour Carrée at the Louvre.
[2] Claude Perrault (1613-88) served with Louis Le Vau and Charles Le Brun on a committee which designed the Colonnade.

There has been another immense improvement: the groves of the Bois de Boulogne, formerly the rendezvous of duellists, footpads, and gipsies, have been transformed as if by the hand of an enchanter, and flowers and foliage, velvet turf, cascades, and winding streams combine to delight the senses and invigorate the health of the promenaders. Here lovers, idlers, poets, the humble and the wealthy, lounge their hours away amid joyous scenes, where art and skill have successfully combined the varied charms of nature.

HAIRDRESSING FIFTY YEARS SINCE, AND VAILS TO SERVANTS

Nobody in the present day can conceive the inconvenience of our military costume when I first entered the Guards in 1813, or the annoyance to which we were subjected at being constantly obliged to seek the assistance of a *coiffeur* to powder our hair. Our commanding officers were very severe with respect to our dress and powdering; and I remember, when on guard, incurring the heavy displeasure of the late Duke of Cambridge for not having a sufficient quantity of powder on my head, and therefore presenting a somewhat piebald appearance. I received a strong reprimand from HRH, and he threatened even to place me under arrest should I ever appear again on guard in what he was pleased to call so slovenly and disgraceful a condition. The hairdresser was not only required at early dawn, before our field-days or parades, but again in the evening, if we dined out, or went to parties or balls.

The most fashionable *coiffeur* was Rowland, or Rouland, a French *émigré*. His charge for cutting hair was five shillings; and his shop was next door to the Thatched-House Tavern in St James's Street. He was the inventor of the famous Macassar oil, and made a large fortune.[1] He came to London with the Bourbons on the breaking out of the French Revolution, and followed them back to France in 1814.

There was another custom in my young days which has luckily fallen into disuse. If one dined at any of the great houses in London, it was considered absolutely necessary to give a guinea to the butler on leaving the house. One hundred and thirty years ago this very had habit (as I

---

[1] Macassar oil was said to be made from ingredients obtained from Makasar in Indonesia. Its application necessitated the use of antimacassars, the coverings placed over the backs of chairs and sofas which became so common a feature of Victorian drawing rooms.

always considered it) prevailed to an even greater extent; for Pope the poet,[1] whenever he dined with the Duke of Montagu, finding that he had to give five guineas to the numerous servants at Montagu House, told the Duke that he could not dine with him in future unless his grace sent him five guineas to distribute among his myrmidons.[2] The Duke, an easy, good-natured man, used ever after, on sending an invitation to the great poet, to enclose at the same time an order for the tribute-money: he preferred doing this to breaking through a custom which had grown to be looked upon by servants as a right, and the abolition of which they would have considered as a heavy grievance.

Dining and Cookery in England Fifty Years Ago

England can boast of a Spenser, Shakspeare, Milton, and many other illustrious poets, clearly indicating that the national character of Britons is not deficient in imagination; but we have not had one single masculine inventive genius of the kitchen. It is the probable result of our national antipathy to mysterious culinary compounds, that none of the bright minds of England have ventured into the region of scientific cookery. Even in the best houses, when I was a young man, the dinners were wonderfully solid, hot, and stimulating. The *menu* of a grand dinner was thus composed: – Mulligatawny and turtle soups were the first dishes placed before you; a little lower, the eye met with the familiar salmon at one end of the table, and the turbot, surrounded by smelts, at the other. The first course was sure to be followed by a saddle of mutton

---

[1] Alexander Pope (1688–1744), poet. His *Essay on Criticism* was published in 1711, his *Dunciad* in 1726.

[2] Montagu House, Bloomsbury, was rebuilt in the late seventeenth century after a fire had destroyed its predecessor. This first house had been designed by Robert Hooke for the first Duke, Charles II's Ambassador to Paris, who repaired the fortune it had dissipated by marrying the second Duchess of Albemarle, an extremely rich but insane woman who, having declared she would marry no one but a crowned head, was persuaded to believe that Montagu was the Emperor of China and, in the role of Empress, was served at Montagu House on bended knee. In 1755 the house was sold for the housing of the newly established British Museum.

The system of tipping, which prevailed here in its heyday, was not in the least uncommon. Foreign visitors complained that it was cheaper to pay for a good meal in a tavern than accept an invitation from a man of quality. In some houses the servants actually adopted a fixed scale of rates for the different services provided for guests; and a guest who declined to pay was liable to have his hat cut to pieces, a punishment inflicted, according to the *London Chronicle*, by an admiral's valet in 1761 on a parsimonious friend of his master. The custom of vails collecting, as tipping was known, died out towards the end of the century except in one or two of the grander houses.

or a piece of roast beef; and then you could take your oath that fowls, tongue, and ham would as assuredly succeed as darkness after day.

Whilst these never-ending *pièces de résistance* were occupying the table, what were called French dishes were, for custom's sake, added to the solid abundance. The French, or side dishes, consisted of very mild but very abortive attempts at Continental cooking; and I have always observed that they met with the neglect and contempt that they merited. The universally-adored and ever-popular boiled potato, produced at the very earliest period of the dinner, was eaten with everything, up to the moment when sweets appeared. Our vegetables, the best in the world, were never honoured by an accompanying sauce, and generally came to the table cold. A prime difficulty to overcome was the placing on your fork, and finally in your mouth, some half-dozen different eatables which occupied your plate at the same time. For example, your plate would contain, say, a slice of turkey, a piece of stuffing, a sausage, pickles, a slice of tongue, cauliflower, and potatoes. According to habit and custom, a judicious and careful selection from this little bazaar of good things was to be made, with an endeavour to place a portion of each in your mouth at the same moment. In fact, it appeared to me that we used to do all our compound cookery between our jaws.

The dessert, if for a dozen people, would cost at least as many pounds. The wines were chiefly port, sherry, and hock; claret, and even Burgundy, being then designated 'poor, thin, washy stuff.' A perpetual thirst seemed to come over people, both men and women, as soon as they had tasted their soup; as from that moment everybody was taking wine with everybody else till the close of the dinner; and such wine as produced that class of cordiality which frequently wanders into stupefaction. How all this sort of eating and drinking ended was obvious, from the prevalence of gout, and the necessity of every one making the pillbox their constant bedroom companion.

FASHION IN PARIS

It has been said of the French that they are constant only in their fickleness, worshipping one day what they execrate the next, and throwing down with their own hands from its pedestal the idol they themselves had set up a few weeks before. But there is one deity to whom they have never proved faithless; at whose shrine they bow with the same devotion to-day as they did centuries ago, whose fiat is law, and whose dictates none dare resist. This capricious, exacting, ever-changing goddess is Fashion.

I remember once expressing my admiration for a very handsome, charming lady, in the presence of a Parisian 'man-milliner of modern days.' During all my encomiums the Gaul preserved a stern silence. 'Do you not admire Lady X——?' I asked, rather provoked by his disdainful looks. 'She has purple gloves,' he replied, with a look of supreme contempt, which was truly amusing to behold. Though it is now the fashion in Paris to imitate the fast generation of perfidious Albion in many articles of dress, such as looped-up petticoats, wideawake hats, nets for the hair, and Balmoral boots,[1] in former days no English lady who had not been brought up at the feet of some female Parisian Gamaliel,[2] could be supposed by any possibility to know anything about *la toilette*.

Those who, like myself, are old enough to recollect the beautiful Lady Blessington in her brightest days, can remember that she always wore a peculiar costume, chosen with artistic taste to suit exactly her style of beauty. The cap she was in the habit of wearing [was] drawn in a straight line over the forehead, where, after a slight fulness on each temple, giving it a little the appearance of wings, it was drawn down close over the cheeks, and fastened under the chin. Nothing could have been more cunningly devised to show off the fine brow and beautifully-shaped oval face of the deviser, or to conceal the too great width of the cheeks, and a premature development of double chin. Lady Blessington had also a style of dress suitable to her figure, which was full, but then not 'of o'er-grown bulk.' She always wore white in the morning, a thick muslin dress, embroidered in front and lined with some bright colour, and a large silk bonnet and cloak to match. This was her costume in London, but, on her arrival in Paris, two or three French ladies got hold of her, declared she was *horriblement fagotée*, and insisted on having her dressed in quite a different style by a fashionable *modiste*; they managed so completely to transform her that, in the opinion of myself and all who had seen her in England, her defects were brought out, and all her beauty disappeared. But, nevertheless, in her new and unbecoming attire, she was pronounced *charmante* by a jury of fashionable dames, and forced, *nolens volens*, to take an eternal farewell to the lovely and becoming costumes of her youth.

[1] A kind of boot with lacing in front, fashionable in the 1860s.
[2] A pedant, the name of several Rabbis celebrated in the first and second centuries AD, in particular Rabban Gamaliel, a Palestinian master of the Jewish Oral Law.

Fashion has such a wonderful power over the French mind, that it can actually transform the body so as to suit the exigency of the moment. In former days, we old fellows may remember that the French type of womankind was *une petite femme mignonne et brune*. In the whole of society, thirty or forty years ago, one could scarcely have numbered more than half-a-dozen tall women. They were looked upon as anomalies, and saluted not unfrequently with such very uncomplimentary appellations as '*chameaux*,' '*gens darmes*,' '*asperges*,' &c., &c. Now that it is the fashion to be tall and commanding, one sees dozens of gigantic women every day that one goes out, with heels inside as well as outside their boots; perhaps even stilts under those long sweeping petticoats. I know not how the change has been effected, but there it is.

Frenchwomen used to have dark hair; blondes were not generally admired, and tried by every possible means to darken their hair; but now, since the Empress has made fair hair *à la mode*, all the women must be blondes, and what with gold powder and light wigs they do succeed. As to complexions, a dark one is now unknown; roses and lilies abound on every cheek: even some young men of fashion have not disdained the use of cosmetics, but have come out from the hands of the *coiffeur* romantically pale or delicately tinted.

Fashion is very capricious, and it does not suffice to sit in high places in order to govern *la mode*. With the exception of the Duke of Orleans, so prematurely cut off in the flower of his youth, not one of Louis Philippe's family, male or female, ever exercised the smallest influence over this capricious goddess. There were young and handsome princesses, always well and tastefully dressed, but they were pronounced *rococo*;[1] and no one ever dreamt of wearing any particular bonnet or cloak, because the beautiful Duchesse de Nemours, or the graceful Princesse de Joinville had appeared in a similar one.

It is not because the Empress Eugénie is the wife of Napoleon III that she sets the fashion, even to those who don't go to court, and who turn up their noses at her *entourage*.[2] She is considerably older and certainly not handsomer than was the Duchesse de Nemours, when she left France to die in exile; but she has the *chic*, if I may use such a word, that the Orleans princesses did not possess; and the quietest dowager, before

[1] In this sense meaning old-fashioned rather than elaborate.
[2] The Empress Eugénie (1826–1920) was the daughter of a Spanish nobleman who had fought for the French in the Peninsular War. She came to live in exile in England in 1870 after the French defeat in the Franco-Prussian War.

she ventures to adopt a *coiffure*, as well as the gayest lady of the *demi-monde*, will cast a look to see what the Empress wears. Strange to say, the supreme good taste and elegance which reign in her Majesty's *toilettes* were by no means conspicuous in her younger days; for, as Mademoiselle Montijo, she was voted beautiful and charming, but very ill-dressed.

The style of French cookery has also changed as completely as the style of dress, at the dictates of Fashion. Modern attire and modern cookery are alike over ornamented. Thirty years ago, simplicity in dress, especially in the morning, was the right thing: if by any extraordinary chance a Parisian lady of rank condescended to take a walk (a rare occurrence), she could only be remarked by the extreme plainness and neatness of her attire; and any article of dress that could in anywise resemble what might be worn by the *lorette* of that day was studiously shunned. To be taken for anything of a lower grade than what she was, and spoken to by an unknown person, would have been looked on as an insult so great that the humiliating incident would never have been breathed to mortal ear; but now-a-days it is considered only a good joke. How astonished and horror-struck would be the great ladies of the Restoration, if they could rise from their graves and behold their granddaughters emulating the *demi-monde* in their dress, language, and manners; *affichant* their *liaisons* in the sight of the sun; walking into their lovers' houses unveiled, undisguised, or riding with them publicly, and having their carriages called under their own names at the restaurants, or small theatres, where they have been *tête-à-tête*!

The dignified, artful, proud, but perhaps not more virtuous, grandmother would have been unutterably disgusted, not so much at the immorality as at the bad taste displayed in such arrangements; which then existed just as much as now, but were supposed to be unknown.

Literary Salons in France

One of the most agreeable *salons* in Paris was held by the late Madame Emile de Girardin,[1] the Mrs Norton of France.[2] Like our own gifted

[1] The wife of the journalist and founder of *La Presse*, Émile de Girardin (1806–81), she was formerly Delphine Gay, daughter of the novelist Sophie Gay. She was also a novelist, as well as a poet, and contributed a gossip column to *La Presse* under the pseudonym of Charles de Launay.

[2] Caroline Elizabeth Sarah Norton (1808–77), wife of a barrister, the Hon. George Chapple Norton, who instituted divorce proceedings because of her friendship with Lord Melbourne. A beautiful woman, the granddaughter of R. B. Sheridan, she was a poet and novelist, a talented artist and musician as well as a highly entertaining conversationalist.

countrywoman, she was endowed not only with poetic genius, but
likewise with great conversational wit and much personal beauty.

She was a tall, good-looking woman, with the aspect of a Muse, or
rather of what one fancies a Muse ought to be. She had an abundance
of beautiful fair hair, large blue eyes, an aquiline nose, and very fine
teeth, and bore a striking resemblance to the pictures of Marie-
Antoinette.

She had many great and estimable qualities. Her mind and heart,
like her outward frame, were on a large and grand scale. She was above
all the littlenesses that too often disfigure women's characters. She was
(a rare thing in a woman) an enthusiastic admirer of beauty even in her
own sex, and took pleasure in drawing round her the women most
distinguished for their personal or mental qualities. She possessed a
peculiar knack of making her guests appear to the best advantage,
drawing them out, and placing them in the little circle where they
would be sure to shine and be appreciated; for she felt that she could
afford to subdue the light of her brilliant wit, and allow the little
glowworms around her to twinkle to their own satisfaction.

You were sure to meet in the *salon* of Madame E. de Girardin all the
celebrities of the day, whether fashionable, literary, or political. Every
one felt at ease, - the women looked their best, the men made themselves
agreeable, and the charming hostess seemed happy in the enjoyment of
those around her.

In addition to her great gifts as a prose writer, she was also a poetess
of the highest order; and her *pièces de théâtre* enjoyed the greatest
popularity, and met with well-deserved success.

Though in reality far superior to her husband, both in cleverness and
judgment, she had a high and even exaggerated opinion of his merits as
a politician. In the darkest days of that melancholy experiment yclept
the *République française* of 1848, an intimate friend was sitting one
morning in Madame de Girardin's boudoir. They were lamenting over
the miserable state of things which had succeeded the era of constitutional liberty. After discussing the dangers and difficulties of the
moment, Madame de Girardin added, with a grave expression of
countenance, and a deeper intonation of voice, 'Happily, there is one
above who can restore order and tranquillity to the country; and he
alone can save us.' The visitor, somewhat astonished at what he thought
a pious observation coming from a lady of rather Voltairian principles,
muttered out something about Providence, and good coming out of evil.
'That's not the question,' said Madame de Girardin; 'I am not talking
about Providence, but of my husband, who is at this moment overhead,

and engaged in writing an article for the *Presse*, which will appear to-morrow, and set everything to rights.'

Salons like that of the gifted Madame Emile de Girardin are extremely rare now-a-days, owing greatly to the unlimited extension of what is called society; and also, perhaps, in some measure, to the strong line of demarcation drawn by political animosity. The thirst for noisy active pleasure has well-nigh destroyed the charming little *coteries* of the olden time, where men did not think it beneath them to be well-bred and amiable, where they consented to speak of other things besides their horses and mistresses, and where women were not satisfied with being pretty and well-dressed, but aimed also at being thought clever and agreeable.

One of the pleasantest of these *salons* was that of the Comtesse Merlin.[1] In a different way, that lady was almost as remarkable a person as Madame Emile de Girardin. She was a Spanish Creole by birth; and though even when I made her acquaintance, some thirty years ago, she was what our English novelists call 'somewhat *embonpoint*,' her beauty was still of the very highest order. Her face was one which, once beheld, could never be forgotten; the perfect oval of the contour, the small regular features, fine brow, and dark flashing eyes were in perfect harmony. Though she had the Spanish defect of a too long *corsage*, and a somewhat thick waist, yet her bust and arms were faultless.

And she was not only surpassingly beautiful, but possessed a voice equal to those of any of the first-rate singers who have appeared upon the stage. In her later years what once had been so great a charm became the terror of her friends; for she did not feel her declining powers, and her voice, which had become uncertain, and even hoarse, sounded in her own ears as mellow and enchanting as ever. She was one of those who will not grow old. As she approached sixty, her gowns became more *décolletées*, and her bravuras more frequent. She used to have all her grey hairs plucked out.

But perhaps these illusions as to her appearance and perpetual youth enabled Madame Merlin up to the end of her life to remain the same kind, generous-hearted, agreeable woman she had been in her young days, when all the world was at her feet. She still thought herself far superior to the young beauties who had succeeded her; and no doubt even the sere and yellow leaf of her autumnal time was more attractive than the spring of many younger ones around her.

[1] Mercedes Jaruco, Countess Merlin (1788–1852).

She had less wit and more genuine good-nature than Madame de Girardin. She might have a moment of violent anger, but bore no malice; and she had too much reliance on the variety of her attractions to fear any rivalry.

Madame Merlin gave charming concerts, followed by very agreeable suppers. Her house was a sort of neutral ground, where the ministers of the Orleans dynasty met the leaders of the Legitimist party, and the most celebrated writers of the day; where Duchesses sat down with singers, and all aristocratic pretensions were laid aside. Madame Merlin, among her many good qualities, had one which is rare and admirable, and is the stamp of a truly noble nature. She was thoroughly independent. The poor wayworn musician who formed one of a chorus met with as civil and kind a reception as the Duke or Count just arrived from the Faubourg St Germain. There was the kind, beaming, southern smile of recognition for the second-rate artiste, when met in some great house where he or she was kept at arm's length. There was in her no respect of persons for their rank or position, no cringing to the debasing laws of social etiquette. She possessed what is much rarer than we all imagine, – a truly kind heart; and she reaped her reward, for though Madame Merlin had not always a great regard for appearances, no one had the courage to fling a stone at the generous-minded, warm-hearted woman.

ENGLISH CATHOLICS IN ROME

When I was last at Rome I was much disgusted at the absurd over-zeal of the English perverts, who were first and foremost in every procession, prostrating themselves on the saliva-covered floor of the churches before the most grotesque idols or absurd relics, and kissing, with a display of the most ardent devotion, St Peter's well-worn toe,[1] just after the same ceremony had been performed by some filthy Trasteverine reeking of garlic and covered with vermin.[2] It used to be said, at the time of the Restoration in 1815, that many of the followers of Louis XVIII were more *royalistes que le roi*; and the same saying may be applied to our vulgar English perverts, who are more Popish than the Pope, and make

---

[1] The bronze statue of St Peter seated on a marble throne was thought in Gronow's time to date from the fifth or sixth century. It is now believed to be by Arnolfo di Cambio (c. 1296).

[2] The Trastevere, a working-class transpontine quarter of Rome, was much decayed in Gronow's time.

themselves the laughing-stock of Antonelli,[1] and the great majority of cardinals and abbés, who believe in nothing at all.

PIO NONO'S FLIGHT TO GAETA

All who are personally acquainted with Pope Pius IX are aware that he is a man of extremely benevolent disposition, naturally liberal in his political views, and desirous of promoting the welfare and happiness of mankind.[2] Political events in 1847–48 were singularly calculated to bring out the peculiar characteristics of a sovereign Pontiff who was called upon to exercise his temporal power in an exceptional period of modern Italian history. Pius IX believed that it was not incompatible with the attributes of the Papacy, to participate in that great liberal movement which shook so many thrones in the year 1848.

The College of Cardinals, and especially the conspicuous members of the order of the Jesuits, became alarmed at the Pontiff's liberal ideas. Knowing well his character, and observing the progress of that overwhelming tide of popular opinion which was sweeping sovereigns from their thrones, and shaking the very foundations of government, they did not at first openly oppose the Pontiff's views, but gradually and insidiously set about creating alarm in his mind, and, above all, sought to awaken doubts in the conscience of 'the Vicar of Christ.' They calculated, and correctly, that if they could not deter him from bestowing mundane and political benefits on the Roman people, they could at least make him believe that in doing so he was betraying the interests and influences of the Catholic Church, and they succeeded in arousing a tempest of indignation and alarm in the mind of Pio Nono, until he felt it his duty to take to flight, more in the cause of the Roman Catholic Church than from fears concerning personal safety.

The golden tints of an Italian sunset had faded into that brief twilight which heralds darkness, when a female, dressed in humble attire, was admitted to the garden of the Vatican by a gentleman in the confidence of the Pope. Neither of the persons spoke as they made their way to a

---

[1] Cardinal Giacomo Antonelli (1806–76), the charming and none too scrupulous Secretary of State to Pius IX, was firmly opposed to constitutional government in the Papal States.

[2] Pius IX (1792–1878) was scarcely the 'naturally liberal' Pope that Gronow suggests, although expected to be so when elected. His pontificate, the longest in history, was marked by opposition to the spirit of the Risorgimento, by the declaration of the dogma of Immaculate Conception and the doctrine of Papal Infallibility. He was obliged to leave Rome for Gaeta in 1848.

portion of the palace not generally inhabited. On arriving at the foot of
a dark and narrow staircase, the gentleman took from his pocket one of
those little knots of twisted wax-taper which the Italians carry about
with them, and lighted it; then, without uttering a word, he beckoned
the lady to follow him, and proceeded up the narrow stone staircase,
which, after many windings, led to a door, on which three raps were
given by the mysterious guide. Almost immediately the door was
opened by Pio Nono himself, and the guide, making way for the lady,
retired. This was Madame Dodwell, to whom I alluded [elsewhere] as
one of the most beautiful women of her time;[1] she was the widow of an
Englishman, though a Roman by birth, and married *en secondes noces* to
the Bavarian minister, and she had come to the Vatican in order to
arrange the clandestine flight of the Pontiff from Rome.

His Holiness appeared to have lost all presence of mind, and
trembled as he took the lady by the hand, and, gazing earnestly on her
still beautiful face, said, 'I look to you, madam, for arranging all details.
I have the utmost confidence in your discretion, and I know the firmness
of your character.' The lady replied, 'Has any plan of escape suggested
itself to your Holiness?' 'Yes,' said the Pontiff in a low voice; 'I think the
best thing I can do is to put on the gown of an ordinary priest, and at
daybreak to-morrow morning walk out of the gates which conduct to
the Fondi road. You, madam, in your carriage, will have preceded me,
and, waiting at a convenient distance, you will take me up. I have made
arrangements with my good and faithful friend, Ferdinand, King of
Naples, for a safe retreat at Gaeta; and I have no doubt that you, with
your passport as Ambassadress of Bavaria, can pass the customs
authorities with little or no difficulty.' 'Holy father,' replied the lady,
pressing the Pontiff's hand, 'the scheme seems to me in every way
satisfactory. I shall bring with me a confidential servant, a clever
coachman, willing to brave any danger.' The Pope rose, and bestowing
his blessing on the lady, ushered her to the door, adding, 'I retire to pass
the night in prayer.' 'I shall be one mile from the gate on the Fondi
road,' said the lady in a whisper, 'by four o'clock to-morrow morning.'

At that hour a carriage might have been seen in a bend of the road
which leads to Naples. On the box-seat beside the coachman sat a
female, dressed as a domestic servant, who anxiously gazed around
while waiting the arrival of the Pope. She did not wait long before she
beheld approaching a thickset and somewhat corpulent priest, who
advanced towards the carriage with a rapid step, and covered with dust.

[1] See note, p. 191.

In a few moments Pio Nono was seated in the carriage with the ambassadress, and the horses were whipped into a gallop, and did not halt until they reached the small custom-house of Fondi.

It was now ten o'clock, and they were immediately surrounded by the custom-house officers, who demanded their passports. The chief official, looking into the carriage, observed, 'I do not find on your passport the name of the priest who accompanies your excellency.' 'Oh,' replied the lady, 'he is only my confessor.' Unfortunately, the priest showed signs of uneasiness and alarm, which excited the suspicion of the officer, who said, 'In these times our orders are very strict, and I cannot permit the *padre confessore* to pass. I must beg him to descend, and shall be obliged to detain him until I get permission from Rome for his release.' The Pope, hearing this, was in a great state of excitement; he caught hold of the man's hand, and whispered in his ear, '*Caro amico*, you don't know who I am, – I am your sovereign and father, Pius IX.' Whereupon the officer turned round to a little group of persons who had collected, and exclaimed, 'Per Baccho, here is a fellow who calls himself our Pope!' The crowd peered into the carriage, and indulged in a volley of ribaldry, evidently not believing in the identity of the sovereign Pontiff. Matters were becoming serious, when the Pope placed a bag of gold coin in the hands of the officials, whilst the ambassadress threw handfuls of scudi to the mob. A loud cheer was raised by all present, and in a few minutes the carriage was going at full speed, without fear of pursuit, on the road to Gaeta.

Then and Now

Perhaps it is because I am growing old, and woman has less power to charm than heretofore; but, whatever may be the reason, I cannot help thinking that, in 'the merry days when I was young,' or 'in my hot youth, when George the Third was king,' the women of England were more beautiful, better-bred, and more distinguished in appearance, and, above all, in manner, than they are now-a-days. How grand they used to look, with their tall, stately forms, small thoroughbred heads, and long, flowing ringlets, dreamlike fair, and queenly! You could not help feeling somewhat elated and self-satisfied, if perchance one of those sidelong glances, half-proud, half-bashful, like a petted child's, fell upon you, leaving you silent and pensive, full of hopes and memories.

I do not mean to say that there are not now, as there always have been in every state of society, beautiful and amiable women, combining good sense and high principle; but there are too many who seem to have

taken for their ideal a something between the dashing London horse-
breaker and some Parisian *artiste dramatique* of a third-rate theatre; the
object of whose ambition is to be mistaken for a *femme du demi-monde*, to
be insulted when they walk out with their petticoats girt up to their
knees, showing (to do them justice) remarkably pretty feet and legs, and
to wearing wide-awake hats over painted cheeks and brows, and walk
with that indescribable, jaunty, 'devil-may-care' look which is considered 'the right thing' now-a-days, – to make sporting bets, – to address
men as Jack, Tom, or Harry, – to ride ahead in the Park, – to call the
paterfamilias 'governor,' and the lady-mother 'the old party,' – to talk
of the young men who 'spoon' them, and discuss with them the merits
of 'Skittles'[1] and her horses, or the last scandalous story fabricated in the
bay window at White's, the very faintest allusion to which would have
made their mother's hair stand on end with dismay and horror: – this
is to be pleasant, and 'fast,' and amusing. The young lady who is weak
enough to blush if addressed rather too familiarly, and so unwise as
to ignore the existence of *les dames aux camélias*,[2] is called 'slow,' and
distanced altogether: in the London steeplechase after husbands she is
'nowhere' – an outsider – a female muff. The girl of the year 1862 who
is not 'fast' is generally dull and *blasée*, pleased with nothing, and
possesses neither the wisdom of age nor the *naïveté* of youth.

How unspeakably odious – with a few brilliant exceptions, such as
Alvanley and others – were the dandies of forty years ago. They were a
motley crew, with nothing remarkable about them but their insolence.
They were generally not high-born, nor rich, nor very good-looking,
nor clever, nor agreeable; and why they arrogated to themselves the
right of setting up their own fancied superiority on a self-raised pedestal,
and despising their betters, Heaven only knows. They were generally
middle-aged, some even elderly men, had large appetites and weak
digestions, gambled freely, and had no luck. They hated everybody,
and abused everybody, and would sit together in White's bay window,
or the pit boxes at the Opera, weaving tremendous crammers.[3] They
swore a good deal, never laughed, had their own particular slang,

---

[1] Catherine Walters, the celebrated courtesan, mistress of the Marquess of Hartington,
later eighth Duke of Devonshire, amongst many other admirers and protectors. Her
nickname 'Skittles' was derived from her days as an employee in a bowling alley in
Liverpool. The Prince of Wales, later Edward VII, slept with her in Paris.
[2] Courtesans like Marguerite Gautier in Alexander Dumas's novel *La Dame aux camélias*
(1848).
[3] Telling tall stories.

looked hazy after dinner, and had most of them been patronised at one time or other by Brummell and the Prince Regent.

These gentlemen were very fond of having a butt. Many years ago Tom Raikes filled this capacity; though he did kick out sometimes, and to some purpose. They gloried in their shame, and believed in nothing good, or noble, or elevated. Thank Heaven, that miserable race of used-up dandies has long been extinct! May England never look upon their like again!

With regard to France, I should say that the general run of French dandies now-a-days is a sorry mixture of coxcombry and snobbishness. Young France thinks he has done wonders when he has ascended the giddy height of a hideous dog-cart, with a gigantic groom fastened on behind by some mysterious adhesive process, which does not seem altogether to reassure John (all Frenchmen's grooms rejoice in this appellation; be their names Pierre or Paul, when once they put on leathers and boots they become John). Another amusement of the Parisian *élégants* which surprises Englishmen, is to drive about in solitary glory in a brougham or barouche and pair. You see fifteen-stone men, with tremendous whiskers and moustaches, who ought to be taking violent exercise on horseback or on foot, driven up and down the fashionable promenade by the lake in the Bois de Boulogne, lolling on well-stuffed rose-coloured cushions, and ogling through their eye-glasses the fair and frail damsels in gorgeous equipages who frequent this drive.

Index

Page numbers of biographical notes are in italic.

Concorde, 273; Place de la Madeleine, 272; Place Vendôme, 174, 286; Quai d'Orsay, 279; Rue du Bac, 254; Rue Basse du Rempart, 284; rue Gassini, 184; Rue Lepelletier, 159; Rue Mandar, 150; Rue de la Michodière, 166; Rue de la Paix, 145; Rue de Richelieu, 35, 150, 285; Rue des St Pères, 257; Théâtre des Italiens, 209; Tuileries, 144, 145, 160, 195, 254, 258 *people in:* Lady Aldborough, 167; Balzac, 184; Lady Blessington, 293; Blücher, 161; Lord and Lady Castlereagh, 166; Scrope Davies, 12; Devonshire, 166, Dumas, 184; Mademoiselle Duthé, 119, 120; Fanny Elssler, 199; Lord and Lady Granville, 165; Gronow, xi–xii, 26, 68, 106, 143–6, 150, 169, 182; Leopold of the Belgians, 34; Luttrell, 184; Mercandotti, 6; Montrond, 174; Moore, 192; Napoleon and Hare, 195; Normanby, 229; d'Orsay, 106; Rogers, 182; Rossini, 207; Sue, 184, 186; Lady Waldegrave, 68

Pasta, Giuditta, *206*, 209

Peacocke, Sir Warren, 62

Peel, Sir Robert, 2nd baronet, xvi, 5, 87, 180, 241

Peninsular War, xiii, *13*; battle of the Nivelle, 55–7; battle of Orthes, 57; battles of the Pyrenees, 62–3; battle of Toulouse, 58; battle of Vittoria, 45, 68; Bayonne invested, 58; Brown Bess, 61; cavalry, 214; correspondence in *Morning Chronicle*, 47–8; crossing of Adour, 58; discipline, 52–3; dysentery, 64–5; French soldiers, 47; Gronow, 45–6, 50–1, 59–60; Guards at Bordeaux, 59–60; Guards and umbrellas, 60–1; hunting in the Pyrenees, 63–4; militia regiments in Bordeaux, 69–70; peace treaty signed, 69; St Jean de Luz, 49–50; siege of San Sebastian, 45; Waters, 53–5

Percival, Captain, 137

Pergami, Bartolommeo, 79

Perrault, Claude, *289*

Persigny, duc de, *282*, 283–4

Petersham, Viscount, *7*, 109–10

Phillip, Arthur, 111

Picton, Sir Thomas, *65*, and Gronow, xiii; 125; killed, 135; and O'Keefe, 65–6;

talent and discretion, 246; Waterloo campaign, 126, 127, 133, 135; and Wellington, 126–7

Piozzi, Hester, 204

Pitt, William, the Younger, *95*, 221, 226–7, 229

Pius IX, Pope, *299*, 299–301

Pole, Long Wellesley, *97*

Poltimore, 1st Baron, *287*

Poltimore, Lady, *287*

Pompadour, Marquise de, *266*, 266–7

Poniatowski, Prince, *280*

Ponsonby, the Hon. Sir Frederick, *60*, 136, 140–1

Ponsonby, Sir Henry Frederick, *60*

Ponsonby, Sir William, 141

Pope, Alexander, *291*

Porteus, Beilby, *42*

Portland, 3rd Duke of, 238

Portland, 4th Duke of, *76*

Queensberry, 4th Duke of, 77, 100, *120*

Rachel, Mademoiselle, *201*, 201–3

Raggett, George, *82*, 83

Raikes, Robert, 108

Raikes, Thomas, *108*, 303

Ramolino, Letizia, *263*

Récamier, Madame, *213*, 240

Regent, Prince, *see* George IV, King

regiments, *see* army

Reichstadt, Duke of, *199*

Richards, 'Tom Pipes', 245–6

Richardson, Samuel, 263

Richmond and Lennox, 4th Duke of, *126*, 134, 246–7

Richmond and Lennox, 5th Duke of, *57*, 126

Robespierre, Maximilien Marie de, 150, *258*

Rocca, Madame de, 256

Rogers, Samuel, *174*, 182–3, 203

Rome, 2, 298–9

Romilly, Frederick, 214

Rossini, Gioacchino Antonio, *106*, *207*, 207–9

Rothschild, Gudule, *243*, 243–4

Rothschild, Nathan Meyer, *243*

Rowland the *coiffeur*, 290

Roxburgh, 5th Duke of, 82

Rubini, Giovanni Battista, *205*

Rundell, Philip, *249*

Russell, Francis, *62*, 62–3